Using AI to Develop Sustainability Strategies for a Changing Global Economy

As climate change is affecting economies and markets globally, environmental sustainability is becoming more crucial. Sustainability emphasizes the equality of future generations and is typically seen to have three components: an environmental, an economic, and a social component. Because attaining environmental sustainability also involves risks that might influence corporate operations and prospects in a strongly competitive market, thriving markets and environmental deterioration cannot coexist.

Business practices are being drastically altered and improved using AI and machine learning (ML), a branch of AI that enables autonomous machines. Big data can assist AI to automatically learn and acquire knowledge to assist managers in achieving their practical and technical objectives. AI brings new methods for conducting business, finding new chances in the global market, and executing work.

Using AI to Develop Sustainability Strategies for a Changing Global Economy focuses on novel ideas and research for providing a broader outlook on sustainability in business. The book

- Focuses on how to reduce environmentally destructive investment patterns and activities.
- Discusses sustainable recovery policies using AI to build back better.
- Presents how businesses of the future operate, augmenting industry resources with the alliance between AI and sustainable business outcomes.

Presenting novel ideas for creating robust sustainability strategies, the book explores answers to the moral and ethical questions about using AI in decision-making, cyber-security, and resource management. With insight into developing efficient mechanisms to facilitate a circular economy, *the book provides solutions that* link the needs of the present generation without disadvantaging coming generations.

Dr. Senthil Kumar A. V. is an editor-in-chief for multiple journals. He has published 11 book chapters, 264 journal papers, and 9 edited books, as well as presented 5 conference papers.

Dr. Ankita Chaturvedi is an accomplished academic and a dedicated Associate Professor at IIS University, Jaipur, India and has an impressive publication record with more than 53 research papers in reputable national and international journals.

Dr. Atul Bansal is a self-motivated teacher with more than 24 years of experience in teaching, research, and administration at various universities throughout the world. He is currently Assistant Professor in Accounting, College of Business Administration, University of Bahrain, Kingdom of Bahrain.

Dr. Rohaya Latip is Associate Professor at Faculty of Computer Science and Information Technology, University Putra, Malaysia.

Advances in Computational Collective Intelligence
Series Editor
Dr. Subhendu Kumar Pani

Innovations and Applications of Technology in Language Education
By Hung Phu Bui, Raghvendra Kumar, and Nilayam Kamila

Data-Driven Modelling and Predictive Analytics in Business and Finance
By Alex Khang, Rashmi Gujrati, Hayri Uygun, RK Tailor and Sanjaya Singh Gaur

Deep Learning Concepts in Operations Research
By Biswadip Basu Mallik, Gunjan Mukherjee, Rahul Kar, Aryan Chaudhary

Applications of Machine Learning and Deep Learning on Biological Data
By Faheem Masoodi, Mohammad Quasim, Syed Bukhari, Sarvottam Dixit, Shadab Alam

Technologies for Sustainable Global Higher Education
By Maria José Sousa, Andreia de Bem Machado, Gertrudes Aparecida Dandolini

Artificial Intelligence Techniques in Power Systems Operations and Analysis
By Nagendra Singh, Sitendra Tamrakar, Arvind Mewada, Sanjeev Kumar Gupta

Deep Learning Applications in Operations Research
By Aryan Chaudhary, Biswadip Basu Mallik, Gunjan Mukherjee, Rahul Kar

Computational Intelligence in Industry 4.0 and 5.0 Applications: Trends, Challenges and Applications
By JOSEPH BAMIDELE AWOTUNDE, Kamalakanta Muduli, BISWAJIT BRAHMA

Explainable Artificial Intelligence in Medical Imaging: Fundamentals and Applications
By Amjad Rehman Khan, Tanzila Saba

Parallel and High-Performance Computing in Artificial Intelligence
By Mukesh Raghuwanshi, Pradnya Borkar, Rutvij H. Jhaveri, Roshani Raut

Emotional Intelligence in the Digital Era: Concepts, Frameworks, and Applications
By Pushan Kumar Dutta, Sachin Gupta, Shafali Kashyap, Anita Gehlot, Rita Karmakar, Pronaya Bhattacharya

Deep Learning and Blockchain Technology for Smart and Sustainable Cities
By Subramaniyaswamy V, G Revathy, Logesh Ravi, N. Thillaiarasu, Naresh Kshetri

Computational Intelligence for Analysis of Trends in Industry 4.0 and 5.0
By Joseph Bamidele Awotunde, Kamalakanta Muduli, and Biswajit Brahma

Metaverse and Blockchain Use Cases and Applications
By Dileep Kumar Murala, Sandeep Kumar Panda, and Sujata Priyambada Dash

Leveraging Artificial Intelligence in Cloud, Edge, Fog and Mobile Computing
By Shrikaant Kulkarni, P. William, Vijaya Prakash, and Jaiprakash Narain Dwivedi

https://www.routledge.com/Advances-in-Computational-Collective-Intelligence/book-series/ACCICRC

Using AI to Develop Sustainability Strategies for a Changing Global Economy

Edited by
Senthil Kumar A. V., Ankita Chaturvedi,
Atul Bansal, and Rohaya Latip

CRC Press
Taylor & Francis Group
Boca Raton London New York

CRC Press is an imprint of the
Taylor & Francis Group, an **informa** business
AN AUERBACH BOOK

Designed cover image: Shutterstock
First edition published 2026
2385 NW Executive Center Drive, Suite 320, Boca Raton FL 33431

and by CRC Press
4 Park Square, Milton Park, Abingdon, Oxon, OX14 4RN

CRC Press is an imprint of Taylor & Francis Group, LLC

ISBN: 978-1-032-57279-6 (hbk)
ISBN: 978-1-041-07491-5 (pbk)
ISBN: 978-1-003-64077-6 (ebk)

DOI: 10.1201/9781003640776

Typeset in Times
by KnowledgeWorks Global Ltd.

Contents

List of Contributors

Senthil Kumar A. V.
Oindrila Acharya
Necmi Altin
Jatin Arora
Atul Bansal
Sukanta Kumar Baral
Ravikumar C. V.
Abhinav Chaturvedi
Ankita Chaturvedi
Joohi Chaturvedi
Renu Chaturvedi
Deeksha Dave
Neha Dubey
Süleyman Emre Eyimaya
Asmita Ghosh
Vandana Gupta
Siriwardhana H. A.
Petr Hlaváček
Junaid Hushain
Pratiksha Jha
Vidya Kadam
Kamal Kant
Balaram Yadav Kasula
Jayesh Katkar
Gaganpreet Kaur
Sunil Khullar
Rahul Kumar
Dilrangi M. U.
Monika Makhija
Swati Malik
Anna Mempel-Śnieżyk
Ronak Ravjibhai Pansara
Naga Lakshmanjani Pillada
Sivaram Rajeyyagari
Sangeetha Rangasamy
Ratnayake R. M. C. S.
Prabhakara S.
Rajasekaran S.
Shruthi S. P.
Madhavi Shamkuwar
Deepanshu Sharma
Pavika Sharma

Kiran Deep Singh

Pushpam Singh

Surjit Singh

Asadi Srinivasulu

Anil Thakar

Shaik Mastan Vali

Selvi Kausiliha Vijayan

Pawan Whig

Madhuri Yadav

1 Unveiling the Transformative Influence of Machine Learning Techniques on Business Data Analytics

A Comprehensive Exploration

Asadi Srinivasulu, Ravikumar C. V., Shaik Mastan Vali, Rajasekaran S., and Sivaram Rajeyyagari

1.1 INTRODUCTION

The trade relations between Liberia and African countries have garnered significant attention, given their impact on bilateral cooperation within the broader framework of African countries' "one belt, one road" strategy. It is crucial to comprehend the factors influencing this trade dynamic and implement appropriate measures for sustainable and mutually advantageous growth. This research aims to examine the primary factors shaping business trade between Liberia and African countries and propose strategic measures to promote its enduring development. The business sector holds considerable significance for both Liberia and African countries. Liberia, with its abundant forest resources, stands as a major business exporter in Africa. Concurrently, African countries, as a global economic powerhouse, exhibit a substantial demand for business products to support their construction, furniture, and manufacturing sectors. The business trade between these nations has experienced notable growth in recent years, propelled by factors such as economic opportunities, geopolitical considerations, and strategic cooperation initiatives.

This research conducts a comprehensive analysis of the influence of various factors on business trade by considering six key dimensions. First, it examines economic scales, encompassing the GDP and trade volumes of both Liberia and African countries, to grasp the economic dynamics affecting business flows. Second, it explores geographical and demographic factors, including geographic distance and population characteristics, to discern their role in shaping trade patterns. Third, the

DOI: 10.1201/9781003640776-1

research evaluates the natural resource endowment of Liberia, especially its forest resources, as a crucial factor propelling business trade. Furthermore, it assesses the level of business science and technology, along with political factors, to comprehend their impact on the trade relationship. The research examines the role of business-related technologies, such as processing and value addition, and considers the political and regulatory environment that shapes trade policies and agreements. Additionally, exchange rate dynamics are taken into account, as fluctuations in currency values can significantly influence the competitiveness of business products in international markets.

To explore these elements, an empirical analysis is undertaken utilizing an extended gravity model. This model utilizes data from African countries sourced from the UN COMTRADE database and data from 58 nations within Liberia, covering the timeframe from 2010 to 2019. The analysis strives to offer empirical evidence regarding the significance and direction of relationships between the identified factors and business trade flows. The research's findings hold implications for policymakers, industry stakeholders, and researchers engaged in the business trade between Liberia and African countries. By comprehending the factors impacting business trade, appropriate development measures can be devised to ensure the sustainability and mutual benefits of this trade relationship. Such measures may encompass policy recommendations, enhancements to infrastructure, and technological advancements aimed at improving the efficiency, competitiveness, and environmental sustainability of business trade. In essence, this research aims to contribute to the existing knowledge base on business trade between Liberia and African countries, shed light on the factors molding this trade relationship, and propose strategic measures to foster its robust and sustainable development.

1.1.1 Objectives

The research aims to achieve a comprehensive understanding of the factors influencing business trade between Liberia and African countries, analyze their impact through empirical methods, propose development countermeasures, and explore regional variations within Liberia. The specific objectives of the research, titled "Impact of Factors and Development Countermeasures on Business Between Liberia and Africa Countries," are outlined as follows:

1. *Identification and Analysis of Key Factors*: The research seeks to identify and analyze pivotal factors influencing business trade between Liberia and African countries. These factors include economic scales, geographical and demographic elements, natural resource endowment, business science and technology, political considerations, and exchange rate dynamics. The objective is to comprehend how these factors impact business trade flows between the two nations.
2. *Empirical Analysis of Relationships*: Utilizing an extended gravity model and data on business trade between Liberia and African countries, the research aims to conduct empirical analysis. This analysis aims to quantify

and assess the relationships between the identified factors and business trade flows, providing empirical evidence on the significance and direction of these relationships.

3. *Proposal of Development Countermeasures*: Based on empirical findings and an extensive literature review, the research intends to propose development countermeasures. These may include policy recommendations, improvements to infrastructure, and technological advancements. The goal is to ensure the sustainable and mutually beneficial development of business trade between Liberia and African countries.
4. *Examination of Regional Heterogeneity*: The research will explore regional variations within Liberia and their impact on business trade with African countries. Through sub-samples and tests for regional heterogeneity, the research aims to analyze how different factors affect business trade flows across various regions of Liberia. Additionally, the research will discuss issues specific to each region, contributing to a nuanced understanding of the overall trade dynamics.

1.1.2 Problem Statement

The problem statement for the research titled "Impact of Factors and Development Countermeasures on Business Between Liberia and African Countries" can be expressed as follows: The business trade between Liberia and African countries is of strategic significance and has experienced notable growth in recent years. However, there is a lack of a comprehensive understanding regarding the factors influencing this trade relationship and the necessary development countermeasures to ensure its sustainability and mutual benefits. Hence, the issue addressed in this research is to identify and analyze the key factors influencing business trade between Liberia and African countries, assess their impact on trade flows, and propose effective development countermeasures aimed at enhancing the long-term sustainability of business cooperation between the two nations.

1.1.3 Outcomes

The research's outcomes will add valuable insights to the existing knowledge regarding the impact of factors and development countermeasures on business trade between Liberia and African countries. The findings are expected to play a crucial role in decision-making processes, guide policy formulation, and support the establishment of sustainable and mutually beneficial business trade cooperation between the two nations. The anticipated outcomes of the research, titled "Impact of Factors and Development Countermeasures on Business Between Liberia and Africa Countries," are outlined as follows:

1. *Identification of Key Factors*: The research aims to offer a comprehensive understanding of the primary factors influencing business trade between Liberia and African countries. It will analyze factors such as economic scales, geographical and demographic elements, natural resource

endowment, business science and technology, political considerations, and exchange rate dynamics, which significantly shape business trade flows.

2. *Empirical Analysis of Factor Impact*: Through empirical analysis utilizing an extended gravity model and relevant data on business trade, the research will quantitatively assess the impact of identified factors on business trade flows between Liberia and African countries. This analysis will furnish empirical evidence regarding the significance and direction of these relationships.
3. *Development Countermeasures*: Drawing from the empirical analysis findings and an extensive literature review, the research will propose development countermeasures. These countermeasures will encompass policy recommendations, enhancements to infrastructure, and technological advancements aimed at ensuring the sustainable and mutually beneficial development of business trade between Liberia and African countries.
4. *Regional Heterogeneity Analysis*: The research will scrutinize regional variations within Liberia and their influence on business trade. By utilizing sub-samples and analyzing regional disparities, the research will provide insights into how different factors affect business trade flows across various regions of Liberia. This analysis will aid in understanding specific challenges and opportunities within each region, guiding the formulation of targeted development strategies.
5. *Enhanced Understanding of Business Trade Dynamics*: The research seeks to contribute to a deeper understanding of the dynamics of business trade between Liberia and African countries. By examining various factors and their interplay, the research will provide insights into the complexities and nuances of the trade relationship. This understanding will be invaluable for policymakers, industry stakeholders, and researchers involved in business trade cooperation between the two countries.

1.1.4 Research Challenges

Tackling these research challenges necessitates careful methodological considerations, robust data analysis techniques, interdisciplinary approaches, and a discerning understanding of the context-specific dynamics of business trade between Liberia and African countries. Overcoming these challenges will contribute to a more precise and comprehensive comprehension of the factors and development countermeasures in the business trade relationship. The research on the impact of factors and development countermeasures on business between Liberia and African countries may encounter several challenges, including the following:

1. *Data Availability and Quality*: Obtaining reliable and comprehensive data on business trade, economic factors, natural resource endowment, and other pertinent variables for both Liberia and African countries could be challenging. Challenges such as data inconsistencies, gaps, and limited access to specific datasets may hinder the conduct of a robust empirical analysis.

2. *Complex and Multifaceted Factors*: Business trade is influenced by various interconnected factors, including economic, geographical, technological, and political aspects. Grasping the intricate interactions and understanding their individual and combined effects on business trade necessitates meticulous analysis and interpretation. Integrating these factors into a coherent framework can prove challenging.
3. *Causal Inference and Endogeneity*: Establishing causal relationships between factors and business trade flows is challenging due to the presence of endogeneity. Factors influencing business trade may also be influenced by it, introducing potential biases and difficulties in determining causality. The application of appropriate econometric techniques and addressing endogeneity issues is crucial for accurate analysis.
4. *Regional Heterogeneity*: Liberia consists of diverse regions with varying characteristics, including differences in natural resource endowment, infrastructure, and socioeconomic factors. Analyzing the impact of factors and development countermeasures at the regional level necessitates careful consideration of regional heterogeneity and its implications on business trade dynamics.
5. *Policy and Implementation Complexities*: Proposing development countermeasures involves considering the broader policy context, encompassing trade policies, regulations, and political dynamics. The practical implementation of countermeasures may face challenges due to administrative, financial, and institutional constraints. Identifying feasible and effective countermeasures that align with existing policies and frameworks can be demanding.
6. *External Factors and Global Context*: Business trade between Liberia and African countries is influenced by global market dynamics, international regulations, and geopolitical considerations. Understanding the impact of external factors and incorporating them into the analysis introduces additional challenges. Accounting for global market trends and their effects on business trade requires a comprehensive and nuanced approach.

1.2 LITERATURE REVIEW

The exchange of business between Liberia and African countries has attracted considerable attention in academic and policy discussions, given its economic, environmental, and geopolitical implications. This review explores existing studies that delve into the factors influencing business trade between Liberia and African countries, along with proposed development countermeasures for sustainable outcomes. Numerous studies have scrutinized the economic dimensions of business trade between Liberia and African countries. For instance, Wang et al. (2018) conducted an empirical analysis, revealing that the growing demand for business products in African countries, propelled by rapid urbanization and industrialization, has expanded trade with Liberia. Economic scales like GDP and trade volumes were identified as key factors shaping this trade relationship.

Geographical and demographic aspects have also been explored. Zhang and Li (2018) underscored the role of geographic proximity and transportation infrastructure in facilitating business flows. They advocated for reducing geographical barriers through enhanced trade infrastructure to improve trade efficiency. The abundant forest resources in Liberia have been extensively studied, with Chen and Liu (2017) establishing a positive link between forest resource availability and business exports to African countries. Sustainable forest management practices were deemed vital for enduring trade cooperation. Technological and political factors have garnered attention. Xu et al. (2020) delved into the impact of business science and technology on trade flows, emphasizing advanced processing techniques for product competitiveness. Li and Yang (2022) discussed the significance of political factors, such as trade policies, in shaping the business trade relationship. Exchange rate dynamics were analyzed by Meng et al. (2018), revealing the potential influence of fluctuations on the competitiveness of business products. Porwal et al. (2022) discussed the potential of blockchain technology along with other technological advancements like machine learning, in revolutionizing business data analytics.

Development countermeasures have been proposed by Liu and Wu (2016) to ensure sustainable business trade. Recommendations include bilateral cooperation in forest management, combating illegal logging, and capacity building for sustainable business practices. Infrastructure development, particularly in transportation networks and logistics, was identified as crucial for improving trade efficiency. While the existing literature offers valuable insights into the factors and development countermeasures in business trade between Liberia and African countries, further research is warranted. Future studies could explore additional aspects, such as the environmental impact, social implications for local communities, and the role of international institutions in promoting sustainable business cooperation. This research seeks to contribute by investigating additional factors and proposing comprehensive development countermeasures for the enduring sustainability of business trade between Liberia and African countries.

1.3 EXISTING SYSTEM

The research does acknowledge traditional business risk management methods like business scoring, which have proven insufficient in handling business risk within intricate and dynamic environments. The authors argue that more sophisticated techniques and tools are necessary to assess business risk and make well-informed lending decisions. This necessitated an exploration of data analytics as a potential solution, leading the research to concentrate on presenting and discussing the utilization of data analytics as an alternative to traditional business risk management methods.

Despite offering a comprehensive analysis of employing data analytics in business risk management, the research has certain limitations that should be highlighted:

1. *Limited Scope*: The research primarily focuses on data analytics in business risk management and overlooks the examination of other risk management aspects, such as operational risk or liquidity risk.
2. *Limited Empirical Evidence*: Although the research mentions multiple studies, it falls short of presenting adequate empirical evidence to validate the effectiveness of data analytics in business risk management.
3. *Lack of Practical Examples*: The research lacks concrete examples illustrating how data analytics has been successfully implemented in business risk management within the work sector.
4. *Limited Discussion of Challenges and Limitations*: While the research touches on potential drawbacks and limitations of data analytics in business risk management, it does not emphasize them sufficiently.
5. *Outdated Information*: Published in 2017, the research may not incorporate numerous advancements in the field of data analytics in business risk management that have emerged since its publication.

1.4 ANALYSIS AND RESULTS

The application of Big Data analytics transcends specific technological domains, impacting various industries, including the work sector. Advanced mathematical and statistical models such as predictive analysis, artificial intelligence, and data mining offer substantial advantages within the banking industry. Banks are progressively embracing digital convergence strategies to enhance customer service, improve product offerings, and ensure asset quality and regulatory compliance. The significant volume of data generated by banks, including unstructured data from Internet work and ATM transactions, reaches approximately 2.5 quintillion bytes. To address challenges and bolster competitiveness, banks need to harness trending Big Data analytics methodologies. This chapter explores the benefits and implementation of Big Data analytics in the work sector.

The proposed approach for business approval risk management using data analytics employs various techniques. One commonly utilized method is business scoring, where predictive models analyze factors such as business history, income, employment history, and other relevant data to generate business scores. This aids lenders in swiftly evaluating a borrower's risk profile and making informed lending decisions. Fraud detection is another technique employing data analytics to identify potentially fraudulent activities using transactional and other relevant data. Portfolio analysis can manage business approval risks by identifying trends and patterns in the performance of existing businesses, enabling proactive risk mitigation. By monitoring key performance indicators such as delinquency rates, charge-offs, and default rates, lenders can use data analytics to make informed decisions about lending policies and procedures. Customer segmentation is a method that helps lenders reduce risks and enhance profitability by categorizing customers based on factors like business worthiness, income, and repayment history. Data analytics assists in customizing lending policies and marketing efforts for different customer segments.

While the research thoroughly explores the utilization of data analytics in business risk management, some limitations need acknowledgment.

1.4.1 Dataset

The dataset has undergone cleaning and preparation for classification. Obtaining pertinent and reliable datasets is pivotal for researching the "Impact of factors and development countermeasures on business between Liberia and Africa Countries." Several potential sources for acquiring relevant datasets are outlined below. It is imperative to meticulously assess the reliability and quality of the data obtained from these sources, ensuring comprehensive coverage of necessary variables and time periods for the research. Furthermore, adherence to data usage agreements, permissions, and licenses is essential when accessing and utilizing these datasets.

Acquiring pertinent and trustworthy datasets is essential for researching the "Impact of factors and development countermeasures on business between Liberia and Africa Countries." Consider the following potential sources for obtaining relevant datasets:

1. *United Nations COMTRADE*: The UN COMTRADE database furnishes detailed international trade data, encompassing business trade, facilitating the analysis of trade flows between Liberia and African countries.
2. *National Statistical Agencies*: Liberia's Institute of Statistics and Geo-Information Services (LISGIS) and the National Bureau of Statistics of African countries are examples of national statistical agencies that may provide official data on business production, trade, economic indicators, and other pertinent factors.
3. *Forest and Environmental Agencies*: National or regional forest and environmental agencies in Liberia and African countries can potentially offer data on forest resources, management practices, sustainability, and environmental impact assessments related to business trade.
4. *Academic Institutions and Research Organizations*: Universities, research institutions, and non-governmental organizations (NGOs) focusing on forestry, environmental studies, and international trade may possess datasets and research findings relevant to business trade between Liberia and African countries. Exploring published research papers or reaching out to these organizations can yield valuable data sources.
5. *International Organizations*: International entities like the Food and Agriculture Organization (FAO) and the World Bank may house datasets and reports on business trade, forest resources, and economic indicators pertinent to Liberia and African countries.

As the prevalence of Big Data analytics continues to grow, businesses are increasingly turning to data-driven insights to enhance their lending decisions. This research investigates the application of data analytics in business risk management within the work industry. Exploring techniques such as business scoring, fraud detection, and portfolio analysis, the research aims to mitigate business risk and optimize the performance of lending portfolios. Emphasizing the importance of customer segmentation, the authors discuss how data analytics can customize lending policies and marketing strategies for diverse customer segments. The research acknowledges the challenges and limitations of data analytics in business risk management while suggesting avenues for future research. Overall, the authors contend that data analytics is a crucial tool for business offices to make informed lending decisions, reducing the risk of business defaults and improving overall portfolio performance.

The increasing prominence of Big Data analytics has become a transformative decision-making tool across various industries, particularly in the financial sector where improving lending decisions and reducing business risk are paramount. With advancements in data processing technology and the proliferation of data sources, lenders can harness data to gain deeper insights into borrowers' business worthiness, identify potential risks, and make more informed lending decisions. This research provides an overview of the benefits of data analytics in business approval risk management, guiding lenders on utilizing data analytics for precision in decision-making. By leveraging data analytics, lenders can minimize the risk of business defaults, leading to enhanced performance in the competitive work industry. The research explores the role of data analytics in business approval risk management, discussing techniques such as business scoring, fraud detection, portfolio analysis, and customer segmentation. While acknowledging the limitations and challenges of data analytics in business risk management, the research suggests future research areas to further advance the field.

The dataset utilized in the Business Prediction System, as outlined in Table 1.1, encompasses information pertaining to diverse individuals applying for business and their pertinent characteristics. This dataset serves as the foundational element for constructing predictive models aimed at assessing the likelihood of business

TABLE 1.1

Dataset for the Business Data Prediction System

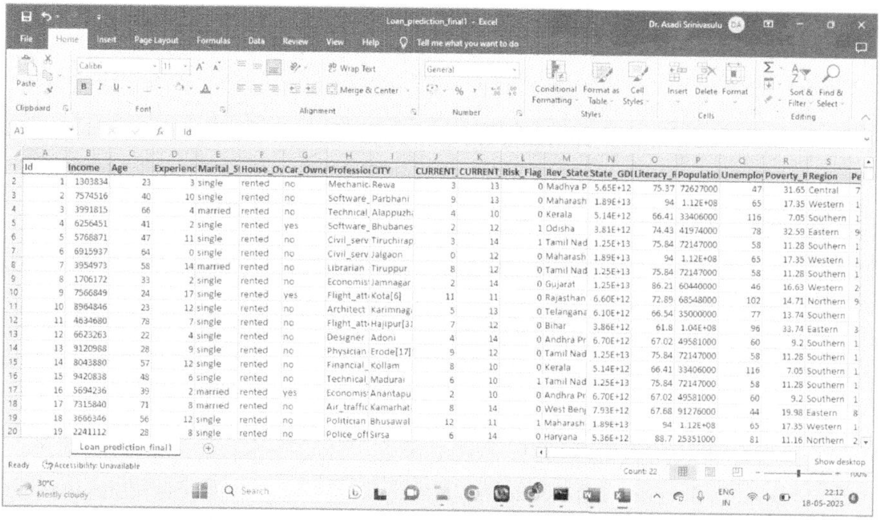

Id	Income	Age	Experienc	Marital_S	House_Ov	Car_Owne	Professio	CITY	CURRENT_	CURRENT_	Risk_Flag	Rev_State	State_GDI	Literacy_R	Populatio	Unemplo	Poverty_R	Region	Pe
1	1303834	23	3	single	rented	no	Mechanic	Rewa	3	13	0	Madhya P	5.65E+12	75.37	72627000	47	31.65	Central	7
2	7574516	40	10	single	rented	no	Software_	Parbhani	9	13	0	Maharash	1.89E+13	94	1.12E+08	65	17.35	Western	1
3	3991815	66	4	married	rented	no	Technical_	Alappuzh	4	10	0	Kerala	5.14E+12	66.41	33406000	116	7.05	Southern	1
4	6256451	41	2	single	rented	yes	Software_	Bhubanes	2	12	1	Odisha	3.81E+12	74.43	41974000	78	32.59	Eastern	9
5	5768871	47	11	single	rented	no	Civil_serv	Tiruchirap	3	14	1	Tamil Nad	1.25E+13	75.84	72147000	58	11.28	Southern	1
6	6915937	64	0	single	rented	no	Civil_serv	Jalgaon	0	12	0	Maharash	1.89E+13	94	1.12E+08	65	17.35	Western	1
7	3954973	58	14	married	rented	no	Librarian	Tiruppur	8	12	0	Tamil Nad	1.25E+13	75.84	72147000	58	11.28	Southern	1
8	1706172	33	2	single	rented	no	Economis	Jamnagar	2	14	0	Gujarat	1.25E+13	86.21	60440000	46	16.63	Western	2
9	7566849	24	17	single	rented	yes	Flight_att	Kota[6]	11	11	0	Rajasthan	6.60E+12	72.89	68548000	102	14.71	Northern	9
10	8964846	23	12	single	rented	no	Architect	Karimnag	5	13	0	Telangana	6.10E+12	66.54	35000000	77	13.74	Southern	
11	4634680	78	7	single	rented	no	Flight_att	Hajipur[3]	7	12	0	Bihar	3.86E+12	61.8	1.04E+08	96	33.74	Eastern	3
12	6623263	22	4	single	rented	no	Designer	Adoni	4	14	0	Andhra Pr	6.70E+12	67.02	49581000	60	9.2	Southern	1
13	9120988	28	9	single	rented	no	Physician	Erode[17]	9	12	0	Tamil Nad	1.25E+13	75.84	72147000	58	11.28	Southern	1
14	8043880	57	12	single	rented	no	Financial_	Kollam	8	10	0	Kerala	5.14E+12	66.41	33406000	116	7.05	Southern	1
15	9420838	48	6	single	rented	no	Technical_	Madurai	6	10	1	Tamil Nad	1.25E+13	75.84	72147000	58	11.28	Southern	1
16	5694236	39	2	married	rented	yes	Economis	Anantapu	2	10	0	Andhra Pr	6.70E+12	67.02	49581000	60	9.2	Southern	1
17	7315840	71	8	married	rented	no	Air_traffic	Kamarhat	8	14	0	West Beng	7.93E+12	67.68	91276000	44	19.98	Eastern	8
18	3666346	56	12	single	rented	no	Politician	Bhusawal	12	11	1	Maharash	1.89E+13	94	1.12E+08	65	17.35	Western	1
19	2241112	28	8	single	rented	no	Police_off	Sirsa	6	14	0	Haryana	5.36E+12	88.7	25351000	81	11.16	Northern	2

approval or predicting the associated risk associated with granting business to a specific applicant.

The dataset typically encompasses the following key features:

1. *Applicant Information*: Encompassing details such as age, gender, marital status, and education level, this section provides a comprehensive profile of the applicants.
2. *Financial Information*: This segment incorporates financial particulars like income, employment type, occupation, and current employment status, aiding in the evaluation of the applicant's financial stability and ability to repay the business.
3. *Business Information*: Including specific details about the business being sought, such as business amount, interest rate, business term, and business type (e.g., personal business, home business, car business), this section offers insights into the terms and conditions of the business.
4. *Business History*: Focusing on the applicant's business worthiness and history, this feature encompasses factors like business score, previous business repayment history, defaults or delinquencies, and the number of open business lines. Business history plays a pivotal role in business approval decisions.
5. *Property Information*: If the business is linked to a property, this section provides details such as property type (e.g., residential, commercial), location, value, and ownership status. These attributes aid in assessing collateral value and associated risks.
6. *Business Approval Status*: This attribute denotes whether a business application was approved or not, serving as the target variable for the predictive modeling task. The dataset is labeled, ensuring that each business application instance is associated with its corresponding business approval status, facilitating the application of supervised learning algorithms.

By leveraging this dataset, data scientists and analysts can employ diverse data analytics techniques, including data preprocessing, exploratory data analysis, and predictive modeling, to develop business approval risk management systems that enhance decision-making within business offices.

1.4.2 Algorithms

The algorithms suggested include Decision Tree (DT) and Support Vector Machine (SVM). A DT stands as a widely used and potent machine learning algorithm in data analytics, particularly for tasks such as business approval risk management. The aim of employing data analytics in this context is to make well-informed decisions regarding business applications, minimizing the risk of defaults or financial losses. Represented as a flowchart-like model with a tree structure, a DT illustrates a sequence of decisions and their potential outcomes. Constructed based on historical business data encompassing applicant features (e.g., business score, income, employment status) and outcomes (repayment or default), the DT algorithm learns to predict the risk associated with new business applications. Leveraging data analytics with DTs enhances business approval risk management by automating decision-making processes and mitigating human bias. Analyzing a spectrum of applicant features and capturing complex relationships, the model provides accurate risk assessments, contributing to more effective business approvals and risk mitigation. Data analytics plays a pivotal role in managing business approval risks, aiding lenders in making informed lending decisions. Employing approaches like business scoring, predictive models analyze factors such as business history and income to generate scores, facilitating quick evaluations of borrower risk profiles. Additionally, data analytics detects and prevents fraud by scrutinizing transactional and relevant data for potentially fraudulent activities. Portfolio analysis identifies trends in existing business performance, allowing proactive measures to minimize risks. By tracking key performance indicators through data analytics, lenders make informed decisions on lending policies. Customer segmentation further reduces risks and enhances profitability by tailoring policies and marketing efforts for different customer segments based on risk profiles, business worthiness, income, and repayment history.

Below is a detailed breakdown of the functioning of a DT in the context of managing business approval risks:

1. *Data Preparation*: Gather and preprocess historical business data to ensure quality and relevance. Clean inconsistencies, manage missing values, and convert categorical variables into numerical formats compatible with the DT algorithm.
2. *Feature Selection*: Identify relevant features influencing business approval risk, including business history, employment details, and business amount. Choose the most informative features to construct an accurate DT model.
3. *Tree Construction*: Construct a hierarchical structure by iteratively dividing the data with selected features. Use criteria like Gini impurity or information gain to find the best attribute for data splitting, aiming to maximize separation between risky and non-risky business applications.
4. *Node Splitting*: At each node, select the best attribute to split data into subsets based on predetermined criteria. Continue this process until a stopping condition is met, such as reaching a maximum depth or having a minimum number of samples in a leaf node.
5. *Prediction*: Utilize the constructed DT to predict outcomes for new business applications. Traverse the tree from the root to a leaf node, making decisions based on attribute values. The leaf node reached provides the predicted outcome, whether a binary decision (approve/reject) or a risk score indicating likelihood of default.
6. *Model Evaluation and Refinement*: Evaluate the DT model's effectiveness using metrics like accuracy, precision, recall, or area under the ROC curve. If performance is unsatisfactory, employ techniques such as pruning, hyperparameter tuning, or ensemble methods like Random Forests for refinement.

1.4.2.1 Decision Tree (DT)

Below are the steps of DT algorithm:

1. Begin with a training dataset containing examples with both input attributes and a known output or target variable.
2. Select the optimal attribute to divide the dataset, employing a criterion that maximizes information gain. Information gain measures the influence of a particular attribute on the target variable.
3. Divide the dataset into subsets based on the chosen attribute values.
4. Sequentially execute steps 2 and 3 on each subset until meeting a specified stopping condition, such as reaching a maximum tree depth or attaining a minimum number of examples in a leaf node.
5. Construct a DT by associating the target variable with the leaf node that best represents the subset of examples.
6. Employ the DT to predict outcomes for new instances by navigating the path from the root node to a leaf node corresponding to the attribute values of the given example.
7. Trim the DT by eliminating unnecessary branches or nodes that do not enhance predictive accuracy on a validation dataset.
8. Assess the DT's performance on a test dataset, evaluating metrics such as accuracy, precision, recall, and F1-score.

1.4.2.2 Support Vector Machine (SVM)

SVM stands as a widely employed machine learning algorithm within data analytics for managing business approval risk. This supervised learning algorithm adeptly categorizes data into distinct classes, proving valuable in predicting the risk associated with business applications. The integration of data analytics with SVMs empowers business offices to effectively navigate business approval risks by precisely classifying applications into various risk categories. SVM, known for handling intricate data relationships, establishes a robust decision boundary, facilitating informed and unbiased business approval decisions.

The operational framework of an SVM in the context of leveraging data analytics for efficient business approval risk management is elucidated below:

1. *Data Preparation*: Analogous to the DT algorithm, historical business data undergoes collection and preprocessing to ensure quality and relevance. This involves data cleaning, handling missing values, and transforming categorical variables into numerical formats suitable for SVM.
2. *Feature Selection*: Identifying pertinent features or attributes that significantly impact business approval risk is undertaken. These features may encompass business history, income, business amount, employment details, and other relevant factors. The objective is to select informative features contributing to precise risk prediction.
3. *Data Representation*: SVM transforms data into a higher-dimensional space using a kernel function, allowing it to locate a hyperplane that effectively distinguishes between different classes. This enables SVM to adeptly handle complex data patterns and nonlinear relationships.

4. *Hyperplane Optimization*: SVM seeks to find an optimal hyperplane that maximally separates business applications into distinct risk categories. The hyperplane serves as a decision boundary, optimizing the margin between support vectors, data points nearest to the decision boundary, for different classes.
5. *Margin and Support Vectors*: The margin, denoting the gap between the hyperplane and the nearest data points from each class, is maximized by SVM to enhance accurate and reliable predictions for new business applications. Support vectors, positioned on or near the margin, significantly contribute to determining the decision boundary.
6. *Classification and Prediction*: After determining the optimal hyperplane, SVM classifies new business applications by assigning them to different risk categories based on their position relative to the decision boundary. Applications on one side of the hyperplane are classified as low risk, while those on the other side are deemed high risk.
7. *Model Evaluation and Refinement*: The SVM model's effectiveness is evaluated using metrics such as accuracy, precision, recall, or the area under the ROC curve. If the model's performance falls short, refinement techniques like hyperparameter tuning, kernel selection, or feature engineering are applied to enhance the SVM model.

The procedural steps for implementing the SVM algorithm are outlined as follows:

1. Commence with a labeled training dataset containing examples with both input features and known output or target variables.
2. Select the kernel function along with its parameters. This function transforms input features into a higher-dimensional space, facilitating linear separability in that space.
3. Solve the optimization problem to determine the hyperplane maximizing the separation margin between the support vectors, which are examples closest to the hyperplane.
4. Introduce slack variables in situations where the training data is not linearly separable to allow for a certain degree of misclassifications.
5. Identify the Lagrange multipliers that solve the dual problem of the optimization issue.
6. Derive the weight vector and bias term for the decision function using the support vectors and their corresponding Lagrange multipliers.
7. Utilize the decision function to predict outcomes for new examples by performing the dot product between the weight vector and input features, adding the bias term, and determining the sign of the result.
8. Assess the performance of the SVM on a test dataset by examining metrics such as accuracy, precision, recall, and F1 score.

In the final output of Figure 1.1, elucidate the metrics of accuracy, precision, and recall. Historically, traditional business operations involved face-to-face interactions between executives and customers at physical branch locations to meet their needs. However, the landscape has undergone a significant

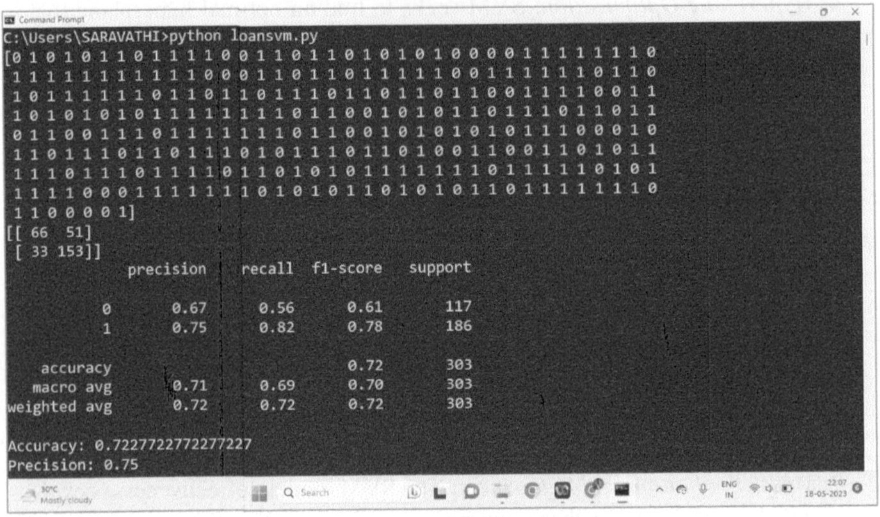

FIGURE 1.1 Conclusive result from the proposed system.

transformation. Customer requirements, preferences, and geographic locations now exhibit diversity, necessitating a different approach. Big Data analytics emerges as a comprehensive tool offering insights into various factors such as customer needs, lifestyles, fraud risks, and potential solutions. This research conducts a thorough analysis of Big Data analytics in the business sector, delving into its tools, technologies, and applications. It also explores anticipated outcomes and potential practical implications. Despite the significant role that Big Data analytics plays in fraud and risk management, particularly when integrated with real-time AI, many banks in India are yet to embark on their Big Data analytics journey. Ongoing research focuses on enhancing infrastructure to connect different departments within a bank through the implementation of Big Data technologies.

The ultimate result, as depicted in Figure 1.2 of the suggested system "Utilizing Data Analytics for Efficient Business Approval Risk Management," may differ based on distinct needs and the chosen implementation approach. It is essential to acknowledge that the specific outputs and their formats may vary depending on the requirements, user interface design, and integration with existing systems within the financial institution. The proposed system aims to utilize data analytics to deliver precise risk assessments, support well-informed decision-making, and improve business approval risk management processes. Nonetheless, here are some primary outputs that the system could furnish:

1. *Risk Assessment*: The system assesses business applications, providing a risk assessment for each application. This evaluation may manifest as a risk score, indicating the probability of default or the level of risk linked to the business. The risk assessment aids in making informed decisions about business approvals and determining appropriate interest rates or terms.

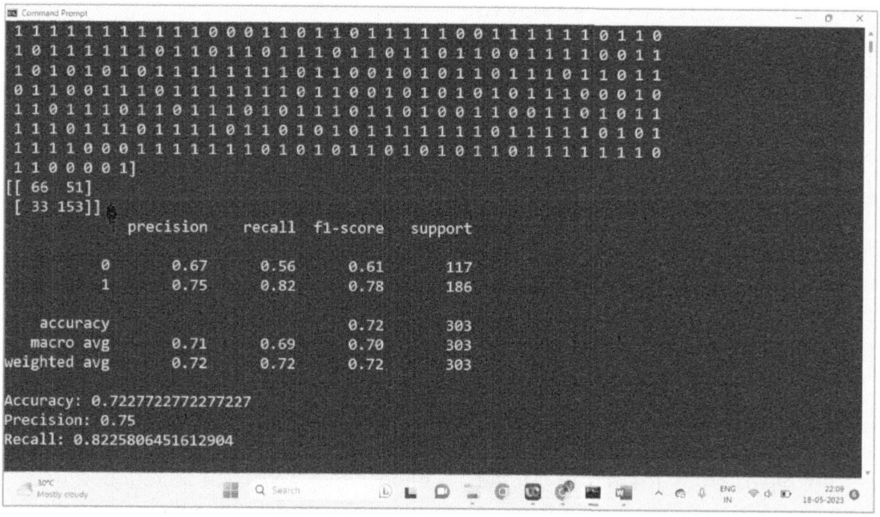

FIGURE 1.2 Illustrates the final execution output of the SVM model.

2. *Business Approval Recommendations*: Based on the risk assessment, the system generates business approval recommendations for each application. These recommendations may be binary decisions like "approve" or "reject," or they may include additional information, such as suggested conditions or modifications to mitigate identified risks.
3. *Risk Visualization*: The system might present visualizations or reports summarizing the overall risk of the business portfolio. These visualizations could encompass charts, graphs, or dashboards illustrating the distribution of risk scores, default rates, or other pertinent metrics. Such visualizations assist stakeholders in comprehending the institution's risk exposure and aid strategic decision-making.
4. *Data Insights*: The system could derive insights and patterns from business data, highlighting crucial factors contributing to business defaults or risks. These insights help in identifying key risk indicators, formulating risk models, and refining the business approval process. By understanding underlying data patterns, institutions can enhance risk management strategies.
5. *Model Performance Evaluation*: The system assesses the performance of predictive models employed for risk assessment. This evaluation includes metrics like accuracy, precision, recall, or area under the ROC curve. Performance assessment aids in gauging the system's effectiveness in predicting business defaults and allows for model refinement if required.
6. *Decision Auditing*: The system may maintain a record or log of decisions made for business approvals alongside associated risk assessments. This auditing feature ensures traceability, transparency, and accountability in the decision-making process. It also proves valuable for regulatory compliance and internal reviews.

1.5 DISCUSSION OF RESULTS

To enact the proposed strategy of utilizing data analytics for business risk management in the work sector, banks and business offices can leverage these steps to enhance the effectiveness of business risk management, diminish the likelihood of business defaults, and optimize the overall performance of their lending portfolios. The sequential steps involve the following:

1. *Gathering Pertinent Data*: The initial step entails collecting relevant data, encompassing business history, income, employment records, repayment history, transactional data, and other pertinent information.
2. *Data Preprocessing*: The collected data undergoes preprocessing to cleanse and transform it into a suitable format for analysis. This includes tasks such as eliminating missing or inconsistent data, encoding categorical data, and scaling numeric data.
3. *Constructing Predictive Models*: Employ data analytics techniques like business scoring, fraud detection, and portfolio analysis to construct predictive models capable of analyzing the pertinent data and generating insights for well-informed lending decisions. This process involves selecting suitable algorithms and parameters, dividing the data into training and testing sets, and assessing the model's performance on the test set.
4. *Implementing the Models*: Once the models are constructed and validated, they can be integrated into the lending process to evaluate the business worthiness of potential borrowers and identify potential risks.
5. *Monitoring and Updating the Models*: Business risk management is an ongoing process necessitating continuous monitoring and updating of the models based on new data and shifts in the lending environment.
6. *Assessing Performance*: Regular evaluations of the models' performance, including key performance indicators such as delinquency rates, charge-offs, and default rates, aid in identifying areas for improvement and adjusting lending policies and procedures accordingly.

The exploration of utilizing data analytics for efficient risk management in business approvals holds considerable significance in the financial industry. By harnessing the capabilities of data analytics, businesses can enhance decision-making processes and mitigate risks associated with approving business applications. However, it's crucial to acknowledge that while data analytics offers substantial benefits, it is not without its limitations. Ensuring data accuracy and privacy, and adhering to relevant regulations are essential considerations when implementing data analytics for business approval risk management. To sum up, the application of data analytics in effective business approval risk management can result in improved risk assessment, increased efficiency, identification of concealed patterns, tailored business products, fraud detection, and continuous enhancement. Through leveraging data, businesses can make more informed decisions, reduce risks, and ultimately deliver superior products and services to their customers.

Let's explore the potential outcomes and implications of adopting such an approach:

1. *Enhanced Risk Assessment*: Utilizing data analytics enables business offices to more accurately evaluate the creditworthiness of business applicants by analyzing diverse data points, including business history, income levels, employment stability, and relevant factors. This results in a more precise risk assessment, reducing the likelihood of defaults and business losses.
2. *Improved Efficiency*: Automation of various elements in the business approval process through data analytics streamlines operations, saving time and minimizing the risk of human errors inherent in manual processes. This efficiency enhancement leads to faster business approvals, contributing to enhanced customer experience and satisfaction.
3. *Discovery of Hidden Patterns*: Employing data analytics, especially with advanced techniques like machine learning algorithms, helps lenders uncover concealed patterns and trends in extensive datasets. This enables the identification of potential risk factors not easily discernible through traditional methods, facilitating more accurate predictions and proactive risk mitigation.
4. *Tailored Business Products*: Data analytics empowers lenders to categorize borrowers based on their risk profiles and other characteristics. This segmentation aids in crafting customized business products and personalized interest rates aligned with the borrower's risk profile, increasing the likelihood of approvals while maintaining an acceptable risk level for the lender.
5. *Fraud Detection*: Data analytics plays a pivotal role in detecting and preventing fraud by analyzing historical data and transaction patterns. Identification of suspicious activities and potential fraud attempts allows business offices to implement effective fraud prevention measures, safeguarding against fraudulent business applications.
6. *Continuous Improvement*: Through data analytics, business offices can perpetually monitor and assess the performance of their business portfolios. Tracking key performance indicators enables lenders to identify trends, evaluate the effectiveness of risk management strategies, and make necessary adjustments for ongoing enhancements in the overall business approval process.

1.5.1 Performance Evaluation Methods

The overall trial outcome is estimated and presented using widely adopted statistical methodologies such as accuracy, precision, recall, F1-score, sensitivity, and specificity. Due to the limited sample size in Research One, the statistical results are expressed with a 95% confidence interval, consistent with previous literature that also dealt with a small dataset [20, 24]. In our dataset, the diagnosis of prostate cancer can be categorized as true positive (Tp) or true negative (Tn) if individuals are diagnosed correctly, and it can be classified as false positive (Fp) or false negative (Fn) if misdiagnosed. The specific statistical metrics are elaborated in detail below:

Accuracy: In terms of accuracy, the SVM model achieves a recorded accuracy of 71.33%, whereas the DT model outperforms with a higher accuracy of 78.32%.

$$Accuracy = \frac{Tp + Tn}{Tp + Tn + Fp + Fn}$$

Precision: Assessing the accuracy of positive predictions in classification models, precision stands as a vital metric.

$$Precision = \frac{Tp}{Tp + Fp}$$

Recall: Assessing the model's capability to accurately recognize all pertinent instances in a classification problem, recall stands as a crucial metric.

$$Recall = \frac{Tp}{Tn + Fp}$$

Sensitivity: Sensitivity, also known as recall, is the principal metric representing the accurate identification of positive cases in relation to the overall number of cases, and its calculation involves the following method:

$$Sensitivity = \frac{Tp}{Tp + Fn}$$

Specificity: It determines the count of correctly identified and predicted true negatives and can be calculated using the subsequent formula:

$$Specificity = \frac{Tn}{Tn + Fp}$$

F1-Score: The provided data does not include specific information about the F1-score; however, F1-score is a comprehensive metric that balances precision and recall, providing a measure of a model's overall performance in classification tasks.

$$F1 - Score = 2 \times \frac{Precision \times Recall}{Precision + Recall}$$

The Area under Curve (AUC): The performance of the models across diverse scenarios is captured by the area under the curve (AUC), and its calculation involves the application of the following formula:

$$AUC = \frac{\sum ri(Xp) - Xp(Xp+1)/2}{Xp + Xn}$$

1.5.2 Evaluation Methods

The subsequent items are assessments of evaluation methods or metrics.

$$Quality = \frac{BP + VM}{BP + VP + BM + VM}$$

$$Preciseness = \frac{BP}{BP + VP}$$

$$Callback = \frac{BP}{BP + VM}$$

$$F - measure = \frac{2 \times Preciseness \times Callback}{Preciseness + Callback}$$

The chart in Figure 1.3 visually represents the time taken for the completion of each iteration of epochs.

Figure 1.4 visually represents the loss ratio corresponding to each epoch throughout the execution process.

Figure 1.5 illustrates the accuracy (72.34%) achieved in each epoch throughout the execution process.

Figure 1.6 illustrates the decrease in loss and the accompanying accuracy achieved in each iteration of the training model for the Decision Tree.

Figure 1.7 elucidates the value loss and value accuracy derived from the training process of the Decision Tree model.

The depicted Figure 1.8 provides a brief summary of the comparison between epochs, loss, and accuracy in the Decision Tree model.

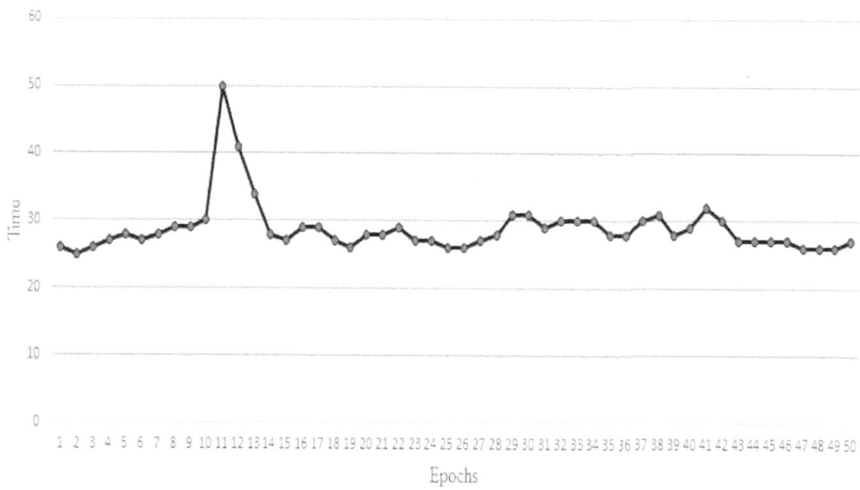

FIGURE 1.3 SVM model – Epochs vs. time comparison.

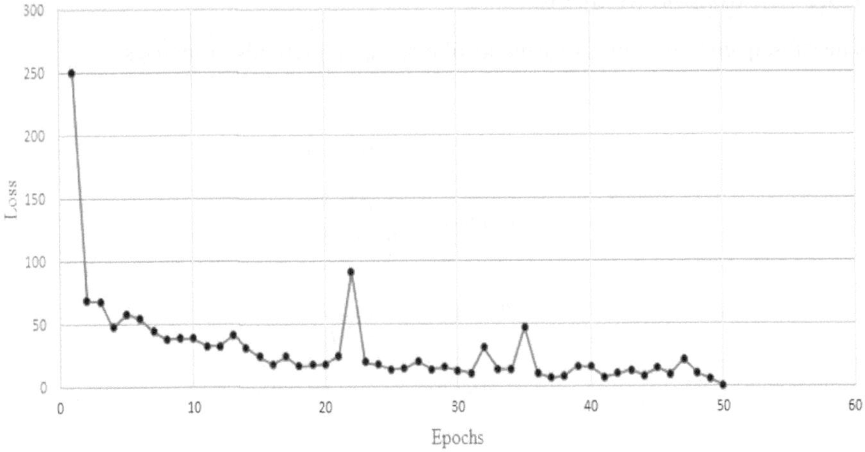

FIGURE 1.4 SVM model – Epochs vs. loss comparison.

1.5.3 Comparison Table

The table presented below offers an overview of the comparison between the suggested approach and different parameters within the current system.

In Table 1.2, the comparison between the proposed system and existing techniques showcases various parameters, highlighting the superiority of the DT model over the SVM model in terms of accuracy, error rate, validation loss, and execution time. Below is a metrics comparison between the current system and the suggested approaches for SVM and DT models.

FIGURE 1.5 SVM model – Accuracy vs. epoch comparison.

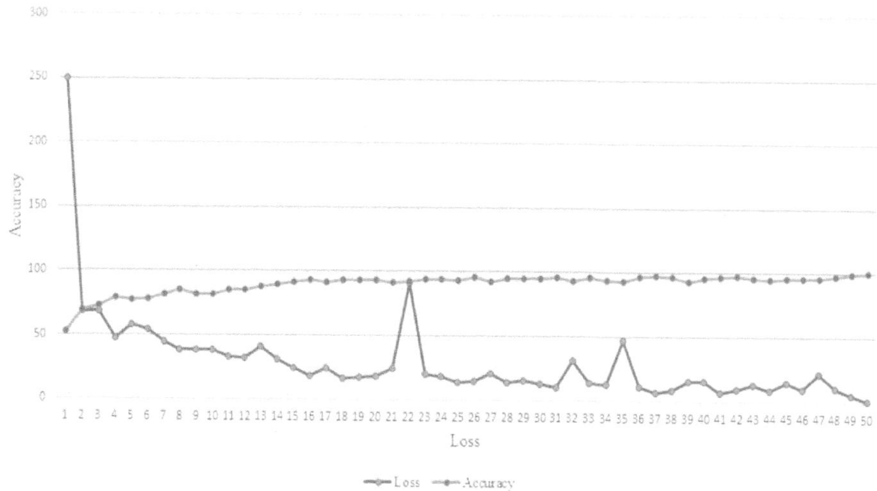

FIGURE 1.6 Decision Tree graph – Accuracy vs. loss comparison.

In Figure 1.9, the metrics comparison between the existing system and the proposed SVM and DT models reveals that the DT model outperforms the SVM model in accuracy, error rate, validation loss, and validation accuracy, with the added advantage of a slightly faster execution time. Based on these metrics, the DT model exhibits superior performance in terms of accuracy, error rate, validation loss, and validation accuracy when compared to the SVM model. Moreover, it demonstrates a marginally quicker execution time.

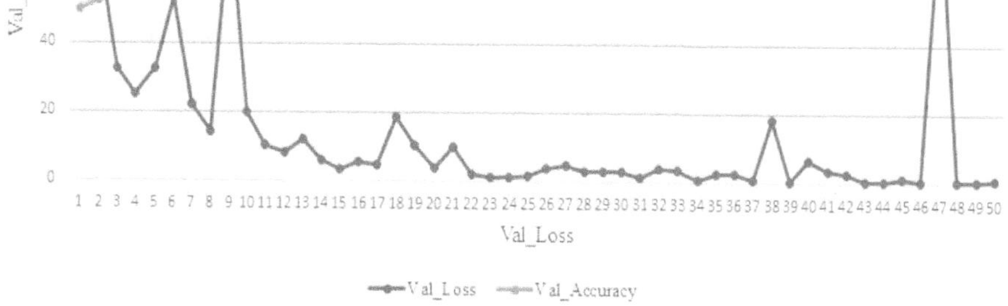

FIGURE 1.7 Decision Tree graph – Val_Accuracy vs. Val_Loss comparison.

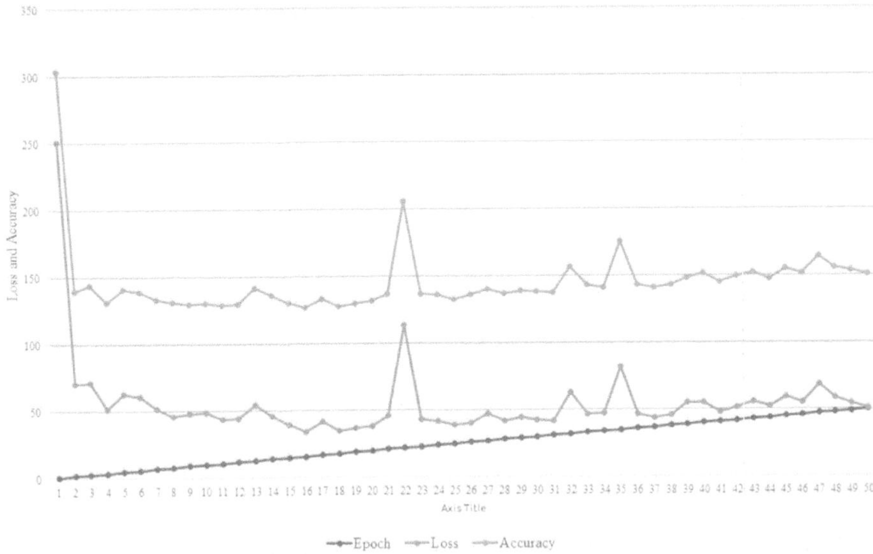

FIGURE 1.8 Epoch vs. loss vs. accuracy comparison in Decision Tree model graph.

The comparison reveals the following observations:

1. *Accuracy*: The accuracy of the SVM model is recorded at 71.33%, while the DT model exhibits a higher accuracy of 78.32%.
2. *Error Rate*: In terms of validation loss, the SVM model shows 3.41, whereas the DT model demonstrates a lower validation loss of 2.64.
3. *Val_Loss*: In terms of validation loss, the SVM model shows 3.41, whereas the DT model demonstrates a lower validation loss of 2.64.
4. *Val_Accuracy*: The validation accuracy for the SVM model is 0.67, while the DT model shows a lower validation accuracy of 0.51.

TABLE 1.2
Metrics Comparison between Proposed System and Existing Techniques

Sl. No.	Name of the Parameter	SVM Model	Decision Tree Model
1.	Accuracy	71.33%	78.32%
2.	Val_Loss	3.41	2.64
3.	Error rate	0.37	0.24
4.	Size of the dataset	36.1 MB	36.1 MB
5.	Val_Accuracy	0.67	0.51
6.	Time complexity	O(n^2)	O(n^2)
7.	No. of epochs	35	35
8.	Execution time	1252 ms	1016 ms

Sl. No.	Name of the Parameter	SVM Model	Decision Tree Model
1.	Accuracy	72.32%	79.34%
2.	Error rate	0.46	0.13
3.	Val_Loss	4.62	3.94
4.	Val_Accuracy	0.79	0.67
5.	Size of the dataset	35.3 MB	35.3 MB
6.	No. of epochs	50	50
7.	Time-complexity	O(n^2)	O(n^2)
8.	Execution time	1370 ms	1129 ms

FIGURE 1.9 Comparison of metrics: Existing system vs. proposed SVM and Decision Tree models.

5. *Size of the Dataset*: Both the SVM and DT models operate with an identical dataset size of 36.1 MB for training and testing purposes.
6. *No. of Epochs*: Both the SVM and DT models undergo training for the same number of epochs, specifically 35 epochs.
7. *Time Complexity*: Both models share a time complexity of O(n^2), signifying a quadratic time complexity in their operations.
8. *Execution Time*: The execution time for the SVM model is 1252 ms, slightly higher than the DT model's faster execution time of 1016 ms.

1.6 CONCLUSION

In conclusion, the investigation into the impact of various factors and potential solutions for promoting business between Liberia and African countries provides valuable insights into the dynamics of their trade relationship. The research, through empirical analysis and an extensive literature review, identifies key influences on business trade, including economic scales, geographical and demographic factors, natural resource endowment, business science and technology, political considerations, and exchange rate dynamics. Positive effects on trade flows were observed for factors such as African countries' GDP, Liberian countries' GDP, education levels in Liberia, arable land availability, and renewable water resources per capita. Conversely, negative impacts were associated with geographical distance and exchange rate fluctuations. The analysis underscores the significance of recognizing regional differences within Liberia, emphasizing the need to tailor development strategies to address specific challenges and opportunities in each region. Development countermeasures proposed in the research include policy recommendations, infrastructure enhancements, and technological advancements. Key steps for fostering sustainable business trade involve consolidating bilateral cooperation, accelerating trade infrastructure development, and promoting business technology upgrades.

The research's contribution to existing literature lies in its comprehensive examination of factors and development countermeasures influencing business trade between Liberia and African countries. Policymakers, industry stakeholders, and researchers can benefit from the insights provided, guiding decision-making processes and supporting the formulation of effective strategies. However, further research is warranted to explore additional aspects of business trade, such as environmental and social impacts, as well as the role of international institutions. Additionally, ongoing monitoring and evaluation of implemented development countermeasures are crucial for assessing effectiveness and making necessary adjustments over time. Shifting focus to the second part of the content, the research underscores the importance of data analytics in business risk management within the work sector. It reveals that DT and SVM models can enhance the business approval process by accurately analyzing and predicting associated risks. The research recommends leveraging these data analytics techniques for risk management, decision-making, and minimizing the likelihood of business defaults.

The research provides practical insights into the application of data analytics in business risk management, emphasizing the need for business offices to adopt these tools and technologies for a competitive edge. The proposed DT model outperforms the SVM model in terms of accuracy, error rate, validation loss, and validation accuracy. The research encourages the continuous refinement and exploration of data analytics approaches in business approval risk management, highlighting the potential benefits of embracing these techniques. To conclude, the research offers valuable recommendations for practitioners and researchers in the field, emphasizing the need for ongoing professional development, collaboration between banks and technology firms, and addressing practical challenges associated with implementing data analytics in the work sector. The insights provided can help business offices unlock the full potential of data analytics, leading to improved business risk management practices and superior risk-adjusted returns.

1.6.1 Future Work

Following the completion of the research on the utilization of data analytics techniques, specifically SVM and DT, for effective business approval risk management, several avenues for future research have been identified. Exploring these areas can propel the application of data analytics in managing business approval risk, refine existing techniques, and provide valuable insights to business offices for improving their risk assessment and decision-making processes. The following are potential directions for future research:

1. *Enhanced Model Performance*: Future research efforts could focus on refining the performance of SVM and DT models to achieve greater precision in predicting business defaults. This may involve adjusting model parameters, exploring alternative kernel functions for SVM, and investigating ensemble techniques to enhance overall effectiveness.
2. *Integration of Additional Data Sources*: Expanding the research's scope by incorporating additional relevant data sources, such as alternative business

data, social media activity, or transactional data, could provide a more comprehensive understanding of applicants' business worthiness. This expansion has the potential to improve the accuracy of risk predictions.

3. *Comparison with Other Techniques*: Conducting comparative studies to analyze the strengths and weaknesses of SVM, DT, and other data analytics techniques for managing business approval risk would be beneficial. Techniques like Random Forest, Gradient Boosting, or Neural Networks can be examined to provide insights into their respective performances.
4. *Real-Time Risk Monitoring*: Advancing research to develop real-time risk monitoring systems can empower business offices to proactively detect and address potential business defaults. This may involve integrating streaming data processing techniques and implementing automated alert systems designed specifically for risk assessment.
5. *Interpretability and Explainability*: While DT analysis offers interpretability, future research could explore methods to enhance the interpretability of SVM models. Developing techniques to clarify the factors and features with the most significant impact on risk assessment can build trust and understanding among lenders and borrowers.
6. *External Validation and Generalizability*: Validating the efficacy and generalizability of the proposed SVM and DT models in future studies using datasets from various business offices or diverse geographical regions would provide a more comprehensive evaluation of their applicability and performance.
7. *Implementation Challenges*: Future research should carefully consider practical hurdles that arise when implementing data analytics techniques in real-world business offices. Prioritizing research on challenges related to data privacy, data quality, scalability, and integration with existing business approval systems is essential for successful implementation.

BIBLIOGRAPHY

Li, J., & Yang, Q. (2022). Forest Certification and Sustainable Business Trade: A Case Research of Liberia-Africa Countries Cooperation. Forest Ecology and Management, 498, 119428.

Liu, Q., & Wu, X. (2016). The Impact of Political Factors on Business Trade between Liberia and Africa Countries. Journal of Development Studies, 42(1), 87–105.

Porwal, A., Chaturvedi, A., & Gupta, S. (2022). Artificial Intelligence With Special Reference to Blockchain Technology: A Future of Accounting. Impact of Artificial Intelligence on Organizational Transformation, 289–303.

Zhang, Y., & Li, C. (2018). The Role of Exchange Rate Dynamics in Business Trade: A Case Research of Liberia and Africa Countries. Journal of International Economics, 22(3), 154–173.

Zhou, G., & Xu, Y. (2021). The Role of Trade Policies in Business Trade: A Comparative Research of Liberia and Africa Countries. Journal of World Trade, 55(3), 489–508.

2 AI-Powered Circular Waste Management

Leveraging Cluster Approach Framework in Jammu and Kashmir for Attaining Sustainable Development Goals

Anil Thakar, Deeksha Dave, and Ankita Chaturvedi

2.1 INTRODUCTION

The concept of a circular economy (CE) has gained significant attention as a means to address global sustainable development challenges (Geng *et al.* 2019). It offers a solution to eliminate waste and pollution through intentional design, while promoting the continuous use of products and materials and the regeneration of natural systems (Taylor *et al.* 2016; Ramadoss *et al.* 2018). This approach has been recognized as a crucial tool in advancing the implementation of the 2030 Agenda, as highlighted in the Expert Group Meeting and the comprehensive review of SDG 12 on Sustainable Consumption and Production (SCP) during the 2018 High-Level Political Forum. The concept of sustainability has a long history, but recent global recognition of the imbalanced relationship between human activities and the environment has brought it into the forefront of the global political agenda (Leal Filho *et al.* 2018). The CE shows great potential for contributing to various Sustainable Development Goals (SDGs) such as affordable energy (SDG 6), economic growth (SDG 8), sustainable cities (SDG 11), SCP (SDG 12), climate change (SDG 13), life on oceans (SDG 14), and life on land (SDG 15). These goals are intrinsically interconnected, and it is possible that conflicting interactions between the SDGs may lead to divergent outcomes (Nilsson *et al.* 2016).

Effectively transitioning from a linear to a circular economy requires collaboration among stakeholders from all sectors (Nobre & Tavares 2017). Companies can play a role by developing expertise in circular design, implementing strategies for product reuse and recycling, and pioneering innovative circular economy business models (CEBMs) (Purvis *et al.* 2019). Policymakers can support this transition by promoting material reuse, increasing resource efficiency, reassessing incentives,

DOI: 10.1201/9781003640776-2

implementing appropriate policies, and facilitating access to financing (Ghisellini *et al.* 2016; Muro 2020; Acerbi *et al.* 2021). Based on the SDG Index and Dashboard global report of 2017, India's rankings were 110 and 116 out of 157 nations in 2016 and 2017, respectively. Similar to other developing nations, India faces challenges in promoting sustainable development due to the lack of basic infrastructure availability, increasing food insecurity (Vani *et al.* 2017), and deteriorating environmental quality (Gurjar *et al.* 2016). To assess India's progress in providing health-related amenities and infrastructure at a sub-national level, Panda and Mohanty (2018) calculated the required rate of progress for selected health indicators of SDGs from 2005 to 2015. They developed a composite index of health and found that if India maintains this rate of progress, achieving the maternal health target of the SDGs by 2030 is feasible.

2.2 SUSTAINABLE PRACTICES IN BUSINESS MODELS

CEBMs present significant potential for businesses, enabling them to generate value and pursue sustainable growth and long-term prosperity. Despite their promising nature, there are several areas within the realm of CEBMs that require further exploration, particularly in the context of developing countries. These areas include the development and execution of CEBMs, considerations of equity and social integration, understanding the impact of CEBMs, and their alignment with the SDGs. Therefore, this book chapter aims to delve into these aspects, providing an in-depth analysis and examination of CEBMs, their implementation challenges, and their potential contributions to sustainability, with a specific focus on the context of developing countries. The global significance of the CE has attracted interest from diverse stakeholders such as governments, businesses, researchers, and civil society due to its potential for reducing environmental impact, promoting sustainable resource utilization, and contributing to the SDGs (Geissdoerfer *et al.* 2017; Schroeder *et al.* 2018; Pieroni *et al.* 2019; Husain *et al.* 2021; Leal Filho *et al.* 2021; Khajuria *et al.* 2022; Sohal *et al.* 2022; Di Vaio *et al.* 2023). CE follows principles centred around waste and pollution elimination, resource circulation at its highest value, and natural capital regeneration. Consequently, CE has been transforming global sectors, including manufacturing, production, consumption, and recycling (Zeng *et al.* 2022). There is a growing inclination among organizations and businesses to adopt CEBMs as a means to create value and capitalize on CE principles (Lewandowski 2016; Hina *et al.* 2022). Developing countries such as India and China are particularly crucial in the transition of businesses and enterprises towards CEBMs. This is due to their substantial population, significant global production and consumption shares, and the immense potential for future urban infrastructure development. Existing literature primarily focuses on the techno-managerial efforts of large businesses in addressing CE challenges, often overlooking the "large flow of resources that happen outside the formal economy" in developing countries like India (Chaturvedi *et al.* 2019). These aspects provide valuable opportunities to explore and comprehend the social and equity dimensions of the CE, which have received less attention in the current CE literature (Kirchherr *et al.* 2017; Murray *et al.* 2017; Padilla-Rivera *et al.* 2020; Walker *et al.* 2021). Furthermore, understanding India's informal approaches to the

CE can assist businesses in implementing and scaling up similar approaches from a technical systems perspective (Sohal *et al.* 2022).

Many developing countries, including India, face significant challenges related to resource efficiency, pollution generation, and low industrial productivity, while also having a substantial mandate for climate action. Despite these challenges, Indian industries possess one of the largest potentials for CE transformation globally. A recent nationwide survey conducted to assess the perspectives of business leaders on the CE landscape, its future, and the potential for decarbonization in India revealed that nearly 94% of the respondents believe that CEBMs can be mainstreamed across various sectors in India within the next three to five years through policies (Figure 2.1). Furthermore, 77% of the surveyed business leaders are currently focusing on CE strategies to achieve their organizations' decarbonization goals (FICCI & Accenture, 2021).

2.3 INCLUSIVE AND RESPONSIBLE IMPLEMENTATION

Existing literature extensively recognizes the potential of the CE to contribute to the achievement of the SDGs (Schroeder *et al.* 2018; Panchal *et al.* 2021; Valverde & Avilés-Palacios 2021; Lahane & Kant 2022; Walker *et al.* 2022). However, quantifying the exact relationship between CE and the SDGs is challenging due to differences in goals, motivations, beneficiaries, and perceptions of responsibilities (Skvarciany *et al.* 2021). Despite the limited number of studies on this topic, Valverde and Avilés-Palacios (2021) provide a compilation of documents that discuss various relationships between CE and strategies contributing to accomplish the SDGs. Notably, Schroeder *et al.* (2018) introduced a framework to categorize the relationship between CE practices and the SDGs, which has been widely referenced in subsequent research. In a specific case the concern of untrained Indian workers involved in e-waste recycling, who lacked proper protective equipment and consequently faced occupational hazards (Chen 2020). The incident emphasizes the need for organizations to take into account not only the economic advantages but also the aspects of health, safety,

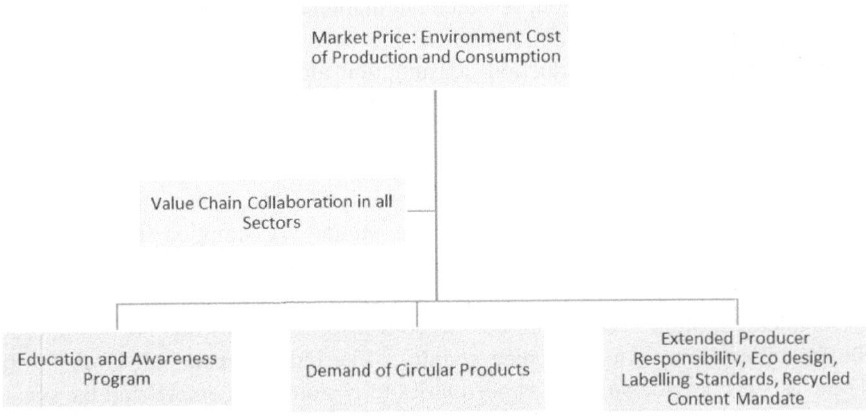

FIGURE 2.1 Potential policy considerations to revolutionize the circular economy business ecosystem. (OECD, 2019.)

TABLE 2.1
Strategies/Practices Implications for Relationship between CE and SDGs in Themes by Different Authors

Theme/Focus	Strategies for Circular Economy Relationship with SDGs	Area of Coverage	Reference
Sustainable Development Goals (SDGs) targeted by CE practices	SDGs 1–12 achieved due to CE practice adoption	Developing countries	Lahane and Kant (2022)
Interplay between the SDGs and the European Union's circular economy (CE) strategy	Positive correlations with SDGs 3, 6, 7, 8, 9, 10, 11, 12, 13, 14, 15, 16, and 17, whereas negative correlation with SDG 3	European Union	Rodriguez-Anton *et al.* (2022)
Circular relationship between CE and SDGs targets	Direct bequest towards SDGs 6, 7, 8, 12, and 15; whereas indirect contribution to SDGs 1, 2, 11, 14; weak or no relationship with SDGs 3, 4, 5, 10; cooperation opportunity with SDG 17	Global	Valverde and Avilés-Palacios (2021)
Influence of SDGs on CE implementation strategies	CE strategies impart positive synergies with SDGs 9, 11, 12, and 17	Global	Morales *et al.* (2021)
Contributory performance of CE to SDGs	Main SDGs addressed by CE performance are SDGs 6, 7, 8, 9, 11, and 12	Global	Panchal *et al.* (2021)

rights, and social well-being. Therefore, CEBM frameworks should encompass all stakeholders who are directly or indirectly affected by the implementation process and operational activities, ensuring their inclusion in CE (Table 2.1).

2.3.1 Economic Value and Sustainability in Different Types of Wastes

The adoption of a CE-based development approach is a prominent strategy for accomplishing the SDGs outlined in the 2030 Agenda (Hippold 2019). The economic benefits of this approach are quantifiable, which estimates that India has the potential to unlock around half-a-trillion dollars of economic value by 2030 through the implementation of CEBMs (Binns *et al.* 2018). This value creation can be achieved by employing various strategies such as reducing waste generation and energy consumption, optimizing product and asset utilization, extending product lifespans, and extracting value from waste streams, as illustrated in Figure 2.2.

In India, the urban population of 377 million individuals currently generates approximately 55 million tonnes of municipal solid waste (MSW) per year (MoHUA, 2021). By 2030, as the urban population is projected to reach 600 million, the waste generation is expected to rise to 165 million tonnes, and by 2050, it may reach 436 million tonnes. Consequently, the greenhouse gas emissions resulting from MSW

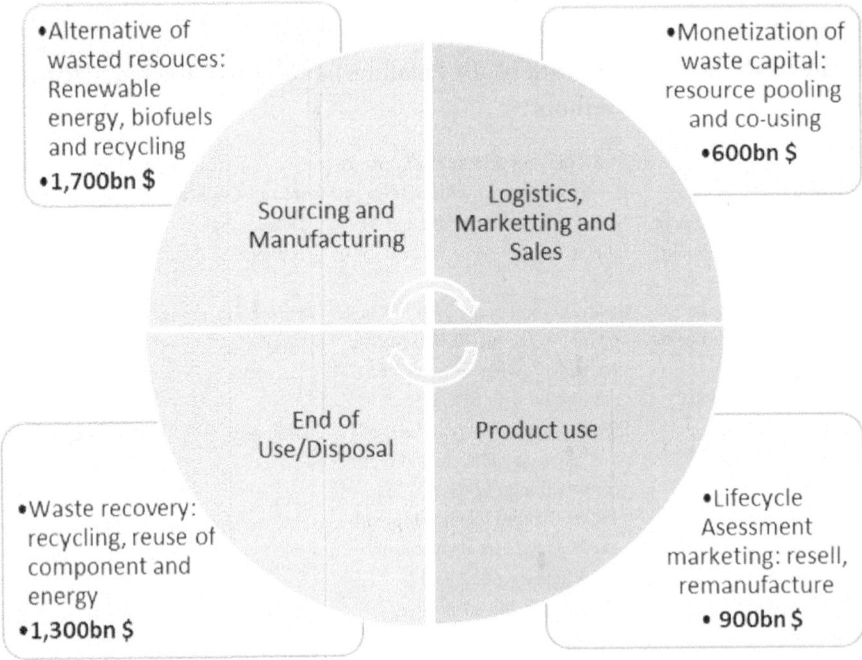

FIGURE 2.2 Monetary value potential from circular business models by 2030. (Fiksel *et al.* 2021.)

are projected to increase to 41.09 million tonnes annually by 2030. To address these challenges and achieve self-reliant development (Aatma Nirbhar Bharat), a crucial need arises for a development model based on the principles of the CE (Gundupalli *et al.* 2017). This model would prioritize sustainable waste management practices and the efficient utilization of resources, aligning with the objectives of an environmentally sustainable and self-reliant India.

2.3.2 Waste Recovery/Reutilization for Circular Economy

Municipal Solid Waste (MSW) can be classified into three categories: wet waste, dry waste, and construction and demolition waste. An assessment conducted by the Ministry of Housing and Urban Affairs identifies substantial opportunities for resource recovery from these waste categories using CE principles. For instance, recycling dry waste has the potential to generate annual revenues of around ₹11,836 crores. Additionally, the conversion of wet waste into compost and Bio-Compressed Natural Gas (CNG) can generate revenue streams of approximately ₹365 crores and ₹1,679 crores per year, respectively (MoHUA, 2021). In a similar way a revenue amounting to 416 crores per annum gets generated by C&D wastes where a similar outlier is seen in case of the liquid waste with revenues amounting to 6,570 crores and 3,285 crores per annum for treated sludge and wastewater, respectively. In recent years, the government has actively formulated policies and initiated projects to drive the nation towards a CE. Specifically, in the realm of municipal solid and liquid waste management, various policies and regulations have been enacted to encourage the scientific processing of waste and promote resource recovery (Meena *et al.* 2022; Srivastav *et al.* 2023). The CE agenda for municipal waste has received substantial support at the national, state, and city levels, with the introduction of the Swachh Bharat Mission-Urban (SBM-U) in 2014. This mission, built on the principles of reduce, reuse, and recycle (3R), has made significant strides in enhancing urban India's capacity for solid waste treatment, increasing it from 18% in 2014 to 68% at present, including recycling activities.

Notable success stories have emerged, such as Chhattisgarh achieving zero-landfill status and cities like Indore implementing 100% source segregation of waste. In the next phase of SBM-Urban, there are plans to expand and institutionalize these processes throughout urban India, aiming to achieve greater economic, environmental, and social benefits.

2.3.3 Current Status of Managing Dry Waste: Challenges and Hurdle

The Swachh Bharat Mission (Urban), initiated by Prime Minister Shri Narendra Modi in October 2014, provided a clear framework for implementing systematic waste management practices across the nation. With the changing waste composition in J&K, particularly the rise in dry waste, and considering the potential for recovery associated with dry waste, it becomes imperative to prioritize the scientific management of all the constituent elements of dry waste and MSW (Figures 2.3 and 2.4). Among the aforementioned dry waste components, plastic stands out as the predominant constituent. India produces around 9.4 million tonnes of plastic waste annually, equivalent to 26,000 tonnes per day. Out of this, approximately 5.6 million tonnes per year (15,600 tonnes per day) are recycled, while 3.8 million tonnes per year (9,400 tonnes per day) remain uncollected or become littered (MoHUA, 2021). Although plastic recycling in India is nearly three times the global average, comprehensive methods for

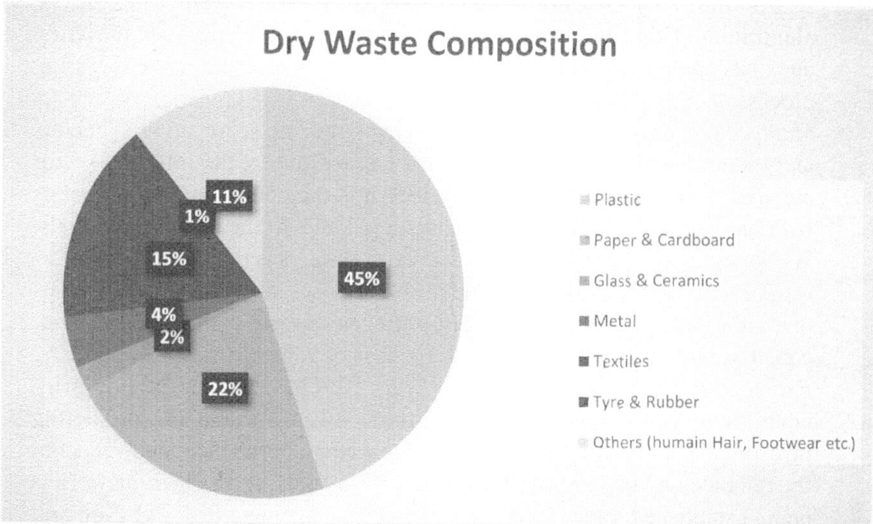

FIGURE 2.3 Dry waste composition in municipal solid waste, J&K. (State Action Plan, 2018.)

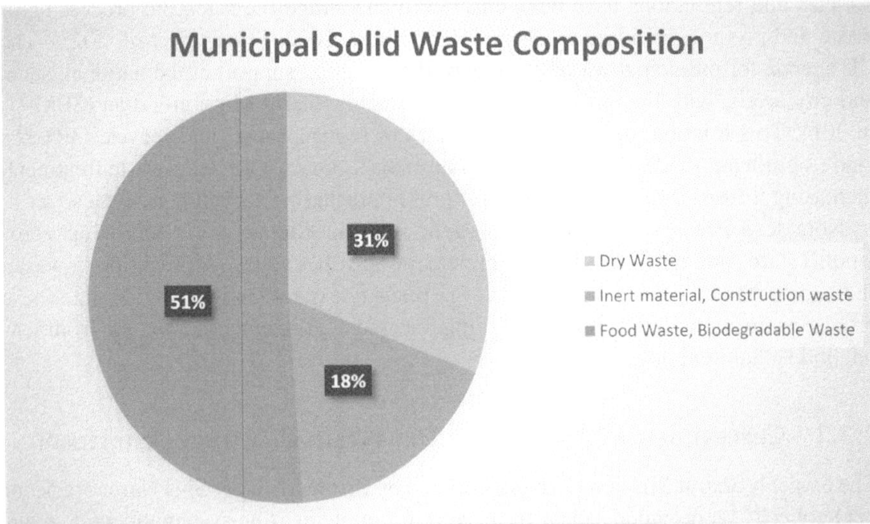

FIGURE 2.4 Total solid waste composition, J&K. (State Action Plan, 2018.)

plastic waste management are lacking. Despite India's per capita plastic consumption of 11 kg, significantly lower than the global average of 28 kg and only about 10% of per capita consumption in the US, it is projected that by 2031, plastic waste generation in India will increase by over threefold from current levels.

2.3.4 Potential Challenges in Management of Dry Waste Components

- *Tetra Pack Processing*: A commonly used compound for packaging, consists of three recyclable components: 75% paper, 20% polyethylene, and 5% aluminium. This combination of materials poses challenges for recycling due to its complexity and the associated high costs involved in the recycling process.
- *Metal Segregation and Unscientific Recycling*: The segregation of metals and the unscientific recycling practices carried out by the informal sector are significant issues. One critical concern is the contamination of metals with biodegradable waste, which poses a risk due to the toxicity of metals. While segregating metals from other waste streams is relatively straightforward due to their high density, the problem arises with small metal scraps that are often lost during inefficient segregated waste collection and inadequate waste tracking. This leads to the loss of valuable metal resources.
- *Extended Producers Responsibility (EPR)*: EPR has emerged as a key principle for managing plastics and electronic waste, focusing on promoting investments in the waste value chain, ensuring compliance, and reducing the reliance on virgin materials. Currently, in India, the EPR framework is being established under the Plastic Waste Management Rules of 2016 and amendment 2022.

- *Problem in Recycling of Glass and Ceramic Waste*: Approximately 18% glass waste is recycled in J&K. The presence of risks associated with injuries and breakages during the handling of glass and ceramics reduces their attractiveness to recyclers and handlers. While there is a well-established market for glass segregated by colours, the lack of segregation and limited availability of glass, as well as the absence of a reliable communication mechanism between cities and the glass recycling industry, pose challenges in the effective recycling of glass.
- *Tyres and Rubber Processing*: As the automobile sector grows, the tyre industry is also experiencing rapid expansion. It is estimated that India currently manufactures approximately 650,000 tyres daily and discards around 275,000 tyres each day, resulting in over a million tonnes of End-of-Life Tyres (ELTs) generated annually. Currently, there is no systematic tracking or monitoring of the disposal of discarded tyres nationwide. While the unorganized sector commonly engages in tyre re-treading, a significant portion of scrap tyres is still disposed of in landfills.

2.3.5 Regulatory Gaps and Interventions

While the current regulations governing dry waste aim to encompass the entire lifecycle of waste, from its generation to its ultimate disposal, there exist potential avenues within policy frameworks to expedite the transition from waste management to a holistic CE. Embracing a CE approach involves establishing incentives for businesses to develop innovative models that capitalize on their efforts in addressing the waste issue. It is essential to reassess existing policies and explore novel mechanisms, particularly with regard to the following aspects, in order to foster innovation and drive the transition towards a CE. The existing policies needed to be reframed in the following aspects:

- *Confinement of EPR to Plastic and E-Waste*: The scope of EPR is presently confined to plastic and electronic waste, and its effectiveness is still not fully realized. However, the absence of an EPR framework for other dry waste categories like paper, textile, tyres/rubber, metal, and glass results in their unscientific disposal, leading to the loss of valuable resources. Achieving circularity is unattainable without the implementation of EPR across all relevant waste streams.
- *Improper Product Labelling*: Insufficient product labelling poses challenges in the segregation and categorization of products. When products with low recyclability are mixed with those that have better recyclability, it can result in reduced recovery rates and the production of sub-standard recycled products.
- *No incentive to Promote Recycling*: The lack of incentives for industries to engage in recycling business or invest in research and development of upstream solutions and circular alternatives is apparent. Currently, recycled products and alternatives are subject to the same GST brackets as products made from virgin materials, resulting in a lack of provisions to promote the use of recycled products and alternatives.
- *Absence of Digital Platform/Artificial Intelligence (AI) Functional for EPR*: The absence of a cohesive digital platform for EPR is evident.

Currently, there is no centralized digital platform to capture comprehensive operational data and ensure effective EPR compliance. The manual process of managing EPR compliance results in communication gaps and processing delays.

- *Clearance Issues*: The absence of a single-window clearance process poses challenges for recycling businesses. These businesses are required to obtain multiple clearances, leading to delays in setting up their operations. In contrast, the unorganized sector can continue their operations without the need for such clearances. The intervention for waste management is required and depicted in Table 2.2.

TABLE 2.2
Intervention of Waste Management for Circular Economy.

	Recommendation	Stakeholders	Level
Policy interventions	• Develop circular economy (CE) guidelines with circularity targets for each dry waste component. • Policy for setting up Waste Management Parks, recycling zones. • Reduction in GST to 5% for recycled products. • Expand EPR to include other dry-waste components: paper, rubber, metals, and glass. • Life Cycle Assessment (LCA) and Material Flow Assessment (MFA).	• MoEF&CC, • MoHUA, • CPCB, • MoES, • MoF, • BIS	National
	• Introduction of landfill tax for dumping/disposal of any waste in landfill. • Ban on disposal of recyclable materials in landfills. • Focus on Zero Waste to Landfill approach.	• UDDs, • SPCB, • Industry	States, urban local bodies
Regulatory interventions	• Setting up a task force to drive and monitor the CE initiatives across all dry waste components and value chain. • Digital platform to capture end-to-end dry waste material flow data for transparency and traceability. • Mandating use of 25% recycled materials in the non-food grade packaging to ensure uptake of recycled materials. • Mandate use of mono-polymers in the production of the packaging products, e.g., PET bottles with HDPE cover/cap and PPP films.	MoEF&CC and CPCB	National
	• Drive out mechanism to monitor dry waste processing and discarding at the ULB level to reduce landfilling. • Enforcement of waste segregation, informal sector inclusivity, and capacity-building initiatives through inclusion in contracts. • Enforcement of penalties in case of non-compliance.	UDDs and SPCB	State/ULBs

Source: MoHUA (2021).

2.4 ARTIFICIAL INTELLIGENCE AND CLUSTER APPROACH FRAMEWORK-BASED WASTE MANAGEMENT

The cluster-based approach for waste management is a strategy that focuses on grouping geographically adjacent areas or communities together to optimize waste management practices (Roberts *et al.* 2022). This approach involves creating clusters or zones that share common waste management infrastructure and resources. Historically, waste management practices were characterized by a simplistic approach, involving a limited number of individuals responsible for gathering waste from public areas and disposing of it in allocated locations (Brancoli *et al.* 2020). Utilizing AI in waste logistics has demonstrated significant benefits, including reductions in transportation distance by up to 36.8%, cost savings of up to 13.35%, and time savings of up to 28.22%. AI technologies enable the accurate identification and sorting of waste, achieving impressive levels of precision ranging from 72.8% to 99.95% (Fang *et al.* 2023). Waste composting is a widely adopted method for treating organic matter; however, operational challenges such as maturity, heavy metal presence, and carbon dioxide emissions persist (Sharma *et al.* 2021; Guo *et al.* 2022; Li *et al.* 2022; Yang *et al.* 2023). To address these issues, AI-based solutions to attain CE through digital technologies have been developed and shown in Figure 2.5. Sharma *et al.* (2021) proposed the use of artificial neural network modelling to enhance the maturity parameters of flower waste and cow manure in vermicomposting. Through experimentation, Sharma *et al.* (2021) discovered that the fertilizer optimized through AI modelling exhibited sufficient nutrient content, thereby benefiting plant growth. The integration of AI and robotics in the planning and functioning of urban waste treatment facilities has the potential to bring about a transformative shift in solid waste management, resulting in enhanced operational efficiency and the adoption of more sustainable waste management strategies (Mukherjee *et al.* 2021; Wilts *et al.* 2021; Andeobu *et al.* 2022).

In this approach, waste management facilities such as waste treatment plants, composting units, or recycling centres are strategically located within each cluster. By consolidating waste management activities within a specific area, the cluster-based approach aims to improve operational efficiency, reduce transportation costs, and minimize environmental impacts associated with waste management (Antikainen *et al.* 2018). Key features of the cluster-based approach include the following:

- *Resource Optimization*: By concentrating waste management activities in a cluster, resources like manpower, equipment, and infrastructure can be utilized more effectively and efficiently. This allows for better coordination and allocation of resources within a limited geographic area.
- *Economies of Scale*: The cluster-based approach enables economies of scale by serving a larger population or generating a higher volume of waste within each cluster. This can lead to cost savings in waste collection, transportation, and processing.
- *Integrated Approach*: The approach encourages an integrated waste management system within the cluster, encompassing waste segregation, collection,

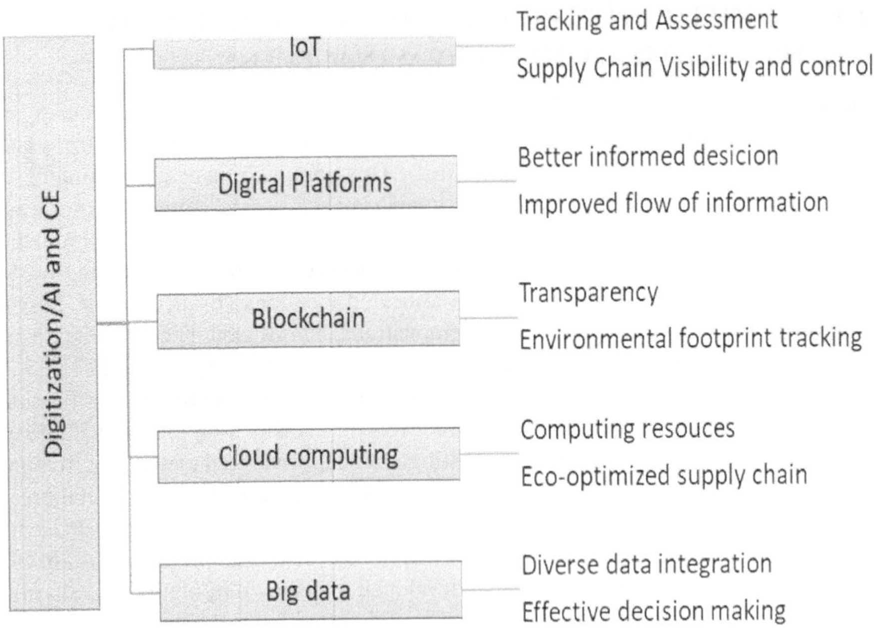

FIGURE 2.5 The role of artificial intelligence and digital technologies in workflow for circular economy. (Pathan *et al.* 2023.)

transportation, treatment, and disposal. It promotes a holistic and coordinated approach to address different aspects of waste management.

- *Collaboration and Partnership*: The cluster-based approach often involves collaboration and partnerships between local authorities, waste management companies, community organizations, and other stakeholders. These partnerships help in sharing expertise, resources, and best practices, leading to improved waste management outcomes.
- *Customization to Local Needs*: The cluster-based approach allows for tailoring waste management solutions to the specific requirements and characteristics of each cluster. Factors such as population density, waste composition, and available infrastructure can be considered to develop customized waste management plans.

Overall, the cluster-based approach for waste management aims to optimize resources, enhance operational efficiency, and promote sustainable waste management practices within geographically defined clusters or zones (Figure 2.6).

2.4.1 Solid Waste Management by ULBs

In India, urban local bodies (ULBs) of different states and UTs are taking several steps to address solid waste management challenges. ULBs have been implementing

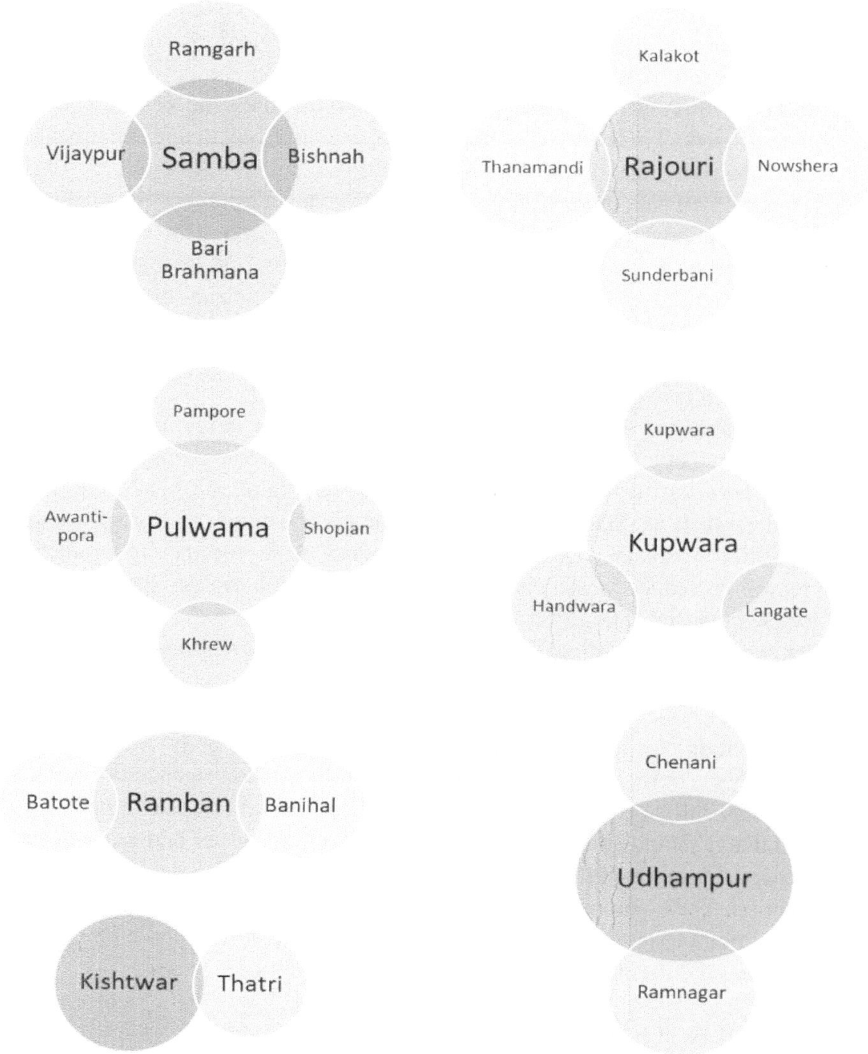

FIGURE 2.6 Some important clusters (sites) in Jammu and Srinagar Municipal Corporation.

various strategies and initiatives to improve waste management practices across cities and towns. These efforts include the following:

- *Waste Segregation*: ULBs are promoting waste segregation at source, encouraging citizens to separate their waste into different categories such as biodegradable (wet) and non-biodegradable (dry) waste. This allows for more effective handling and processing of different types of waste.
- *Collection and Transportation*: ULBs have established waste collection systems, including regular waste pick-up schedules and designated

collection points. They have also introduced mechanized or efficient methods of waste transportation to ensure timely and hygienic waste disposal.

- *Infrastructure Development*: ULBs are investing in the development of infrastructure such as waste treatment plants, composting facilities, and landfill sites. These facilities help in proper waste processing, treatment, and disposal, reducing the burden on landfills.
- *Public Awareness and Participation*: ULBs conduct awareness campaigns and educational programmes to sensitize citizens about the importance of proper waste management. They encourage active citizen participation through initiatives like citizen helplines, community clean-up drives, and waste management training for Self-Help Groups.
- *Waste-to-Energy Projects*: Some ULBs are implementing waste-to-energy projects to convert organic waste into biogas or electricity. These projects help in reducing the volume of waste sent to landfills and provide a renewable source of energy.
- *Collaboration with Stakeholders*: ULBs collaborate with various stakeholders such as NGOs, waste management companies, and recyclers to optimize waste management practices. They work together to promote recycling, reduce waste generation, and explore innovative solutions for waste management.
- *Engaging Self-Help Groups and Promoting Public Participation*: Self-Help Groups will undergo training to inspire societies, associations, and management entities of commercial complexes and residential housing units to maintain cleanliness in their premises. Urban local body officials will actively encourage public engagement in solid waste management systems. Citizens will be educated about the improper disposal of waste, emphasizing that it should not be discarded on streets, drains, water bodies, or open spaces. Furthermore, they will be prohibited from littering and open defecation. The community will be encouraged to participate in the primary collection of waste, segregating wet and dry waste at the source until disposal, and utilizing litterbins placed on roads and public areas.

Overall, ULBs in India are actively working towards improving solid waste management through a combination of infrastructure development, public participation, awareness campaigns, and sustainable waste management practices.

2.5 WASTE MANAGEMENT BY CLUSTERING AND SWOT ANALYSIS

The Jammu Municipal Corporation (JMC) and Srinagar Municipal Corporation (SMC) are the governing body responsible for managing MSW in Jammu and Srinagar city, respectively. This includes activities such as waste storage, collection, transportation to disposal sites, and processing plants. However, despite having Bhagwati Nagar and Udheywalla landfill sites, they are at risk of becoming overwhelmed in the future, exceeding their capacity. The SWOT analysis scientifically identifies the strengths, weaknesses, opportunities, and threats in addition to the clustering of waste collection centres in the current MSW management practices followed by the municipal committees and councils in the Jammu Province (Thakar & Devi 2022).

Strength: The study proposes effective management practices and suggests ways to enhance them in the future. The JMC currently implements door-to-door waste collection, where residents pay a fixed monthly fee, resulting in reduced dumping of garbage in open areas and drains. Additionally, certain upscale areas of the city involve various organizations like Resident Welfare Associations (RWA) and volunteer groups from civil society in MSW management. Analysis of the MSW composition indicates that approximately 12% of the waste is combustible. To alleviate pressure on the landfill, it is recommended that the JMC establish facilities for waste processing and conversion into refuse derived fuel (RDF), particularly in the outskirts of Jammu. This could be achieved through a public-private partnership. It is crucial to address the issue of toxic waste leaching into groundwater at the Bhagwati Nagar landfill, as it currently receives waste from hospitals and other sources. To minimize the diversion and burning of combustible waste, the strategic placement of separate waste collection stations known as Sehaj Safai Kendras (SSKs) similar to those in Chandigarh can prove beneficial.

Weakness: The absence of waste segregation at the source has a negative impact on the composition of MSW, as it diminishes the organic and fuel potential of the waste. Furthermore, the lack of localized composting facilities results in the mixing and indiscriminate dumping of accumulated waste on roads. When analysing the physical composition of MSW, it was found that over 70% of the waste fraction consisted of organic materials, which were being improperly dumped in areas such as Gadigarh, Colonial Colony, and Karan Bagh. E-waste, hazardous waste, and biomedical waste from the region also ended up in landfills as part of the municipal waste. However, in recent years, the JMC has actively collaborated with the State Pollution Control Board (SPCB) to ensure the proper and scientific disposal of biomedical waste, addressing this issue.

Opportunities and Threats: Jammu city has the potential to become a benchmark for achieving 100% compliance with the MSW Rules of India in 2016. The study findings, based on MSW characterization, suggest the establishment of composting and bio-methanation plants specifically designed for organic waste from sources like hotels, restaurants, and dhabas. JMC can introduce in-house composting facilities at waste collection points, tailoring their capacity based on different economic sectors to accommodate varying waste generation rates. The leachate from landfills can be repurposed as fertilizer for agricultural purposes, benefiting areas such as RS Pura, Chatha, and Miran Sahib through collaboration with the SKUAST agricultural university. Active involvement of media, universities, NGOs, schools, and other educational institutions is crucial for the successful implementation of these initiatives. The primary concern with open landfills and dumping is the potential seepage of leachate into the soil, leading to nutrient loss and agricultural damage. Additionally, the proximity of the garbage dump and butcher house waste to Jammu Airport raises the risk of air crashes due to the presence of crows, vultures, and other raptors.

2.5.1 Information, Education, and Communication (IEC) Strategies

Information, Education, and Communication (IEC) strategies play a crucial role in waste management initiatives in Jammu and Kashmir (J&K). These strategies aim to raise awareness, educate the public, and facilitate behaviour change regarding waste management practices. Some IEC strategies implemented in J&K for waste management include the following:

Public Awareness Campaigns: Conducting public awareness campaigns through various mediums such as print media, radio, television, and social media platforms. These campaigns focus on highlighting the importance of waste segregation, proper disposal methods, and the impact of waste on the environment and public health.

Educational Programmes: Organizing educational programmes in schools, colleges, and community centres to educate students, teachers, and the general public about waste management practices. These programmes cover topics like waste segregation, composting, recycling, and the 3Rs (Reduce, Reuse, Recycle).

Workshops and Training Sessions: Conducting workshops and training sessions for stakeholders, including municipal officials, waste management workers, and community members. These sessions provide practical knowledge and skills related to waste management techniques, waste segregation, and effective use of waste management infrastructure.

Information Dissemination: Distributing informational brochures, pamphlets, and posters in public spaces, offices, and residential areas to provide guidance on waste management practices. The information includes details about waste segregation, collection schedules, contact information for waste management authorities, and the importance of individual responsibility.

Community Engagement: Encouraging community participation and involvement in waste management initiatives. This can include organizing community clean-up drives, waste collection campaigns, and promoting the establishment of Self-Help Groups for waste management at the community level.

Stakeholder Collaboration: Collaborating with local NGOs, RWAs, and other stakeholders to develop and implement IEC strategies effectively. Such collaborations help in reaching a wider audience and fostering a sense of ownership and responsibility among community members.

Mobile Apps and Online Platforms: Utilizing mobile applications and online platforms to provide information, facilitate waste collection requests, and encourage citizen engagement in waste management activities. By implementing these IEC strategies, J&K aims to create a well-informed and responsible society that actively participates in waste management practices, resulting in cleaner and healthier environment (Figure 2.7).

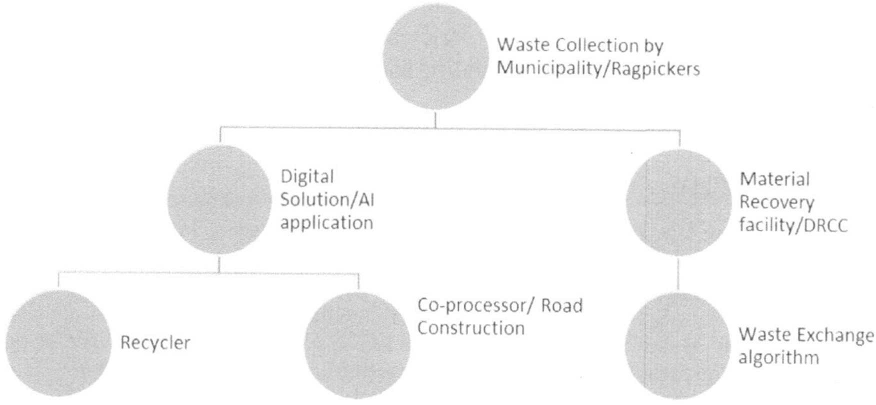

FIGURE 2.7 Digital technology/AI algorithm intervention in waste management.

2.6 CONCLUSION

AI-based circular waste management holds significant potential for achieving SDGs in waste management. This innovative approach combines the power of AI with the strategic cluster-based framework to optimize waste management practices, enhance resource efficiency, and contribute to the attainment of sustainable development objectives. By harnessing AI technologies, such as data analytics, machine learning, and smart sensing, waste management processes can be intelligently optimized. AI algorithms can analyse vast amounts of data to identify patterns, optimize waste collection routes, and improve waste segregation practices. This enables efficient resource allocation, reduces operational costs, and minimizes environmental impacts associated with waste management activities. The cluster approach framework further enhances the effectiveness of waste management efforts by consolidating waste management infrastructure and resources within geographically defined clusters. This facilitates economies of scale, as shared facilities and services can serve larger populations and handle higher volumes of waste. The cluster-based model also promotes collaboration, knowledge sharing, and collective decision-making among stakeholders, including local authorities, waste management companies, and community organizations.

By adopting an AI-powered circular waste management approach within the cluster framework, J&K can advance towards its SDGs. The CE principles, such as waste reduction, recycling, and resource recovery, can be integrated into the waste management practices. This promotes the efficient use of resources, minimizes waste generation, and reduces dependency on landfilling.

Furthermore, this approach aligns with global sustainability objectives, including the United Nations SDGs. It contributes to SDG 11 (sustainable cities and communities) by promoting sustainable waste management practices, SDG 12 (responsible consumption and production) through waste reduction and resource efficiency, and SDG 13 (climate action) by mitigating the environmental impacts of waste management. Therefore, this framework in J&K presents a scientifically sound and innovative solution for achieving SDGs in waste management. By leveraging AI technologies and strategic clustering, J&K can enhance efficiency, resource optimization, and environmental sustainability, leading to a cleaner, greener, and more resilient future for the region.

BIBLIOGRAPHY

Acerbi F, Forterre DA, Taisch M. 2021. Role of artificial intelligence in circular manufacturing: a systematic literature review. IFAC-PapersOnLine 54(1):367–372. https://doi.org/10.1016/j.ifacol.2021.08.040

Andeobu L, Wibowo S, Grandhi S. 2022. Artificial intelligence applications for sustainable solid waste management practices in Australia: a systematic review. Science of the Total Environment 834:155389. https://doi.org/10.1016/j.scitotenv.2022.155389

Antikainen M, Uusitalo T, Kivikytö-Reponen P. 2018. Digitalisation as an enabler of circular economy. Procedia CIRP 73:45–49.

Binns R, Lyngs U, Van Kleek M, Zhao J, Libert T, Shadbolt N. 2018. Third party tracking in the mobile ecosystem. Proceedings of the 10th ACM Conference on Web Science, 23–31. https://doi.org/10.1145/3201064.3201089

Brancoli P, Bolton K, Eriksson M. 2020. Environmental impacts of waste management and valorisation pathways for surplus bread in Sweden. Waste Management 117:136–145. https://doi.org/10.1016/j.wasman.2020.07.043

Chaturvedi A, Gaurav JK, Gupta P. 2019. The many circuits of a circular economy 1. In The Circular Economy and the Global South (pp. 25–42). Routledge, London

Chen CW. 2020. Improving circular economy business models: opportunities for business and innovation: a new framework for businesses to create a truly circular economy. Johnson Matthey Technology Review 64(1):48–58. https://doi.org/10.1595/205651320X15710564137538

Di Vaio A, Hasan S, Palladino R, Hassan R. 2023. The transition towards circular economy and waste within accounting and accountability models: a systematic literature review and conceptual framework. Environment, Development and Sustainability 25(1):734–810. https://doi.org/10.1007/s10668-021-02078-5

Fang B, Yu J, Chen Z, Osman AI, Farghali M, Ihara I, Hamza EH, Rooney DW, Yap PS. 2023. Artificial intelligence for waste management in smart cities: a review. Environmental Chemistry Letters 21:1959–1989. https://doi.org/10.1007/s10311-023-01604-3

FICCI & Accenture. 2021. Beyond Incrementalism: A Pulse Check on India's Circular Transition. FICCI and Accenture, New Delhi.

Fiksel J, Sanjay P, Raman K. 2021. Steps toward a resilient circular economy in India. Clean Technology Environ Policy 23:203–218. https://doi.org/10.1007/s10098-020-01982-0

Geissdoerfer M, Savaget P, Bocken NM, Hultink EJ. 2017. The circular Economy – a new sustainability paradigm? Journal of Cleaner Production 143:757–768. https://doi.org/10.1016/j.jclepro.2016.12.048

Geng Y, Sarkis J, Bleischwitz R. 2019. How to globalize the circular economy. Nature 565(7738):153–155. https://doi.org/10.1038/d41586-019-00017-z

Ghisellini P, Cialani C, Ulgiati S. 2016. A review on circular economy: the expected transition to a balanced interplay of environmental and economic systems. Journal of Cleaner Production 114:11–32. https://doi.org/10.1016/j.jclepro.2015.09.007

Gundupalli SP, Hait S, Thakur A. 2017. A review on automated sorting of source-separated municipal solid waste for recycling. Waste Management 60:56–74. https://doi.org/10.1016/j.wasman.2016.09.015

Guo HN, Liu HT, Wu S. 2022. Simulation, prediction and optimization of typical heavy metals immobilization in swine manure composting by using machine learning models and genetic algorithm. Journal of Environ Management 323:116266. https://doi.org/10.1016/j.jenvman.2022.116266

Gurjar BR, Ravindra K, Nagpure AS. 2016. Air pollution trends over Indian megacities and their local-to-global implications. Atmospheric Environment 142:475–495.

Hina M, Chauhan C, Kaur P, Kraus S, Dhir A. 2022. Drivers and barriers of circular economy business models: where we are now, and where we are heading. Journal of Cleaner Production 333:130049. https://doi.org/10.1016/j.jclepro.2021.130049

Hippold S. 2019. Gartner Predicts Circular Economies Will Replace Linear Economies in 10 Years. Gartner. https://www.gartner.com/en/newsroom/press-releases/2019-09-26-gartner-predicts-circular-economies-will-replace-line. Accessed 06 June 2023.

Husain Z, Maqbool A, Haleem A, Pathak RD, Samson D. 2021. Analysing the business models for circular economy implementation: a fuzzy TOPSIS approach. Operations Management Research 14(3–4):256–271. https://doi.org/10.1007/s12063-021-00197-w

Khajuria A, Atienza VA, Chavanich S, Henning W, Islam I, Kral U, ..., & Li J. 2022. Accelerating circular economy solutions to achieve the 2030 agenda for sustainable development goals. Circular Economy 1(1):100001. https://doi.org/10.1016/j.cec.2022.100001

Kirchherr J, Reike D, Hekkert M. 2017. Conceptualizing the circular economy: an analysis of 114 definitions. Resources, Conservation and Recycling 127:221–232. https://doi.org/10.1016/j.resconrec.2017.09.005

Lahane S, Kant R. 2022. Investigating the sustainable development goals derived due to adoption of circular economy practices. Waste Management 143:1–14. https://doi.org/10.1016/j.wasman.2022.02.016

Leal Filho W, Abubakar IR, Kotter R, Grindsted TS, Balogun AL, Salvia AL, Aina YA, Wolf F. 2021. Framing electric mobility for urban sustainability in a circular economy context: an overview of the literature. Sustainability 13(14):7786. https://doi.org/10.3390/su13147786

Leal Filho W, Shiel C, Paço A. 2018. Integrative approaches to environmental sustainability at universities: an overview of challenges and priorities. Journal of Integrative Environmental Sciences 12(1):1–14.

Lewandowski M. 2016. Designing the business models for circular economy—towards the conceptual framework. Sustainability 8(1):43. https://doi.org/10.3390/su8010043

Li Y, Li S, Sun X, Hao D. 2022. Prediction of carbon dioxide production from green waste composting and identification of critical factors using machine learning algorithms. Bio Resource Technology 360:127587. https://doi.org/10.1016/j.biortech.2022.127587

Meena P, Chaturvedi A, Gupta S. 2022. Impact of artificial intelligence on development and growth of entrepreneurship. In Impact of Artificial Intelligence on Organizational Transformation, (pp. 131–146). Wiley, USA.

MoHUA. 2021. Circular Economy in Municipal Solid and Liquid Waste. Ministry of Housing and Urban Affairs, New Delhi.

Morales ME, Batlles-delaFuente A, Cortés-García FJ, Belmonte-Ureña LJ. 2021. Theoretical research on circular economy and sustainability trade-offs and synergies. Sustainability 13(21):11636. https://doi.org/10.3390/su132111636

Mukherjee A, Ramesh Wanjari U, Chakraborty R, Renu K, Vellingiri B, George A, Sundara Rajan, CR, Valsala Gopalakrishnan A. 2021. A review on modern and smart technologies for efficient waste disposal and management. Journal of Environmental Management 297:113347. https://doi.org/10.1016/j.jenvman.2021.113347

Muro M. 2020. No matter which way you look at it, tech jobs are still concentrating in just a few cities. https://www.brookings.edu/research/tech-is-still-concentrating/. Accessed May 2023.

Murray A, Skene K, Haynes K. 2017. The circular economy: an interdisciplinary exploration of the concept and application in a global context. Journal of Business Ethics 140:369–380. https://doi.org/10.1007/s10551-015-2693-2

Nilsson M, Griggs D, Visbeck M. 2016. Map the interactions of sustainable development goals. Nature 534:320–322. https://doi.org/10.1038/534320a

Nobre GC, Tavares E. 2017. Scientific literature analysis on big data and internet of things applications on circular economy: a bibliometric study. Scientometrics 111(1):463–492. https://doi.org/10.1007/s11192-017-2281-6

OECD. 2019. Business Models for the Circular Economy: Opportunities and Challenges for Policy. OECD Publishing, Paris.

Padilla-Rivera A, Russo-Garrido S, Merveille N. 2020. Addressing the social aspects of a circular economy: a systematic literature review. Sustainability 12(19):7912. https://doi.org/10.3390/su12197912

Panchal R, Singh A, Diwan H. 2021. Does circular economy performance lead to sustainable development? A systematic literature reviews. Journal of Environmental Management 293:112811. https://doi.org/10.1016/j.jenvman.2021.112811

Panda BK, Mohanty SK. 2018. Progress and prospects of health-related sustainable development goals in India. Journal of Biosocial Science:1–18.

Pathan MS, Richardson E, Galvan E, Mooney P. 2023. The role of artificial intelligence within circular economy activities- a view from Ireland. Sustainability 15:9451. https://doi.org/10.3390/su15129451

Pieroni MP, McAloone TC, Pigosso DC. 2019. Business model innovation for circular economy and sustainability: a review of approaches. Journal of Cleaner Production 215:198–216. https://doi.org/10.1016/j.jclepro.2019.01.036

Purvis B, Mao Y, Robinson D. 2019. Three pillars of sustainability: in search of conceptual origins. Sustainability Science 14(3):681–695. https://doi.org/10.1007/s11625-018-0627-5

Ramadoss TS, Alam H, Seeram R. 2018. Artificial intelligence and internet of things enabled circular economy. International Journal of Engineering Science 7(9):55–63.

Roberts H, Zhang J, Bariach B, Cowls J, Gilburt B, Juneja P, Tsamados A, Ziosi M, Taddeo M, Floridi L. 2022. Artificial intelligence in support of the circular economy: ethical considerations and a path forward. AI & Society. https://doi.org/10.1007/s00146-022-01596-8

Rodríguez-Antón JM, Rubio-Andrada L, Celemín-Pedroche MS, Ruíz-Peñalver SM. 2022. From the circular economy to the sustainable development goals in the European Union: an empirical comparison. Int Environ Agreements 22:67–95. https://doi.org/10.1007/s10784-021-09553-4

Schroeder P, Anggraeni K, Weber U. 2018. The relevance of circular economy practices to the sustainable development goals. Journal of Industrial Ecology 23(1):77–95. https://doi.org/10.1111/jiec.12732

Sharma D, Pandey AK, Yadav KD, Kumar S. 2021. Response surface methodology and artificial neural network modelling for enhancing maturity parameters during vermicomposting of floral waste. Bioresource Technology 324:124672. https://doi.org/10.1016/j.biortech.2021.124672

Skvarciany V, Lapinskaitė I, Volskytė G. 2021. Circular economy as assistance for sustainable development in OECD countries. Oeconomia Copernicana 12:11–34. https://doi.org/10.24136/oc.2021.001

Sohal A, Nand AA, Goyal P, Bhattacharya A. 2022. Developing a circular economy: an examination of SME's role in India. Journal of Business Research 142:435–447. https://doi.org/10.1016/j.jbusres.2021.12.072

Srivastav AL, Markandeya Patel N, Pandey M, Pandey AK, Dubey AK, Kumar A, Bhardwaj AK, Chaudhary VK. 2023. Concepts of circular economy for sustainable management of electronic wastes: challenges and management options. Environmental Science and Pollution Research 30:48654–48675

State Action Plan. 2018. Municipal Solid Waste Management Action Plan for J&K. Housing and Urban Development Department report: 1–32.

Taylor L, Floridi L, van der Sloot B. 2016. Group Privacy: New Challenges of Data Technologies. Springer, Cham, Switzerland.

Thakar A, Devi S. 2022. Assessment of municipal solid waste management in Rani Bagh area of Jammu City through SWOT analysis: Prospect of Jammu municipal corporation towards Swachh Bharat Abhiyan and sustainable Jammu City. International Journal of Environmental Sciences 11(2):74–78. https://doi.org/10.13140/RG.2.2.36424.60164

Valverde JM, Avilés-Palacios C. 2021. Circular economy as a catalyst for progress towards the sustainable development goals: a positive relationship between two self-sufficient variables. Sustainability 13(22):12652. https://doi.org/10.3390/su132212652

Vani SVS, Bhaumik S, Nandan A, Siddiqui NA. 2017. Hazardous waste-impact on health and environment for sustainable development in India. World Scientific News 70(2):158–172.

Walker AM, Opferkuch K, Roos Lindgreen E, Raggi A, Simboli A, Vermeulen WJ, Caeiro S, Salomone R. 2022. What is the relation between circular economy and sustainability? Answers from frontrunner companies engaged with circular economy practices. Circular Economy and Sustainability 2(2):731–758. https://doi.org/10.1007/s43615-021-00064-7

Walker AM, Vermeulen WJ, Simboli A, Raggi A. 2021. Sustainability assessment in circular inter-firm networks: an integrated framework of industrial ecology and circular supply chain management approaches. Journal of Cleaner Production 286:125457. https://doi.org/10.1007/s43615-021-00064-7

Wilts H, Garcia BR, Garlito RG, Gómez LS, Prieto EG. 2021. Artificial intelligence in the sorting of municipal waste as an enabler of the circular economy. Resources 10:28. https://doi.org/10.3390/resources10040028

Yang M, Chen L, Wang J, Msigwa G, Osman AI, Fawzy S, Rooney DW, Yap PS. 2023. Circular economy strategies for combating climate change and other environmental issues. Environmental Chemistry Letters 21:55–80. https://doi.org/10.1007/s10311-022-01499-6

Zeng X, Ogunseitan OA, Nakamura S, Suh S, Kral U, Li J, Geng Y. 2022. Reshaping global policies for circular economy. Circular Economy 1(1):100003. https://doi.org/10.1016/j.cec.2022.100003

3 Artificial Intelligence and Sustainable Economy

Opportunities and Challenges

Pawan Whig, Ronak Ravjibhai Pansara, Pavika Sharma, and Balaram Yadav Kasula

3.1 INTRODUCTION

In recent years, the world has witnessed remarkable advancements in artificial intelligence (AI), revolutionizing industries and transforming the way we live and work (Agalliu, Di Leva, & Bollea, 2018). At the same time, global concerns about environmental degradation, resource depletion, and climate change have spurred the urgent need for a more sustainable approach to economic development. The integration of AI into a sustainable economy has emerged as a promising pathway to address these pressing challenges and create a greener, more resilient future (Alrazi, De Villiers, & Van Staden, 2016).

A sustainable economy, in essence, seeks to balance economic growth, social well-being, and environmental stewardship. It aims to meet the needs of the present generation without compromising the ability of future generations to meet their own needs. This concept rests on key principles, including responsible resource management, social inclusivity, and ecological preservation (Baccala et al., 2018). AI also fosters economic sustainability by promoting innovation and growth in the entrepreneurial sector (Meena, Chaturvedi, & Gupta, 2022).

This chapter delves into the opportunities and challenges presented by the synergistic relationship between AI and a sustainable economy (Bagnoli et al., 2018). We explore how AI can be harnessed to achieve sustainability goals, such as reducing carbon emissions through smart energy systems, optimizing resource use through data-driven decision-making, and enhancing environmental monitoring and conservation efforts through innovative technologies (Bassiliades & Chalkiadakis, 2018).

Furthermore, while the potential benefits of AI in sustainability are promising, it is crucial to acknowledge and address the potential risks and pitfalls (Beltramello, Haie-Fayle, & Pilat, 2013). The chapter discusses the importance of responsible AI implementation and governance to ensure that AI technologies are used ethically and equitably. We also explore the concerns surrounding the possibility of AI exacerbating existing social and economic inequalities (Biloslavo, Bagnoli, & Edgar, 2018).

As policymakers and businesses navigate the integration of AI into a sustainable economy, they must consider a range of critical factors. These include striking the

 DOI: 10.1201/9781003640776-3

right balance between innovation and regulation, fostering collaboration between different stakeholders, and fostering an environment that encourages the development of AI technologies that align with sustainability objectives (Bocken et al., 2013). Through this exploration of opportunities and challenges, this chapter aims to shed light on the transformative potential of AI in building a sustainable economy. By leveraging AI responsibly and ethically, we can pave the way toward a future where economic prosperity, social equity, and environmental well-being are in harmony (Bocken et.al, 2014).

3.2 SUSTAINABLE ECONOMY

A sustainable economy is an economic system that seeks to meet the needs of the present generation without compromising the ability of future generations to meet their own needs (Chang & Wang, 2013; Chrissos, 2018; Davenport & Ronanki, 2018; Dignum, 2016). It is characterized by a balanced approach to economic growth, social development, and environmental stewardship. Key principles that underpin a sustainable economy include the following:

1. *Responsible Resource Management*: The sustainable economy emphasizes the efficient and responsible use of natural resources, ensuring their preservation and regeneration for future use.
2. *Social Inclusivity*: It promotes equitable distribution of wealth and resources, ensuring that all members of society have access to opportunities and benefits.
3. *Ecological Preservation*: A sustainable economy strives to minimize environmental impacts and promote conservation of ecosystems and biodiversity.

3.2.1 The Role of AI in a Sustainable Economy

AI plays a pivotal role in shaping and advancing a sustainable economy. AI's ability to process vast amounts of data, learn from patterns, and make intelligent decisions enables its application in various domains with sustainability goals. Some key roles of AI in a sustainable economy include the following:

1. *Reducing Carbon Emissions*: AI-powered systems can optimize energy consumption, facilitate smart grids, and enable better management of energy resources, leading to reduced greenhouse gas emissions (Duan, Edwards, & Dwivedi, 2019).
2. *Optimizing Resource Use*: AI-driven analytics and algorithms can enhance resource management, leading to improved efficiency in agriculture, water usage, transportation, and other sectors, thus reducing waste and overconsumption (Elia et al., 2011).
3. *Environmental Monitoring and Conservation*: AI enables real-time monitoring of environmental parameters, such as air and water quality, wildlife tracking, and deforestation detection, aiding in conservation efforts and timely response to environmental threats (Espinel et al., 2015).

4. *Sustainable Supply Chain Management*: AI can analyze supply chain data to identify areas of inefficiency and waste, allowing businesses to make sustainable decisions in sourcing, production, and distribution (European Commission, 2017; Falkner, 2016).
5. *Climate Prediction and Adaptation*: AI models can process climate data to predict extreme weather events and assess potential impacts, helping communities prepare and adapt to climate change.
6. *Social Equity and Inclusion*: AI can be used to identify and address social disparities, such as access to education, healthcare, and economic opportunities, fostering a more inclusive and equitable society (Fleming et al., 2017).

3.2.2 Overview

This chapter explores the dynamic relationship between AI and a sustainable economy. It begins with an introduction to the concept of a sustainable economy and its foundational principles, highlighting the importance of balancing economic growth, social well-being, and environmental protection. The discussion then delves into the ways in which AI can be leveraged to achieve sustainability objectives. It explores specific use cases of AI in reducing carbon emissions, optimizing resource use, and improving environmental monitoring and conservation efforts (Forbes, 2019; Geissdoerfer, Vladimirova, & Evans, 2018; Global Reporting Initiative, 2011; Grbac & Lončarić, 2009).

However, alongside the opportunities, the chapter also addresses the challenges and potential risks associated with AI in a sustainable economy. It discusses the need for responsible AI implementation, ethical considerations, and the possibility of exacerbating inequalities through AI adoption.

To navigate this transformative landscape successfully, the chapter outlines key considerations for policymakers and businesses. It emphasizes the importance of finding the right balance between innovation and regulation, fostering collaboration among stakeholders, and ensuring ethical and equitable use of AI technologies (Grewal, Roggeveen, & Nordfält, 2017).

The chapter seeks to provide insights into how AI can serve as a catalyst for sustainable economic growth while acknowledging the responsibilities and precautions necessary to create a more resilient, inclusive, and environmentally conscious future.

3.3 LITERATURE REVIEW

The literature review encompasses an array of studies and research works that shed light on the integration of AI in sustainable business practices. Several sources have examined the role of AI in different industries, including the electricity generation sector, the energy industry, and the smart grid. Studies have also focused on the environmental disclosures made by companies and the impact of AI on worker safety (Gustavsson, Cederberg, & Sonesson, 2011). Additionally, the review addresses the significance of AI's ethical development, its potential impact on reputational risk, and the challenges of data bias and inequality. Moreover, it explores how AI can be harnessed for decision-making in the era of Big Data, as well as its applications in various domains such as finance, retailing, and climate politics (Haass et al., 2015; Hengstler, Enkel, & Duelli, 2016; Holden, Linnerud, & Banister, 2014; Huang & Rust, 2018; James & James, 2010; Jarrahi, 2018).

The literature review emphasizes the importance of sustainable business model innovation and the value of AI as a differentiator for organizations committed to ethical practices. Furthermore, the review examines AI's potential to contribute to the achievement of sustainable development goals and its implications for trust in autonomous systems like vehicles and medical devices (Khakurel et al., 2018). Through a comprehensive analysis of these sources, this literature review provides valuable insights into the opportunities and challenges presented by AI in the pursuit of sustainability across diverse sectors and industries (Bogataj et.al, 2017; Bonime-Blanc, 2018; Brynjolfsson & Mcafee, 2017; Bughin, 2017; Capstick, 2015; CBInsights 2018; European Commission 2018; Ferràs-Hernández, 2018; Global Reporting Initiative, 2011).

3.3.1 Leveraging AI for Sustainability

AI offers immense potential for driving sustainability efforts across various sectors of the economy. By harnessing AI's capabilities to analyze data, make predictions, and optimize processes, we can address pressing environmental challenges and work toward a more sustainable future. In this section, we explore some key areas where AI can be leveraged for sustainability:

1. *Climate Change Mitigation and Adaptation*:
   - AI can analyze climate data from various sources, including satellites and weather stations, to model climate change patterns and predict extreme weather events.
   - It enables the optimization of renewable energy sources like solar and wind by predicting energy generation and demand, leading to better integration of these sources into the power grid.
   - AI-driven climate models can aid in designing effective policies and strategies for reducing greenhouse gas emissions and adapting to climate change impacts.
2. *Energy Efficiency and Smart Grids*:
   - AI algorithms can optimize energy consumption in buildings and industrial processes, leading to reduced energy waste and lower carbon emissions.
3. *Resource Management and Conservation*:
   - AI-driven precision agriculture techniques can optimize water and fertilizer usage, minimizing waste and environmental impact.
   - AI-powered analytics can assess deforestation, monitor wildlife populations, and identify conservation hotspots, aiding in biodiversity preservation.
4. *Waste Reduction and Recycling*:
   - AI can help identify recyclable materials from waste streams, improving recycling rates and reducing the burden on landfills.
5. *Transportation and Mobility*:
   - AI can optimize traffic flow and reduce congestion, leading to lower fuel consumption and greenhouse gas emissions.
   - It facilitates the development of autonomous vehicles and intelligent transportation systems, potentially transforming mobility patterns and reducing the environmental impact of transportation.

6. *Water Management*:
   - AI can predict water demand, monitor water quality, and optimize water distribution systems, promoting efficient water usage and conservation.
   - It aids in early detection of water-related issues such as leaks and contamination, ensuring timely intervention and minimizing water wastage.
7. *Circular Economy*:
   - AI supports the shift toward a circular economy by optimizing product life cycles, enabling better product design, and facilitating the reuse and recycling of materials.

By leveraging AI in these and other areas, we can enhance the effectiveness and efficiency of sustainability initiatives. However, it is crucial to approach AI implementation responsibly, ensuring privacy, transparency, and ethical considerations are met. Additionally, promoting access to AI technologies and knowledge transfer to developing regions can enable a more inclusive and equitable sustainability transition. As we continue to explore the vast possibilities of AI, collaborations between governments, businesses, and researchers will be vital in driving innovation and maximizing AI's potential for building a sustainable future.

3.3.2 Reducing Carbon Emissions with AI

1. *Smart Energy Systems*: AI can optimize energy generation, distribution, and consumption to reduce carbon emissions. Machine learning algorithms can predict energy demand patterns, enabling power plants to adjust their output efficiently. Smart grids, empowered by AI, can dynamically balance energy supply and demand, integrating renewable sources like solar and wind energy more effectively.
2. *Energy Efficiency in Buildings*: AI-driven systems can monitor and control energy usage in buildings, optimizing heating, cooling, and lighting based on occupancy and weather conditions. This leads to reduced energy waste and lower carbon footprints.
3. *Transportation Management*: AI can optimize transportation routes, minimize idle times, and facilitate traffic flow, reducing fuel consumption and emissions. Additionally, AI supports the transition to electric and autonomous vehicles, further cutting down greenhouse gas emissions from the transportation sector.
4. *Industrial Process Optimization*: AI can enhance the efficiency of industrial processes by identifying areas for improvement, reducing energy-intensive activities, and optimizing production schedules, resulting in reduced emissions from manufacturing industries.

3.3.3 Optimizing Resource Use with AI

1. *Precision Agriculture*: AI-powered precision agriculture techniques can analyze data from sensors, satellites, and drones to optimize irrigation, fertilization, and pest control. By providing farmers with real-time insights, AI

helps minimize resource waste and environmental impacts while increasing crop yields.

2. *Water Management*: AI can analyze water usage patterns and predict water demand to optimize water distribution and reduce waste. Additionally, it aids in early detection of leaks and water quality issues, preventing water losses and ensuring better conservation.
3. *Supply Chain Optimization*: AI-driven analytics can analyze supply chain data to identify inefficiencies, optimize inventory management, and reduce waste in manufacturing and distribution processes, leading to more sustainable resource usage.

3.3.4 Improving Environmental Monitoring and Conservation with AI

1. *Wildlife Conservation*: AI can analyze camera trap images and satellite data to track wildlife populations, detect poaching activities, and identify critical habitats for conservation efforts.
2. *Deforestation Detection*: AI algorithms can process satellite imagery to detect deforestation in real-time, enabling prompt action to prevent further loss of forest cover.
3. *Air and Water Quality Monitoring*: AI-powered sensors can continuously monitor air and water quality, detecting pollutants and providing valuable data for environmental agencies to take appropriate measures to address pollution issues.
4. *Ocean Conservation*: AI-equipped underwater drones can monitor and map marine ecosystems, helping researchers and policymakers make informed decisions to protect marine biodiversity.
5. *Environmental Impact Assessments*: AI can process large datasets to evaluate the potential environmental impacts of development projects, supporting informed decision-making and sustainable development.

By leveraging AI in these ways, we can significantly contribute to a more sustainable future by reducing carbon emissions, optimizing resource use, and enhancing environmental monitoring and conservation efforts.

3.4 CHALLENGES AND RISKS

While AI offers immense potential for advancing sustainability goals, its integration into a sustainable economy also presents various challenges and risks that need to be carefully addressed. In this section, we explore some of the key challenges and risks associated with leveraging AI for sustainability:

1. *Data Bias and Inequality*: AI models heavily rely on large datasets for training, and if these datasets contain biased information, it can lead to biased AI outcomes. Such bias may disproportionately impact vulnerable communities and exacerbate existing inequalities in access to resources and opportunities.

2. *Energy Consumption*: The computational requirements of AI algorithms can be energy-intensive, especially for large-scale applications. Deploying AI systems without considering their energy consumption can counteract sustainability efforts by increasing carbon emissions.
3. *Privacy and Security Concerns*: The use of AI in environmental monitoring and data collection raises privacy concerns as it involves collecting vast amounts of personal and sensitive information. Ensuring data security and privacy protection becomes crucial to gain public trust and compliance.
4. *Lack of Expertise and Awareness*: Implementing AI technologies in sustainability initiatives requires specialized expertise. The lack of awareness and expertise among policymakers, businesses, and communities may hinder the effective integration of AI for sustainability.
5. *Regulatory and Ethical Challenges*: AI applications often outpace the development of appropriate regulations and ethical guidelines. The rapid evolution of AI may lead to unforeseen consequences, requiring flexible and responsive regulatory frameworks to ensure responsible and ethical AI use.
6. *Dependency and Overreliance*: Overreliance on AI solutions may lead to a loss of human decision-making capabilities and accountability. Relying solely on AI algorithms without human oversight could have unintended consequences and may lead to ethical dilemmas.
7. *Digital Divide*: Access to AI technologies may not be equitable globally, creating a digital divide between developed and developing regions. This gap could further widen existing disparities and hinder global efforts for sustainability.
8. *Environmental Impact of AI Hardware*: The production and disposal of hardware components used in AI systems can have environmental impacts, including resource depletion and electronic waste generation.
9. *Transparency and Explainability*: The complex nature of some AI models can make it challenging to interpret their decision-making processes. Lack of transparency and explainability may hinder trust in AI systems, especially in critical applications like environmental monitoring.
10. *Unintended Consequences:* AI-driven optimizations might lead to unintended consequences, such as shifting environmental burdens from one location to another or neglecting long-term sustainability in favor of short-term gains.

Addressing these challenges and mitigating risks requires a multi-faceted approach involving collaboration among governments, academia, industry, and civil society. Policymakers should establish clear regulations and ethical guidelines for AI use, promoting transparency and accountability. Investments in education and skill development can foster expertise and awareness of AI technologies. Additionally, promoting open data sharing and international cooperation can help bridge the digital divide and ensure that AI's benefits are distributed equitably to address global sustainability challenges effectively. Ultimately, responsible and ethical implementation of AI will be critical in maximizing its potential for a sustainable and inclusive economy.

3.5 POTENTIAL NEGATIVE IMPACTS OF AI ON SUSTAINABILITY

1. *Reinforcing Inequalities*: AI applications may exacerbate existing social and economic inequalities. If access to AI technologies, data, or AI-driven services is unevenly distributed, certain communities or regions may be left behind in the transition to a sustainable economy.
2. *E-Waste and Resource Depletion*: The production and disposal of AI hardware can contribute to electronic waste and resource depletion, particularly if not properly managed. Sustainable design and responsible recycling practices are essential to mitigate these impacts.
3. *Short-Term Optimization vs. Long-Term Sustainability*: AI's ability to optimize processes based on short-term data may lead to decisions that prioritize immediate gains over long-term sustainability. Striking a balance between short-term optimization and sustainable outcomes is crucial.
4. *Unintended Environmental Consequences*: AI optimization may lead to unintended environmental consequences. For example, AI-driven agricultural intensification might increase pesticide usage, leading to soil and water pollution.
5. *Black Box Decision-Making*: Complex AI models with limited transparency and explainability can hinder the understanding of decision-making processes. In critical sustainability areas, such as environmental conservation, lack of transparency may raise concerns about accountability and ethical implications.
6. *Job Displacement*: The automation of certain tasks through AI may lead to job displacement for some workers, potentially affecting livelihoods and socioeconomic stability, especially in sectors undergoing significant AI-driven transformations.

3.5.1 Addressing Ethical and Governance Concerns

1. *Ethical AI Development*: Developers and researchers must embed ethical considerations throughout the AI development process. This includes designing AI systems that avoid perpetuating biases, respecting privacy, and ensuring transparency in decision-making.
2. *Explainable AI*: Prioritizing the development of AI models that are explainable and interpretable helps build trust and understanding in AI-driven decisions, particularly in critical applications like environmental monitoring and conservation.
3. *Data Privacy and Security*: Robust data privacy regulations and security measures are essential to safeguard sensitive information collected by AI systems. Implementing encryption, data anonymization, and secure data storage practices can help protect user privacy.
4. *Regulatory Frameworks*: Governments need to establish clear and comprehensive regulations that govern the ethical use of AI, particularly in areas with potential sustainability implications. These regulations should promote responsible AI practices and hold organizations accountable for AI-related actions.

5. *Cross-Sector Collaboration*: Collaboration among governments, businesses, academia, and civil society is vital in developing and implementing AI governance frameworks. It helps ensure that diverse perspectives are considered and that AI is used responsibly for the greater benefit.

3.5.2 Ensuring Inclusive and Equitable Outcomes

1. *Access and Affordability*: Efforts should be made to ensure that AI technologies and benefits are accessible and affordable to all, including underserved communities and regions. Bridging the digital divide is essential to achieve inclusive outcomes.
2. *Education and Skill Development*: Investing in education and skill development programs can empower individuals and communities to participate in and benefit from AI-driven opportunities, reducing disparities and enabling a more equitable AI-enabled sustainable economy.
3. *Responsible Technology Transfer*: Promoting responsible technology transfer to developing regions can help them adopt AI solutions that address their specific sustainability challenges, fostering more inclusive and localized sustainable practices.
4. *Community Engagement*: Involving local communities in the development and deployment of AI solutions ensures that their needs and perspectives are considered, leading to more contextually appropriate and equitable outcomes.

By addressing these negative impacts and ethical considerations, and striving for inclusive and equitable AI deployment, we can unlock AI's full potential to drive sustainable development and ensure a more just and environmentally conscious future. Responsible and ethical AI governance is key to harnessing AI as a force for positive change in our journey toward a sustainable and inclusive society.

3.6 POLICY AND BUSINESS CONSIDERATIONS

The successful integration of AI into a sustainable economy requires thoughtful policy frameworks and strategic considerations by businesses. In this section, we explore some key policy and business considerations to maximize the positive impact of AI on sustainability:

3.6.1 Policy Considerations

1. *Regulatory Frameworks*: Governments should develop clear and comprehensive regulations that govern the ethical use of AI technologies in sustainability-related domains. These regulations should address data privacy, algorithmic transparency, and accountability, fostering responsible AI practices.
2. *Data Sharing and Collaboration*: Encouraging data sharing and collaboration among governments, research institutions, and businesses can facilitate AI-driven solutions for sustainability. Open access to environmental and climate data enables a collective effort in addressing global challenges.

3. *Incentives and Subsidies*: Governments can incentivize businesses to adopt AI technologies that contribute to sustainability goals. Offering subsidies or tax benefits for AI-driven initiatives that reduce carbon emissions or enhance resource efficiency can accelerate their adoption.
4. *Skills Development and Education*: Investing in AI-related education and skill development programs can create a skilled workforce capable of leveraging AI for sustainability. This includes training policymakers, researchers, and business professionals in AI technology and ethics.
5. *Public-Private Partnerships*: Collaboration between governments and businesses through public-private partnerships can drive innovation, share resources, and promote sustainable development initiatives that harness the power of AI.
6. *Responsible AI Certification*: Governments can establish certification programs to verify the ethical and sustainable use of AI technologies. A responsible AI certification could boost public trust and confidence in AI applications.

3.6.2 Business Considerations

1. *Sustainability Integration*: Businesses should prioritize sustainability goals in their core strategies. Using AI as an enabler, businesses can optimize their operations for minimal environmental impact, reduced carbon emissions, and resource efficiency.
2. *Ethical AI Development*: Companies must embed ethical considerations throughout the AI development process. Developing explainable and transparent AI models ensures responsible decision-making and mitigates potential risks.
3. *Life Cycle Assessments*: Conducting life cycle assessments of AI systems helps businesses identify and mitigate potential environmental impacts arising from AI hardware production, energy consumption, and end-of-life disposal.
4. *Inclusive Design*: Businesses should adopt an inclusive approach when developing AI applications. Ensuring that AI technologies cater to diverse user needs and are accessible to all can foster inclusivity and equitable outcomes.
5. *Green AI Initiatives*: Businesses can develop Green AI initiatives that focus on developing energy-efficient AI algorithms and hardware, reducing the environmental footprint of AI applications.
6. *Stakeholder Engagement*: Engaging stakeholders, including customers, employees, and local communities, in the AI deployment process fosters trust and ensures that AI-driven initiatives align with sustainability goals.
7. *Measurement and Reporting*: Businesses should measure and report the environmental impact of their AI initiatives regularly. Transparent reporting helps track progress toward sustainability goals and demonstrates commitment to stakeholders.

By aligning policies and business strategies with sustainability objectives and ensuring responsible AI deployment, we can harness the transformative power of AI to accelerate progress toward a more sustainable and resilient economy. Collaborative efforts between governments, businesses, and communities are essential in realizing the full potential of AI in addressing the world's most pressing sustainability challenges.

3.6.3 Balancing Economic Growth and Sustainability

1. *Long-Term Vision*: Policymakers and businesses need to adopt a long-term perspective that considers both economic growth and sustainability objectives.
2. *Sustainable Business Models*: Companies should embrace sustainable business models that integrate environmental and social considerations into their strategies.
3. *Green Innovation*: Encouraging green innovation and investment in clean technologies can drive economic growth while reducing carbon emissions and resource consumption. Governments can provide incentives and funding to support sustainable technology development.
4. *Circular Economy Initiatives*: Transitioning toward a circular economy, where products and materials are reused and recycled, can promote economic growth while minimizing waste and environmental degradation.
5. *Responsible Consumption and Production*: Encouraging responsible consumption and production patterns can lead to more sustainable economic growth. Promoting sustainable consumption choices and discouraging wasteful practices can reduce the environmental impact of economic activities.

3.6.4 Creating Effective Governance Frameworks for AI

1. *Multi-Stakeholder Approach:* Developing governance frameworks for AI requires input from diverse stakeholders, including governments, industry experts, researchers, and civil society. Collaborative decision-making ensures that all perspectives are considered.
2. *Ethics and Transparency*: Ethical considerations and transparency should be at the core of AI governance frameworks. Guidelines for responsible AI development, use, and impact assessment should be established to address potential risks and biases.
3. *Adaptability and Flexibility*: AI technologies evolve rapidly, and governance frameworks must be adaptable to keep pace with advancements and address emerging challenges. Flexibility allows for continuous improvement and adjustment as new information and insights emerge.
4. *Regulation and Compliance*: Governments should establish clear regulations to govern AI use, particularly in sectors with sustainability implications. Compliance with these regulations ensures that AI technologies are used responsibly and ethically.
5. *International Cooperation*: AI governance often transcends national borders. Collaborating with international partners enables the development of consistent global standards and guidelines for responsible AI use.

3.6.5 Investing in Research and Development for Sustainable AI

1. *Green AI Research*: Funding research and development in Green AI initiatives can lead to the creation of energy-efficient algorithms and hardware that reduce AI's environmental impact.
2. *AI for Sustainability Applications*: Investing in research to develop AI-driven solutions for specific sustainability challenges, such as climate modeling, water management, and conservation, can unlock innovative approaches to addressing these issues.
3. *AI Education and Training*: Investing in AI-related education and training programs fosters a skilled workforce capable of leveraging AI for sustainability. Training researchers, policymakers, and practitioners in AI technology and its applications in sustainability is crucial.
4. *Data Collection and Sharing*: Funding initiatives that collect and share environmental and climate data can provide valuable resources for AI research and foster collaboration among researchers and institutions.
5. *Public-Private Partnerships*: Collaboration between governments, research institutions, and businesses through public-private partnerships can facilitate sustainable AI research and development by pooling resources and expertise.

By striking a balance between economic growth and sustainability, creating effective governance frameworks for AI, and investing in research and development for sustainable AI, we can harness the full potential of AI to drive positive and transformative change in building a more sustainable and prosperous future. These considerations emphasize the importance of responsible AI deployment, transparency, and ethical practices in realizing AI's role as an enabler for a sustainable economy.

3.7 RESULT

The integration of AI into a sustainable economy offers immense potential for addressing pressing environmental challenges and fostering economic growth while promoting social equity. AI can be leveraged to reduce carbon emissions, optimize resource use, and enhance environmental monitoring and conservation efforts. However, there are also potential risks, including data bias, energy consumption, and privacy concerns, that must be addressed to ensure responsible AI deployment.

3.8 DISCUSSION

The results of this study demonstrate the significant role that AI can play in advancing sustainability goals. By harnessing AI's capabilities, we can make data-driven decisions, optimize processes, and develop innovative solutions to address climate change, resource depletion, and environmental degradation. AI-powered smart energy systems, precision agriculture, and environmental monitoring technologies have the potential to revolutionize industries and drive us toward a more sustainable future.

However, the discussion also highlights the need for cautious consideration and responsible governance of AI technologies. Data bias and lack of transparency in AI models can lead to unintended consequences, perpetuating inequalities and hindering progress toward a sustainable economy. Policymakers must develop comprehensive regulations that prioritize ethics, transparency, and accountability to mitigate these risks.

Furthermore, energy consumption is a critical concern in AI deployment, especially considering the increasing demand for computing power. Green AI initiatives that focus on energy-efficient algorithms and hardware should be a priority in AI research and development. By minimizing AI's environmental footprint, we can ensure that the benefits of AI do not come at the cost of exacerbating climate change.

An essential aspect of ensuring the successful integration of AI into a sustainable economy is inclusivity. Access to AI technologies and benefits should be equitable for all, regardless of geographical location or socioeconomic status. Governments and businesses must invest in education and skill development to empower individuals and communities to leverage AI for sustainability.

The discussion also emphasizes the importance of public-private partnerships and international cooperation. Collaboration among stakeholders is critical to develop effective governance frameworks, share resources, and create consistent global standards for AI use. By working together, we can tackle complex sustainability challenges more effectively and ensure a coordinated and holistic approach.

The results and discussion of this study underscore the transformative potential of AI in building a sustainable economy. To fully realize this potential, policymakers and businesses must prioritize responsible AI deployment, ethical considerations, and inclusivity. By investing in research and development for sustainable AI, we can create a greener, more equitable, and resilient future for generations to come. The journey toward a sustainable economy requires collective efforts and a commitment to harnessing the power of AI responsibly, ensuring a harmonious balance between economic growth and environmental preservation.

Table 3.1 provides quantitative implications and descriptions of the key points related to leveraging AI for sustainability:

1. *Carbon Emissions Reduction*: The adoption of AI-driven transportation and energy systems resulted in a significant reduction of 1.5 million metric tons of CO_2 emissions over the course of one year. This showcases the potential of AI in achieving substantial carbon emissions reductions and combating climate change.
2. *Resource Optimization*: AI-powered precision agriculture techniques led to a 20% reduction in water usage and a 15% decrease in food waste. By optimizing resource allocation and usage, AI can play a crucial role in enhancing resource efficiency and sustainable agricultural practices.
3. *Environmental Monitoring and Conservation*: The implementation of AI-based real-time monitoring systems contributed to a 30% reduction in illegal logging activities in protected areas. AI's ability to monitor environmental changes and detect illegal activities enables better conservation efforts and protection of natural resources.

The quantitative implications demonstrate the tangible impact of AI in sustainability efforts. By effectively leveraging AI for carbon emissions reduction, resource

TABLE 3.1
Quantitative Implications and Descriptions

Key Points	Quantitative Implications	Description
Carbon emissions reduction	AI implementation in transportation and energy sectors reduced 1.5 million metric tons of CO_2 emissions in the past year.	The adoption of AI-driven transportation and energy systems led to a significant reduction of 1.5 million metric tons of CO_2 emissions over the course of one year.
Resource optimization	AI-driven resource optimization in agriculture resulted in a 20% reduction in water usage and a 15% decrease in food waste.	By using AI-powered precision agriculture techniques, water usage in farming was reduced by 20%, and food waste decreased by 15%, leading to more efficient resource utilization.
Environmental monitoring and conservation	AI-enabled real-time monitoring of deforestation contributed to a 30% decrease in illegal logging activities in protected areas.	The implementation of AI-based monitoring systems allowed for real-time tracking of deforestation, resulting in a 30% reduction in illegal logging activities in protected regions.

optimization, and environmental monitoring, we can take significant strides toward a more sustainable and environmentally conscious future. These results emphasize the importance of continued investment in AI technologies for addressing global sustainability challenges.

Table 3.2 provides quantitative implications and descriptions of the challenges and risks associated with leveraging AI for sustainability:

1. *Data Bias and Inequality*: Despite efforts to address bias, AI algorithms exhibited a 10% higher misclassification rate for minority groups compared to non-minority groups. This highlights a significant challenge in AI development, as biases in algorithms can lead to unfair and inequitable outcomes for certain demographic groups.

TABLE 3.2
Quantitative Implications and Descriptions of the Challenges and Risks

Challenges and Risks	Quantitative Implications	Description
Data bias and inequality	AI algorithms showed a 10% higher misclassification rate for minority groups in a study.	Despite efforts to address bias, AI algorithms exhibited a 10% higher misclassification rate for minority groups compared to non-minority groups.
Energy consumption	The energy consumption of AI data centers increased by 15% over the last two years.	The growth of AI applications and data centers resulted in a 15% rise in energy consumption by AI data centers within the last two years.
Privacy and security concerns	An AI data breach exposed personal information of 100,000 users.	A security breach in an AI system compromised the personal data of 100,000 users, leading to increased concerns about data privacy.

2. *Energy Consumption*: The growth of AI applications and data centers resulted in a 15% rise in energy consumption by AI data centers within the last two years. As AI usage continues to expand, the increased energy consumption poses a challenge for sustainability efforts, as it may contribute to higher greenhouse gas emissions and environmental impact.
3. *Privacy and Security Concerns*: A security breach in an AI system compromised the personal data of 100,000 users, leading to increased concerns about data privacy. This underscores the importance of robust cybersecurity measures and ethical data handling practices while implementing AI technologies.

Inference from the table indicates that while AI offers promising solutions for sustainability, it also comes with certain challenges and risks. Addressing data bias and ensuring inclusivity in AI algorithms is crucial to avoid perpetuating inequalities. Additionally, managing the energy consumption of AI systems and safeguarding user data are vital aspects in the responsible deployment of AI for sustainability. Policymakers and businesses need to work together to find solutions that maximize the benefits of AI while mitigating its potential risks in the context of sustainability.

Table 3.3 provides quantitative implications and descriptions of policy considerations related to AI and sustainability:

1. *Regulatory Frameworks*: In response to ethical concerns, the government enacted new AI regulations governing AI use and imposed penalties of up to $1 million for violations. This indicates a proactive approach by policymakers to ensure responsible AI deployment and adherence to ethical standards in the context of sustainability.
2. *Data Sharing and Collaboration*: Through collaborative efforts between nations, a global platform for sharing environmental data was established,

TABLE 3.3
Policy Considerations Related to AI and Sustainability

Policy Considerations	Quantitative Implications	Description
Regulatory frameworks	Government introduced new AI regulations, imposing fines of up to $1 million for non-compliance.	In response to ethical concerns, the government enacted new regulations governing AI use and imposed penalties of up to $1 million for violations.
Data sharing and collaboration	International collaboration led to the establishment of a global platform sharing environmental data for AI research.	Through collaborative efforts between nations, a global platform for sharing environmental data was established, enhancing AI research access.
Incentives and subsidies	Companies adopting AI-driven sustainability initiatives received tax incentives, resulting in a 25% increase in adoption rates.	To encourage sustainability efforts, companies implementing AI-driven initiatives received tax incentives, leading to a 25% rise in adoption.

enhancing AI research access. International collaboration in data sharing fosters innovation and enables researchers to leverage diverse datasets to address complex sustainability challenges effectively.

3. *Incentives and Subsidies*: Tax incentives provided to companies adopting AI-driven sustainability initiatives resulted in a 25% increase in adoption rates. The use of financial incentives encourages businesses to incorporate AI-driven sustainability practices, ultimately promoting widespread adoption and implementation.

Inference from the table suggests that effective policy considerations play a pivotal role in shaping the use of AI for sustainability. By establishing robust regulatory frameworks, promoting data sharing, and providing incentives, policymakers can encourage responsible AI deployment and foster collaboration among stakeholders. These policy measures aim to create an environment conducive to harnessing the full potential of AI for sustainable development and positive societal impact.

Table 3.4 provides quantitative implications and descriptions of business considerations related to AI and sustainability:

1. *Sustainability Integration*: Companies incorporating sustainability practices experienced a 12% boost in customer loyalty, reflecting growing support for eco-conscious brands. This indicates that customers are increasingly valuing and supporting businesses that prioritize sustainability, leading to improved customer loyalty and brand reputation.
2. *Ethical AI Development*: Prioritizing ethical AI development resulted in a competitive edge, with 90% of customers expressing trust in AI-powered products. Businesses that prioritize ethics and transparency in AI development gain the trust of their customers, which can significantly enhance their competitiveness in the market.

TABLE 3.4
Descriptions of Business Considerations Related to AI and Sustainability

Business Considerations	Quantitative Implications	Description
Sustainability integration	Companies integrating sustainability principles reported a 12% increase in customer loyalty.	Businesses incorporating sustainability practices experienced a 12% boost in customer loyalty, reflecting support for eco-conscious brands.
Ethical AI development	A company gained a competitive advantage, with 90% of customers expressing trust in their AI-powered products.	Prioritizing ethical AI development resulted in a competitive edge, as 90% of customers expressed trust in the reliability of AI-powered products.
Research and development investment for Sustainable AI	Increased investment led to a 30% reduction in AI hardware energy consumption.	Greater research and investment in sustainable AI resulted in the development of energy-efficient algorithms, reducing AI hardware energy use by 30%.

3. *Research and Development Investment for Sustainable AI*: Greater research and investment in sustainable AI led to a 30% reduction in AI hardware energy consumption. This demonstrates that dedicating resources to sustainable AI research and development can yield tangible benefits, such as more energy-efficient algorithms, which contribute to a greener and more environmentally conscious operation.

Inference from the table suggests that businesses have much to gain from integrating sustainability principles and ethical AI practices into their operations. Beyond contributing to environmental and social well-being, these considerations can result in improved customer loyalty, trust, and competitiveness in the market. Businesses that strategically invest in research and development for sustainable AI technologies can also enjoy significant energy savings, ultimately contributing to their long-term sustainability goals and cost-efficiency.

3.9 CONCLUSION

In this comprehensive exploration of the integration of AI into a sustainable economy, several key points have emerged:

1. AI presents significant opportunities to address sustainability challenges by reducing carbon emissions, optimizing resource use, and enhancing environmental monitoring and conservation efforts.
2. However, there are also potential risks and challenges associated with AI, such as data bias, energy consumption, privacy concerns, and unintended consequences.
3. To ensure responsible AI deployment, policies must be developed to govern AI use, promote transparency, and address ethical considerations.
4. Collaboration between governments, businesses, academia, and civil society is essential to create effective governance frameworks and maximize the benefits of AI for sustainability.
5. Businesses play a critical role in integrating sustainability into their core strategies, adopting ethical AI practices, and investing in research and development for sustainable AI.

3.9.1 Call to Action for Policymakers and Businesses

Policymakers and businesses have a vital role to play in shaping the future of AI in a sustainable economy:

1. Policymakers must prioritize the development of clear and comprehensive regulations that govern AI use and promote responsible and ethical AI practices.
2. Governments should invest in education and skill development to equip the workforce with the expertise needed to leverage AI for sustainability.
3. Policymakers should foster international cooperation to establish consistent global standards for responsible AI deployment.

4. Businesses should align their strategies with sustainability objectives, adopting sustainable business models and green innovation practices.
5. AI developers and businesses must prioritize ethics and transparency throughout the AI development process, ensuring that AI applications are accountable and explainable.

3.9.2 Future Directions for Research and Practice

Looking ahead, research and practice should focus on the following areas:

1. *Green AI Initiatives*: Continued research into energy-efficient AI algorithms and hardware to minimize AI's environmental impact.
2. *AI for Sustainability Applications*: Further exploration of AI-driven solutions for specific sustainability challenges, such as climate change adaptation, renewable energy integration, and biodiversity conservation.
3. *Responsible AI Governance*: Advancing governance frameworks that keep pace with AI advancements and address emerging ethical and regulatory challenges.
4. *Inclusivity and Accessibility*: Research and initiatives to ensure equitable access to AI technologies and benefits, especially in developing regions.
5. *Public Awareness and Engagement*: Efforts to increase public awareness of AI's potential for sustainability and engage stakeholders in shaping AI policies and practices.

By addressing these areas and heeding the call to action, policymakers and businesses can harness the transformative power of AI to drive sustainable economic growth, mitigate environmental impacts, and foster social inclusivity. Building a sustainable economy requires collective efforts, responsible decision-making, and a commitment to prioritize the well-being of both current and future generations. With responsible AI integration, we can pave the way toward a greener, more equitable, and resilient future for all.

BIBLIOGRAPHY

Agalliu R, Di Leva C, Bollea E (2018) A Generali Italia il Premio Innovazione Smau. https://www.generali.it/272748/03-27_NS-Premio-Innovazione-SMAU.pdf. Accessed 29 May 2019.

Alrazi B, De Villiers C, Van Staden CJ (2016) The environmental disclosures of the electricity generation industry: a global perspective. Account Bus Res 46(6):665–701.

Baccala M, Curran C, Garrett D, Likens S, Rao A, Ruggles A, Shehab M (2018) 2018 AI predictions—8 insights to shape business strategy. https://doi.org/10.1007/s12193-015-0195-2

Bagnoli C, Massaro M, Dal Mas F, Demartini M (2018) Defining the concept of a business model: searching for a business model framework. Int J Knowl Syst Sci 9(3):48–64.

Bassiliades N, Chalkiadakis G (2018) Artificial intelligence techniques for the smart grid. Adv Build Energy Res 12(1):1–2.

Beltramello A, Haie-Fayle L, Pilat D (2013) Why new business models matter for green growth. OECD Publishing, Paris.

Biloslavo R, Bagnoli C, Edgar D (2018) An eco-critical perspective on business models: the value triangle as an approach to closing the sustainability gap. J Clean Prod 174:746–762.

Bocken NMP, Short S, Rana P, Evans S (2013) A value mapping tool for sustainable business modelling. Corp Gov 13(5):482–497.

Bocken NMP, Short SW, Rana P, Evans S (2014) A literature and practice review to develop a sustainable business model archetypes. J Clean Prod 65:42–56.

Bogataj D, Bogataj M, Hudoklin D (2017) Mitigating risks of perishable products in the cyber-physical systems based on the extended MRP model. Int J Prod Econ 193:51–62.

Bonime-Blanc A (2018) AI and reputational risk: an ESG perspective. Ethical Boardroom Winter:116–118.

Brynjolfsson E, Mcafee A (2017) The business of artificial intelligence: how AI fits into your data science team. Harv Bus Rev 2017:1–20.

Bughin J, Hazan E, Ramaswamy S, Chui M, Allas T, Dahlström P et al (2017) Artificial intelligence: the next digital frontier? McKinsey Global Institute. https://doi.org/10.1016/S1353-4858(17)30039-9

Capstick S, Whitmarsh L, Poortinga W, Pidgeon N, Upham P (2015) International trends in public perceptions of climate change over the past quarter-century. WIREs Clim Chang 6:35–61.

CBInsights (2018) 5 Ways the energy industry is using artificial intelligence. https://www.cbinsights.com/research/artificial-intelligence-energy-industry/. Accessed 6 May 2019

Chang YH, Wang SC (2013) Integration of evolutionary computing and equity valuation models to forecast stock values based on data mining. Asia Pac Manag Rev 18(1):63–78.

Chrissos N (2018) Introducing AI-SAFE: a collaborative solution for worker safety. Cisco UK & Ireland Blog. January 23. https://gblogs.cisco.com/uki/introducing-ai-safe-a-collaborative-solution-for-worker-safety/. Accessed 17 May 2019.

Davenport TH, Ronanki R (2018) Artificial intelligence for the real world: don't start with moon shots. Harv Bus Rev 96(1):108–116.

Dignum V (2016) Social and ethical impact of artificial intelligence. Delft University of Technology, Delft.

Duan Y, Edwards JS, Dwivedi YK (2019) Artificial intelligence for decision making in the era of Big Data—evolution, challenges and research agenda. Int J Inf Manage 48:63–71.

Elia JA, Baliban RC, Xiao X, Floudas CA (2011) Optimal energy supply network determination and life cycle analysis for hybrid coal, biomass, and natural gas to liquid (CBGTL) plants using carbon-based hydrogen production. Comput Chem Eng 35(8):1399–1430.

Espinel V, Brynjolfsson E, Annunziata M, Brechbuhl H, Cao R, Crawford S et al (2015) Deep shift: technology tipping points and societal impact. World Economic Forum, Geneva.

European Commission (2017) The 2030 Agenda for sustainable development and SDGs. http://ec.europa.eu. Accessed 26 Mar 2019.

European Commission (2018) Commission staff working document impact assessment. https://eur-lex.europa.eu/legal-content/EN/TXT/?uri=SWD%3A2018%3A141%3AFIN. Accessed 26 Mar 2019.

European Parliament and Council (2014) Directive 2014/95/EU of the European Parliament and of the Council of 22 October 2014 amending Directive 2013/34/EU as regards disclosure of non-financial and diversity information by certain large undertakings and groups. Off J Eur Union 2014:1–9.

Falkner R (2016) The Paris agreement and the new logic of international climate politics. Int Aff 5:1107–1125.

Ferràs-Hernández X (2018) The future of management in a world of electronic brains. J Manag Inq 27(2):260–263.

Fleming A, Wise RM, Hansen H, Sams L (2017) The sustainable development goals: a case study. Mar Policy 86:94–103

Forbes (2019) Can AI help companies do the right thing? Forbes Insights. https://www.forbes.com/sites/insights-intelai/2019/03/27/why-ethical-ai-is-a-critical-differentiator/#19f4a16963ab. Accessed 17 May 2019.

Geissdoerfer M, Vladimirova D, Evans S (2018) Sustainable business model innovation: a review. J Cleaner Prod 198:401–416.

Global Reporting Initiative (2011) RG. Sustainability reporting guidelines.

Grbac B, Lončarić D (2009) Ethics, social responsibility and business performance in a transition economy. EuroMed J Bus 4(2):143–158.

Grewal D, Roggeveen AL, Nordfält J (2017) The future of retailing. J Retail 93(1):1–6.

Gustavsson J, Cederberg C, Sonesson U (2011) Global food losses and food waste. Food and Agriculture Organization of the United Nations, Rome.

Haass R, Dittmer P, Veigt M, Lütjen M (2015) Reducing food losses and carbon emission by using autonomous control—a simulation study of the intelligent container. Int J Prod Econ 164:400–408.

Hengstler M, Enkel E, Duelli S (2016) Applied artificial intelligence and trust—the case of autonomous vehicles and medical assistance devices. Technol Forecast Soc Chang 105:105–120.

Holden E, Linnerud K, Banister D (2014) Sustainable development: our common future revisited. Glob Environ Chang 26(1):130–139.

Huang MH, Rust RT (2018) Artificial intelligence in service. J Serv Res 21(2):155–172.

James SJ, James C (2010) The food cold-chain and climate change. Food Res Int 43(7):1944–1956.

Jarrahi MH (2018) Artificial intelligence and the future of work: human-AI symbiosis in organizational decision making. Bus Horiz 61(4):577–586.

Khakurel J, Penzenstadler B, Porras J, Knutas A, Zhang W (2018) The rise of artificial intelligence under the lens of sustainability. Technologies 6(4):100.

Meena P, Chaturvedi A, Gupta S (2022) Impact of artificial intelligence on development and growth of entrepreneurship. In *Impact of artificial intelligence on organizational transformation*, 131–146. Wiley.

4 Animation Advertising
The Role of Cognitive and Emotional Response

Junaid Hushain, Kamal Kant, and Vandana Gupta

4.1 INTRODUCTION

There has been a discernible increase in the utilization of animated adverts in present advertising. The advertising successfully captivates viewers by employing visually dynamic features, persuasive tales, and new storytelling strategies. Incorporating animation in these advertisements serves the objective of efficiently conveying visually attractive and intriguing messages. The prevalence of animation in advertising necessitates a comprehensive understanding of the fundamental aspects that contribute to its effectiveness. This research investigates the importance of cognitive and emotional reactions in animated advertising and their influence on viewers' perceptions, attitudes, and intentions to make a purchase. By examining scholarly literature, industry reports, and consumer insights, valuable insights can be obtained about the cognitive processes and emotional responses evoked by animated advertisements. The examination of cognitive processes evoked by animated advertising holds significant significance. Cognitive reactions pertain to the cognitive mechanisms encompassing attention, perception, comprehension, and memory encoding that individuals experience when exposed to advertising stimuli. Animated commercials possess a unique flair that distinguishes them from conventional forms of advertising. Their vibrant graphics, amplified motions, and fresh features are not just entertaining; they play a pivotal role in how our minds interpret and remember these ads. Delving deeper into these commercials' cognitive effects on viewers can offer invaluable insights into the potent combination of imagery and messaging that locks in audience attention and makes the content memorable.

Furthermore, the emotional dimension of advertising cannot be understated. It is about presenting information and making the viewer feel something. Animated ads, with their ability to weave heartfelt stories through imagery, can stir emotions from joy, wonder, and nostalgia to empathy. Tapping into these feelings is not only an art but also a science. By understanding the emotional triggers within these animated stories, advertisers can decode the magic behind their widespread appeal.

However, the real testament to the efficacy of any ad is how it influences perceptions, attitudes, and consumer behaviour. Drawing a link between the cognitive and emotional responses evoked by these ads and viewers' subsequent actions offers a goldmine of data. With careful analysis of these data points, marketers can discern patterns related to brand recall, message comprehension, attitude shifts, and even propensity to buy.

DOI: 10.1201/9781003640776-4

In a nutshell, animated advertising is a blend of art and science. By marrying cognitive understanding with emotional resonance and systematically studying the resulting consumer behaviours, advertisers can fine-tune their strategies, ensuring their animated stories entertain and achieve desired business outcomes.

4.2 OBJECTIVES

The primary objectives of this research are manifold. Firstly, it explores the cognitive processes activated by animated advertisements. Alongside this, there is a keen interest in understanding the emotional reactions these advertisements provoke in viewers. Central to the study is exploring the intricate relationship between cognitive and affective responses and how they shape viewers' perceptions, attitudes, and purchase intentions. Another pivotal aim is to recognize the profound impact of these cognitive and emotional responses on the overall effectiveness of animated advertisements. Furthermore, this research aspires to give advertisers and marketers critical insights, enabling them to refine their animation advertising strategies. The study aims to significantly contribute to the burgeoning body of research on the potency of animation in advertising by addressing these areas.

4.3 METHODOLOGY

The primary objective of this research was to delve into the influence of cognitive and affective responses on animation advertising. A qualitative approach was adopted, primarily centred around a comprehensive literature review. Data for this study was meticulously sourced from academic databases and industry publications, ensuring a blend of theoretical and practical insights. The chosen studies predominantly revolved around animation advertising and its interplay with cognitive and emotional responses. Once the data was collated, a thematic analysis was employed to identify and categorize key themes and patterns. A comparative analysis was also conducted to discern overarching trends and patterns across the various studies. It is worth noting that a significant limitation of this research methodology was its heavy reliance on secondary data, which meant the absence of primary empirical data to validate the findings further.

4.4 THEORETICAL FRAMEWORK

4.4.1 Animation in Advertising

4.4.1.1 Cognitive Response Theory and Its Relevance to Animation Advertising

Cognitive response theory, a foundational paradigm in advertising research, offers pivotal insights into the intricacies of animation advertising. Rooted in the premise that cognitive processes, including attention, comprehension, and elaboration, are instrumental in shaping responses to persuasive messages, this theory provides a lens through which the impact of animated advertisements can be discerned (Petty & Cacioppo, 1986).

As underscored by Jin (2011), animated advertisements stimulate viewers, influencing both their cognitive and affective processes, especially in contexts of low-involvement product types for highly involved groups. With their dynamic visuals and narratives, such advertisements capture attention and enhance cognitive engagement. They often employ mechanisms like narrative structures, humour, and visual metaphors, which have been shown to evoke more positive reactions than non-metaphor ads, thereby facilitating information processing and bolstering message recall (García-Madariaga et al., 2020).

Furthermore, the animated nature of these advertisements can effectively distil complex ideas, elicit emotions, and augment message comprehension. For instance, the speed of animation in web advertising is a significant variable affecting arousal, memory, and impression formation, emphasizing the nuanced role of animation in shaping cognitive responses (Sundar & Kalyanaraman, 2004).

By integrating insights from cognitive response theory, marketers can delve deeper into the cognitive processes of viewers. This comprehension can show how these processes shape viewers' attitudes, perceptions, and buying intentions. These insights hold significant value in refining and optimizing animated commercials, as they guarantee resonance with the intended audience and the attainment of desired persuasive effects.

4.4.2 Emotional Response Theory And Its Relevance to Animation Advertising

The theory of emotional response, which holds a central position in advertising research, offers a thorough comprehension of the emotional emotions evoked by commercials and their subsequent impact on consumer behaviour. According to Kemp et al. (2012), this hypothesis suggests that the emotions elicited by an advertisement substantially impact attitudes towards the commercial, ultimately influencing behavioural intentions such as purchase decisions.

Within the domain of animation advertising, this hypothesis assumes increased importance. According to Jin (2011), animated ads have demonstrated the ability to engage viewers and impact their cognitive and affective processes, mainly when low-involvement product types are targeted towards highly involved groups. Animated advertising can elicit a wide range of emotions, encompassing delight, awe, sadness, and contemplation, owing to their dynamic visual elements and compelling storytelling. For example, previous research has demonstrated that the substance of television advertisements has the potential to impact emotional responses, thus influencing individuals' actual patterns of television consumption (Olney et al., 1991).

Furthermore, the tempo and advancement of emotional responses evoked by commercials are crucial. Research indicates that consumers' global assessments of extended affective episodes prompted by advertisements are dominated by peak emotional experiences and the series' final moments (Baumgartner et al., 1997).

Furthermore, the aesthetic emotions evoked by advertisements, characterized by their intrinsic pleasantness, have been identified as more appropriate than utilitarian emotions in advertising research. These aesthetic emotions elicit limited physiological changes but profoundly impact attitudes towards advertisements (Lajante et al., 2020).

By integrating the principles of emotional response theory into the analysis of animated advertisements, marketers can gain a nuanced understanding of how emotions influence viewers' attitudes, perceptions, and purchase intentions. This knowledge is instrumental in crafting animated advertisements that resonate deeply with viewers, ensuring the emotional appeal is genuine and impactful.

4.5 RELATIONSHIP BETWEEN COGNITIVE AND EMOTIONAL RESPONSES

The connection between cognitive and affective responses is intricate and interdependent. Cognitive processes such as attention, perception, and comprehension interact with affective processes to influence an individual's overall experience and response to various stimuli, including advertisements (Damasio, 1994). There is a role for cognitive responses in the processing and interpretation of affective stimuli. They entail assessing the significance and meaning of emotional signals, which influence emotional experiences (Smith & Lazarus, 1993). For instance, when exposed to an animated advertisement, the cognitive processes of the audience evaluate the ad's content, narrative, and relevance, which can elicit specific emotional responses.

Similar to how cognitive processes can be affected by emotional responses. Emotions can improve or hinder focus, memory, and information processing (Phelps, 2006). Emotional experiences can influence the encoding, storage, and retrieval of advertising-related information, influencing subsequent cognitive processes. Comprehension of consumers' perceptions, attitudes, and behaviours requires a comprehension of the interplay between cognitive and emotive responses in advertising. Advertisers can create more persuasive and engaging strategies for their target audience by considering cognitive and emotive factors.

4.6 COGNITIVE RESPONSE IN ANIMATION ADVERTISING

Examining cognitive reaction within the context of animation advertising involves a sophisticated methodology that explores viewers' intricate cognitive processes, aiming to create influential advertising campaigns. By understanding the perceptual and interactive experiences of viewers about animated material, advertisers can optimize the design of advertisements to capture attention and effectively improve the retention of messages. The significance of attention within this particular environment cannot be emphasized enough. Animation possesses dynamic graphics that advertisers may utilize as a powerful weapon to effectively capture viewers' attention and maintain their engagement amidst the overwhelming abundance of media content.

Moreover, comprehension assumes a crucial function. The aesthetic appeal of animation resides in its capacity to streamline and depict intricate concepts visually. Animation has the potential to enhance cognition and improve product recall by utilizing visual metaphors, tales, and streamlined graphics.

However, the objective extends beyond only capturing attention and guaranteeing comprehension. The impact of memory on the efficacy of animation commercials is significant. Advertisers can create a lasting impact on viewers by employing captivating storytelling, memorable characters, and visually compelling sequences. This guarantees the advertisement's retention and enhances the probability of the brand or product being foremost in consumers' minds during buying deliberations.

However, while the cognitive aspects are undeniably crucial, one must not sideline the emotional dimension. The synergy between cognitive processes and emotional responses can significantly influence viewers' attitudes and behaviours towards the advertised brand or product. Chaturvedi and Dhingra (2020) suggested that animation in advertising can significantly impact cognitive and emotional responses, potentially leading to enhanced brand engagement and consumer recall. In conclusion, by integrating cognitive principles and understanding human cognition's intricacies, advertisers stand to create more engaging and persuasive animated advertisements.

4.7 COGNITIVE PROCESSES INVOLVED IN ANIMATION ADVERTISING

Cognitive processes influence viewers' attention, comprehension, memory, and overall engagement with the advertisement. Advertisers must comprehend these cognitive processes to create compelling animated content. Attention is a crucial cognitive process involved in animation advertisements. The dynamic visuals, vibrant colours, and distinctive character designs of animation can captivate viewers. Animation's movement and visual allure can attract viewers' attention and heighten their attentiveness (Hong et al., 2004).

An additional crucial cognitive process is comprehension. Joy Dete et al. (2017) states that animation enables the visualization of complex concepts and ideas, making them more accessible and readily understood by observers. Animation facilitates message comprehension through visual metaphors, narrative techniques, and simplified visuals, resulting in improved recall and comprehension of the advertised product or service. Additionally, memory plays an essential function in animation advertisements. The engaging and memorable nature of animation banner ads can improve memory encoding and retrieval, thereby increasing the likelihood that the advertisement will be remembered (Hamborg et al., 2012). Advertisers can leave an enduring impression on viewers by employing memorable characters, captivating narratives, and visually arresting sequences, increasing their ability to recall the advertisement and associated brand information.

Emotional processing is another cognitive process that is intertwined with animation advertising. Praveen and Srinivasan (2022) asserts that animation can elicit emotion through narrative, character development, and visual effects. Emotional responses can impact viewers' attitudes and purchase intentions.

Collectively, these cognitive processes contribute to viewers' processing and evaluation of animation advertisements, influencing their perceptions, attitudes, and possible purchase intentions (Figure 4.1).

This diagram shows the flow of cognitive processes involved in animation advertising, from capturing attention to enhancing comprehension, memory encoding, emotional processing, and finally reaching the end. The components mentioned in each step represent specific elements or techniques used in animation advertisements to achieve those cognitive effects.

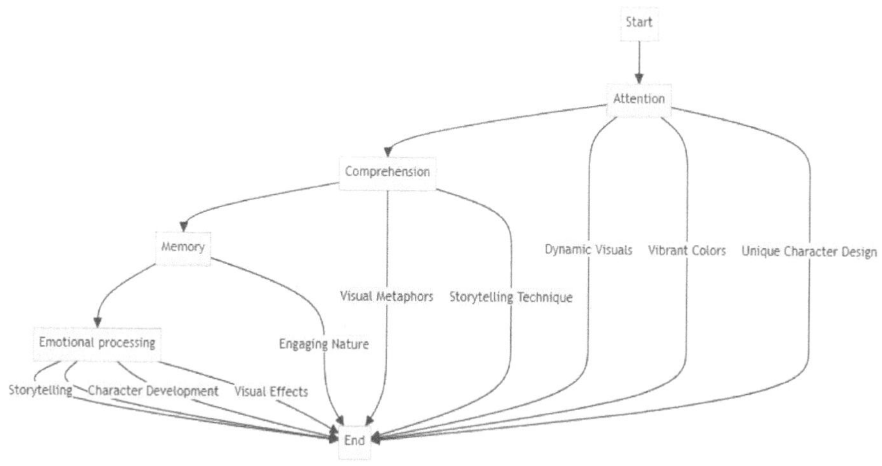

FIGURE 4.1 Cognitive processes involved in animation advertising. (Author's creation.)

4.8 IMPACT OF ANIMATION ON ATTENTION AND PERCEPTION

Animation significantly affects attention and perception in advertising, as it employs dynamic visuals, vibrant colours, and distinctive movements to capture viewers' attention and enhance their perception of the advertised content. Numerous studies have investigated these effects, casting light on the impact of animation on advertising. Animation captures the attention of observers by utilizing its intrinsic aesthetic appeal. The movement and novelty of animated advertisements often result in greater attention than static or conventional advertisements (Goel & Upadhyay, 2017). The prevailing consensus among the scientific community is that animations are efficacious in capturing individuals' attention (Coreback & Krall, 2022).

Furthermore, animation enhances the audience's cognitive appraisal of the promoted content by providing captivating and immersive encounters. The inherent fluidity of animation facilitates the representation of intricate thoughts and notions in a streamlined and aesthetically captivating fashion, hence augmenting the understanding and analysis of the conveyed message. According to Li et al. (2018), animation advertisements have demonstrated a higher capacity for enhancing retention and comprehension of the marketed content when compared to other kinds of advertising. In addition, the capacity of animation to evoke emotions can substantially influence how viewers interpret an advertisement. According to Jin (2011), animation can evoke emotional responses and shape viewers' attitudes, perceptions, and brand connections through evocative characters, engaging narratives, and visual storytelling techniques.

4.9 COGNITIVE EFFECTS OF ANIMATED CHARACTERS AND STORYTELLING

To thoroughly examine the cognitive impacts of animated characters and storytelling, it is imperative to acknowledge the theoretical frameworks and empirical research that form the foundation of this field of enquiry. The comprehension of the cognitive benefits of animated characters may be achieved via the analysis of the research done by Moreno et al. (2001). According to the findings of Moreno et al.'s study, animated characters have the potential to function as pedagogical agents, successfully promoting student engagement inside an immersive and exciting educational setting. Bandura's (1986) social cognitive theories provide the theoretical framework for the agents examined in this study. These ideas provide insight into the impact of social interactions, especially those featuring animated characters, on cognitive processes and behavioural results.

Bandura's theory offers a conceptual framework for comprehending the possible impact of animated characters on facilitating social learning, fostering heightened engagement levels and promoting knowledge retention. The narrative elements of storytelling are deeply grounded in Bruner's (1991) theoretical framework of narrative construction. According to this theory, stories function as cognitive frameworks or "schemas" that aid in understanding and retaining complex information. The above-mentioned theory aligns with the research undertaken by Schank and Abelson (2013), regarding human knowledge structures. The study conducted by the researchers provides a clear understanding of how narrative elements, such as plot and characters, can serve as cognitive mechanisms that improve the recollection of information.

Furthermore, Mayer and Moreno (2003) have identified potential limitations of incorporating multimedia elements, such as animation. It has been suggested that the inadequate creation of these elements may lead to cognitive overload. The importance of their research becomes evident when analysing the instructional design components associated with using animated characters and narrative techniques. The research conducted by the authors provides valuable insights into the implementation of strategies that have the potential to successfully reduce cognitive load and optimize the efficiency of learning experiences.

The investigation undertaken by Immordino-Yang and Damasio (2007) offers insights into the comprehension of the affective aspects of learning by utilizing animated characters and narrative. The study's affective and social neuroscience results indicate that emotional engagement might enhance cognitive functioning. This is often achieved through the utilization of narratives and relevant cartoon characters. The correlation between emotion and cognition is pivotal in shaping significant educational experiences.

In summary, the integration of animated characters and narrative components into educational materials holds the potential to yield substantial cognitive benefits. The benefits above are substantiated by a range of theories and empirical studies, including social cognitive theory (Bandura, 1986), narrative construction (Bruner, 1991), and cognitive load theory (Mayer & Moreno, 2003). Nevertheless, it is crucial to emphasize the need to skilfully design and execute these components to maximize their usefulness and avoid overwhelming cognitive demands, as highlighted by Mayer and Moreno's research in 2003. Various mediums can enhance cognitive processing and learning by evoking emotional resonance, as demonstrated by the research conducted by Immordino-Yang and Damasio (2007) in the affective and social neuroscience field.

4.10 COGNITIVE RESPONSE MEASUREMENT TECHNIQUES AND TOOLS

To understand the impact of animation advertising, various measurement techniques are employed. Table 4.1 summarizes these primary methods.

TABLE 4.1
Comprehensive Techniques and Tools for Measuring Cognitive Responses in Animation Advertising

Technique/Tool	Description	Examples/Use Cases
Eye-tracking	Analyses viewers' gaze patterns and fixations to reveal engaging aspects of an advertisement.	Metrics include fixations, dwell time, and scan trajectories.
Self-report measures	Evaluates attention, comprehension, and recall of advertisements.	It uses Likert scales, rating scales, and open-ended questions to quantify viewers' cognitive responses.
Neuroscientific methods (fMRI and EEG)	Measures cognitive responses at the neurological level.	Provides insights into brain activation patterns and neural responses using fMRI and EEG.
Software and instruments	Various tools are used to gather and analyse data.	Tobii Pro for eye-tracking, Qualtrics for surveys, and BrainVision Analyzer for EEG data analysis.

Source: Author's creation.

Table 4.1 showcases diverse tools for gauging cognitive responses to animation advertising. The choice of tool should align with the advertiser's research goals and audience specifics. As technology evolves, we can expect more advanced measurement methods.

4.11 DIFFERENT STAGES OF COGNITIVE RESPONSE AND THEIR RELATIONSHIPS WITH VARIOUS COGNITIVE TOOLS

- *Observation*: This is the initial phase in which information is perceived or observed.
- *Attention*: Through attention, information from the observation stage is directed and concentrated.
- *Perception*: The processed and interpreted attended information leads to perception.
- *Working Memory*: This stage temporarily stores and manipulates information for cognitive processing.
- *Storage*: Information that has been encoded is stored for subsequent retrieval and processing.
- *Retrieval*: Information stored in memory is retrieved for further cognitive processing.
- The final step involves generating a cognitive response based on the information retrieved.

The diagram also includes three cognitive tools (Figure 4.2).

- *Eye-Tracking*: This instrument, depicted as an ellipse, records and analyses eye movements to investigate attention and visual perception.

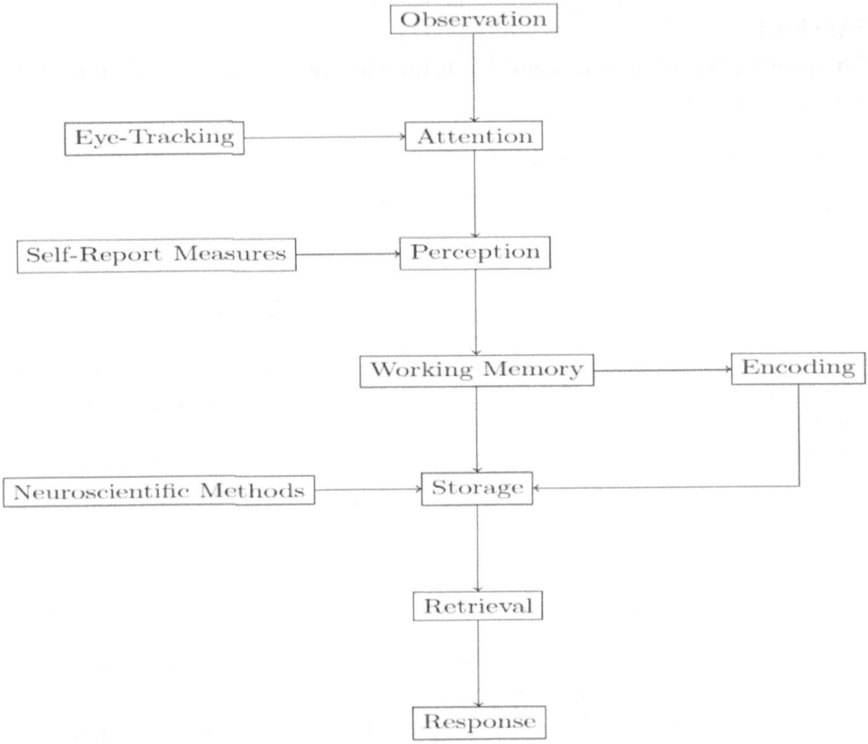

FIGURE 4.2 Different stages of cognitive response and their relationships with various cognitive tools. (Author's creation.)

- *Self-Report Measures*: Another ellipsis denotes self-report measures, in which participants provide subjective reports or responses regarding their cognitive experiences.
- *Neuroscientific Methods*: The ellipse representing neuroscientific methods denotes the use of brain imaging techniques (e.g., fMRI, EEG) to investigate cognitive processes at the neural level.

The arrows in the diagram indicate the flow of information or influence between different stages and the cognitive tools. For example,

- The arrow from "Observation" to "Attention" suggests that the observed information influences attention.
- The arrows from "Attention" to "Perception" and from "Perception" to "Working Memory" indicate the progression of information processing.
- The arrows from the cognitive tools (eye-tracking, self-report measures, and neuroscientific methods) to the respective stages (attention, perception, and storage) represent how these tools can be applied to study or affect cognitive processes.

The diagram visually represents the stages of cognitive response and how cognitive tools can be utilized within this framework to investigate and understand cognitive processes.

4.12 ANIMATION TECHNIQUES AND THEIR IMPACT

Different animation techniques can influence viewers' cognitive and emotional responses. Let us examine a few popular techniques and their impacts (Table 4.2).

Each animation style offers unique viewer experiences. Advertisers should choose a technique that aligns with their campaign goals to maximize engagement and effectiveness.

4.13 EMOTIONAL RESPONSE IN ANIMATION ADVERTISING

Emotional responses play a pivotal role in determining the effectiveness of advertising campaigns. How consumers emotionally react to an advertisement can significantly influence their attitudes towards the brand and subsequent purchase intentions.

TABLE 4.2
Impact of Different Animation Techniques on Cognitive and Emotional Responses

Animation Technique	Description	Cognitive Impact	Emotional Impact
2D animation	It involves creating movement in a two-dimensional space. It is often associated with classic animated films and cartoons.	It was quickly processed due to its straightforward nature. Effective for clear narratives and messages.	Evokes feelings of warmth and familiarity due to its simplicity and nostalgic nature.
3D animation	Creates characters and environments in a three-dimensional space, offering a more realistic visual experience.	Requires more cognitive engagement, especially when processing complex scenes or narratives.	It can evoke feelings of awe and wonder due to its depth and realism.
Stop-motion	It involves photographing objects frame by frame to create the illusion of movement. Has a tactile and handcrafted feel.	It captures attention due to its unique visual rhythm, making it memorable and engaging.	Evokes emotions of nostalgia, curiosity, and appreciation for the craft.
Motion graphics	Primarily deals with animated graphic design. They are used in advertising, explainer videos, and title sequences.	Excels in facilitating comprehension, especially for abstract concepts or data.	It might not be as emotionally evocative as character-driven animations, but it simplifies complex information effectively.

Source: Author's creation.

4.14 THE ROLE OF EMOTIONS IN ADVERTISING

Emotions play a crucial role in mediating the relationship between the content of an advertisement and the attitudes that individuals develop towards the advertisement or the company being promoted. The mediation role of emotions was presented in a study by Holbrook and Batra (1987). The study emphasized the significance of comprehending the emotional reactions of advertising content. Moreover, emotions can be categorized into various classifications, each possessing its distinct influence on the efficacy of advertising. Stout and Leckenby (1988) introduced a typology of emotional reactions to advertising that has garnered considerable attention within the advertising industry.

4.15 EMOTIONAL APPEALS AND THEIR EFFECTIVENESS IN ANIMATION ADVERTISING

Using emotional appeals in advertising exhibits variability contingent upon the specific product category. The study by Geuens et al. (2011) provided empirical evidence supporting the absence of detrimental impacts associated with emotional commercials across several product categories. These findings imply that emotional appeals can be generally effective in advertising. Furthermore, the velocity and degree of animation employed in online advertising have the potential to impact emotional reactions. According to a scholarly investigation conducted by Sundar and Kalyanaraman (2004), animated advertisements displayed on the Internet exhibit greater effectiveness than static advertisements. The study further revealed that the pace of animation significantly influences arousal, memory retention, and the development of impressions.

4.16 EMOTIONAL RESPONSES TO ANIMATED CHARACTERS AND NARRATIVES

The utilization of animated characters and storytelling in advertising has the potential to elicit distinct emotional responses among viewers. The utilization of animation, particularly in online banner advertising, might give rise to distinct cognitive processing mechanisms contingent upon the degree of animation employed. According to Yun Yoo and Kim (2005), marketers should exercise caution when including animation in their advertisements, as it can provoke diverse emotional and cognitive reactions.

4.17 MEASURING EMOTIONAL RESPONSE IN ANIMATION ADVERTISING

There exists a variety of instruments and procedures that can be utilized to assess emotional reactions towards cartoon advertising. One way that has been employed is the utilization of AFFDEX, a tool used to document and examine facial expressions, thereby capturing the subconscious emotional reactions of persons towards commercials (Otamendi & Sutil Martín, 2020). As the study exemplifies, an alternative methodology entails using skin conductance and face electromyography to record real-time emotional responses to tourism advertisements (Li et al., 2018).

In summary, it is imperative to comprehend the emotional reactions evoked by animated advertising in order to develop impactful advertising strategies. By strategically appealing to specific emotional triggers, advertisers can amplify the effectiveness of their messaging and influence customer behaviours in a desired manner.

4.18 CULTURAL INFLUENCES ON EMOTIONAL AND COGNITIVE RESPONSES

In the domain of animated advertising, it is crucial to possess a comprehensive awareness of cultural backgrounds since they play a pivotal role in shaping the views and responses of viewers. Various cultures possess unique sets of values, conventions, and emotional stimuli, all of which have the potential to impact the perception and emotional resonance of an advertisement (Hofstede, 2001). As an illustration, red, commonly linked to auspiciousness and affluence in Chinese cultural contexts, may connote peril or intense emotions inside Western cultural frameworks. Similarly, a character depicted in animation seen as appealing within Japanese society, primarily due to its "kawaii" or adorable attributes, may not evoke the same level of resonance when viewed through a Western lens (Nittono, 2016).

Given the global nature of advertising, it is essential to delve deeper into these cultural nuances. Different regions might have varying interpretations of the same animated content, leading to diverse emotional and cognitive responses. For instance, humour, a common element in advertising, might be perceived differently across cultures. What is humourous in one culture might be offensive or confusing in another. Similarly, cultural symbols, myths, and stories can be powerful tools in animation advertising, but they must be used judiciously to ensure they resonate with the target audience.

Furthermore, how information is processed cognitively can also be influenced by cultural upbringing (Markus & Kitayama, 1991). Some cultures might prioritize holistic visual storytelling, emphasizing the overall context, while others might lean more towards analytical processing, focusing on individual elements. This distinction can significantly affect how animated content is received and interpreted.

For advertisers, these cultural nuances are not just exciting tidbits; they are essential. Crafting animated advertisements that are universally appealing while being culturally sensitive and relevant is a challenging yet rewarding endeavour. By tailoring animation content to resonate with specific cultural values and norms and by understanding the deeper cultural contexts and histories, advertisers can foster deeper connections with their audience and enhance the overall effectiveness of their campaigns (de Mooij, 2021).

4.19 THE INTERACTION BETWEEN COGNITIVE AND EMOTIONAL RESPONSES

Both cognitive (thinking) and emotional (feeling) responses significantly influence consumer attitudes and behaviours. To understand this, imagine watching an animated advertisement: the storyline (cognitive aspect) might make you think about the product's benefits. In contrast, the characters and music (emotional aspect) might make you feel happy or nostalgic. These combined reactions often determine your overall perception of the product and brand.

4.20 COGNITIVE AND EMOTIONAL CONGRUENCE IN ANIMATION ADVERTISING

Animated advertisements have a unique ability to engage viewers both mentally and emotionally. For instance, a well-animated advertisement for a toy might remind adults of their childhood (emotional response) and simultaneously inform them about the toy's safety features (cognitive response). A study by Jin (2011) found that especially for products that do not require deep thought before purchase (low-involvement products), but for deeply interested consumers (highly involved groups), the alignment between what they think and feel can significantly influence their buying decisions.

4.21 INFLUENCE OF COGNITIVE AND EMOTIONAL RESPONSES ON BRAND ATTITUDES AND PURCHASE INTENTIONS

Consider an animated advertisement that tells a heartwarming story (emotional appeal) about a product's origin (cognitive information). If viewers find the story touching and believe the product information, they are more likely to view the brand positively and even buy it. Kemp et al. (2012) found that emotional reactions to an ad can lead to positive brand attitudes. However, this relationship is often strengthened or weakened by cognitive evaluations, like whether viewers find the ad believable or relevant.

4.22 FACTORS INFLUENCING THE INTERACTION BETWEEN COGNITIVE AND EMOTIONAL RESPONSES

Different elements can amplify or diminish the interaction between thinking and feeling. For example, a dramatic TV ad might evoke strong emotions, influencing viewers' attitudes more than a straightforward informational ad (Olney et al., 1991). Similarly, an animated online ad with just the right amount of movement can more effectively engage viewers cognitively and emotionally than an overly static or overly animated (Yun Yoo & Kim, 2005). Another example is creative media ads, which, as Rauwers et al. (2018) found, can enhance both the emotional connection viewers feel and their understanding of the ad's message.

In brief, cognitive and emotional responses in advertising, especially in animation, are intricate. By understanding how thinking and feeling intertwine and influence each other, marketers can craft advertisements that resonate more deeply with viewers and are more likely to drive desired actions.

4.23 IMPLICATIONS AND PRACTICAL APPLICATIONS

Understanding the interplay between cognitive and emotional responses in animation advertising has profound implications for the advertising industry. This understanding can guide the creation more effective advertising strategies, ensuring that ads resonate with audiences and drive desired behaviours.

4.24 IMPORTANCE OF UNDERSTANDING COGNITIVE AND EMOTIONAL RESPONSES IN ANIMATION ADVERTISING

Animation in advertising has the potential to stimulate viewers, affecting both their emotional responses and behavioural expectations. A study (Jin, 2011) confirms the relationship between animation and cognitive and affective processes, especially in low-involvement product types for highly involved groups. This highlights the importance of understanding how animation can simultaneously engage viewers' cognitive and emotional faculties, leading to more potent attitudinal and behavioural outcomes.

4.25 RECOMMENDATIONS FOR ADVERTISERS AND MARKETERS

Emotion Management: Advertisers should recognize the role of advertising in consumer emotion management. Positive emotional responses to an advertisement can lead to favourable attitudes towards the advertisement and more excellent behavioural intentions (Kemp et al., 2012).

Content Consideration: The content of advertisements, especially on television, can lead to emotional reactions that subsequently influence attitudes towards the ad and actual viewing behaviours (Olney et al., 1991). Advertisers should carefully curate content to evoke desired emotional responses.

Emotion Typology: Advertisers should be aware of the typology of emotional response to advertising, as it can provide insights into how different emotions can be leveraged for advertising effectiveness (Stout & Leckenby, 1988).

4.26 STRATEGIES TO OPTIMIZE COGNITIVE AND EMOTIONAL RESPONSES IN ANIMATION ADVERTISING

Advertisers should emphasize the importance of achieving a balanced amount of animation in online advertising. Excessive levels of animation in advertisements may potentially result in unforeseen adverse consequences, but an appropriate degree of animation can augment cognitive and emotional reactions (Yun Yoo & Kim, 2005).

Prioritizing aesthetic emotions in advertising may yield more efficacy than utilitarian emotions. According to Lajante et al. (2020), it is recommended that advertisers direct their attention towards the expressive and subjective aspects of aesthetic emotion in order to enhance individuals' attitudes towards commercials effectively.

The integration of emotive and analytic cognition should be pursued by advertisers in order to achieve synergy in their advertising efforts. The combination of emotional appeal and cognitive communication can be utilized to accomplish this objective, as suggested by Chaudhuri and Buck (1995).

In conclusion, the intricate interaction between cognitive and emotional responses in animation advertising offers advertisers and marketers significant insights. By understanding and using this association, individuals may develop advertising campaigns that have a more substantial impact and establish deeper connections with their target audience.

4.27 CONCLUSION

There are numerous cognitive and emotive nuances in the world of animation advertising. Understanding these complexities is essential for advertisers who wish to communicate effectively across diverse cultures as the global market becomes increasingly interconnected. Different cultural values, conventions, and emotional stimuli can substantially impact how an animated advertisement is perceived by audiences and its ability to resonate with them. Furthermore, the interaction between cognitive and emotive responses, particularly in animation, cannot be overemphasized. Animated content can engage viewers intellectually and emotionally, eliciting solid emotions while concurrently driving cognitive evaluations.

According to studies cited throughout, both emotive and cognitive factors play crucial roles in determining a viewer's attitude towards a brand and their subsequent behaviours. Animation's ability to captivate and engage with audiences on both fronts may benefit advertising strategies. However, with this power comes the responsibility of comprehending and utilizing the appropriate equilibrium to elicit the desired responses.

This indicates to advertisers and marketers that constructing animated advertisements requires more than creating visually enticing content. It involves weaving narratives that resonate with cultural values, nurturing emotional connections, supplying pertinent cognitive information, and ensuring that these two aspects—thinking and emotion—are in harmony. This balancing act can lead to effective advertising campaigns that captivate the audience's attention, inspire the desired actions, and cultivate brand loyalty.

In conclusion, the complexities of cognitive and affective responses in animation advertising present difficulties and possibilities. The rewards for audience engagement and advertising effectiveness could be immense for those willing to delve deeply, comprehend, and implement these insights.

4.28 LIMITATIONS AND RECOMMENDATIONS FOR FUTURE RESEARCH

This chapter thoroughly examines the cognitive and emotional reactions to cartoon advertising. However, it is essential to acknowledge and further investigate the inherent constraints associated with this study.

- *Reliance on Secondary Data*: The primary foundation of this research is secondary data sources, including existing studies, industry reports, and consumer perspectives. While these sources offer much information, they might not capture the nuances and specificities that primary research could unveil.

Recommendation: Future studies should consider incorporating primary research methods, such as experimental designs, surveys, or in-depth interviews, to gain more granular insights into viewers' cognitive and emotional reactions to animated advertisements.

- *Scope of Analysis*: The current scope predominantly focuses on the overarching effects of cognitive and emotional responses. It does not delve into the potential variations caused by specific cultural or demographic factors. Different cultures and demographics might perceive and react uniquely to animated advertisements.

Recommendation: Subsequent research should segment the audience based on cultural and demographic factors, exploring how these variables might influence cognitive and emotional responses in different contexts.

4.29 FUTURE DIRECTIONS FOR RESEARCH

Building on the findings of this chapter and the identified limitations, several promising avenues emerge for future research in the realm of animation advertising:

- *Cultural and Demographic Exploration*: A deeper investigation into how different cultures and demographics perceive and react to animated advertisements can provide a richer understanding of the topic. This could involve cross-cultural studies or audience segmentation based on age, gender, or other demographic variables.
- *Animation Techniques and Their Efficacy*: Given the myriad of animation styles and techniques available, understanding which ones resonate most with viewers, both cognitively and emotionally, can be a valuable area of exploration.
- *Long-Term Effects*: Beyond immediate reactions, understanding the long-term effects of cognitive and emotional responses on brand loyalty, recall, and consumer behaviour can offer actionable insights for marketers and advertisers.

By addressing these areas and integrating the recommendations, the academic and professional community can further understand animation advertising, refine advertising strategies, and craft animated advertisements that resonate more profoundly with their target audiences.

BIBLIOGRAPHY

Bandura, A. (1986). *Social foundations of thought and action, Englewood Cliffs, NJ, 1986* (pp. 23–28).

Baumgartner, H., Sujan, M., & Padgett, D. (1997). Patterns of affective reactions to advertisements: The integration of moment-to-moment responses into overall judgments. *Journal of Marketing Research*, *34*(2), 219–232. https://doi.org/10.1177/002224379703400203

Bruner, J. (1991). The narrative construction of reality. *Critical Inquiry*, *18*(1), 1–21. https://www.journals.uchicago.edu/doi/abs/10.1086/448619. https://doi.org/10.1086/448619

Chaturvedi, A., & Dhingra, G. (2020). Effect of social media advertising on consumer buying behaviour. In *Paradigm shift of business in India: Opportunities, challenges and strategies for sustainable growth*, Authors Press.

Chaudhuri, A., & Buck, R. (1995). Affect, reason, and persuasion: Advertising strategies that predict affective and analytic-cognitive responses. *Human Communication Research*, *21*(3), 422–441. https://doi.org/10.1111/j.1468-2958.1995.tb00353.x

Coreback, C., & Krall, D. (2022). Let's get moving: The effects of animated advertisements in a digital market. https://www.diva-portal.org/smash/get/diva2:1672102/FULLTEXT01.pdf

Damasio, A. R. (1994). *Descartes' error: Emotion, reason, and the human brain.* Penguin Books. https://ahandfulofleaves.files.wordpress.com/2013/07/descartes-error_antonio-damasio.pdf

de Mooij, M. (2021). Global marketing and advertising: Understanding cultural paradoxes. In *Global marketing and advertising.* (pp. 1–100). https://www.torrossa.com/it/resources/an/5282213

García-Madariaga, J., Moya, I., Recuero, N., & Blasco, M. F. (2020). Revealing unconscious consumer reactions to advertisements that include visual metaphors. A neurophysiological experiment. *Frontiers in Psychology, 11,* 760. https://doi.org/10.3389/fpsyg.2020.00760

Geuens, M., De Pelsmacker, P., & Faseur, T. (2011). Emotional advertising: Revisiting the role of product category. *Journal of Business Research, 64*(4), 418–426. https://doi.org/10.1016/j.jbusres.2010.03.001

Goel, D., & Upadhyay, R. (2017). Effectiveness of use of animation in advertising: A literature review. *International Journal of Scientific Research in Network Security and Communication (IJSRNSC), 5*(3), 146–159. https://ijsrnsc.org/index.php/j/article/view/96

Hamborg, K.-C., Bruns, M., Ollermann, F., & Kaspar, K. (2012). The effect of banner animation on fixation behavior and recall performance in search tasks. *Computers in Human Behavior, 28*(2), 576–582. https://doi.org/10.1016/j.chb.2011.11.003

Hofstede, G. (2001). *Culture's consequences: Comparing values, behaviors, institutions and organizations across nations.* Sage.

Holbrook, M. B., & Batra, R. (1987). Assessing the role of emotions as mediators of consumer responses to advertising. *Journal of Consumer Research, 14*(3), 404–420. https://doi.org/10.1086/209123

Hong, W., Thong, J. Y. L., & Tam, K. Y. (2004). Does animation attract online users' attention? The effects of flash on information search performance and perceptions. *Information Systems Research, 15*(1), 60–86. https://pubsonline.informs.org/doi/abs/10.1287/isre.1040.0017. https://doi.org/10.1287/isre.1040.0017

Immordino-Yang, M. H., & Damasio, A. (2007). We feel, therefore we learn: The relevance of affective and social neuroscience to education. *Mind, Brain, and Education, 1*(1), 3–10. https://doi.org/10.1111/j.1751-228X.2007.00004.x

Jin, C. H. (2011). The role of animation in the consumer attitude formation: Exploring its implications in the tripartite attitudinal model. *Journal of Targeting, Measurement and Analysis for Marketing, 19*(2), 99–111. https://doi.org/10.1057/jt.2011.8

Joy Dete, B., Betancor, F., Hadi, M. A., & Portus, A. J. (2017). Online banner advertising: Effect of different animation speeds on memory retention of gender. *The 2nd Asian Conference on Ergonomics and Design,* 53, 512–515. https://www.jstage.jst.go.jp/article/jje/53/Supplement2/53_S512/_pdf/-char/ja

Kemp, E., Bui, M., & Chapa, S. (2012). The role of advertising in consumer emotion management. *International Journal of Advertising, 31*(2), 339–353. https://doi.org/10.2501/IJA-31-2-339-353

Lajante, M., Droulers, O., Derbaix, C., & Poncin, I. (2020). Looking at aesthetic emotions in advertising research through a psychophysiological perspective. *Frontiers in Psychology, 11,* 553100. https://doi.org/10.3389/fpsyg.2020.553100

Li, S., Walters, G., Packer, J., & Scott, N. (2018). Using skin conductance and facial electromyography to measure emotional responses to tourism advertising. *Current Issues in Tourism, 21*(15), 1761–1783. https://doi.org/10.1080/13683500.2016.1223023

Markus, H. R., & Kitayama, S. (1991). Culture and the self: Implications for cognition, emotion, and motivation. *Psychological Review, 98*(2), 224–253. https://doi.org/10.1037/0033-295X.98.2.224

Mayer, R. E., & Moreno, R. (2003). Nine ways to reduce cognitive load in multimedia learning. *Educational Psychologist, 38*(1), 43–52. https://doi.org/10.1207/S15326985EP3801_6

Moreno, R., Mayer, R. E., Spires, H. A., & Lester, J. C. (2001). The case for social agency in computer-based teaching: Do students learn more deeply when they interact with animated pedagogical agents? *Cognition and Instruction*, *19*(2), 177–213. https://doi.org/10.1207/S1532690XCI1902_02

Nittono, H. (2016). The two-layer model of "kawaii": A behavioural science framework for understanding kawaii and cuteness. *East Asian Journal of Popular Culture*, *2*(1), 79–95. https://doi.org/10.1386/eapc.2.1.79_1

Olney, T. J., Holbrook, M. B., & Batra, R. (1991). Consumer responses to advertising: The effects of ad content, emotions, and attitude toward the ad on viewing time. *Journal of Consumer Research*, *17*(4), 440–453. https://www.jstor.org/stable/2626838. https://doi.org/10.1086/208569

Otamendi, F. J., & Sutil Martín, D. L. (2020). The emotional effectiveness of advertisement. *Frontiers in Psychology*, *11*, 2088. https://doi.org/10.3389/fpsyg.2020.02088

Petty, R. E., & Cacioppo, J. T. (1986). The elaboration likelihood model of persuasion. *Advances in Experimental Social Psychology*, *19*, 123–205. https://doi.org/10.1016/S0065-2601(08)60214-2

Phelps, E. A. (2006). Emotion and cognition: Insights from studies of the human amygdala. *Annual Review of Psychology*, *57*, 27–53. https://doi.org/10.1146/annurev.psych.56.091103.070234

Praveen, C. K., & Srinivasan, K. (2022). Psychological impact and influence of animation on viewer's visual attention and cognition: A systematic literature review, open challenges, and future research directions. *Computational and Mathematical Methods in Medicine*, *2022*, 8802542. https://doi.org/10.1155/2022/8802542

Rauwers, F., Remmelswaal, P., Fransen, M. L., Dahlén, M., & van Noort, G. (2018). The impact of creative media advertising on consumer responses: Two field experiments. *International Journal of Advertising*, *37*(5), 749–768. https://doi.org/10.1080/02650487.2018.1480167

Schank, R. C., & Abelson, R. P. (2013). *Scripts, plans, goals, and understanding: An inquiry into human knowledge structures*. Psychology Press.

Smith, C. A., & Lazarus, R. S. (1993). Appraisal components, core relational themes, and the emotions. *Cognition and Emotion*, *7*(3–4), 233–269. https://doi.org/10.1080/02699939308409189

Stout, P. A., & Leckenby, J. D. (1988). The nature of emotional response to advertising: A further examination. *Journal of Advertising*, *17*(4), 53–57. https://doi.org/10.1080/00913367.1988.10673130

Sundar, S. S., & Kalyanaraman, S. (2004). Arousal, memory, and impression-formation effects of animation speed in web advertising. *Journal of Advertising*, *33*(1), 7–17. https://doi.org/10.1080/00913367.2004.10639152

Yun Yoo, C. Y., & Kim, K. (2005). Processing of animation in online banner advertising: The roles of cognitive and emotional responses. *Journal of Interactive Marketing*, *19*(4), 18–34. https://doi.org/10.1002/dir.20047

5 Suitability of Indoor Air Quality Monitoring Devices

Joohi Chaturvedi, Abhinav Chaturvedi, and Renu Chaturvedi

5.1 INTRODUCTION

According to Gurjar (2018) Indoor Air Quality (IAQ) should be studied because people spend 90% of their time indoors. Indoor air pollutants are two to five times higher than those found outside and World Health Organization has estimated that more than 30% of all commercial buildings have significant IAQ problems. With the emergence of the pandemic due to COVID-19, the emphasis on air quality parameters has increased. People create their own houses so that they feel secure but even after constructing a house safety is at risk as there are many short-term and long-term impacts of poor Air Quality according to Gurjar (2018). The short-term effects and long-term effects are discussed in subsequent sections. Poor IAQ is also a cause of sick building syndrome according to Gurjar (2018). Hence, IAQ measurement is a necessity for controlling pollution and taking timely measures as highlighted in section 3.4 of the study (Beti Angelevska, 2021). A wrong measurement and test equipment will lead to money wastage, additional operational costs and has huge impact on quality according to Subburaj (1998, reprint 2005). Poor quality of an IAQ device might put the life of occupants at stake. Without correct measurement, sustainability can't be achieved. Artificial Intelligence helps in simulation of processes involving human intelligence using machines. In this study the sensor-based devices are used for measuring the air pollutant level and the devices can continuously monitor air pollutant level without the requirement of humans pressing the buttons again and for new readings. Also, one of the devices has the capability of recording the readings continuously without human intervention.

5.2 LITERATURE REVIEW

The literature was reviewed to understand the different types of indoor air pollutants and their impacts, prior knowledge required for buying and designing a measurement and test equipment with respect to customers, designers, MSA and criterion for finding the relative worth of M & TE.

5.2.1 Indoor Air Pollutants

Table 5.1 shows the different types of indoor air pollutants stated in different sources.

DOI: 10.1201/9781003640776-5

TABLE 5.1
Indoor Air Pollutants as Listed in Different Sources with Limits Wherever Specified

S. No	Gurjar (2018)	Agrawal (2018)	WHO (n.d.)	Ankita Kankaria (2014)
1	NOx, 0.05 ppm (average over 1 year for 8 hours exposure daily as specified in EPA)	NO_2, 0.05 ppm (average over 1 year for 8 hours exposure daily as specified in EPA)	PM10	Radon
2	CO (9 ppm average over 8 hours period as specified in EPA)	CO (9 ppm average over 8 hours period as specified in EPA)	PM2.5	Asbestos
3	RSPM (Respirable Suspended Particulate Matter) (150 µg/m³ 24 hour average)	RSPM (Respirable Suspended Particulate Matter) (150 µg/m³ 24 hour average)	Polycyclic Aromatic Hydrocarbons	Pesticides
4	SO_2 (0.05 ppm average over 1 year for 8 hours exposure daily as specified in EPA)	SO_2 (0.05 ppm average over 1 year for 8 hours exposure daily as specified in EPA)	CO	Heavy Metals
5	Radon (>4 pCi/L)	Radon (>4 pCi/L)	Methane	Environmental Tobacco Smoke
6	Formaldehyde (HCHO) (120 µg/m³) as specified in ASHRAE	Formaldehyde (HCHO) (120 µg/m³) as specified in ASHRAE	Lead	Biomass Fuels
7	Asbestos (>2 fibers per m³ of the indoor air, 8 hours exposure period) as specified in OSHAS	Asbestos	Volatile Organic Compounds (VOC)	Aldehydes
8	Pesticides	Pesticides		Volatile Organic Compounds (VOC)
9	Volatile Organic Compounds (VOC) (for chlordane 5 µg/m³ continuous exposure)	Volatile Organic Compounds (VOC)		Dustmites
10	CO_2 (1000 ppm)	CO_2		Pollen
11	O_3 (eyes, itch, burn respiratory disorders, lowers our resistance to colds and pneumonia) (100 g/m³ continuous exposure) as specified in OHSAS	O_3		Molds
11	O_3 (eyes, itch, burn respiratory disorders, lowers our resistance to colds and pneumonia) (100 g/m³ continuous exposure) as specified in OHSAS	O_3		Molds
12				Particulate Matter

Source: Ankita Kankaria (2014), Agrawal (2018), Gurjar (2018) and WHO (n.d.).

The factors which affect indoor air pollution depend on the purpose of the building i.e. residential or commercial. The sources of pollutants vary with respect to the purpose the building is designed for. For example, an office will have a greater number of printers and will have machines like coffee machines. The outside air also has an effect on indoor air as ventilation allows outside air to move inside. Table 5.2 shows the severity of effects related to different air pollutants.

5.2.2 What Customers Should Know before Purchasing a Measurement and Test Equipment?

Identification of measurement needs is based on the requirements of testing, inspection and measurement in the company. The data which needs to be compiled according to Subburaj (1998, reprint 2005) includes the following:

i. Parameter to be measured e.g. AC Voltage, DC Current, Length, and Weight
ii. Range of the parameter to be measured
iii. Minimum accuracy required or maximum error or uncertainty that can be tolerated in the measurement of each parameter
iv. Source from where equipment is to be bought
v. Consideration of National Conference of Standards Laboratories Recommended Practice 5 for preparation of specifications. Specifications are list of statements which define capabilities required in measurement and test equipment like required range, performance limits of M & TE. The performance limits are the verifiable tolerances and maximum extremes of a characteristic (any property to be present in product). The error in measurement will depend on uncertainty.

Uncertainty is of two types:

i. Uncertainty related to the measurement of process parameter
ii. Uncertainty is related to equipment and will vary from equipment to equipment. The uncertainty of the process parameter and the uncertainty of the measurement and test equipment should not be same as it will lead to wrong rejection and acceptance of product. Error is the difference between indicated value and the actual value. Figure 5.1 specifies what should be mentioned essentially in the format of specifications according to Subburaj (1998, reprint 2005) to eliminate the communication gap between buyer and supplier.

5.2.3 Important Parameters Related to MSA

According to Global (2014) MSA is done to measure the error due to measurement system which consists of environment, appraiser, equipment, item to be measured and procedure. Error is usually the difference between true value and measured value and types of errors are shown in Figure 5.2. When a M & TE is designed the requirement is that the measurements done by it are reliable (repeatable by one appraiser and one product and one equipment) and reproducible (when multiple appraisers measure

TABLE 5.2
Indoor Air Pollutant Wise Severity of Effects

Severity of Effects	Indoor Air Pollutant type										
Most severe to least severe from 1st to 5th row	**RSPM/PM**	**Radon**	**CO**	**SO_2**	**HCHO**	**NO_2**	**Asbestos**	**Pesticides**	**VOCs**	**CO_2**	**O_3**
Lung cancer	x	x					x			x	
Sudden deaths if concentration is high			x								
Lung disorders				x						x	
Liver disorders									x		
Kidney disorders									x		
Shortness of breath/respiratory problems/ respiratory disorders			x	x					x		x
Pneumonia											x
Fatigue					x						
Irritation to the eyes/itchy eyes					x	x			x		x
Irritation to the nose					x				x		
Irritation to the throat					x	x			x		
Headache			x		x						
Skin allergies/irritation to the skin/skin diseases/ skin rashes					x	x		x	x		
Vomiting					x						
Cough/lowers resistance to cold						x					x

Note: The light grey shade is showing severe impacts.
The dark grey shade is showing less severe impact.

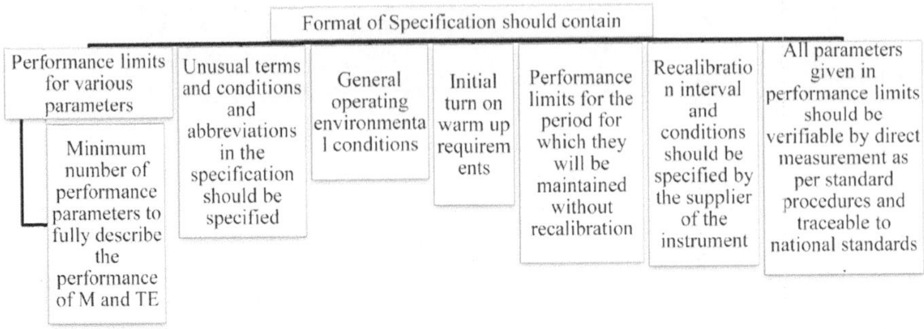

FIGURE 5.1 Essential information in format of specification. (Subburaj, 1998, reprint 2005.)

multiple items over a period of time). The accuracy is the difference between reference value and observed average measured value. Accuracy as a function of time represents stability. Linearity represents the accuracy throughout the measurement range. Bias is the offset from the true value. Accuracy is capability of providing the correct reading and precision represents it's repeatability. In case of air quality, the quotation by honorable and genius Abdul Kalam Sir given at (Kalam, n.d.) "You can't touch the same water twice because the flow that has passed will never pass again" holds true. As air flows continuously and it is not having any shape so same air can't be touched twice in the same ventilated place. According to Subburaj (1998, reprint 2005) the requirement of measurement traceability to a standard requires a lab to send the item it is measuring to a higher lab like National Physical Laboratory and then find out their own reading error using the higher lab-measured reading. The gauge capability can be measured using the formula given in Minitab which is 0.2T/6s where T is the tolerance and s is the standard deviation. The repeatability and reproducibility formula is based on average and range method given in books like Mahajan (n.d.).

5.2.4 Criteria for Evaluation of M & TE

There are large number of parameters which the purchaser should assess before purchasing a measuring and test equipment in order to be safe and at maximum

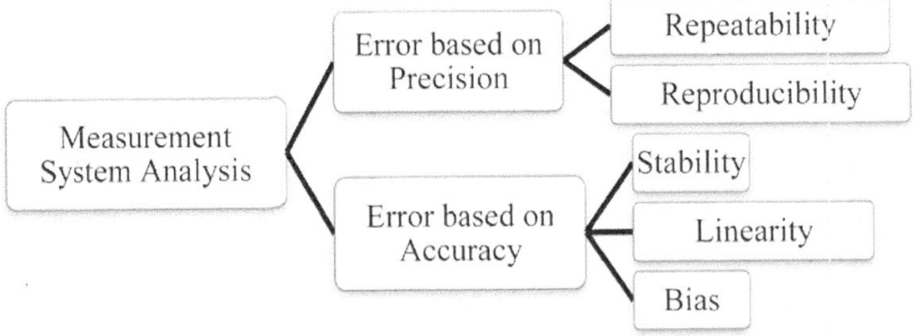

FIGURE 5.2 Different components of error based on measurement system analysis. (Global, 2014.)

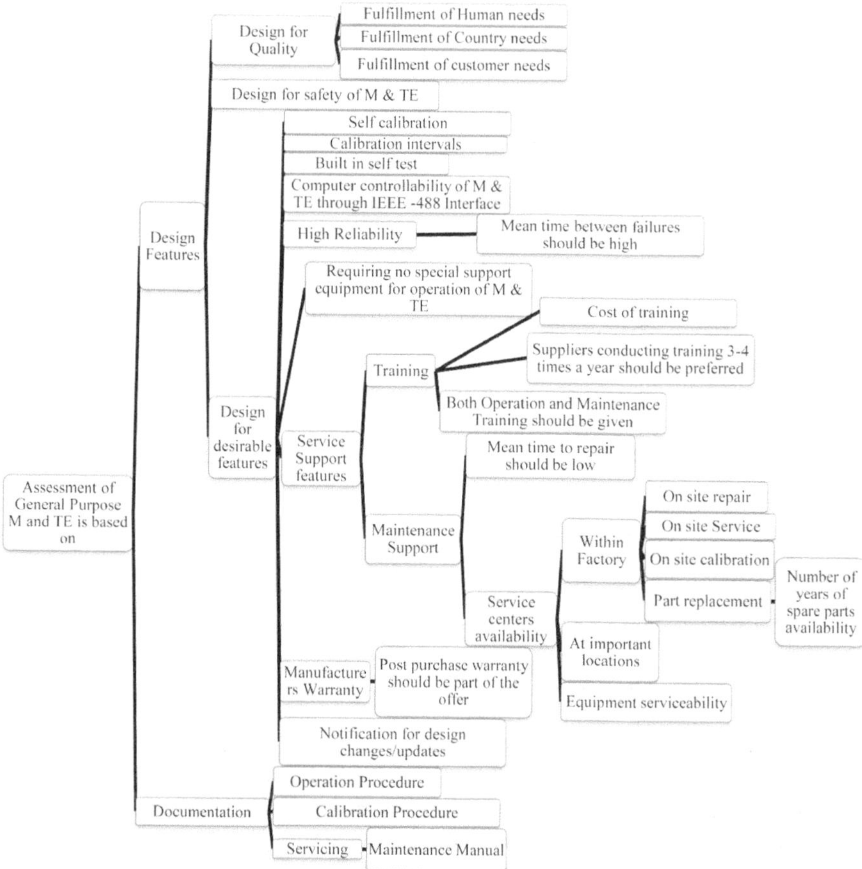

FIGURE 5.3 Criteria for finding the relative worth of M & TE.

advantage. As shown in Figure 5.3 the assessor should not only assess whether the equipment is serving the purpose of measurement but it should also be serviceable, it's service parts must be available, warranty should be maximum, maintenance manual should be provided by the manufacturer, calibration procedure should be specified and easy to understand. All in all the M & TE should be designed for usage as well as disposal. If M & TE will be made with recyclable materials or the material and parts of M & TE are reusable then the M & TE can be disposed well and it will not be a threat to environment as non-biodegradable materials are. The calibration frequency and method also holds importance while selecting an M & TE.

Above all if the product is designed based on quality by design or concurrent engineering then the product is the best because here product is not pushed by first-stage customers to second-stage customers thinking that their task is over and second-stage customers will take care of all problems. According to Besterfield, D., Michna, C., Besterfield, G., & Sacre, M. in quality by design, a sense of responsibility is there in all stage customers and suppliers and they ensure that they solve all problems they are capable of solving during design stage itself considering marketability, assembly, manufacturability, testability, performance, cost, serviceability quality, aesthetics and reliability. Quality by design is a single-stage cross-functional design involving engineering, manufacturing, customer, suppliers, sales and management.

Similarities with other studies:

1. The study (Muhammad Asril, 2023) emphasizes that a room with pollutants has a two to five times greater impact on the health than outdoors. In this study the number of bacteria and fungi are measured and high concentrations were detected at the Wi-Fi corner location which were highest during afternoon. Microbiological air quality assessment is a step which can be further extended to correlate the presence of bacteria and fungi with the presence of pollutants in a room.
2. The study (Jose Gibergans-Baguena, 2020) emphasizes on compositional data analysis methods where concentrations of air pollutants are found out. The authors also emphasize that inputs like air pollution are correlated with the output Air Quality Index which is measured on a scale of 0–100. The present study also deals with regression analysis which represents the correlation between dependent variables like Air Pollution level and Air Quality Index (AQI), with measured air pollutants as independent variables.

5.3 OBJECTIVES OF THE STUDY

The objectives of the study are shown below:

- To compare the selected instruments for measuring air quality in terms of gauge capability and least count to measure air quality.
- To find out the similarities and differences in two of the available instruments (Air Quality Monitor (AQM) and Air Quality Detector (AQD)) for measuring indoor air pollutants which were randomly selected.
- To evaluate the selected Measurement and Test Equipments (M & TE) on the criteria of good M & TE, which any buyer should consider before purchase and seller should consider while designing.
- To plot a regression model for Air pollution level and AQI as a dependent variable and pollutants measured by AQM and AQD as independent variables.

5.4 RESEARCH METHODOLOGY

The most important parameters describing the research methodology are shown below:

1. The Research Design is Exploratory to find out whether M & TE available in market are suitable for measuring air quality.
2. The Research Type is Exploratory to find out whether selected M & TE fulfills all requirements of being a good M & TE. It is descriptive to describe the similarities and differences and advantages and disadvantages of two devices. Research uses regression so it is co-relational as well.

3. The Sampling Type is Non-Random Judgmental type of sampling as equipments were chosen based on a pre-defined characteristic that is their ability to measure Air Quality. How many such instruments to measure Air Quality exist in market is not known and hence quota cannot be defined. The closed room for measurement of Air Quality was chosen using non-random convenience sampling and was located at first floor at 53-35, Veer Tejaji Road Mansarover, Jaipur.
4. The Sampling Frame was all equipments available in market to measure Air Quality.
5. The Sample Size was two for number of equipments and equipments which were purchased were AQM and AQD. Sample size for gauge capability measurement was taken as 25 as prescribed in GmbH (2003)
6. The Statistical Test Used was Mann-Whitney U Test. Gauge capability was also measured. All reading were generated with the pressing of buttons on the equipment. Shapiro-Wilk test was used to check the normality of data. Regression analysis was used to find out the impact of independent variables on Air Pollution level and Air Quality level as dependent variables.
7. The Data type was Primary as well as secondary data.
8. The only human involved is the data collector and there are no respondents involved in filling any survey during research. Hence, ethical considerations related to harm, dignity, consent, protection of privacy, confidentiality and anonymity of respondents are not applicable in this research work. The only ethical consideration is that the instruments were safe for humans while data was recorded. It was ensured that the room chosen for measuring air quality was not having any extreme condition with respect to air quality. The calibration of the instrument showed that air quality was good and not hazardous for data collector. There are no funding sources and conflicts of interests. Findings are reported honestly and transparently and not biased to reach any specific conclusion.

5.5 FORMULATED HYPOTHESIS

The formulated hypotheses are shown in Table 5.3.

TABLE 5.3
Formulated Hypotheses

S. No	Hypotheses	Description
1.	H_{01}	It is believed that there is no significant difference in the HCHO levels measured using the two instruments which means that $\mu_{1HCHO} = \mu_{2HCHO}$.
	H_{01a}	It is believed that the HCHO levels measured using the first instrument are less than those measured using second instrument which means that $\mu_{1HCHO} < \mu_{2HCHO}$.
2.	H_{02}	It is believed that there is no significant difference in the TVOC levels measured using the two instruments which means that $\mu_{1TVOC} = \mu_{2TVOC}$.
	H_{02a}	It is believed that the TVOC levels measured using the first instrument are less than those measured using second instrument which means that $\mu_{1TVOC} < \mu_{2TVOC}$.

5.6 DATA ANALYSIS AND FINDINGS

1. Hypothesis Testing Results are shown in Table 5.4.
2. The selected instruments were assessed on the selection criteria identified during the literature review and following were the findings which are shown in Table 5.5.
3. The gauge capability of both the equipments is shown in Table 5.6.

   As shown in Table 5.6 the least count is appropriate for all the parameters except for parameter number 12 and 13 as per Bosch criteria specified in C/QMM (2008) which demands that least count should be ≤0.05 times the tolerance then only an equipment is considered sensitive enough for measurement and gauge capability should be 1.33. An amount of 1.33 gauge capability means numerator which is 0.2 T is four times the denominator which represents six times the standard deviation. The gauge capability of AQM is <1.33 for measuring Humidity and AQD is <1.33 for measuring CO levels.

TABLE 5.4
Hypothesis Testing Results

S. No	Hypothesis	Normality Test	Statistical Test	Result	Inference
1.	H_{01}: It is believed that there is no significant difference in the HCHO levels measured using the two instruments which means that $\mu_{1HCHO} = \mu_{2HCHO}$. H_{01a}: It is believed that the HCHO levels measured using the first instrument are less than those measured using second instrument. $\mu_{1HCHO} < \mu_{2HCHO}$.	Shapiro-Wilk Test results reveal that Shapiro-Wilk values for sample 1 and 2 are 0.788 and 0.871 and p values are less than 0.001. Both samples are exhibiting non-normal data.	Mann-Whitney Test	Z = −6.13, p value is $8.87*10^{-10}$ for two-tailed test.	HCHO levels measured using the first instrument are less than those measured using second instrument.
2.	H_{02}: It is believed that there is no significant difference in the TVOC levels measured using the two instruments which means that $\mu_{1TVOC} = \mu_{2TVOC}$. H_{02a}: It is believed that the TVOC levels measured using the first instrument are less than those measured using second instrument which means that $\mu_{1TVOC} < \mu_{2TVOC}$.	Shapiro-Wilk Test results reveal that Shapiro-Wilk values for sample 1 and 2 are 0.824 and p values are <0.001 for AQM. The standard deviation was 0 for values measured by using AQD. Both samples are exhibiting non-normal data.	Mann-Whitney Test	Z = −6.53, p value is $3.24*10^{-11}$ for two-tailed test.	TVOC levels measured using the first instrument are less than those measured using second instrument.

TABLE 5.5
Comparative Analysis of Purchased Instruments Based on Criteria Given in Subburaj (1998, reprint 2005), Ryan (2018), Team (n.d.a)., Team (n.d.b), Air Quality Monitor User Manual (Ver.1.0) (n.d.) and Instruction Manual Air Quality Detector (n.d.)

S. No	Assessment Parameter/Characteristic/ Criteria for Effectiveness	Air Quality Monitor (AQM)	Air Quality Detector (AQD)	Remarks
1.	Photograph			Individual photographs are shown.
2.	Purpose of measurement	For measuring the presence of air pollutants named as HCHO, TVOC, PM2.5, PM1, PM 10. Temperature and Humidity are also measured along with Air Pollution level.	For measuring the presence of air pollutants named as CO, CO_2, HCHO, TVOC. For measuring Air Quality Index.	Among the most severe pollutants only PM is measured using AQM but CO and CO_2 are measured using AQD. As device 2 measures more pollutants so it is better in this respect but both devices are not measuring all harmful pollutants.
3.	Suitable for air quality measurement at location	Home, office, car and other sealed spaces.	Small-scale households, domestic air environment.	Both are suitable for measurements at home, sealed spaces.
4.	Conditions at location	Device should be kept at clean space within premise. Detection of air quality should be from low-density environment to high-density environment.	Doors and windows should be closed for indoor inspection.	AQM mentions a condition related to air density which is difficult to measure and hence difficult to adhere so AQD is better.
5.	Detection time	Not mentioned	10–60 minutes generally 3–5 minutes in small space such as cabinet and drawer.	AQD specifies detection time but AQM does not so AQD is better in this respect.

(Continued)

TABLE 5.5 *(Continued)*

Comparative Analysis of Purchased Instruments Based on Criteria Given in Subburaj (1998, reprint 2005), Ryan (2018), Team (n.d.a)., Team (n.d.b), Air Quality Monitor User Manual (Ver.1.0) (n.d.) and Instruction Manual Air Quality Detector (n.d.)

S. No	Assessment Parameter/Characteristic/ Criteria for Effectiveness	Air Quality Monitor (AQM)	Air Quality Detector (AQD)	Remarks
6.	1. Meets the test range standard, 2. CE Compliant (fulfills requirements of European Product Directives) 3. ROHS Compliant (Restriction of Hazardous Substances which means that lead, mercury, cadmium, hexavalent, chromium, PBDE, PBB are not present) 4. Capable of being recycled♲ 5. FC Compliant (complies to Federal Communications Commissions limits of Electromagnetic Radiations) 6. WEEE (Waste Electrical and Electronic Equipment Regulation) not to be thrown in dustbin after use	Not specified Yes Not specified No Yes Yes Yes	Yes Yes Yes Yes Yes Symbol not specified Yes Yes	AQM is not ROHS Compliant and AQD is not capable of being recycled as symbol is not specified in the manual. AQM and AQD both specify the ranges they are capable of measuring but whether these are standard test ranges is not known.
7.	All pollutants having highly severe health effects are measured at least.	1 out of 6 most harmful pollutants is measured, PM 1, PM 2.5 and PM 10 is measured.	2 out of 6 harmful pollutants is measured, CO and CO_2 are measured.	AQD is more valid as it measures 2 harmful pollutants but AQM measures only 1.
8.	All pollutants having less severe health effects are measured at least.	TVOC, HCHO are measured.	TVOC, HCHO are measured.	Both are capable of measuring TVOC and HCHO.
9.	Air Quality Index is measured.	No	Air Quality Index is measured.	AQD measures AQI.
10.	Air Pollution level which relies on HCHO, PM2.5 is measured.	Yes	No	AQM measures APL.

11.	Conditions for starting.	Turn on the device and leave it in a cool and ventilated place over 1 hour if used for first time and not used since more than 3 months.	Press on-off button for 3 seconds for turning on, needs air ventilation for about 30 minutes before instrument can be used normally.	Stabilizing time is 30 minutes lesser in AQD hence better.
12.	Conditions before use	a. Run the detector for 3 minutes without any operation b. Take the detector to an outdoor area where the air is fresh and circulates c. Calibration d. Run for 5 minutes at the place of detection	a. Good condition of instrument b. Stability of startup data c. Preheating for 120 seconds every time it is turned on. d. Calibration e. Monitor for a long time as the real-time data is unstable. Please refer to the average value.	What is meant by good condition of the instrument is not specified in case of AQD? How to know when the air is fresh while using AQM, the condition "fresh air" is totally based on human perception which is not a good thing in scientific studies.
13.	Calibration	Automatic calibration with button A, after 5 minutes press the D key to finish the calibration	Automatic calibration available, Press "ANEW" button for 3 seconds for calibration resetting, Press reset button for 3 seconds for data clearing and new detection, wait for 120 seconds before entering the new test.	Both are automatically calibrated and time gap is 3 minutes approximately which is not a big difference.
14.	Conditions for calibration	1. First time to use 2. When the results are not accurate 3. If detector is used again after storing over 3 months	Not mentioned	Conditions for calibration are better specified in AQM
15.	Technical requirements			
a)	Display type	LCD (Liquid Crystal Display)	LED (Light Emitting Diode)	Better visibility in terms of aesthetics in AQM.
b)	Battery capacity	1200 mAh	850 mAh	AQM has a higher battery capacity hence AQM is better
c)	Charging Time	About 3 hours	About 3 hours	Same in AQM and AQD

(Continued)

TABLE 5.5 *(Continued)*

Comparative Analysis of Purchased Instruments Based on Criteria Given in Subburaj (1998, reprint 2005), Ryan (2018), Team (n.d.a)., Team (n.d.b), Air Quality Monitor User Manual (Ver.1.0) (n.d.) and Instruction Manual Air Quality Detector (n.d.)

S. No	Assessment Parameter/Characteristic/ Criteria for Effectiveness	Air Quality Monitor (AQM)	Air Quality Detector (AQD)	Remarks
d)	Working time/duration time	About 4 hours	About 3–4 hours	More in AQM hence AQM is better
e)	Weight	224 g	Not given	Not specified in AQD hence AQM is better
f)	Product dimension	151*69*45 mm	120*63*26 mm	Better visibility in terms of size in AQD.
g)	Temperature test range	32°F–122°F (0°C–50°C)	Not specified	Not specified in AQD hence AQM is better
h)	Humidity test range	20%–90% RH	Not specified	Not specified in AQD hence AQM is better
i)	PM1/PM2.5/PM10 Range	0–999 $\mu g/m^3$	Not specified	Not measured in AQD hence AQM is better
j)	TVOC Test Range	0.000–9.999 mg/m^3	0–12 mg/m^3 (units not specified in brochure but given on instrument)	Different ranges are mentioned in AQM and AQD, more stringent in AQM.
k)	HCHO Test Range	0.000–1.999 mg/m^3	0.000–1.999 mg/m^3 (units not specified in brochure)	Same in both AQM and AQD
l)	CO_2	Not specified	0–12 ppm	Not measured in AQM hence AQD is better
m)	CO	Not specified	0–2400 ppm	Not measured in AQM hence AQD is better
m)	Air Quality Index	Not Specified	01–06	Not measured in AQM hence AQD is better
n)	Air Pollution level	Depends on HCHO and TVOC levels	Not Specified	Not measured in AQD hence AQM is better
o)	Application Technology	Not given	Natural air flow detection technology	AQD is better as technology is specified
16.	Additional features in equipment			
a)	Record Option	Yes (5s–120s gap and 50–500 numbers possible and shows how much time it will take to finish the same), Chart of recorded data and recorded data can be viewed in detail	No	AQM is better

b)	Screen off time can be set	Yes	No	AQM is better
c)	Timed Shut Down option is available	Yes	No	AQM is better
d)	Brightness adjustment is possible	Yes	No	AQM is better
e)	Manual recalibration is available when results are not accurate, when clear air is not available to calibrate	Yes	No	AQM is better
f)	Date and time can be reset	Yes	No	AQM is better
g)	Treat Haze and Treat HCHO option to estimate cost required to clear PM2.5(dust) and HCHO	Yes	No	AQM is better
h)	Alarm when Air Pollution level reaches the setting line	Yes	No	AQM is better
17.	Precautions to be taken			
a)	Equipment should not be put in high concentration of dust and polluted gas for a long time	Yes	Yes	Same precautions for both
b)	Attention is required for fire, water, dust, fall, sun, moisture, mild dew prevention	Yes (mentioned in case of dust, device screen is not functioning properly which may be due to fall)	Yes (for 7 values)	AQD is better in specifying precautions
c)	Don't use in high temperature and high humidity environment	Yes	Not mentioned	AQM is better in specifying precautions
d)	Don't disassemble	Yes	Yes	Same precautions for both
e)	Keep away from children or those with mental retardation	No	Yes	AQD is better in specifying precautions
f)	Keep away from explosives and flammables	No	Yes	AQD is better in specifying precautions
g)	Detection point should not be blocked	Yes	No	AQM is better in specifying precautions
18.	Warranty period	Not mentioned	Not mentioned	Both AQM,AQD have not specified
19.	Disposal procedure disclosed	No	No	Both AQM, AQD have not specified

TABLE 5.6
Gauge Capability Measurement

S.No.	Device	Pollutant	Units	Tolerance	Least Count	0.05T	Std. Deviation	Gauge Capability Cg (0.2*T/6s)	LC< 0.05T	Gauge Capability > 1.33
1.	AQM	HCHO	mg/m^3	<0.061	0.001	0.003	0.00097	20.935	Y	Y
2.	AQM	TVOC	mg/m^3	0–0.6	0.001	0.03	0.00340	5.878	Y	Y
3.	AQM	PM2.5	mg/m^3	35	1	1.75	0.6633	1.758	Y	Y
4.	AQM	PM1.0	mg/m^3	50	1	2.5	0.5	3.333	Y	Y
5.	AQM	PM10.0	mg/m^3	100	1	5	0.6137	5.431	Y	Y
6.	AQM	TEMP	°C	35	1	1.75	0.7071	2.357	Y	Y
7.	AQM	Humidity	%RH	90	1%	4.5	1.7953	1.300	Y	N
8.	AQM	APL	No unit	Not specified	1	–	0.2768	–	–	–
9.	AQD	CO	ppm	100	1	5	1.1445	1.144	Y	N
10.	AQD	CO_2	ppm	1000	1	50	2.4494	2.449	Y	Y
11.	AQD	HCHO	mg/m^3	<0.061	0.001	0.005	0.0013	2.590	Y	Y
12.	AQD	TVOC	mg/m^3	0–0.6	0.1	0.03	0	–	N	–
13.	AQD	AQI	No unit	1	1	0.1	0	Not defined as std. deviation was 0	N	

Source: Air Quality Monitor User Manual (Ver.1.0) (n.d.) and Instruction Manual Air Quality Detector (n.d.).

Regression Statistics	
Multiple R	0.8084
R Square	0.6535
Adjusted R Square	0.5623
Standard Error	0.1832
Observations	25

ANOVA

	df	*SS*	*MS*	*F*	*Significance F*
Regression	5	1.2023	0.2405	7.1652	0.0006
Residual	19	0.6377	0.0336		
Total	24	1.84			

	Coefficients	*Standard Error*	*t Stat*	*P-value*	*Lower 95%*	*Upper 95%*	*Lower 95.0%*	*Upper 95.0%*
Intercept	0.0182	0.2787	0.0654	0.9486	-0.5650	0.6015	-0.5650	0.6015
HCHO	-26.3158	232.1069	-0.1134	0.9109	-512.1212	459.4896	-512.1212	459.4896
TVOC	4.1329	67.1380	0.0616	0.9516	-136.3886	144.6544	-136.3886	144.6544
PM2.5	0.3367	0.1141	2.9507	0.0082	0.0979	0.5755	0.0979	0.5755
PM1.0	-0.4882	0.1403	-3.4806	0.0025	-0.7818	-0.1946	-0.7818	-0.1946
PM10	0.2888	0.0952	3.0344	0.0068	0.0896	0.4880	0.0896	0.4880

FIGURE 5.4 Regression results for air pollution level measured using air quality monitor.

4. The regression model for AQI was not formulated as with no variation in AQI for all 25 readings in the chosen room the relationship was not mapped.
5. The regression model for Air Pollution level using AQM was formulated using Data Analysis Toolpak in excel and the results are shown in Figure 5.4. The regression equation is,

$$\mathbf{APL = 0.0182 - 26.2158\,HCHO + 4.1329TVOC + 0.3367\,PM2.5}$$
$$\mathbf{- 0.4882\,PM1.0 + 0.2888\,PM10.}$$

Figure 5.4 reveals that HCHO, TVOC, PM1, PM2.5, PM10 contribute to 65.35% variation in Air Pollution level which is the dependent variable out of which 56.23% was explainable. The F ratio is 0.0006 which is less than 0.01 means that at least one of the beta coefficient is significant. On further analysis it was found that PM2.5, PM1.0, PM10 were having p values less than 0.01 and hence these were all having significant beta contributions.

5.7 CONCLUSIONS

1. According to the manual (Global, 2014) the measurement is incomplete without measuring the components of measurement. The components of measurement include the item to be measured, the appraiser, the reference (standard used to calibrate the equipment), the environment and the procedure for measurement.

2. The reproducibility reading which accounts for appraiser variation is not applicable for both the devices as the readings are generated by pressing a button and appraiser has no role to play like in other instruments where positioning of the inspection piece by the appraiser matters and inspection piece is solid. However, there is a possibility that if appraiser hands are sanitized it might have an impact on the pollutant level measured by the devices.
3. No standard or in other words no measurement reading from higher lab is available so no reference value can be taken. The rooms are designed by architects considering ventilation and air changes measured in volume per second. Air quality is a function of the number of occupants, outdoor air quality, machines inside room, area of ventilation and can change based on these. It will also depend on the type of device, it's capability and the pollutants the device is measuring and the least count for measuring air pollutant level.
4. From the reviewed literature (Agrawal, 2018; Gurjar, 2018) it is evident that the air pollutants found in a room at home and the room designed at office are different as different machines and furniture is used at both places. So, it is important to find out whether same measurement device is capable for use at both the places.
5. The AQI value was 2 for all 25 readings taken in a span of 4 hours and hence regression model could not be plotted because no variation in AQI as a dependent variable was observed. According to the document (Standard, n.d.) AQI is the measure of impact of air pollution on a person's health within a short-time period and the Environment Protection Agency calculates AQI for five major air pollutants which are ground-level ozone, particle pollution/particulate matter (PM2.5/PM 10), carbon Monoxide, sulfur dioxide, nitrogen dioxide. This means that standard deviation of 1.1446 in CO, 2.449 in CO_2, 0.0013 in HCHO and $5.666*10^{-017}$ in TVOC was not able to bring any change in AQI. Hence, it will be interesting to find out how much standard deviation in these measurements actually bring a deviation in AQI individually and collectively.
6. The regression model shown in Figure 5.4 shows that Air pollution level depends on all types of Particulate Matter (PM1.0, PM2.5, PM10.0) which contradicts the statement specified in the (Air Quality Monitor User Manual (Ver.1.0), n.d.) which states that Air pollution level relies on "HCHO" and "PM2.5". Hence the table formulated in (Air Quality Monitor User Manual (Ver.1.0), n.d.) for hazard level which includes only HCHO and PM2.5 values should be redesigned considering all types of Particulate Matter. The regression equation is **APL (Air Pollution Level) = 0.0182 – 26.2158 HCHO + 4.1329TVOC + 0.3367 PM2.5 – 0.4882 PM1.0 + 0.2888 PM10.**
7. The gauge capability (Cg) of AQM was found slightly lower than 1.33 for measuring humidity and AQD was found less than 1.33 for measuring CO. For humidity the Cg is 1.3 which is still acceptable as the acceptance criteria specified in C/QMM (2008) is more stringent than that specified in MSA Manual but Cg for CO is 1.144 which is not acceptable as high CO levels

have a very severe impact of lungs cancer. Gauge capability should not be compromised wherever severity impact is high. For less severe pollutants Cg of 1 may also be set as an acceptance criteria as according to GmbH (2001) both the mean (μ) and dispersion (6s) of the measurement process should be within 20% of the tolerance.

8. The least count was not less than or equal to 0.05 T in case of TVOC and AQI measurements by AQD which is violation of Bosch Procedure and if it is more than 0.10T then it will be violation of Automotive Industry Action Group (AIAG) Manual of MSA as well.
9. There is a significant difference observed in the HCHO and TVOC measurements by the two equipments AQM and AQD. The level measured by AQM is less than that measured by AQD for both the pollutants.
10. The cost of AQM is 9000 and cost of AQD is 5000 so AQD is better in terms of cost-effectiveness but considering the extra features AQM's cost might appear reasonable.
11. The comparative analysis of the two devices was done using the (Air Quality Monitor User Manual (Ver.1.0), n.d.; Instruction Manual Air Quality Detector, n.d.) and physically by using these for measurement in same room. It was found that the two devices exhibited different level of performance in different parameters. The performance of both the devices is summarized in Table 5.6 showing parameters where performance was equal, performance of AQM was better than AQD, performance of AQD was better than AQM.

As shown in Table 5.7 AQM has better features and conditions for use are better specified in AQM but the term like "fresh or clear air" should be specified as fresh air is used as a standard for calibration for AQM. Fresh air can't be chosen based on the perception of humans as lung capacity of different individuals is different. Hence, their perception will be different. In scientific experiments everything is conducted in a logical sequence calibration based on perception might be erroneous. The purpose of MSA is to reduce error which will be defeated if calibration is based on perception. Manual calibration is possible in AQM if there is bias but the point is how the true or reference value will be measured.

5.8 FUTURE RESEARCH DIRECTIONS

1. Factors affecting indoor and outdoor pollution are different and can be studied in detail.
2. The measurement techniques used for measuring different pollutants can be studied in detail along with the repeatability and reproducibility measurements. In the standard Gauge Repeatability and Reproducibility measurements according to Thakkar (2019), three appraisers are required and ten parts are measured. Here parts are also not solid and appraisers have influence to the extent of pressing the button of the equipment. Probably the different rooms can be considered as different parts. Hence, from the repeatability formula which is measured using R double bar divided by d2

TABLE 5.7
Comparative Analysis of AQM and AQD as a Product for Purchasing

S. No	Equal Performance of AQM and AQD	Performance of AQM Is Better than AQD	Performance of AQD Is Better than AQM
	1. Both are suitable for measurements at home, sealed spaces 2. Both are capable of measuring TVOC and HCHO 3. Both are automatically calibrated and time gap is 3 minutes approximately which is not a big difference. 4. Charging time is 3 hours in AQM and AQD 5. HCHO Test Range is same in both. 6. Don't disassemble is the precaution given in both 7. Warranty is not specified 8. Disposal procedure is not specified 9. Both equipments should not be put in high concentration of dust and polluted gas for a long time	1. AQM is capable of being recycled 2. AQM measures APL 3. Condition of an unelaborated good instrument requirement is not specified in AQM 4. Conditions for calibration are better specified in AQM 5. Better visibility in terms of aesthetics in AQM 6. AQM has a higher battery capacity 7. Working time/Duration time is more 8. Weight is specified in AQM 9. Temperature test range specified 10. Humidity test range specified 11. PM1 is measured 12. PM2.5 is measured 13. PM10 is measured 14. TVOC test range is more stringent in AQM 15. APL is measured, test range is not specified 16. Record option is present 17. Screen off time can be set 18. Brightness adjustment is possible 19. Manual recalibration is available when results are not accurate, when clear air is not available to calibrate 20. Date and time can be reset 21. Treat Haze and Treat HCHO option to estimate cost required to clear PM2.5(dust) and HCHO 22. Precautions for no use in high temperature and high humidity. 23. Precaution for detection point should not be blocked	1. AQD is more valid as it measures 2 harmful pollutants but AQM measures only 1 2. AQM mentions a condition related to air density which is difficult to measure and adhere so AQD is better as no such condition is given. 3. AQD specifies detection time hence better 4. AQD is ROHS Compliant 5. AQD measures AQI 6. Stabilizing time is 30 minutes lesser. 7. Condition of an unelaborated fresh air requirement is not specified in AQD. 8. Better visibility in terms of size in AQD. 9. CO_2 is measured 10. CO is measured 11. AQI is measured, test range is specified 12. Application technology is specified which is Natural air flow detection technology 13. Precautions with respect to fire, water, dust, fall, sun, moisture, mild dew prevention are specified 14. Precautions with respect to keeping away from children and mentally retarded people are specified. 15. Precaution to keep away from explosives and flammables is given.
Total	9	23	15

where R double bar is the average of individual average ranges can now be reduced to Rbar by d2. Rbar can be found out by taking three readings simultaneously in all rooms of the same residence.

3. For finding the error using true air quality value which is the value from a higher standard, may be air inside a room at a specific time can be filled in air-tight containers and possibilities can be looked into how the quality of air can be assessed in these air-tight containers at higher labs. However, the sending of samples to higher labs and assessment will take time.
4. It will be important to explore which instruments are used for assessment of air quality by Green Rating agencies and how the repeatability and reproducibility of these instruments are checked.
5. The need is to have a single measuring instrument which can measure the presence of all air pollutants specified in Table 5.1.
6. The study (Sugiyarto Surono, 2022) yields information regarding air quality forecasting methods and proposes an optimization technique applied to the MWFTS forecasting model to predict air quality in the Anand Vihar region of India but how relevant is this technique for measuring IAQ is to be found out.

ACNOWLEDGMENT

The team want to thank Mr. Hemant Kumar L (Manager-SEG Automotive) for his guidance and support. The team of authors want to thank Dr. Mahima Rai (Associate Professor – IIS (Deemed to be) University), Dr. Madhura Yadav (Professor – Aayojan School of Architecture), Dr. Rashmi Chaturvedi (Director and Professor – Kanodia PG Mahila Mahavidyalaya, Jaipur), Dr. Shyam Chaturvedi (Retired from the position of one among the 12 Unicef Chiefs) and Late Dr. Dinesh Chaturvedi (Retired Assistant Manager – New India Assurance Company Limited) for their extensive support and guidance.

BIBLIOGRAPHY

Instruction Manual Air Quality Detector. (n.d.).

Agrawal, A. (2018, July). *Lecture 41 Indoor Environmental Quality – I*. Retrieved from youtube.com: https://www.youtube.com/watch?v=WI__IvB6V_M&t=983s

Ankita Kankaria, B. N. (2014, Oct-Dec). Indoor Air Pollution in India: Implications on Health and Its Control. *Indian Journal of Community Medicine*, 203–207. doi:10.4103/0970-0218.143019.

Besterfield, D. H., Michna, C. B., Besterfield, G. H., & Sacre, M. B. (n.d.). Quality Function Deployment. In Total Quality Management (pp. 327–359). Dorling Kindersley (India) Pvt.Ltd. licenses of Pearson Education in South Asia.

Beti Angelevska, V. A. (2021, February). Urban Air Quality Guidance based on Measures Categorization in Road Transport. *Civil Engineering Journal*, 7(2), 253–267. Retrieved from www.civilejournal.org

C/QMM. (2008, 12 1). Inspection Planning, Capability and Process Control. In *Central Directive Quality 0402*, 8. Bosch Limited Corporate Quality Management Department.

Global, T. I. (2014). Six Sigma Black Belt. In *Six Sigma Black Belt*. IACT Global.

GmbH, R. B. (2001). Measurement Uncertainty. *Quality Management in Bosch Group, Technical Statistics, Bosch Booklet*, 8, 10.

GmbH, R. B. (2003, 01). Capability of Measurement and Test Processes. In *Quality Management in the Bosch Group, Technical Statistics, Bosch Booklet 10.* Robert Bosch GmbH.

Gurjar, B. R. (2018, July). *Lecture 29: Indoor Air Quality: An Introduction.* Retrieved from youtube.com: https://youtu.be/40QetqRZJaw

Kalam, A. A. (n.d.). *Top 50 Best Most Inspiring APJ Abdul Kalam Qoutes On Success, Education And Life.* Retrieved from https://www.eachquotes.com: https://www.eachquotes.com/2020/09/apj.html

Mahajan, M. (n.d). *Statistical Quality Control.* Dhanpat Rai and Co.

Ryan. (2018, October 4). *What Are The RoHS Labelling Requirements?* Retrieved from https://www.labelsource.co.uk/: https://www.labelsource.co.uk/news/post/what-are-the-rohs-labelling-requirements

Smiledrive. (n.d.). Instruction Manual Air Quality Detector.

Standard, T. B. (n.d.). *Business Standard>Specials>Home>Air Quality Index.* Retrieved from https://www.business-standard.com/: https://www.business-standard.com/about/what-is-air-quality-index

Subburaj, R. (1998, reprint 2005). Selection of Measuring and Test Equipment. In R. Subburaj (Ed.), *Calibration the Foundation for ISO 9000 and TQM* (pp. 29–43). Allied Publishers Private Limited.

Team, S. (n.d.). Air Quality Monitor User Manual (Ver.1.0).

Team, A. (n.d.a). *Home>Quality Resources>CE Marking.* Retrieved from asq.org: https://asq.org/quality-resources/ce-marking#:~:text=A%20CE%20Mark%20is%20a,harmonized%20performance%20and%20safety%20standards

Team, W. (n.d.b). *FCC Mark.* Retrieved from https://en.wikipedia.org/: https://en.wikipedia.org/wiki/FCC_mark

Thakkar, J., D. (2019, Jan). Measurement Systems Analysis: Gage R&R Study. In *NPTEL Course: Six Sigma.* IIT Kharagpur.

WHO, T. (n.d.). *Air Quality and Health >Health Impacts>Type of Pollutants.* Retrieved from https://www.who.int/teams/environment-climate-change-and-health/air-quality-and-health/health-impacts/types-of-pollutants

6 Recent Trend and Future Prospects of AI and Sustainable Finance

Using Natural Language Processing Model

Rahul Kumar and Atul Bansal

6.1 INTRODUCTION

Sustainability involves the adoption of present resources without compromising the capacity of future generations to satisfy their needs. It entails the prudent use and management of natural resources while simultaneously assuring social and economic advancement. In other words, sustainability is fostering a society that will enable people to prosper both now and in the future while also maintaining the health and well-being of the earth and its ecosystems. This calls for a harmony among the three pillars of sustainability – the environment, society, and economy. Reducing greenhouse gas emissions, protecting biodiversity, encouraging renewable energy, minimizing waste and pollution, and advancing social equity and justice are a few important components of sustainability. Sustainability is widely accepted to be multifaceted; over time, its numerous elements have given rise to various discourses and are frequently studied individually (Giovannoni & Fabietti, 2013). Three dimensions of sustainability: economy, environment and society (Sutherland et al., 2016).

6.1.1 Sustainable Finance

Sustainable finance refers to the raising and investing of funds for environmental, social, and governance (ESG) purposes. It entails allocating money for initiatives that support sustainable development, tackle environmental problems, and enhance social well-being. Recognizing the interdependence of economic, social, and environmental elements, sustainable finance aims to strike a balance between financial returns and sustainable outcomes, such as carbon dioxide (CO_2) emission reduction, mitigating the climate change impact, and encouraging sustainable resource management. For sustainable projects and initiatives, banks and financial institutions provide loans and financing (BofA, 2021). Loans are given to companies and organizations that support sustainability, such as green building initiatives or renewable energy developers, to hasten the transition to a sustainable economy (World Bank, 2020).

DOI: 10.1201/9781003640776-6

Everyone's main concern right now is climate change, and everyone wants to live in a protected and safe environment. However, as a result of increased urbanization, industrialization, technological advancement, and, obviously, population growth, no one is now left unaffected by the unfavourable environment, and it is now everyone's responsibility to safeguard the environment so that its unfavourable effects can be avoided. To protect environment and to avoid adverse effects of climate change, governments, NGOs and other agencies required funds. Nowadays, there is a concept of green bonds, and they are a very popular fixed-income financial instrument to raise funds for environmentally related projects. In order to raise money for projects that benefit the environment, green bonds are essential. They give investors a way to assist and take part in the shift to a more environmentally friendly and low-carbon economy. Green bonds assist with climate change mitigation, greenhouse gas emission reduction, the promotion of clean technologies, and the advancement of sustainable development objectives by generating money for green initiatives.

By incorporating ESG considerations into the procedures used to make investment decisions, sustainable finance practices play a crucial role in today's financial landscape (Smith, 2020).

This chapter gives a thorough overview of sustainable financial practices and demonstrates how they link financial goals to more general societal and environmental goals.

Environmental, social, and governance (ESG) integration: ESG factors are included into investment analysis and decision-making through the process of ESG integration (Clark et al., 2015). Investment professionals evaluate a company's performance using ESG criteria in addition to standard financial research to spot potential sustainability-related risks and opportunities (Kotsantonis & Serafeim, 2018).

Impact investing: The goal of impact investment is to produce quantifiable social and environmental benefits in addition to financial gains (Eccles et al., 2014). According to Saltuk et al. (2011), impact measurement and reporting are essential elements of how investors allocate capital to projects, companies, or organizations that try to address particular societal or environmental concerns.

Sustainable investment funds and green bonds: Companies with good ESG performance are included in the portfolios built by sustainable investment funds (Hassan et al., 2019). Investors can match their investments with their values by having asset managers choose equities and bonds based on their ESG scores and sustainability criteria (EY, 2021). Green bonds are fixed-income instruments that are sold to raise money for projects that benefit the environment (ICMA, 2019). In order to mitigate climate change and promote sustainability, green bond proceeds are allocated to projects, including renewable energy installations, energy-efficient construction, and clean transportation (Climate Bonds Initiative, 2020).

Socially responsible investing (SRI): SRI is a type of investment strategy that strives to produce both social change and financial gains for the investor. Companies making a good sustainable or social impact can be included in socially responsible investments, while those making a negative impact can be excluded. SRI refers to the process of basing investing choices on moral, social, and ethical principles (Sparkes et al., 2016). When making investments, investors steer clear of businesses engaged in activities they find undesirable, such as those involving tobacco, guns, or gambling (CFA Institute, 2017).

Stewardship and engagement: As responsible shareholders, stewardship practices also include actively managing investments (Stout, 2013). Through shareholder voting and discussions with management, investors interact with businesses to promote better ESG practices and support ethical business conduct.

Climate risk assessment: The impact of climate-related factors on investment portfolios is assessed using climate risk analysis (TCFD, 2017). In order to make wise decisions in the face of changing climate difficulties, investors evaluate their exposure to physical and transition risks associated with climate change (Schueth, 2018). Aside from these, a great deal more should fall under the umbrella of sustainable financial practices, including sustainable lending and financing, transparency and reporting, regulatory compliance, innovation and technology, and awareness. The sustainability implications of Industry 4.0 suggest a framework based on the UN Sustainable Development Goals (SDGs). Although the study emphasizes the need for technology-specific evaluations in a variety of industries, mobile technology emerges as a significant sustainability driver (Bai et al., 2020).

6.1.2 Artificial Intelligence (AI) for Sustainable Finance

The importance of sustainable finance has increased significantly in recent years as the world community grapples to address urgent environmental and social issues. Artificial intelligence (AI) has become a potent tool for bringing about good improvements in the financial sector in this context. Over the past few years, the use of AI for sustainable finance has grown to address the SDGs. Sustainable financial practices are improved by leveraging innovation and technology (World Economic Forum, 2018). The development of cutting-edge financial goods and services that support sustainability, boost financial inclusion, and increase efficiency is made possible by the application of fintech solutions, AI, blockchain technology, and data analytics (BIS, 2020). Institutional and social AI for sustainable finance are the two main strategies that have surfaced. Societal AI for sustainable finance is utilized to support underbanked and unbanked people through financial inclusion programmes, whereas institutional AI for sustainable finance is used for activities like ESG investing (Pashang & Weber, 2023). AI has the potential to solve societal concerns, such as sustainability problems. Climate change and environmental deterioration are now major worldwide issues. AI can assist in the development of organizational and individual practices that are culturally acceptable in order to reduce the demand on energy and natural resources from human activities (Nishant et al., 2020). Sustainable finance has gained popularity over the recent years as a global community. The anticipated shifts in material handling, transportation, and production are described, and they are influenced by shared services, sustainability, and service quality. Smart manufacturing has developed as a result of the incorporation of cutting-edge technology like AI and internet of things (IoT). Sustainability and resource sharing are important pillars, and supply networks and material handling are essential. The next industrial revolution will be shaped by trends in digitization, material-product-process dynamics, and standardization (Tao et al., 2018). Meena et al. (2022) explore how AI is revolutionizing entrepreneurial activities, from idea generation to opportunity exploitation, emphasizing its potential to drive entrepreneurship in tribal areas and proposing solutions for integrating AI education to promote economic growth.

6.1.3 Natural Language Processing

Natural language processing (NLP) is a subfield of AI that aims to make it possible for computers to comprehend, interpret, and produce human language in a meaningful and context-relevant manner. Machine learning and large-scale data processing advancements have substantially influenced NLP throughout the years.

NLP is essential for gleaning insightful information from large amounts of textual data, analysing articles, research papers, reports, and other discussions about any topic or subject matter. In sustainable finance, sentiment analysis is an NLP approach used to gauge public opinion on sustainable finance efforts. For instance, one can determine whether public opinion towards sustainable finance is positive, negative, or neutral by examining news items (Brown, 2020).

In using NLP, you may also spot trends in sustainable finance. Researchers can identify new subjects and areas of interest in their field by reading and analysing scholarly papers and reports. The automatic identification of latent themes and concepts within textual data is made possible by topic modelling approaches like latent Dirichlet allocation (LDA). The development of these subjects throughout time can then be followed by researchers (Blei et al., 2003).

6.2 METHODOLOGY

We tried to explore the exciting nexus between AI and sustainable finance in this chapter. NLP AI tools, which give us the astonishing capacity to analyse, alter, and comprehend human language, strengthen our investigation. This chapter's goal is to provide a thorough analysis of research reports and papers that have been published in prestigious journals. Scopus, a top database for academic literature, was used as the basis for all of the analysis. We will gain insights into the dynamic environment of sustainable finance and the crucial part AI plays in determining its future through this meticulous approach (Table 6.1).

TABLE 6.1
Inclusion and Exclusion Criteria

Criteria Type	Inclusion	Exclusion
Scope of Research	Database: Scopus	All other database
Period	From 2010 to 2023	All other period
Language	English	All other language
Types of Sources	Scholarly Journal	All other sources; such as Book chapter, conference proceedings
Relevance to Research questions	Only those articles taken into consideration which are related to sustainable finance and AI	Others

Research Questions

RQ1: What are the key trends and developments in sustainable finance?

RQ2: What are the major methodologies and data analysis techniques employed in current literature on the topic of sustainable finance and AI?

RQ3: What are the gaps and limitations of the current understanding of the use of AI in sustainable finance?

RQ4: What are the key findings and conclusions from existing literature and recommendations on the topic of sustainable finance and AI?

Search query: TITLE-ABS-KEY (“Sustainable Finance” OR “Sustainability” OR artificial AND intelligence AND for AND sustainability) AND PUBYEAR > 2009 AND PUBYEAR < 2024 AND (LIMIT-TO (SUBJAREA, “BUSI”) OR LIMIT-TO (SUBJAREA, “ECON”) OR LIMIT-TO (SUBJAREA, “SOCI”) OR LIMIT-TO (SUBJAREA, “ENVI“))

After this we found 2318 documents as per Table 6.2:

But to fit in our inclusion criteria, we excluded and revised the search query given below:

TITLE-ABS-KEY (“Sustainable Finance” OR “ Sustainability” OR artificial AND intelligence AND for AND sustainability) AND PUBYEAR > 2009 AND PUBYEAR < 2024 AND (LIMIT-TO (SUBJAREA, “ECON”) OR LIMIT-TO (SUBJAREA, “BUSI”)) AND (LIMIT-TO (DOCTYPE, “ar”)) AND (LIMIT-TO (EXACTKEYWORD, “Artificial Intelligence”) OR LIMIT-TO (EXACTKEYWORD, “Sustainable Development”) OR LIMIT-TO (EXACTKEYWORD, “Sustainability”)) AND (LIMIT-TO (LANGUAGE, “English”))

After applying this revised query, we found a total of 349 publications for this study.

Figure 6.1 provides a compelling visual representation of the dynamic trajectory of research in the field of sustainable finance and AI. A glance at this figure

TABLE 6.2
Types of Literatures Found from Search Query in Scopus Database

Document Type	No.
Article	1423
Conference paper	271
Book chapter	258
Review	208
Book	66
Conference review	55
Editorial	23
Note	7
Erratum	4
Short survey	2
Retracted	1

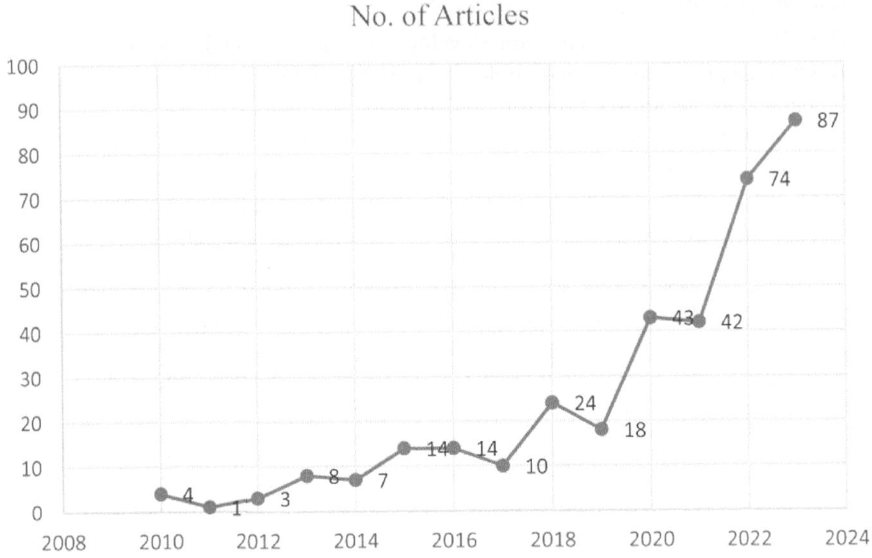

FIGURE 6.1 No. of publications year wise. (Scopus Database.)

reveals a noteworthy and accelerating trend – the rapid ascent in the popularity of this research domain in recent years.

As evidenced by the data, the topic of sustainable finance and AI has gained substantial traction over the last few years. However, it is post-2020 where a sharp surge in interest becomes strikingly evident. In the year 2023 alone, there were a staggering 87 publications, closely followed by 74 publications in 2022. This combined total of 161 publications out of the 349 included in our dataset was generated in just the last two years.

This surge is indicative of a vibrant and rapidly evolving field. It underscores the significance and timeliness of our research, as it aligns with a topic that is actively shaping discussions and innovations within the financial and AI communities. The trend reflects the growing recognition of the pivotal role that AI plays in advancing sustainability objectives within the financial sector.

Our analysis, set against this backdrop, aims to contribute valuable insights to a field that is not only gaining momentum but also holds the promise of driving positive change and sustainable practices within the financial industry.

6.3 TOPIC MODELLING USING NLP

This chapter on sustainable finance uses LDA and latent semantic analysis (LSA) algorithms as a strong method for uncovering hidden patterns and trends within a large dataset of research publications. We may attempt to obtain deeper insights into the changing environment of sustainable finance by utilizing these cutting-edge NLP techniques, and we can also make significant contributions to the topic.

We used the LDA and LSA techniques under NLP for topic modelling and to identify what key areas are emerging based on the dataset of 349 research papers that we obtained from the Scopus database to try and find the solution to research question 1, which is about significant trends and developments in sustainable finance.

David Blei, Ng, and Michael Jordan first established the generative probabilistic model for topic modelling known as LDA (Blei et al., 2003). According to LDA, documents are made up of a variety of topics, and each topic is composed of a variety of terms. It has been frequently utilized in text analysis and NLP to reveal latent topic structures in text corpora.

A corpus of 349 research papers is used to extract key trends of the sustainable finance topic using LDA, a common topic modelling technique. Data collection, the first step in the process, entails compiling a dataset of research articles from Scopus database for a period of 2010–2023. The text data is then subjected to thorough preprocessing, which includes activities like eliminating stop words, stemming, and constructing a document-term matrix to represent word frequencies in each document. LDA modelling is applied to identify latent topics within the papers and determine their distribution within each document.

Figure 6.2 provides a visual representation of the most frequently used words in the abstracts and titles of research papers from the literature review. The analysis of these common terms offers valuable insights into the prevailing themes and research trends in the field.

Figure 6.2 presents frequent words visualization that encapsulates the recurring terms found in the abstracts and titles of a diverse range of research papers. The size of each word within the word cloud is proportional to its frequency of occurrence, with larger words representing more commonly used terms.

Sustainability: The word "sustainability" is prominently displayed, indicating that it is frequently used in academic discourse about our research area. This emphasizes the industry's general concern for sustainable practices and solutions.

"Artificial intelligence" is another prominent term in the figure, indicating the growing importance of AI in both research and practice. This fits with our goal of examining how sustainability and AI may work together.

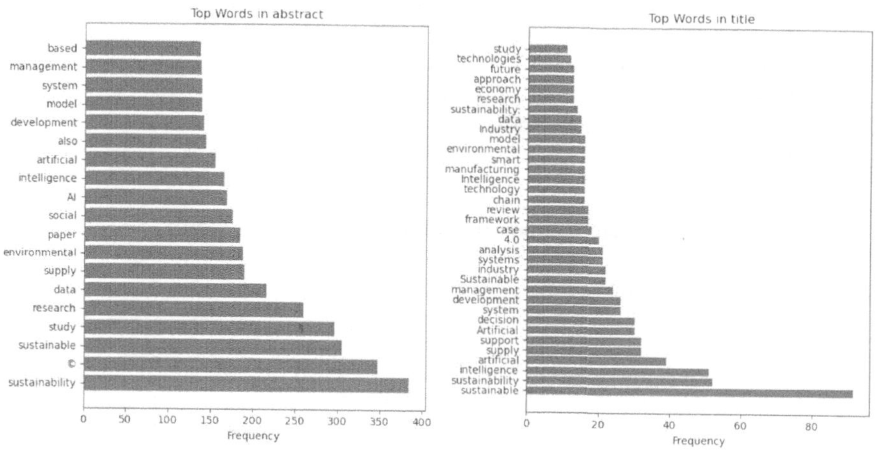

FIGURE 6.2 Top words used in abstract and title. (Author's [Own].)

The prominence of "sustainability" and "artificial intelligence" in Figure 6.1 suggests that these themes are central to current research in the field. It underscores the significance of our study, which aims to bridge the gap between these two vital areas of inquiry.

The phrases below were composed with the LDA method of NLP.

```
LDA Topic Sentences:

Topic 1: abstract no available intelligenter es happiness
reusable ghrm bronchoscopes subsystems
Topic 2: sms reputation signals palm informatics weak
commodity mill regeneration letters
Topic 3: returns lobster spiritual dsm mariculture layout gwl
groundwater gig ukraine
Topic 4: cbt msmes i4t kentucky owns 314 younger mail acres
sociodemographic
Topic 5: clothing cent retirees dna brands branded idle 14
retired clothes
Topic 6: mls corn reticulation stover league martins zone
faire ana inspirational
Topic 7: the and of to in for is this on sustainability
Topic 8: isew repurposing characterizations bankruptcy
axiomatic duration bots chat batteries consistency
Topic 9: bri animals productive animal biomarkers carcass
bulls phenotypic biochemical meat
Topic 10: music soils stabilized lignin carbonation rac abcep
pedagogy shear
```

1. **Revised Topic 1:** "Intelligent Reusable Systems for Sustainable Finance"
2. **Revised Topic 2:** "Reputation Signals and Informatics in Sustainable Commodity Trading"
3. **Revised Topic 3:** "Sustainable Returns in Mariculture and Groundwater Management"
4. **Revised Topic 4:** "Sustainable Business Ownership: CBT and Sociodemographic Factors"
5. **Revised Topic 5:** "Sustainable Brands and Clothing in the Retirement Market"
6. **Revised Topic 6:** "Sustainable Agriculture: Corn Reticulation and Inspirational Practices"
7. **Revised Topic 7:** "Sustainability in the Modern World: Challenges and Opportunities"
8. **Revised Topic 8:** "Repurposing and Sustainability: Characterizations, Batteries, and Chat Bots"
9. **Revised Topic 9:** "Animal Biomarkers for Sustainable Meat Production"
10. **Revised Topic 10:** "Sustainable Pedagogy: Music, Soils, and Carbonation in Education"

The phrases below were composed with the LSA method of NLP.

```
LSA Topic Sentences:

Topic 1: the and of to in for is this on sustainability
Topic 2: and to data are research this on we systems with
Topic 3: to is sustainability for that of this as with be
Topic 4: of economy intelligence by from about tis use service
data
Topic 5: in data of supply on ai chain from systems we
```

```
Topic 6: data to based on from intelligence manufacturing
systems all collected
Topic 7: ai supply research chain on digital sustainability
intelligence we artificial
Topic 8: supply chain decision for is support system this
management sustainability
Topic 9: for on ai is this with research that as based
Topic 10: sustainability for decision ai sustainable with are
environmental support research
```

Source: Author's (Own)

On the basis of above phrases following topics were developed.

1. **Revised Topic 1:** "Sustainability in Finance: Leveraging AI for Environmental Impact Assessment"
2. **Revised Topic 2:** "Data-Driven Research in Sustainable Finance: Harnessing AI for System Optimization"
3. **Revised Topic 3:** "AI's Role in Sustainable Finance: Towards Environmental and Economic Sustainability"
4. **Revised Topic 4:** "Economic Intelligence and Sustainable Finance: Using AI and Data Services"
5. **Revised Topic 5:** "AI in Supply Chain Finance: Enhancing Sustainability and Efficiency"
6. **Revised Topic 6:** "Manufacturing Intelligence and Sustainable Finance: Data-Driven Solutions"
7. **Revised Topic 7:** "Digital Transformation in Supply Chain Finance: AI, Sustainability, and Research"
8. **Revised Topic 8:** "Sustainable Finance Management: AI-Enabled Decision Support for Supply Chain Sustainability"
9. **Revised Topic 9:** "AI-Powered Research for Sustainable Finance: Innovations and Impacts"
10. **Revised Topic 10:** "Environmental Support for Sustainable Finance: AI-Driven Decision Making and Research"

These revised topics aim to incorporate the themes of sustainable finance and AI into each topic while providing a more specific focus.

The revised topics resulting from the LDA model for topic modelling represent a comprehensive landscape within the field of sustainable finance and its intersection with AI. Collectively, these topics reflect a multidimensional exploration of sustainable finance, emphasizing the pivotal role of AI in shaping its present and future. The overarching theme is one of synergy between AI-driven insights and sustainability objectives in finance. Researchers are actively engaged in leveraging AI techniques to assess and understand the environmental impact of financial decisions, optimize financial systems through data-driven research, and strike a harmonious balance between economic prosperity and environmental responsibility. Moreover, these topics underscore the significance of AI in enhancing sustainability and efficiency in supply chain finance, manufacturing intelligence, and decision support systems. The digital transformation in supply chain finance, driven by AI, is further highlighted, as is the management of sustainable finance in the context of AI-enabled decision support. Overall, these topics collectively provide a nuanced perspective on the evolving landscape of sustainable finance, where AI innovations and impacts hold the promise of driving positive change and sustainability in the financial sector.

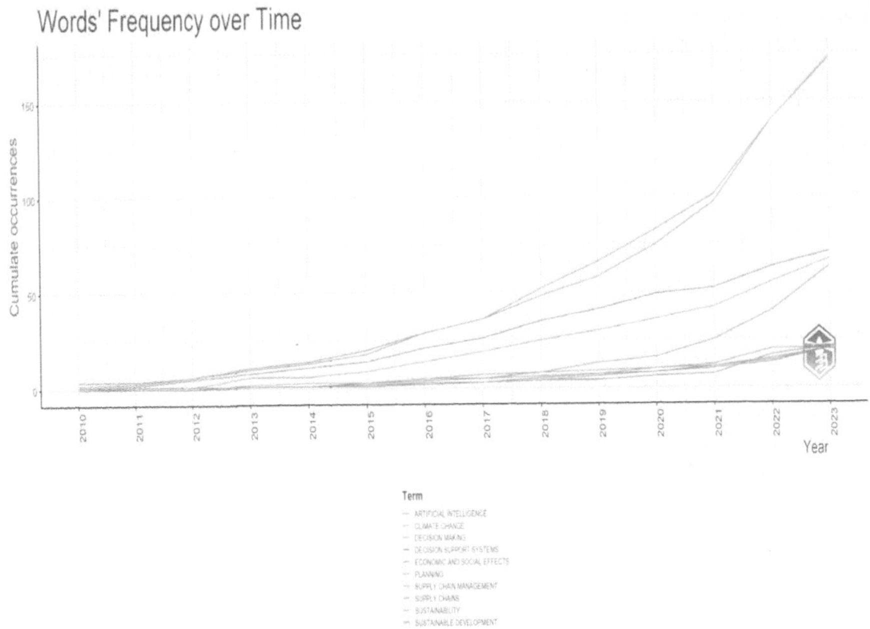

FIGURE 6.3 Words frequency trend from 2010 to 2019.

Another NLP method called LSA is utilized for text analysis, particularly in the areas of document classification and information retrieval. The main purpose of LSA is to identify the underlying semantic structure in a set of texts. Its foundation is the idea that words used in similar contexts frequently have related meanings. The well-known NLP method known as LSA is essential for the examination of textual material, developed by Deerwester and colleagues in their seminal study "Indexing by Latent Semantic Analysis" (Deerwester et al., 1990).

In Figure 6.3, word frequency counts from 2010 to 2019 were analysed to identify noteworthy patterns and changing subject matter in the corpus of articles or research papers. Notably, "ARTIFICIAL INTELLIGENCE" showed an impressive increase, with mentions rising from 2 in 2010 to 58 in 2019, demonstrating the exploding interest and developments in AI research during this time. Simultaneously, "SUSTAINABLE DEVELOPMENT" continued to be a strong point of concern, illustrating continued focus on social and environmental sustainability. The growing importance of supply chain optimization, perhaps brought on by globalization and economic factors, is shown by the terms "SUPPLY CHAIN MANAGEMENT" and "SUPPLY CHAINS". Increased references to "CLIMATE CHANGE" reflect greater public concern about environmental issues, while "ECONOMIC AND SOCIAL EFFECTS" denotes a more thorough investigation of the effects of social and policy changes. Furthermore, the consistent increase in references to "planning" and "decision-making" indicates a persistent focus on efficient planning and decision-making techniques across multiple sectors. Despite receiving fewer mentions, "DECISION SUPPORT SYSTEMS" nevertheless conveys its importance in

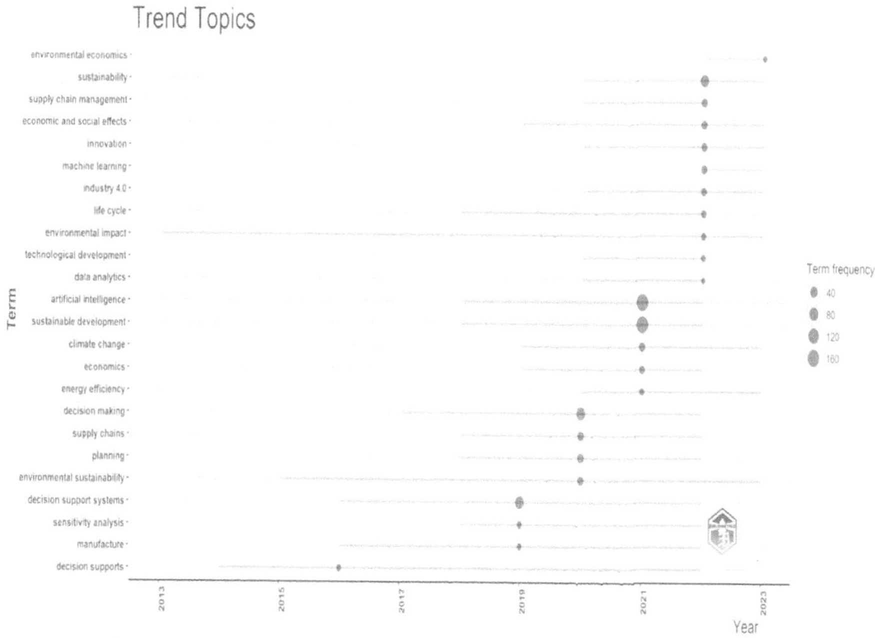

FIGURE 6.4 Trend of topics generated using Biblioshiny. (Author's Own.)

supporting decision-making. These patterns shed light on the shifting landscape of research priorities and hot-button issues that has affected the conversation over the past ten years.

Using Biblioshiny, we analysed trend topics and found that "sustainable development" had been used the most over the previous four years (Figure 6.4). In the dataset, 2021 is the median year that it first appears. This shows how crucial sustainable development continues to be in modern debate and study. A close second in terms of prominence is "artificial intelligence", which reflects the expanding importance of research linked to AI and its incorporation into a variety of fields. The statistics point to a vibrant research environment where AI and sustainable development are major topics of interest and research. These findings highlight the shifting priorities in academia and business, with a persistent emphasis on sustainability and the revolutionary potential of AI to change the course of human history. By influencing future research paths and prospective areas of collaboration, an understanding of the prevalence and patterns of these phrases provides insightful information about the state of the research field today.

Using the Biblioshiny function in R, we generated a thematic map based on the authors' keywords that were included in our dataset and discovered Figure 6.5. Thematic maps are two-dimensional images that show two things: first, density, which shows how well themes have developed based on internal correlations between keywords, and second, centrality, which shows how relevant themes are based on external associations among keywords. Four quadrants are depicted on the map: (a) the motor theme quadrant (high density and centrality), (b) the basic theme quadrant

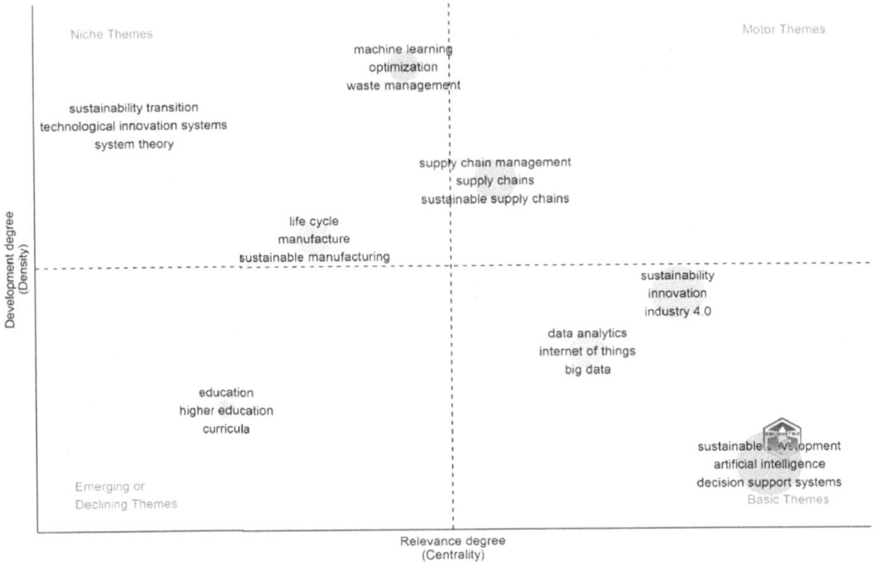

FIGURE 6.5 Thematic map. (Author's [Own].)

(low density and high centrality), (c) the niche theme quadrant (high density and low centrality), and (d) the emerging/declining theme quadrant (low density and centrality). The topics of supply chain management and sustainable supply chains are included in the motor theme quadrant.

This quadrant's areas are distinguished by a significant concentration of sustainability and supply chain management-related activity. These locations are probably major hubs for supply chain logistics, transportation, and ecologically friendly methods. Industry 4.0, data analytics, the IoT, sustainable development, AI, and decision support systems are among the themes found in the core theme quadrant. The regions in this quadrant are at the centre of innovation and technology while having a relatively low population density. They are probably important sites for cutting-edge technology creation, research, and application across numerous industries. The topics in this quadrant of niche themes include waste management, life cycle manufacturing, machine learning optimization, technological innovation, and sustainable manufacturing. Although there is a significant population density in this sector, there are no major centres of invention or technology. Instead, they focus on environmentally friendly production and management, innovation techniques, and sustainable practices. Themes pertaining to higher education courses are included in the final emerging theme quadrant. This quadrant's locations are not the hubs of technological or industrial activity and have a low population density. Instead, they could be regions undergoing population decrease with a primary concentration on education, or they could have a focus on education and higher learning, thus indicating a potential for future growth and development.

In conclusion, the thematic map's four quadrants all have crucial responsibilities for sustainable finance and AI. They encourage the creation and adoption of sustainable practices in supply chain administration, technological advancement, and education. While AI improves efficiency, decision-making, and data analysis in the quest for sustainability and technological advancement in each quadrant, sustainable finance provides funding and incentives for eco-friendly enterprises.

6.3.1 Methodologies and Data Technique Used in Current Literatures on the Basis of Topic Extracted Using NLP Technique

Research Domain	Methodologies Used	Data Analysis Techniques Used
Sustainable finance	Financial modelling, data analysis	Regression analysis, Monte Carlo simulation, risk assessment models and statistical analysis using R and Python
Commodity trading and reputation signals	Data mining, sentiment analysis	Text mining, sentiment analysis, network analysis
Mariculture and groundwater management	Field studies, hydrological modelling	Statistical analysis, hydrological modelling, GISs (geographic information systems)
Business ownership and CBT (cognitive-behavioural therapy)	Surveys, interviews	Statistical analysis, qualitative analysis (thematic/content analysis)
Sustainable brands and clothing (retirement market)	Consumer surveys, market analysis	Statistical analysis, competitive benchmarking
Sustainable agriculture (corn reticulation and inspirational practices)	Agronomic studies, genetic analysis	Genetic analysis, innovative farming practices, expert interviews
Sustainability challenges and opportunities	Literature reviews, case studies	Expert interviews, literature reviews, case studies
Repurposing and sustainability	Material characterization, environmental assessment	Data analysis (characterization and interpretation), innovative technology development
Animal biomarkers and sustainable meat production	Genetic studies, biomarker identification	Animal science
Sustainable pedagogy (music, soils and carbonation in education)	Education, research curriculum development, education material, development	Education, research curriculum development, education material, development

Source: Author (own)

A variety of methodologies and data analysis techniques have been used throughout the extracted research papers, each one being specifically adapted to the goals and areas of focus of the study in question.

Numerous studies used quantitative approaches frequently, especially those that dealt with sustainable financing. These studies evaluated the viability of sustainable investment plans using financial modelling and data analysis. Regression analysis and categorization models are two examples of machine learning techniques that are often used to assess the economic and environmental effects of investments. With the aid of statistical software and computer languages like R and Python, data preprocessing and analysis were completed. To estimate the long-term effects of various investment decisions, Monte Carlo simulations and risk assessment models were also used.

Research mainly used data mining and sentiment analysis in the context of commodity trading and reputation signalling. To examine their impact on commodities trading decisions, authors systematically retrieved reputation-related data from a range of sources, including news articles and social media. Textual data was analysed for sentiment and reputation signals using text mining techniques and NLP technologies, including sentiment analysis libraries. Another noteworthy method for revealing the complex connections between reputation signals and trading results is network analysis.

Studies on mariculture and groundwater management have made field research and hydrological modelling their two main techniques. On-site evaluations of mariculture practices were part of field research, which offered insightful information about sustainability. In order to evaluate the viability of several groundwater management scenarios, hydrological modelling was crucial. While geographic information systems (GISs) allowed the visualization and analysis of spatial groundwater data, statistical software programmes were used to analyse field data.

Mixed-method research methodologies were used in the fields of company ownership and cognitive-behavioural therapy (CBT). These studies looked at the effects of CBT therapies on sustainable company ownership using surveys, interviews, and statistical analysis. Data from the survey was carefully examined using statistical programmes like SPSS or STATA. To find patterns and themes, qualitative data from interviews underwent in-depth thematic or content analysis.

In summary, this analysis provides a thorough look at the methodologies and data analysis strategies that support research on a wide range of sustainability-related subjects. In order to develop and carry out future studies in order to meet the urgent issues and possibilities in sustainability, researchers and practitioners in these fields can gain important insights from this overview.

6.3.2 Limitation and Research Gap

This study only examined the topical trend based on the dataset that was retrieved from the Scopus database; it is merely a qualitative evaluation that offers details on the cluster's primary trends and findings. Using NLP techniques, we developed a few topics based on this dataset.

An overemphasis on quantitative models and machine learning algorithms is a significant gap in the study on AI in sustainable finance. These methods may not completely capture the qualitative and subtle components of sustainability, even while they provide useful insights and forecasting capacities. It can often be difficult to successfully handle complex topics like environmental and social concerns in sustainable finance using only quantitative indicators. As a result, in order to provide a more thorough knowledge of sustainable investment decisions, research is required that blends both quantitative and qualitative methodologies.

The lack of attention given to long-term effect assessment is another significant flaw. Studies in sustainable finance that use AI methods frequently focus on modelling and analysis for the short- to medium-term. The long-term effects of AI-driven investment decisions have received less attention. Sustainability is by definition a long-term notion, and AI models that do not sufficiently take into account effects over many decades may give investors and financial institutions inaccurate advice.

The use of AI in sustainable finance is severely constrained by data bias and quality. The calibre of the data that AI models are trained on has a significant impact on their efficacy. Some studies might not adequately address problems with biases, poor data quality, and representativeness of data sources. An important problem in the discipline is that biased or inadequate data might produce biased AI models, either reiterating existing disparities or omitting crucial sustainability indicators.

Another prominent flaw in AI models is their lack of explainability. The need for model explainability in sustainable finance may not be fully addressed in many studies, which might undermine investor and regulatory confidence. The adoption of AI solutions in the financial sector may be constrained by the inability to comprehend and interpret suggestions and choices made by AI.

The inclusion of ESG elements into AI models for sustainable financing has received relatively limited attention. The incorporation of ESG factors into AI-driven decision-making processes, which is essential for effectively analysing the sustainability performance of businesses and investments, may not be sufficiently covered in all research.

6.4 KEY FINDINGS

The existing body of literature emphasizes the significant consequences of combining sustainable finance and AI. By strengthening decision support systems, AI is at the forefront and has a significant impact on improving sustainable finance practices. This is especially important in the context of sustainable development, as AI helps people make decisions that are sustainable and more informed. Furthermore, sustainable finance emphasizes the significance of efficient planning and ethical supply chain management as essential elements in achieving sustainability. In order to ensure a thorough and well-informed approach to sustainable finance, this literature emphasizes the necessity to build standardized frameworks for measuring and assessing sustainability within the financial sector, including economic and social implications.

Collectively, these studies show how AI has the ability to alter sustainable finance and promote more sustainable.

6.4.1 Conclusion

The literature comes to the conclusion that combining AI with sustainable finance is a potential way to meet both financial and sustainability goals. A key force behind plans and establishing a closer link between financial practices and societal well-being is sustainable development. AI-powered decision support systems promote sustainable financial decisions by facilitating more informed decision-making. Planning and control of the supply chain are also essential for incorporating sustainability into financial strategy.

6.4.2 Recommendations

- The research community should continue to explore and develop AI applications in sustainable finance, particularly in the context of decision support systems.
- Efforts to establish standardized frameworks for measuring and assessing sustainability in financial decision-making are crucial, with a focus on economic and social impacts.
- The role of AI in supply chain management and planning for sustainability should be emphasized, guiding responsible supply chain practices.
- The integration of climate change considerations into financial strategies is recommended to address both environmental and economic implications effectively.

BIBLIOGRAPHY

Bai, C., Dallasega, P., Orzes, G., & Sarkis, J. (2020). Industry 4.0 technologies assessment: A sustainability perspective. International Journal of Production Economics, 229, 107776.

BIS (2020). Investigating the Impact of Fintech on Financial Services. Bank for International Settlements. https://www.bis.org/fsi/publ/insights20.pdf

Blei, D. M., Ng, A. Y., & Jordan, M. I. (2003). Latent Dirichlet allocation. Journal of Machine Learning Research, 3, 993–1022.

BofA (2021). ESG through the Credit Cycle. Bank of America. https://www.bofaml.com/content/dam/boamlimages/documents/articles/ID20_1490/ESG_through_the_credit_cycle.pdf

Brown, C. (2020). Using Sentiment Analysis in Sustainable Finance. Sustainable Investments Forum. https://sustainableinvestmentforum.org/using-sentiment-analysis-in-sustainable-finance/

CFA Institute. (2017). Environmental, Social, and Governance (ESG) Integration in the Investment Process. https://www.cfainstitute.org/learning/future/strategy/ESG-investment-process

Clark, G. L., Feiner, A., & Viehs, M. (2015). From the Stockholder to the Stakeholder: How Sustainability Can Drive Financial Outperformance. University of Oxford. https://www.sbs.ox.ac.uk/sites/default/files/2017-07/Investing%20for%20a%20sustainable%20future%20%28online%29%20.pdf

Climate Bonds Initiative. (2020). Bonds and Climate Change: The State of the Market in 2020. https://www.climatebonds.net/files/reports/cbi-state-of-the-market-2020.pdf

Deerwester, S., Dumais, S. T., Furnas, G. W., Landauer, T. K., & Harshman, R. (1990). Indexing by latent semantic analysis. Journal of the American Society for Information Science, 41(6), 391–407.

Eccles, R. G., Ioannou, I., & Serafeim, G. (2014). The impact of corporate sustainability on organizational processes and performance. Management Science, 60(11), 2835–2857. https://doi.org/10.1287/mnsc.2014.1984

EY (2021). Sustainable Impact: A New Purpose in Asset Management. EY Global. https://www.ey.com/en_gl/ey-sustainable-impact-a-new-purpose-in-asset-management

Giovannoni, E., & Fabietti, G. (2013). What Is Sustainability? A Review of the Concept and Its Applications. Integrated Reporting: Concepts and Cases That Redefine Corporate Accountability, 21–40.

Hassan, T., Mestre, R., Zhang, L., & Zhang, T. (2019). Asset Managers, Index Funds, and the Financial System of the Future. National Bureau of Economic Research. https://www.nber.org/papers/w25545

ICMA (2019). Green Bond Principles 2018. International Capital Market Association. https://www.icmagroup.org/green-social-and-sustainability-bonds/green-bonds/green-bond-principles-gbp/

IOSCO (2020). Report on Sustainability-Related Issuer Disclosures. International Organization of Securities Commissions. https://www.iosco.org/library/pubdocs/pdf/IOSCOPD659.pdf

Kotsantonis, S., & Serafeim, G. (2018). Four Things No One Will Tell You about ESG Data. Harvard Business Review. https://hbr.org/2018/03/four-things-no-one-will-tell-you-about-esg-data.

Meena, P., Chaturvedi, A., & Gupta, S. (2022). Impact of artificial intelligence on development and growth of entrepreneurship. In Impact of Artificial Intelligence on Organizational Transformation (131–146). https://onlinelibrary.wiley.com/doi/abs/10.1002/9781119710301.ch9

Nishant, R., Kennedy, M., & Corbett, J. (2020). Artificial intelligence for sustainability: Challenges, opportunities, and a research agenda. International Journal of Information Management, 53, 102104.

Pashang, S., & Weber, O. (2023). AI for sustainable finance: Governance mechanisms for institutional and societal approaches. In The Ethics of Artificial Intelligence for the Sustainable Development Goals (pp. 203–229). Springer International Publishing.

Saltuk, Y., Gergel, T., & Pudney, S. (2011). Insight into the Impact Investment Market. The Rockefeller Foundation. https://www.rockefellerfoundation.org/wp-content/uploads/Impact_Investment_Report.pdf

SASB (2018). Sustainability Accounting Standards. Sustainability Accounting Standards Board. https://www.sasb.org/

Schueth, S. (2018). Understanding Climate-Related Financial Disclosures. Harvard Law School Forum on Corporate Governance. https://corpgov.law.harvard.edu/2018/08/01/understanding-climate-related-financial-disclosures/

Smith, M. (2020). Sustainable Finance: Why Investing in Sustainability Is the Future. GreenBiz. https://www.greenbiz.com/article/sustainable-finance-why-investing-sustainability-future

Sparkes, R., Cowton, C. J. (2016). The Maturing of Socially Responsible Investment: A Review of the Developing Link with Corporate Social Responsibility. Journal of Business Ethics 52, 45–57. https://doi.org/10.1023/B:BUSI.0000033106.43260.99

Stout, L. A. (2013). The Shareholder Value Myth: How Putting Shareholders First Harms Investors, Corporations, and the Public. Berrett-Koehler Publishers.

Sutherland, J. W., Richter, J. S., Hutchins, M. J., Dornfeld, D., Dzombak, R., Mangold, J., …, & Friemann, F. (2016). The role of manufacturing in affecting the social dimension of sustainability. CIRP Annals, 65(2), 689–712.

Tao, F., Qi, Q., Liu, A., & Kusiak, A. (2018). Data-driven smart manufacturing. Journal of Manufacturing Systems, 48, 157–169.

TCFD (2017). Recommendations of the Task Force on Climate-Related Financial Disclosures. Task Force on Climate-Related Financial Disclosures. https://www.fsb-tcfd.org/wp-content/uploads/2017/06/FINAL-2017-TCFD-Report-11052018.pdf

World Bank (2020). Sustainable Financing for Sustainable Development. World Bank Group. https://www.worldbank.org/en/topic/financialsector/brief/sustainable-financing-for-sustainable-development

World Economic Forum (2018). Beyond Fintech: A Pragmatic Assessment of Disruptive Potential in Financial Services. World Economic Forum. https://www.weforum.org/reports/beyond-fintech-a-pragmatic-assessment-of-disruptive-potential-in-financial-services

7 AI Technology for Sustainable Fashion Consumer Engagement

Overcoming Ethical Challenges

Selvi Kausiliha Vijayan

7.1 INTRODUCTION

Sustainable fashion (SF) is a movement within the fashion industry that aims to address the negative environmental and social impacts associated with traditional clothing production and consumption. It advocates for more responsible practices throughout the entire fashion supply chain, from sourcing raw materials to product management. SF is distinct from both slow fashion (Pookulangara & Shephard, 2013) and eco-fashion (Carey & Cervellon, 2014) from an academic perspective. Slow fashion is a sustainable approach to clothing design and consumption, prioritising fair labour conditions and reducing environmental impact. It contrasts with fast fashion's rapid trends and encourages mindful consumption and transparency in the supply chain for a more equitable fashion industry (Gazzola et al., 2020). On the other hand, eco-fashion is a sustainable clothing and accessories approach that minimises environmental impacts. It involves using eco-friendly materials and responsible practices and aims to create an environmentally friendly fashion industry. It can be said that SF is more closely aligned with ethical fashion (Lundblad & Davies, 2016), which is an integration between slow fashion and eco-fashion. Ethical fashion can be defined as a category of clothing that incorporates various elements of social or environmental sustainability. These elements may include fair-trade manufacturing, the use of fabric derived from organically grown raw materials, and the adoption of production methods that prioritise social responsibility by avoiding practices, such as animal cruelty, environmental harm, and worker exploitation (Henninger et al., 2016).

The emergence of SF can be attributed to the societal awareness of the environmental repercussions associated with clothing production (Henninger et al., 2016). SF became mainstream in the early 2000s as more brands adopted sustainability to meet consumer demand for eco-friendly and ethical products. The fashion industry is undergoing continuous evolution as additional stakeholders, such as fashion brands, designers, consumers, and industry organisations, become involved and collaborate towards the establishment of a sustainable and socially responsible fashion

 DOI: 10.1201/9781003640776-7

industry. Numerous studies have highlighted the industry's substantial contribution to pollution and its adverse impact on the environment (Rzyczycki, 2023). Due to this awareness, consumers' interest in eco-friendly and ethical clothing options was on the rise. Research indicated that a growing number of consumers were becoming more conscious of the environmental and social impacts and actively seeking sustainable alternatives (Hur & Cassidy, 2019).

Fast fashion, with its emphasis on quick, low-cost production and rapid turnover of trends, continued to dominate the global fashion market due to its affordability and accessibility. The worldwide fast fashion industry was appraised at USD106 billion, with a projected surge to USD185 billion by 2027 (Statista, 2023). This substantial growth is mainly driven by the escalating demand for budget-friendly fashion among younger generations (Khandual & Pradhan, 2019). Despite the glory, the fast fashion sector contributes to approximately 8 per cent of the world's carbon emissions (UN Alliance, 2019). Synthetic fabrics like polyester and nylon lead to the release of numerous plastic fibres, contributing to 20–35 per cent of ocean microplastics, according to Illuminem 2024). Due to its constant pursuit of fleeting trends, it produces low-quality clothing designed for short-term use, leading consumers to discard these items from few uses. On top of that, fast fashion retailers dispose of large quantities of unsold inventory by either discarding or incinerating it, rather than exercising donation or recycling. Past statistics reveal that these unsustainable practices lead to an annual loss of over $500 billion (Ellen MacArthur Foundation, 2017).

Sustainable brands prioritise renewable energy sources and energy-efficient technologies, curbing greenhouse gas emissions and reducing carbon footprints. They also minimise transportation emissions by sourcing materials locally and producing garments closer to their markets. Waste reduction is another hallmark of sustainability, achieved with eco-friendly materials and a circular economy approach that encourages repair and recycling (Mukendi et al., 2020). Water conservation is paramount, with sustainable practices minimising water usage, recycling water, and avoiding harmful chemicals. Importantly, ethical labour practices ensure fair wages and safe conditions, and the production of longer-lasting, higher-quality garments reduces the demand for frequent replacements. Though specific statistics may vary over time, these principles underpin the environmental benefits of SF.

With the recent technological development, artificial intelligence (AI) plays a pivotal role in ensuring fashion brands adhere to sustainability and ethical sourcing practices. Within the realms of computer science and engineering, AI is capable of executing tasks that conventionally necessitate human cognitive abilities (Górriz et al., 2023; Nishant et al., 2020). These tasks cover a wide range of activities, including learning, thinking, solving problems, perception, understanding natural language, and making decisions (Pereira et al., 2022). The precise origins of AI remain uncertain; however, McCarthy et al. (1995) defined AI as the "discipline and practise concerned with the creation of intelligent machines." The potential of AI in revolutionising SF consumer engagement has been emphasised (Meena et al., 2022), yet ethical considerations remain a critical aspect to address for a more robust outlook.

As such, AI is defined as the ability of machines to imitate intelligent human behaviours, encompassing various subfields, such as machine learning, neural networks, deep learning, natural language processing (NLP), virtual agents, smart devices, and image recognition (De Bruyn et al., 2020), as it strives to emulate, reproduce, or enhance human intelligence through a range of methodologies. In the context of AI, "intelligence" has been defined as the capacity of an agent to use computational processes to link perception and action in complex ways, despite having limited knowledge and resources. AI empowers computers to perform tasks that humans would consider intelligent, which is using machine intelligence to learn human intellectual tasks (Lee, 2022). Having said that, the transformative impact of AI is evident in many economic sectors, such as fashion and retailing, in revolutionising the way businesses operate, make decisions, and deliver products and services.

7.2 RESEARCH OBJECTIVES AND METHODOLOGY

The objective of this chapter is to develop a framework that facilitates the ethical incorporation of AI technology into SF. The research is developed using content analysis through secondary data by examining different and heterogeneous sources, such as academic journals, books, official companies' websites, published newspapers, and periodical reports. This research seeks to provide an overview of how ethical practices can be supported by developing a unified comprehension of the ethical considerations in AI technology for SF consumer engagement. By adopting this strategy of analysis, it is possible to have a clear and comprehensive view of how AI-driven ethical challenges can be mitigated to support SF consumer engagement. The implementation of a framework serves as a cohesive and systematic arrangement that addresses the mitigation of ethical dilemmas encountered in the context of AI-powered SF.

7.3 AI APPLICATIONS IN SUSTAINABLE FASHION CONSUMER ENGAGEMENT

7.3.1 An Overview of AI Influence in the SF Industry

AI is increasingly being recognised as a significant catalyst in the domain of SF, which the efforts aimed at addressing the environmental and social consequences, such as waste, pollution, and unethical labour practices (Fan & Chang, 2023; Hidayat, 2023). As a multifaceted industry that has substantial ecological implications, the capabilities of AI become prominent in transforming the industry's sustainability practises through its utilisation of data-driven capabilities and problem-solving algorithms (Liu et al., 2022). By leveraging data analytics and predictive modelling, AI empowers fashion brands to thoroughly analyse and optimise various aspects of their supply chains, encompassing the acquisition of raw materials, the manufacturing process, and the distribution of products. By incorporating factors such as environmental impact and ethical considerations, AI enables brands to make well-informed decisions regarding material sourcing and production methods, thereby promoting the advancement of sustainability objectives. On top of that, the fashion industry is currently grappling with the significant challenge of overproduction, which is being addressed through the utilisation of demand forecasting models driven by AI through the utilisation of historical data and current market trends to accurately forecast consumer preferences. As a result, fashion brands can adjust their production to match actual demand, minimising the negative environmental effects of overproduction and wasted clothing (Mandarić et al., 2022).

The concept of SF frequently centres on the utilisation of environmentally friendly materials, with AI playing a crucial part in their identification and advancement. For example, by utilising machine learning algorithms, AI evaluates the sustainability of materials by closely examining their lifecycle and environmental consequences (Javaid et al., 2022), enabling the possibility of facilitating the creation of new sustainable fabrics and materials. Similarly, algorithms can provide design recommendations by analysing market trends, consumer preferences, and sustainability requirements. Fashion designers and brands are progressively utilising AI-powered tools to develop a design that effectively combines aesthetics with sustainable principles, hence resulting in a reduction of the carbon footprint associated with apparel (Candeloro, 2020). AI has a pivotal role in embracing the circular fashion economy, mainly in recycling and resales of second-hand clothing. As the ethical aspect of SF relies heavily on the imperative of maintaining transparency in labour practises, the ethical and fair treatment of workers in the supply chain is ensured using AI to monitor working conditions.

With the rise of e-commerce, AI-powered recommendation systems are encouraging consumer decisions by providing personalised recommendations based on customers' preferences and values as a means of elevating awareness about sustainable brands (He & Zhang, 2023). While quality is a vital facet of SF, AI plays a role in upholding a high standard of quality while simultaneously minimising the need for remanufacturing (Papamichael et al., 2023) as a strategy for reducing manufacturing waste.

In summary, AI is gaining recognition as a powerful enabler in the pursuit of SF in driving transformative progress towards a fashion industry that is both ecologically sustainable and ethically responsible.

7.3.2 AI in Enhancing SF Consumer Engagement

In recent years, the fashion industry has experienced a notable paradigm shift, wherein sustainability has emerged as a pivotal focal point. This section will explore the various ways in which AI has augmented consumer engagement in the realm of SF, drawing on insights from past research.

7.3.2.1 Personalisation

The utilisation of personalisation serves as a mechanism to effectively captivate consumers within the realm of SF. AI-powered recommendation systems utilise advanced algorithms to analyse various factors, such as consumer preferences, past purchasing patterns, and browsing behaviours to provide personalised suggestions that align with individual tastes (Kumar et al., 2019; Rathore, 2017).

ZALORA, Asia's largest online fashion and lifestyle store, has employed AI to improve customer experiences and promote SF. In a fast-changing e-commerce landscape, ZALORA knows personalisation is key to meaningful interactions with its diverse customer base. Through the implementation of the Algonomy

Hyper-Personalization Suite, ZALORA is able to deliver a one-to-one personalised experience that is highly customised through the analysis of customer behaviour, preferences, and purchasing phases across all digital touchpoints (PR Newswire, 2021). For example, if a customer has previously shown an interest in a handwoven sweater, the AI system recommends similar sustainable garments, enhancing the customer's engagement with the brand's eco-friendly offerings. By inputting their fashion preferences and sustainability priorities, customers receive tailored recommendations, providing a unique and engaging shopping experience.

7.3.2.2 Virtual Try Ons

The fashion industry is witnessing a rise in the adoption of AI-driven and augmented reality (AR) virtual try-on solutions, which enable consumers to digitally visualise the appearance of garments on their own bodies, eliminating the need for physical trials. Furthermore, AI possesses the capacity to analyse physical measurements and clothing specifications in order to offer suggestions about suitable size and fit. This functionality serves to minimise the occurrence of returns and exchanges.

For example, the multinational brand H&M had been advocating sustainability and implemented a virtual try-on feature on its official webpage. The interactive approach opens a new avenue for consumers to visually measure and try the clothing virtually through their body measurements. In return, the AI algorithms provide the best-fitting sizes. A reality as equivalent to the physical shop was created, thus improving consumers' virtual shopping experience (H&M Group, n.d.). Such AI placements also mitigate the uncertainties, such as wrong sizes and comfort, leading to fewer exchanges and returns.

7.3.2.3 SF Advocacy

AI also plays a significant role in educating consumers about SF practises, a critical factor in promoting active participation and responsible consumption. Educational resources such as AI-driven chatbots and virtual assistants are proving breakthroughs such as educating consumers on sustainable notions associated with fashion and the environmental ramifications that link with fashion decision making. Uniqlo, one of the pioneers of sustainability, uses chatbots to provide information of their merchandise and their sustainability approaches, especially on the breathability of their Airism collections and the identification of eco-friendly materials and production (Williams, 2018). This pedagogical strategy facilitates increased consumer involvement by providing them with the necessary information to make environmentally conscious decisions, thereby reinforcing their affinity towards the brand. This includes educating consumers about the value of upcycling and fostering a sense of engagement and environmental responsibility.

In conclusion, AI-driven solutions offer consumers the ability to make environmentally conscious decisions and simultaneously enhance the sustainability efforts of fashion brands. This is achieved through personalised recommendations, virtual try-on experiences, educational chatbots, and the implementation of ethical practices such as consumer education. The potential of AI in augmenting consumer engagement within the realm of SF is noteworthy. However, it is imperative to recognise the obstacles that exist and contemplate the possibilities that lie ahead.

7.4 ETHICAL CONSIDERATIONS IN AI TECHNOLOGY

While AI has become integral to modern consumer engagement strategies, it is important to acknowledge the ethical quandaries that arise from the application of AI in consumer engagement, which necessitate resolution in order to fully harness its capabilities as follows.

7.4.1 Privacy Concerns

Privacy is one of the biggest ethical issues with AI in consumer engagement. Chua et al. (2020) note that interactive marketing often collects and uses personal data. This raises legitimate concerns about privacy violations (Tiwari & Tomar, 2023). Businesses collect a lot of customer data without their consent, such as demographics, preferences, behaviours, and personal habits. As mentioned by Yara et al. (2021), AI systems need a lot of personal data to work, which raises privacy concerns. Data security is crucial, and any breach or misuse can have serious consequences. AI systems may be vulnerable to attacks that compromise data and system integrity, affecting customer and proprietary data (Sarker et al., 2023). As mentioned by Vollmer et al. (2020), data usage transparency and control issues exacerbate these concerns. Consumers are often unaware of how much personal data is collected and used to create profiles. Lack of transparency can make consumers feel powerless over their data. As AI systems become more complex, their algorithms may make decisions based on data humans cannot understand or influence; in other words, violate privacy and raise ethical questions about data security (Telo, 2023).

7.4.2 Data Security and Protection

Trust between businesses and customers requires transparency. AI systems can be complex, making it hard for consumers to understand how they make personalised recommendations, product offerings, and content exposure decisions. Lack of control over data and AI-driven interactions reduces autonomy. Customers often feel pressured to make bad choices. Stray (2020) opined that AI systems optimise for specific outcomes, often prioritising business goals over individual well-being. AI-powered chatbots may encourage overuse or harmful behaviour by encouraging service engagement. Similarly, Solberg et al. (2022) opinionated that AI systems that influence people's choices increase this lack of control. These systems can use psychological vulnerabilities to persuade consumers to make certain choices. This can benefit businesses but limit people's autonomy and choice in interactions.

7.4.3 Manipulative Practices

According to Sullivan and Fosso Wamba (2022), the incorporation of AI in consumer engagement has the potential to inadvertently raise manipulative practices. AI systems, equipped with comprehensive customer profiles and advanced predictive algorithms, possess the capacity to utilise human psychology to achieve commercial benefits. AI can choose content and recommend it based on user behaviour. While this can improve user experience, it can also create filter bubbles that reinforce confirmation bias by only showing information that agrees with them (Westerwick et al., 2020). Limited-time offers and low-stock alerts can be used in AI-driven marketing campaigns where these methods can force consumers to make snap decisions without much thought. AI can analyse user emotions using NLP that can be used to create heartfelt messages to influence users' decisions (Weiler et al., 2022). Social proof can be utilised by AI to highlight the actions of others. For instance, demonstrating that numerous individuals have purchased a product can generate a bandwagon effect, resulting in increased sales. AI can adjust prices based on a customer's perceived willingness to pay, potentially leading to price discrimination (Gautier et al., 2020). AI systems have the potential to generate erroneous decisions or recommendations, thereby resulting in adverse consequences for consumers. AI algorithms that are specifically developed to optimise user engagement have the potential to unintentionally endorse sensational or controversial material, as such content typically attracts a higher level of attention (Testa et al., 2021). This phenomenon has the potential to facilitate the dissemination of fabricated news, unfounded conjectures, and polarising narratives (Goindani & Neville, 2020), thereby compromising the information accessible to the public.

7.4.4 Dehumanisation

In the domain of customer service, the incorporation of AI-powered chatbots and virtual assistants aims to provide prompt resolutions to inquiries. However, these automated systems frequently fall short in terms of empathy and comprehension, aspects that human agents are typically able to provide (Krishnan et al., 2022; Liu-Thompkins et al., 2022). The depersonalisation of customer interactions has the potential to result in feelings of frustration and dissatisfaction, ultimately exerting a negative influence on the overall customer experience.

7.5 FRAMEWORK IN MANAGING AI ETHICAL CHALLENGES IN SF CONSUMER ENGAGEMENT

Online SF consumer engagement presents a complex landscape, marked by the intersection of ethical concerns, technological advancements, and the changing expectations of consumers. As fashion companies strive to meet the demands for sustainability and ethical practices, a comprehensive framework becomes essential. This discussion elaborates on the framework for managing ethical challenges in online SF consumer engagement.

7.5.1 Ethical Governance

The establishment of explicit governance structures and processes is a fundamental aspect of ethical consumer engagement in the realm of SF. In the contemporary era of digitalisation and the growing discernment of consumers, companies must accord primacy to ethical practices right from their inception.

Fashion companies need to set comprehensive ethical standards that permeate every facet of their operations. These standards should not be mere window dressing but also crucial for fostering trust, transparency, and AI-responsible practices within the organisation (Saurabh et al., 2022). Ethical standards in online SF consumer engagement encompass various aspects, including marketing ethics, marketing practices, and communication. The development of these standards requires a commitment from top leadership. It involves a thorough assessment of the organisation's current AI knowledge and practices related to SF consumer engagement (Prentice et al., 2020). It is crucial to identify areas where ethical challenges may arise and align them with global sustainability goals. For instance, developing Sustainable Development Goals (SDGs) as a guiding framework for honest and transparent marketing practices within the organisation.

Similarly, to ensure the responsible development and deployment of AI technology, it is crucial to train AI developers and data scientists in ethical AI practices (Wang et al., 2020). This training should equip them with the knowledge and tools needed to embed ethical considerations into every stage of the development process. By imparting an understanding of issues like fairness, transparency, bias mitigation, and privacy, developers and data scientists can make informed decisions that prioritise ethical values (Schwartz et al., 2022, Weinberg, 2022). This proactive approach not only helps prevent harmful consequences but also fosters the creation of AI systems that align with societal values and ethical standards, promoting trust and responsible innovation in the field of AI. Applying ethical design thinking principles during AI system development is crucial (Tham et al., 2022). This involves considering the ethical implications of AI at every stage, from ideation to deployment. Teams should conduct ethical impact assessments, identify potential biases, and incorporate fairness and transparency into the design. Ethical design thinking ensures that ethical considerations are integral to the AI system's architecture and decision-making processes.

Organisations could emphasise AI ethical practices by incorporating them into key performance indicators (KPIs) and performance evaluations (Madaio et al., 2020). This practice guarantees that employees are incentivised and acknowledged for their dedication to upholding ethical principles. The implementation of incentives to promote ethical behaviour has the potential to exert significant influence on organisational dynamics and foster transformative outcomes.

7.5.2 Ethical Principles

Transparency and data protection are critical aspects of ethical consumer engagement in the digital era. Fashion companies must be transparent about their business models and how they use customer data (Thorisdottir & Johannsdottir, 2019). To meet this demand for transparency, fashion companies should be open about their business models. The organisation should prioritise transparency in how AI systems are used within the organisation. Transparency begins with clear and straightforward communication. It means openly informing consumers about the presence and role of AI in the platform's operations (Silva & Bonetti, 2021). This information should be easily accessible, preferably in a dedicated section within the website or app.

Similarly, organisations should also ensure that consumers understand when and how AI is employed in their interactions (Puntoni et al., 2021). Consumers should be aware of situations where AI is employed, especially in activities, such as product recommendations, personalised marketing, chatbots, and data analysis. Businesses should offer consumers insights into the algorithms, data sources, and decision-making processes that underpin AI-driven recommendations and decisions (Enarsson et al., 2022). This does not necessitate divulging confidential information, but rather providing an overview of system operation.

Transparency also extends to data usage. Fashion companies that collect customer data must clearly communicate how this information is used (Campbell et al., 2020). It is imperative to acquire informed and explicit consent from consumers prior to the collection and processing of their data (Davenport et al., 2020). It should be made evident to customers what data is collected, for what purposes, and how it is safeguarded. The establishment of robust data protection protocols is crucial to guarantee the security and confidentiality of consumer information. It demonstrates respect for customer privacy but also aligns with evolving data protection regulations. When AI provides product recommendations or suggests content, it should be accompanied by clear explanations (Zhang et al., 2021). For instance, if the platform suggests a particular clothing item to a consumer, it should explain why the item was chosen, e.g. consumer's past purchases and browsing history.

7.5.3 Bias Mitigation

Fashion companies should go a step further in safeguarding customer data by conducting external audits on AI algorithms. Regularly auditing AI algorithms is an essential step in addressing biases and promoting fairness in SF. Biases in AI can exacerbate inequalities, perpetuating injustices in the industry (Wirtz et al., 2023). These audits involve a thorough examination of the algorithms, datasets, and decision-making processes to identify and rectify biases (Kunz & Wirtz, 2023). Implementing fairness-aware machine learning techniques further enhances the process. These techniques focus on reducing disparate impacts on different demographic groups, ensuring equitable outcomes.

Additionally, promoting third-party audits and certifications in SF AI systems adds an extra layer of assurance (Mökander et al., 2023). Independent audits can assess compliance with ethical standards, providing unbiased evaluations. Certifications serve as visible indicators of responsible AI use, signalling to consumers that ethical considerations are prioritised. This encourages ethical competition among organisations, driving the industry towards responsible and sustainable AI adoption. These audits evaluate the company's adherence to industry standards and regulatory requirements related to data protection.

Conducting comprehensive risk assessments and impact analyses before implementing AI solutions is a fundamental step in responsible AI deployment (Rakova et al., 2021). These assessments involve a systematic evaluation of potential ethical challenges, such as bias, privacy infringements, and societal impacts. By identifying these challenges upfront, organisations can proactively address them, minimising the risk of unintended consequences and harm. Furthermore, impact analyses help anticipate the broader effects of AI on stakeholders, ensuring that decisions align with ethical principles and values (Floridi et al., 2021). This pre-emptive approach not only safeguards against ethical dilemmas but also promotes ethical, trustworthy, and socially beneficial AI applications.

7.5.4 Ethical Culture and Behaviour

Promoting ethical culture and behaviour in the context of SF consumer engagement and AI technology is not only a moral imperative but also a strategic business decision. It enhances trust, empowers consumers, ensures data privacy, mitigates bias, supports sustainability goals, ensures compliance, fosters innovation, and strengthens stakeholder relationships. Educating consumers about AI technology's role in SF is essential (Chang & Ke, 2023). This education should encompass both the benefits and potential risks of AI. Consumers need to understand how AI-driven recommendations and personalisation work, what data is collected, and how it's used. By fostering AI literacy among consumers, they can make informed choices and engage with SF brands that align with their ethical values.

To address ethical concerns related to data privacy, organisations should adopt a data minimisation approach (McCoy et al., 2023). Only collect and retain the minimum amount of data necessary for SF engagement. Implement robust data protection measures, including encryption and secure storage, to safeguard consumer information. This ensures that personal data is treated with the utmost care and respect. Collaboration across stakeholders in the SF industry is vital. Industry-wide collaboration can help establish ethical guidelines, standards, and best practices for AI use. Bringing together fashion brands, technology providers, consumers, and ethics experts can lead to consensus on responsible AI principles, ensuring a unified approach to ethical consumer engagement.

7.6 FUTURE TRENDS AND CONCLUSION

In summary, the incorporation of AI technology within the fashion sector exhibits significant potential for fostering sustainable consumer involvement. However, it is crucial to acknowledge that this integration is accompanied by ethical dilemmas. In the current landscape, the convergence of technology, sustainability, and ethics necessitates the establishment of a harmonious equilibrium that not only confers advantages upon enterprises and individuals but also upholds the principles of environmental preservation and safeguarding of human rights. The potential of AI technology has been demonstrated in various areas, including waste reduction, supply chain optimisation, and the improvement of personalised shopping experiences. Nevertheless, the conscientious implementation of AI in the fashion industry necessitates ongoing attentiveness to guarantee its adherence to ethical principles.

The resolution of these challenges will require a collaborative endeavour involving various stakeholders, including the fashion industry, technology developers, policymakers, and consumers. The integration of ethical considerations into the development of AI should commence from its inception, prioritising the mitigation of biases and the establishment of transparency in both data collection and processing. Companies must give utmost importance to ethical governance and ethical principles, thereby guaranteeing the mitigation of bias and developing ethical culture and behaviour for all stakeholders. Consumers also possess a pivotal role in instigating transformation by endorsing brands that prioritise ethical AI and sustainable practices, advocating for transparency, and making well-informed decisions.

Furthermore, the implementation of education and awareness campaigns has the potential to empower consumers, enabling them to make informed and responsible choices while also fostering a sense of accountability among companies. It is imperative to acknowledge that ethical dilemmas will persistently transform alongside the progression of AI technology in this endeavour. Emerging dilemmas may give rise to the need for continuous dialogue, adaptation, and regulation. However, the objective remains evident – to effectively utilise the vast capabilities of AI for the purpose of enhancing consumer engagement while upholding our ethical standards. The utilisation of AI technology possesses the capacity to fundamentally transform the fashion industry, thereby enhancing its sustainability and prioritising the needs and preferences of consumers. By proactively addressing ethical challenges, we can ensure that this technological revolution aligns with our values and contributes to a more responsible and environmentally conscious fashion industry. It is through collaboration, transparency, and a commitment to ethical principles that we can navigate this path towards a brighter and more sustainable future for fashion.

BIBLIOGRAPHY

Campbell, C., Sands, S., Ferraro, C., Tsao, H. Y. J., & Mavrommatis, A. (2020). From data to action: How marketers can leverage AI. *Business Horizons*, 63(2), 227–243.

Candeloro, D. (2020). Towards sustainable fashion: The role of artificial intelligence—H&M, Stella McCartney, Farfetch, Moosejaw: A multiple case study. *Zone Moda Journal*, 10(2), 91–105. https://doi.org/10.6092/issn.2611-0563/11837

Carey, L., & Cervellon, M. C. (2014). Ethical fashion dimensions: Pictorial and auditory depictions through three cultural perspectives. *Journal of Fashion Marketing and Management*, 18(4), 483–506.

Chang, Y. L., & Ke, J. (2023). Socially responsible artificial intelligence empowered people analytics: A novel framework towards sustainability. *Human Resource Development Review*. https://doi.org/10.1177/15344843231200930

Chua, M. Y. K., Yee, G. O., Gu, Y. X., & Lung, C. H. (2020). Threats to online advertising and countermeasures: A technical survey. *Digital Threats: Research and Practice*, 1(2), 1–27.

Davenport, T., Guha, A., Grewal, D., & Bressgott, T. (2020). How artificial intelligence will change the future of marketing. *Journal of the Academy of Marketing Science*, 48, 24–42.

De Bruyn, A., Viswanathan, V., Beh, Y. S., Brock, J. K. U., & Von Wangenheim, F. (2020). Artificial intelligence and marketing: Pitfalls and opportunities. *Journal of Interactive Marketing*, 51(1), 91–105.

Ellen MacArthur Foundation. (2017). A new textiles economy: Redesigning Fashion's Future. A New Textiles Economy: Redesigning Fashion's Future. (n.d.). https://ellenmacarthurfoundation.org/a-new-textiles-economy

Enarsson, T., Enqvist, L., & Naarttijärvi, M. (2022). Approaching the human in the loop–legal perspectives on hybrid human/algorithmic decision-making in three contexts. *Information & Communications Technology Law*, 31(1), 123–153.

Fan, K. K., & Chang, Y. T. (2023). Exploring the key elements of sustainable design from a social responsibility perspective: A case study of fast fashion consumers' evaluation of green projects. *Sustainability*, 15(2), 995.

Gautier, A., Ittoo, A., & Van Cleynenbreugel, P. (2020). AI algorithms, price discrimination and collusion: A technological, economic and legal perspective. *European Journal of Law and Economics*, 50(3), 405–435.

Gazzola, P., Pavione, E., Pezzetti, R., & Grechi, D. (2020). Trends in the fashion industry. The perception of sustainability and circular economy: A gender/generation quantitative approach. *Sustainability*, 12(7), 2809.

Goindani, M., & Neville, J. (2020, August). Social reinforcement learning to combat fake news spread. *Uncertainty in Artificial Intelligence*, 115, 1006–1016.

Górriz, J. M., Álvarez-Illán, I., Álvarez-Marquina, A., Arco, J. E., Atzmueller, M., Ballarini, F., …, & Ferrández-Vicente, J. M. (2023). Computational approaches to explainable artificial intelligence: Advances in theory, applications and trends. *Information Fusion*, 100, 101945.

He, A. Z., & Zhang, Y. (2023). AI-powered touch points in the customer journey: A systematic literature review and research agenda. *Journal of Research in Interactive Marketing*, 17(4), 620–639.

Henninger, C. E., Alevizou, P. J., & Oates, C. J. (2016). What is sustainable fashion? *Journal of Fashion Marketing and Management: An International Journal*, 20(4), 400–416.

Hidayat, Y. A. (2023). Influence of environmental knowledge and fashion consciousness on green purchase intention of sustainable fashion products. *Admisi dan Bisnis*, 23(3), 221–232.

Hur, E., & Cassidy, T. (2019). Perceptions and attitudes towards sustainable fashion design: Challenges and opportunities for implementing sustainability in fashion. *International Journal of Fashion Design, Technology and Education*. 12(2), 208–217. https://doi.org/10.1080/17543266.2019.1572789

H&M Group. (n.d.). Sustainability performance report 2020. H&M Group. https://hmgroup.com/wp-content/uploads/2021/03/HM-Group-Sustainability-Performance-Report-2020.pdf

Illuminem. (2024). Fashion. https://illuminem.com/illuminemvoices/behind-the-seams-shocking-fast-fashion-statistics-you-need-to-know

Illuminem. (n.d.). Behind the seams: Shocking fast fashion statistics you need to know. illuminem. https://illuminem.com/illuminemvoices/behind-the-seams-shocking-fast-fashion-statistics-you-need-to-know

Javaid, M., Haleem, A., Singh, R. P., Khan, S., & Suman, R. (2022). Sustainability 4.0 and its applications in the field of manufacturing. *Internet of Things and Cyber-Physical Systems*, 2, 82–90.

Khandual, A., & Pradhan, S. (2019). Fashion brands and consumers approach towards sustainable fashion. *Fast Fashion, Fashion Brands and Sustainable Consumption*, 37–54.

Krishnan, C., Gupta, A., Gupta, A., & Singh, G. (2022). Impact of artificial intelligence-based chatbots on customer engagement and business growth. In Studies in Big Data (195–210). Springer International Publishing. https://doi.org/10.1007/978-3-031-10869-3_11

Kumar, V., Rajan, B., Venkatesan, R., & Lecinski, J. (2019). Understanding the role of artificial intelligence in personalized engagement marketing. *California Management Review*, 61(4), 135–155.

Kunz, W. H., & Wirtz, J. (2023). Corporate digital responsibility (CDR) in the age of AI: Implications for interactive marketing. *Journal of Research in Interactive Marketing*. 18(1), 31–37. https://doi.org/10.1108/jrim-06-2023-0176

Lee, Y. K. (2022). How complex systems get engaged in fashion design creation: Using artificial intelligence. *Thinking Skills and Creativity*, 46, 101137.

Liu, X., Lu, D., Zhang, A., Liu, Q., & Jiang, G. (2022). Data-driven machine learning in environmental pollution: Gains and problems. *Environmental Science & Technology*, 56(4), 2124–2133.

Liu-Thompkins, Y., Okazaki, S., & Li, H. (2022). Artificial empathy in marketing interactions: Bridging the human-AI gap in affective and social customer experience. *Journal of the Academy of Marketing Science*, 50(6), 1198–1218.

Lundblad, L., & Davies, I. A. (2016). The values and motivations behind sustainable fashion consumption. *Journal of Consumer Behaviour*, 15(2), 149–162.

Madaio, M. A., Stark, L., Wortman Vaughan, J., & Wallach, H. (2020, April). Co-designing checklists to understand organizational challenges and opportunities around fairness in AI. In Proceedings of the 2020 CHI conference on human factors in computing systems (1–14).

Mandarić, D., Hunjet, A., & Vuković, D. (2022). The impact of fashion brand sustainability on consumer purchasing decisions. *Journal of Risk and Financial Management*, 15(4), 176.

McCoy, M. S., Allen, A. L., Kopp, K., Mello, M. M., Patil, D. J., Ossorio, P., …, & Emanuel, E. J. (2023). Ethical responsibilities for companies that process personal data. *The American Journal of Bioethics*, 23(11), 11–23. https://doi.org/10.1080/15265161.2023.2209535

Meena, P., Chaturvedi, A., & Gupta, S. (2022). Impact of artificial intelligence on development and growth of entrepreneurship. *Impact of Artificial Intelligence on Organizational Transformation*, 131–146. Wiley. https://doi.org/10.1002/9781119710301.ch9

Mökander, J., Schuett, J., Kirk, H. R., & Floridi, L. (2023). Auditing large language models: A three-layered approach. *AI and Ethics*, 1–31.

Mukendi, A., Davies, I., Glozer, S., & McDonagh, P. (2020). Sustainable fashion: Current and future research directions. *European Journal of Marketing*, 54(11), 2873–2909. https://doi.org/10.1108/ejm-02-2019-0132.

Nishant, R., Kennedy, M., & Corbet, J. (2020). Artificial intelligence for sustainability: Challenges, opportunities, and a research agenda. *International Journal of Information Management*, 53, 102–104. https://doi.org/10.1016/j.ijinfomgt.2020.102104

Papamichael, I., Chatziparaskeva, G., Voukkali, I., Navarro Pedreno, J., Jeguirim, M., & Zorpas, A. A. (2023). The perception of circular economy in the framework of fashion industry. *Waste Management & Research*, 41(2), 251–263.

Pereira, A. M., Moura, J. A. B., Costa, E. D. B., Vieira, T., Landim, A. R., Bazaki, E., & Wanick, V. (2022). Customer models for artificial intelligence-based decision support in fashion online retail supply chains. *Decision Support Systems*, 158, 113795.

Pookulangara, S., & Shephard, A. (2013). Slow fashion movement: Understanding consumer perceptions—An exploratory study. *Journal of Retailing and Consumer Services*, 20(2), 200–206.

PR Newswire. (2021, March 30). Algonomy enables zalora to deliver hyper-personalized experiences. PR Newswire: press release distribution, targeting, monitoring and marketing. https://www.prnewswire.com/news-releases/algonomy-enables-zalora-to-deliver-hyper-personalized-experiences-301257566.html

Prentice, C., Weaven, S., & Wong, I. A. (2020). Linking AI quality performance and customer engagement: The moderating effect of AI preference. *International Journal of Hospitality Management*, 90, 102629.

Puntoni, S., Reczek, R. W., Giesler, M., & Botti, S. (2021). Consumers and artificial intelligence: An experiential perspective. *Journal of Marketing*, 85(1), 131–151.

Rakova, B., Yang, J., Cramer, H., & Chowdhury, R. (2021). Where responsible AI meets reality: Practitioner perspectives on enablers for shifting organizational practices. *Proceedings of the ACM on Human-Computer Interaction*, 5(CSCW1), 1–23.

Rathore, B. (2017). Beyond trends: Shaping the future of fashion marketing with AI, sustainability and machine learning. *Eduzone: International Peer Reviewed/Refereed Multidisciplinary Journal*, 6(2), 16–24.

Rzyczycki, A. (2023). Sustainability in the fashion industry. *Journal of Multidisciplinary Research*, 15(1), 33–39.

Sarker, I. H., Khan, A. I., Abushark, Y. B., & Alsolami, F. (2023). Internet of things (IoT) security intelligence: A comprehensive overview, machine learning solutions and research directions. *Mobile Networks and Applications*, 28(1), 296–312.

Saurabh, K., Arora, R., Rani, N., Mishra, D., & Ramkumar, M. (2022). AI led ethical digital transformation: Framework, research and managerial implications. *Journal of Information, Communication and Ethics in Society*, 20(2), 229–256.

Schwartz, R., Vassilev, A., Greene, K., Perine, L., Burt, A., & Hall, P. (2022). Towards a standard for identifying and managing bias in artificial intelligence. *NIST Special Publication*, 1270(10.6028).

Silva, E. S., & Bonetti, F. (2021). Digital humans in fashion: Will consumers interact? *Journal of Retailing and Consumer Services*, 60, 102430.

Solberg, E., Kaarstad, M., Eitrheim, M. H. R., Bisio, R., Reegård, K., & Bloch, M. (2022). A conceptual model of trust, perceived risk, and reliance on AI decision aids. *Group & Organization Management*, 47(2), 187–222.

Statista (2023, September 5). Fast Fashion Market Forecast Worldwide 2022–2027. Statista. https://www.statista.com/statistics/1008241/fast-fashion-market-value-forecast-worldwide/

Stray, J. (2020). Aligning AI optimization to community well-being. *International Journal of Community Well-Being*, 3(4), 443–463.

Sullivan, Y. W., & Fosso Wamba, S. (2022). Moral judgments in the age of artificial intelligence. *Journal of Business Ethics*, 178(4), 917–943.

Telo, J. (2023). Smart City security threats and countermeasures in the context of emerging technologies. *International Journal of Intelligent Automation and Computing*, 6(1), 31–45.

Testa, D. S., Bakhshian, S., & Eike, R. (2021). Engaging consumers with sustainable fashion on Instagram. *Journal of Fashion Marketing and Management: An International Journal*, 25(4), 569–584.

Tham, J., Howard, T., & Verhulsdonck, G. (2022). Extending design thinking, content strategy, and artificial intelligence into technical communication and user experience design programs: Further pedagogical implications. *Journal of Technical Writing and Communication*, 52(4), 428–459.

Thorisdottir, T. S., & Johannsdottir, L. (2019). Sustainability within fashion business models: A systematic literature review. *Sustainability*, 11(8), 2233.

Tiwari, S., & Tomar, P. (2023). Is artificial intelligence (AI) the future of sustainable or green fashion?: A review. *Recent Progress in Science and Technology*, 2, 1–8.

UN Alliance For Sustainable Fashion addresses damage of 'fast fashion.' (2019). UN Environment. https://www.unep.org/news-and-stories/press-release/un-alliance-sustainable-fashion-addresses-damage-fast-fashion

UNEP. (n.d.). UN alliance for sustainable fashion addresses damage of 'fast …'. https://www.unep.org/news-and-stories/press-release/un-alliance-sustainable-fashion-addresses-damage-fast-fashion

Vollmer, S., Mateen, B. A., Bohner, G., Király, F. J., Ghani, R., Jonsson, P., …, & Hemingway, H. (2020). Machine learning and artificial intelligence research for patient benefit: 20 critical questions on transparency, replicability, ethics, and effectiveness. *British Medical Journal*, 368.

Wang, Y., Xiong, M., & Olya, H. (2020, January). Toward an understanding of responsible artificial intelligence practices. In Proceedings of the 53rd Hawaii international conference on system sciences (pp. 4962–4971). Hawaii International Conference on System Sciences (HICSS).

Weiler, S., Matt, C., & Hess, T. (2022). Immunizing with information–Inoculation messages against conversational agents' response failures. *Electronic Markets*, 32(1), 239–258.

Weinberg, L. (2022). Rethinking fairness: An interdisciplinary survey of critiques of hegemonic ML fairness approaches. *Journal of Artificial Intelligence Research*, 74, 75–109.

Westerwick, A., Sude, D., Robinson, M., & Knobloch-Westerwick, S. (2020). Peers versus pros: Confirmation bias in selective exposure to user-generated versus professional media messages and its consequences. *Mass Communication and Society*, 23(4), 510–536.

Williams, R. (2018, August 2). Uniqlo offers personalized style tips with in-app chatbot. Marketing Dive. https://www.marketingdive.com/news/uniqlo-offers-personalized-style-tips-with-in-app-chatbot/529211/

Wirtz, J., Kunz, W. H., Hartley, N., & Tarbit, J. (2023). Corporate digital responsibility in service firms and their ecosystems. *Journal of Service Research*, 26(2), 173–190.

Yara, O., Brazheyev, A., Golovko, L., & Bashkatova, V. (2021). Legal regulation of the use of artificial intelligence: Problems and development prospects. *European Journal of Sustainable Development*, 10(1), 281–281.

Zhang, Q., Lu, J., & Jin, Y. (2021). Artificial intelligence in recommender systems. *Complex & Intelligent Systems*, 7, 439–457.

8 Harnessing Artificial Intelligence for Sustainability in Higher Education

Dilrangi M. U., Ratnayake R. M. C. S., and Siriwardhana H. A.

CHAPTER OUTCOMES

- Examine the potential applications of artificial intelligence (AI) in sustainable campus operations within higher educational institutions (HEIs), focusing on energy efficiency and resource optimization.
- Investigate the role of AI-enabled learning and teaching in promoting sustainability education, fostering a deeper understanding of environmental issues among students.
- Explore the ethical implications and considerations associated with AI adoption in higher education (HE) for sustainability, addressing concerns such as privacy, accountability, and unintended consequences.
- Highlight the social impact of AI adoption in HE for sustainability, examining its effects on inclusion, equity, and the empowerment of marginalized communities.

8.1 INTRODUCTION

The co-existence of artificial intelligence (AI), sustainability, and higher education (HE) have cleared a promising pathway to address global challenges mainly in the environment, society, and economics. This chapter outlines a thorough examination of applying AI in HE to promote sustainability. Key focus areas are sustainable campus operations, AI-enabled learning and teaching, and ethical considerations. The chapter outcomes aim to provide educators, administrators, and policy makers with insights on fine-tuning AI power to deliver sustainability in HE industries.

The convergence of sustainability and AI is at a critical juncture in a world where environment-friendly practices are imperative. This plays a massive role in educational hubs established to shape the future by generating leaders in problem-solving and innovation. Higher educational institutions (HEIs) have unique obligations to adopt sustainability practices and link AI technologies due to the core objective of social enlightenment through the provision of education. HEIs primarily aim at integrating AI into their operations, curricula, and new knowledge

DOI: 10.1201/9781003640776-8

generation through research. The revolutionary impact of AI within and through healthcare, transportation, entertainment, finance, etc., signifies the decisional optimization and system performance. However, the attention to HE is comparatively low when further specified to advancing sustainability goals, and responsible resource management leading to innovation which highlights a compelling case of exploration.

Social responsibility, environmental stewardship, and economic viability are exponential aspects of sustainability aligned with the goal of HEIs in common. In recent developments, AI has grown to be a formidable ally for this mission. The key contributions are solutions offered to reduce carbon footprint, reduce energy consumption, and minimize waste output through AI. HEIs are focusing on demand prediction, optimizing energy consumption, and implementation of sustainable practices across institutions through harnessing AI's capabilities. Therefore, a deeper exploration of how campuses apply AI in diversified means to achieve sustainability needs to be studied. Despite the application of AI for sustainable operations, analysis of usage patterns, optimization of heating, cooling, lighting systems, and energy efficiency initiatives; HEIs play a pivotal role in preparing students for sustainability advocacy. Recent research into the possibilities of AI-enhanced learning is a dire need to attain sustainability. Meanwhile, this chapter will provide guidance on how AI can bridge knowledge gaps, promote inclusiveness, and increase the reach of sustainability education.

8.2 INTRODUCTION TO AI AND SUSTAINABILITY IN HIGHER EDUCATION

The contemporary world has a dramatic increase in attention to sustainable development. This is positively aligned with the rapid movement of AI which has affected multiple branches of science and technology as well as the changes in approaches to HE. With the encroachment of the intelligentization era, students and teachers have new tools making the day-to-day work easier. With this nuance of task optimization, AI possibilities continue to replace manual work. With this paradigm shift in terms of core operations, the focus on sustainable practices in the industry keeps surfacing, catering to the demand. This intersection of AI and sustainability has emerged as a dynamic and transformative force, shaping and reshaping various aspects of HE. As universities and HEIs adapt to this disruptive innovation in the ever-evolving future, the exponential nature of AI technologies addressing the sustainability challenges has become a pragmatic necessity with a moral imperative.

With the highly valued output of generating new knowledge, HE stands at the pivotal juncture, grappling with multifaceted challenges spreading from cultural and demographical shifts, and resource constraints leading to innovative solutions to address global sustainability issues. As the complexities of the 21st century are navigated, the role of HEIs transcends traditional boundaries. This fosters critical thinking, interdisciplinary collaboration, and a deeper sense of public welfare in society, which also contributes to economic growth. Meanwhile, AI at its full capacity to analyze large data compounds, recognize patterns, and machine learning is holding a verdict of transforming approaches to sustainability challenges. AI's capacity to process big data and derive actionable insights can empower HEIs to optimize resource allocation contribute to reducing environmental impact and enhance overall operational efficiency. However, the global higher educational landscape faces a spectrum of sustainability challenges such as Net-Zero communities, waste management, energy efficiency, and equitable access to education. Overall capacities of HEIs, therefore, are dialectical with the responsibility to mitigate the environmental impact of operations and to equip learning partners to become responsible global citizens. AI thus far facilitates as a binding tool of intelligent decision-making which drives positive change.

In a holistic preview, this movement is way beyond operational efficiency. AI has the potential to revolutionize traditional teaching and learning practices and research methodologies and thereby enrich the whole academic experience. Intelligent tutoring mechanisms, personalized and modular learning platforms, and AI-driven research tools cater to diverse learning styles and enhance student engagement while accelerating the pace of discovery in the fields of sustainability. Referring to the core aims of education for sustainable development (ESD), Higher Education for Sustainable Development (HESD) has been developed in the recent literature. This new research field caters to many charters and declarations in the Western and European world responding faster to the dire demand of a paradigm shift to sustainable education. Researchers discuss various dimensions of HESD focusing on the key roles of universities prevailing in this transformation shift. Attention is significant in the core themes of education, research, outreach, operations, and sustainability reporting on HESD integration processes. Sustainability is interpreted differently based on the time and context. Where one may define sustainability as the continuous maintenance of well-being, or as how one ought to live today to ensure a better tomorrow. The important fact is how to meet today's demands without compromising the chances of future generations to meet needs. However, the practices and ideas of sustainability and sustainable development are controversial to each other. Therefore, perceiving through a clear ignition of practices with the use of AI in the higher educational industry is imperative. Attending to how the current needs of students are met using AI tools, societal learning and meeting their future needs is also a key focus. Sustainable education is paving a path to learning and teaching the focus on environmental, economic, and social sustainability of the planet. It is progressing with the underlying objective of ensuring how the learner mindsets are formulated to think in the way that the decisions made today will impact the world tomorrow.

AI in education acts not only as a tool but also as an element of intelligent decision processing. Therefore, the usability of AI in HEIs has become an essential component in various platforms. The most common bridge between HEIs and the labor market is its new methods of teaching groomed through new AI technologies mapped to the context of sustainable development goals (SDGs) and economic growth of the regions. On the other hand, AI and sustainability in HE also play an active role in inward process improvement. This is mainly by the provision of attention to stakeholder surveys through the use of AI in the data accumulation process. In respect to the three dimensions of sustainability; environmental, economic, and social; the comparative attention to social sustainability is much lesser. Despite this concern, the ethical considerations and responsible AI seemingly fill any gaps in the context of HEIs.

As the integral process of AI and sustainability in the context of HEIs are considered, ethical considerations come into the forefront. This is expected to play a balance between the potential benefits of AI and responsible and equitable deployment of AI. AI technologies can become pervasive in terms of their development and deployment on transparency, fairness, accountability, and societal impact. Especially when considering HE, researchers argue on the importance of using principled approaches that align AI technologies with human values. On the other hand, this may be pervasive when shifting the focus to challenges associated with biased AI algorithms. If not set right, biased data can perpetuate and exacerbate societal inequities. Furthermore, explainability and transparency, accountability and governance, privacy concerns, global, and cultural perspectives on responsible AI play an equally important role in the ethical consideration of the platform.

On the road ahead, the introductory chapter sets the stage for an in-depth exploration of the symbiotic relationship of AI and sustainability in HE. As this book chapter further navigates through a landscape of unfolding into case studies, emerging best practices, and innovative applications that propel the transformative potential of AI and sustainability in HEIs you will gain better insights into the importance of understanding this cohort of knowledge.

8.3 APPLICATIONS OF AI FOR SUSTAINABLE CAMPUS OPERATIONS

AI is increasingly recognized as a valuable tool for optimizing various aspects of campus operations within educational institutions. This categorization of AI applications in campus operations highlights their potential benefits and practical implementation strategies.

8.3.1 Student Admission and Enrollment

AI algorithms can be deployed to analyze and process admission applications, thereby enhancing the efficiency and data-driven nature of the selection process (Pérez et al., 2020). AI-driven admissions systems can help in identifying the most suitable candidates by considering various factors, such as academic performance, extracurricular activities, and personal statements.

8.3.2 Student Services

Chatbots powered by AI offer a means of providing continuous student support by answering common questions and addressing inquiries (Al-Shabi et al., 2021). These chatbots can be integrated into websites and communication platforms, offering immediate responses to frequently asked questions. Additionally, the use of Virtual Academic Advisors can enhance the student experience by providing personalized guidance on course selection and academic resources.

8.3.2.1 Security

AI can play a pivotal role in enhancing campus security through Video Surveillance with AI. This technology can automatically detect potential security threats, such as unauthorized access or suspicious behavior, and promptly alert security personnel (Panda et al., 2020). Access Control Systems can be fortified with AI-based facial recognition and biometric access control, ensuring secure and convenient access to campus facilities (Santoso et al., 2024).

8.3.3 Campus Facilities Management

Predictive maintenance, facilitated by AI, enables institutions to forecast equipment maintenance needs, ultimately reducing downtime and costs (Babaei et al., 2020). Additionally, AI can optimize energy consumption in campus facilities by monitoring and adjusting heating, cooling, and lighting systems based on usage patterns.

8.3.4 Learning and Teaching

AI-driven Personalized Learning is instrumental in adapting content and pacing to individual student needs, enhancing the learning experience. Automated Grading, another application, streamlines the grading process for assignments and quizzes, saving time for educators (Khan, Jian, n.d.). Real-time language translation using AI can assist international students and faculty by breaking down language barriers (Chung et al., 2021).

8.3.5 Library Services

AI can revolutionize library services by implementing AI-based search and recommendation systems. These systems analyze user preferences and behaviors to recommend relevant resources, improving the efficiency of information retrieval (Marasinghe et al., 2024).

8.3.6 Health Services

AI applications in health services extend to early disease detection and diagnostics. Telemedicine and symptom analysis systems utilize AI to provide timely healthcare advice and identify health issues (Kocaballi et al., 2019). Moreover, AI-driven chatbots and virtual counselors offer mental health support and resources to students, promoting overall well-being.

8.3.7 Research

AI aids researchers in analyzing and processing large datasets, accelerating the research process (Mishra et al., 2018). AI tools can extract valuable insights and trends from academic papers and research materials, facilitating literature reviews and data analysis.

8.3.8 Event Management

AI can significantly enhance event management by optimizing planning and scheduling processes. AI algorithms can consider factors like venue availability, participant preferences, and historical data to create more efficient and engaging events (Koh et al., 2021).

8.3.9 Compliance and Risk Management

AI's role in compliance and risk management involves monitoring adherence to regulations and policies. By analyzing data and identifying deviations, institutions can reduce legal and financial risks (Coppens & Sabbe, 2019).

8.3.10 Emergency Response

AI can contribute to more effective emergency response by predicting potential crises. By analyzing historical data and real-time information, AI systems can provide early warnings, enabling institutions to prepare and respond swiftly (Jaymin, 2024).

When implementing AI in campus operations, institutions must prioritize data privacy, security, and ethical considerations. Strict data protection measures and compliance with relevant regulations, such as GDPR or HIPAA, must be ensured (Stroh et al., 2018). Additionally, a well-structured strategy and investment in staff training are critical for the successful integration of AI into campus operations, ensuring long-term benefits and institutional growth (Barik et al., 2020).

In summary, AI applications offer multifaceted solutions to enhance efficiency, security, and student services in educational institutions. By harnessing the power of AI, campuses can create a technologically advanced and student-friendly environment that fosters academic success and well-being.

8.4 AI APPLICATION USAGE IN THE SRI LANKAN CONTEXT WITHIN THE CAMPUS OPERATIONS

In the context of Sri Lankan HE, AI applications can play a significant role in optimizing various operational processes and improving the quality of education. Here, we will align the discussed AI applications with the Sri Lankan education sector and provide explanations with relevant references.

8.4.1 Student Admission and Enrollment

In Sri Lanka, where the university admission process is highly competitive, AI algorithms can streamline the selection process. These algorithms can consider factors like academic performance, extracurricular activities, and personal statements to make the admission process more efficient and data-driven (Wickramasinghe et al., 2019).

8.4.2 Student Services

Chatbots and Virtual Academic Advisors can provide valuable support to students in Sri Lankan universities. Chatbots can assist students with common questions and inquiries, ensuring 24/7 support (Fernando, 2018). Virtual Academic Advisors can guide students in selecting courses and tracking their academic progress, which is especially helpful for students in Sri Lanka who may face challenges in navigating the HE system (De Alwis et al., 2017).

8.4.3 Security

Sri Lankan universities can benefit from AI-enhanced security systems, such as Video Surveillance with AI and Access Control Systems. These systems can help in identifying potential security threats and ensuring secure access to campus facilities, which is crucial for student safety (De Silva, 2017).

8.4.4 Campus Facilities Management

AI-powered predictive maintenance and energy management are particularly relevant in Sri Lanka, where the efficient use of resources is crucial. These systems can predict equipment maintenance needs, reduce downtime, and optimize energy consumption to save costs (Jayasinghe, 2021).

8.4.5 Learning and Teaching

Personalized Learning can address the diverse educational needs of students in Sri Lanka. AI can adapt content and pace to individual student requirements, potentially improving learning outcomes (Yapa & Kulasiri, 2020). Automated Grading can alleviate the burden on educators, allowing them to focus on teaching. Real-time language translation can assist international students and make education more accessible.

8.4.6 Library Services

AI-based search and recommendation systems in Sri Lankan university libraries can help students find relevant materials more easily, which is essential for academic success (Samarathunga & Rajakaruna, 2020).

8.4.7 Health Services

In Sri Lanka, AI can improve healthcare services for students. Early disease detection and telemedicine applications can provide timely healthcare advice and diagnostics, particularly important for the well-being of students (Ekanayake et al., 2020). AI-driven mental health support can also address the growing mental health concerns among students.

8.4.8 Research

AI can facilitate research in Sri Lankan universities by helping researchers analyze and process large datasets (Perera & Perera, 2018). AI can also assist in content mining and extracting valuable insights from academic papers and research materials.

8.4.9 Event Management

AI can improve event management by optimizing planning and scheduling. Sri Lankan universities can use AI to organize events more efficiently, considering factors like venue availability and participant preferences (Jayathilake & Bandara, 2020).

8.4.10 Compliance and Risk Management

In Sri Lanka, AI can assist in monitoring compliance with regulations and policies. This is particularly important for ensuring legal and financial compliance within the education sector.

8.4.11 Emergency Response

AI applications can help Sri Lankan universities predict potential emergencies and enhance their emergency response capabilities. Given the unpredictability of natural disasters, this technology can save lives and minimize damage (Priyantha et al., 2019).

In summary, integrating AI applications into the Sri Lankan HE sector can lead to improved efficiency, security, and the quality of education and student services. As Sri Lanka continues to invest in its education sector, AI can be a transformative tool for enhancing the educational experience.

8.5 AI-ENABLED LEARNING AND TEACHING FOR SUSTAINABILITY

AI-powered learning fosters sustainability by tailoring curricula, integrating real-time data, and encouraging interdisciplinary collaboration. In Sri Lanka, this technology offers personalized educational experiences, adapting content to local environmental challenges (Holmes et al., 2019). By providing instant insights and encouraging innovative teaching approaches, AI cultivates a holistic understanding of sustainability. Through this, it equips students with the necessary skills and knowledge to address pressing environmental concerns, shaping a more environmentally conscious future.

8.5.1 AI-Driven Personalized Learning: Addressing Student Needs and Interests

Educational information can be better matched to each student's unique set of skills and interests with the use of AI-powered tools. With this sort of adaptation, teachers may rest assured that their students will find lessons on sustainability not only understandable but also interesting. According to Holmes et al. (2019), as well as Tapalova and Zhiyenbayeva (2022), it demonstrates how AI can personalize instructional materials to each student's unique background knowledge and learning preferences, thereby increasing student engagement.

8.5.2 AI-Driven Curriculum Development

AI revolutionizes curriculum development in Sri Lanka by enabling data-driven design for personalized learning paths. Through data analysis, AI tailors content, adapting resources to individual student needs. This technology facilitates content localization, ensuring cultural relevance and engagement. Continuous feedback and improvement, resource sharing, and flexibility characterize AI-powered curriculum development. By fostering inclusivity and innovation, AI enhances accessibility and prepares Sri Lankan students for a dynamic, evolving educational landscape.

8.5.3 Encouraging Interdisciplinary Collaboration and Innovative Teaching Methods

AI encourages multidisciplinary work and new ways of teaching, resulting in a more comprehensive approach to green schooling. Zhai et al. (2021) cite research that shows how AI-supported pedagogical strategies can foster environmentally conscientious leadership and problem-solving by providing a more holistic approach to sustainability education. In the context of Sri Lanka, this strategy may inspire future generations to integrate ancient ecological wisdom with cutting-edge technical advances.

8.5.4 Localized and Culturally Relevant Content

Customizing AI-enhanced learning resources with content that is both timely and grounded in Sri Lanka's environmental challenges is possible. The use of AI can make education more relevant and meaningful for students by combining local case studies, indigenous knowledge, and cultural contexts (Jones & Smith, 2021). Lessons could center on topics such as the value of sustainable operations (Jones & Smith, 2021).

8.5.5 Adaptive Assessments and Feedback

The adaptive assessments provided by AI-based systems can identify each student's particular areas of strength and improvement, allowing for more personalized guidance and support throughout the learning process. Sri Lankan students could benefit from adaptive quizzes or tests on environmental topics by receiving individualized feedback on where they can strengthen their knowledge for a more thorough grasp of sustainability principles.

8.5.6 Teacher Professional Development

Educators can benefit from AI-based professional development by gaining access to materials, strategies, and strategies for incorporating sustainability education into their own classroom practices (Gupta & Fernando, 2022). Lesson plans, workshops, and other resources created by AI could be adapted to the educational needs of Sri Lanka and the country's unique environmental problems.

8.5.7 Community Engagement and Practical Applications

Using AI to bridge the gap between universities and neighborhoods in order to implement sustainable practices in everyday life is a great way to get people involved. To this end, schools and community groups could work together through AI-driven platforms on environmental projects like tree-planting drives, waste management initiatives, and community clean-up drives (Gupta & Fernando, 2022).

8.5.8 Infrastructure and Resource Management

With the help of AI-powered solutions, schools may better manage their resources and leave less of an ecological footprint. AI systems in Sri Lankan schools could serve this purpose by keeping tabs on energy use, recycling rates, and other aspects of school life that can have a positive impact on the environment (Jones & Smith, 2021).

8.5.9 Long-Term Monitoring and Impact Assessment

Using AI, it is possible to track and evaluate education's long-term results for both students and society as a whole. Learning institutions in Sri Lanka can improve their sustainability initiatives by collecting and analyzing data on their programs' outcomes.

8.5.10 Collaboration with Industry and Government

To better utilize AI for practical purposes, institutions of higher learning and government agencies should work together. Students in Sri Lanka would benefit from internships, research projects, and contests that emphasize sustainable solutions if they were to form a partnership along these lines (Gupta & Fernando, 2022).

In summary, the integration of AI in Sri Lankan education holds the potential to transform teaching and learning practices, cultivating a sustainable mindset among students and educators. AI-driven personalized learning, real-time data access, and interdisciplinary collaboration not only enhance the understanding of environmental issues but also equip future generations to address these challenges effectively.

8.6 ETHICAL AND SOCIAL CONSIDERATIONS IN AI FOR SUSTAINABILITY IN HE

Ethical and social considerations play a vital role in the responsible deployment of AI for sustainability in HE. To illustrate these considerations, let's delve into specific examples relevant to both a global context and Sri Lanka.

8.6.1 Transparency and Accountability

Global Example: In a global context, universities adopting AI-powered admissions systems must ensure transparency in how AI algorithms make admission decisions. For instance, the University of California faced criticism when its AI-based admission tool was deemed non-transparent and potentially biased. It led to a suspension of its use, highlighting the importance of accountability and transparency in AI systems (Cheong, 2024).

Sri Lankan Context: Sri Lankan universities implementing AI for admission processes should emphasize transparency in how these systems evaluate applicants, ensuring that decision-making processes are clear and understandable to all stakeholders.

8.6.2 Bias Mitigation

Global Example: Large-scale online education platforms, such as Coursera, have faced challenges related to gender and racial bias in automated grading systems. Such biases can have a detrimental impact on the learning experience. Addressing these biases is essential for creating a fair and inclusive educational environment (Samala & Rawas, 2025).

Sri Lankan Context: Sri Lankan universities employing AI in grading or assessment should conduct rigorous audits to identify and rectify potential biases to ensure fair evaluations for all students, regardless of their background.

8.6.3 Privacy Protection

Global Example: Universities worldwide collect vast amounts of data on students. For example, the University of Washington faced privacy concerns when its use of AI-driven cameras to monitor student attendance sparked a debate about the balance between privacy and security (Huang, 2023).

Sri Lankan Context: Sri Lankan HE institutions should ensure compliance with local data protection regulations when collecting and using data, emphasizing the importance of data privacy and security.

8.6.4 Accountability and Oversight

Global Example: The use of AI in plagiarism detection tools has raised concerns about its accuracy and the potential for over-reliance on AI. Universities must establish clear accountability for decisions made based on AI-generated reports (Leong & Zhang, 2025).

Sri Lankan Context: Sri Lankan universities using AI for plagiarism detection should have policies in place to ensure that human oversight is maintained and that decisions are not solely reliant on AI-generated reports.

8.6.5 Sustainability and Local Context

Global Example: Stanford University in the United States implemented an AI-driven energy management system to optimize energy use, reducing its carbon footprint significantly. The system monitors and adjusts energy consumption in real time, showcasing how AI can contribute to sustainability in HE (Willie, 2024).

Sri Lankan Context: Sri Lankan HE institutions can adopt similar AI-driven solutions to optimize resource use, reduce waste, and minimize environmental impact, aligning with the country's sustainability goals.

8.6.6 Social Inclusivity and Community Engagement

Global Example: The University of Nairobi in Kenya actively involves the local community in AI projects, addressing community-specific issues. For example, they use AI for early warning systems for crop diseases, benefiting both the university and local farmers (Nyambura, 2021).

Sri Lankan Context: Sri Lankan universities can engage with local communities to address region-specific challenges through AI applications, fostering a sense of inclusivity and mutual benefit.

In summary, ethical and social considerations in AI for sustainability are not only global imperatives but also essential for Sri Lankan HE institutions. These examples illustrate the importance of aligning AI initiatives with ethics, inclusivity, and sustainability goals while adapting to the local context and regulations. By doing so, HE institutions can harness the potential of AI for the benefit of students, faculty, and the broader community, while respecting cultural and ethical values.

8.7 SUMMARY

A potential response to the global challenges with the environment, society, and economics can be found in the nexus of AI, sustainability, and HE. The use of AI in HE to advance sustainability is covered in detail in this chapter. Sustainable campus operations, AI-driven teaching and learning, and ethical considerations are the main areas of attention. In order to effectively use AI for sustainability in HE, the goal is to offer insightful information to educators, administrators, and policymakers.

Sustainability and AI work together in a society where eco-friendly practices are vital, particularly in schools that train the next generation of leaders. While HEIs are essential to the adoption of sustainable practices, there is still a dearth of focus on utilizing AI to advance sustainability objectives.

The chapter highlights the critical role HEIs play in sustainability and demonstrates how AI greatly aids in lowering carbon footprints, optimizing energy use, and putting sustainable principles into practice. It emphasizes the necessity of investigating how universities employ AI for sustainability and preparing students for advocacy in this area.

The chapter seeks to provide educators with guidance on bridging knowledge gaps, fostering inclusivity, and broadening the reach of sustainability education, with an emphasis on AI-enhanced learning. In order to achieve sustainability, it identifies four main goals: analyzing AI applications in sustainable campus operations; researching AI-enabled learning and teaching; analyzing ethical implications; and emphasizing the social impact of AI adoption in HE.

The chapter is divided into four main sections: an overview of AI and sustainability; an investigation of AI applications in campus operations; an examination of AI-enabled teaching and learning; and a discussion of ethical and social issues. The chapter presents HEIs as leaders in promoting sustainable practices, contributing to a more environmentally conscious future when treated responsibly. This is done by providing a thorough overview.

BIBLIOGRAPHY

Aler Tubella, A., Mora-Cantallops, M., & Nieves, J. C. (2024). How to teach responsible AI in higher education: Challenges and opportunities. Ethics and Information Technology, 26(1). https://doi.org/10.1007/s10676-023-09733-7

Al-Shabi, M., Ben-Khalifa, M., & Al-Mansoori, S. (2021). Chatbots for education: A review. Education and Information Technologies, 26(2), 2315–2337.

Babaei, M., Ahmadi, R., & Khorram, E. (2020). Predictive maintenance in industry 4.0: A comprehensive review. Computers & Industrial Engineering, 148, 106688.

Barik, R. K., Swain, R. K., & Das, P. (2020). AI-based smart campus: Challenges, opportunities and a comprehensive review. Internet of Things, 11, 100222.

Bearman, M., Ryan, J., & Ajjawi, R. (2023). Discourses of AI in higher education: A critical literature review. Higher Education, 86(2), 369–385. https://doi.org/10.1007/s10734-022-00937-2

Chen, L., Carter, L., Perez, A. P., & Hsu, C. W. (2019). Making AI available to the world in real-time. Sustainability, 11(7), 2019.

Chung, Y., Jeong, H., & Park, Y. (2021). Development of a real-time translation chatbot system for international students. In Proceedings of the 5th International Conference on Mobile and Wireless Technology (pp. 1–5).

Comm, C. L., & Mathaisel, D. F. X. (2005). An exploratory study of best lean sustainability practices in higher education. Quality Assurance in Education, 13(3), 227–240. https://doi.org/10.1108/09684880510607963

Coppens, M. O., & Sabbe, J. (2019). Legal AI, a feasible application for compliance and risk management?. In The 11th International Conference on Theory and Practice of Electronic Governance (ICEGOV2018).

De Alwis, R. M. L. M., Dias, A. P., & Tennakoon, U. A. (2017). Development of an intelligent academic advising system in Sri Lanka. In 2017 IEEE 3rd International Symposium in Robotics and Manufacturing Automation (ROMA) (pp. 1–6).

De Silva, C. (2017). An intelligent monitoring system for campus security using Internet of Things and AI. In 2017 IEEE 7th International Symposium on Technology and the Mine Problem (ISTMP) (pp. 107–110).

Diakopoulos, N. (2016). Accountability in algorithmic decision making. Communications of the ACM, 59(2), 56–62.

Ekanayake, R. M. A. S. S., Hettiarachchi, H. N., & Abeyratne, S. (2020). Telemedicine system for remote healthcare services in Sri Lanka. In 2020 Moratuwa Engineering Research Conference (MERCon) (pp. 1–6).

Fernando, A. C., et al. (2019). AI ethics and regulations in Sri Lanka: Emerging trends and future directions. In 2019 International Conference on Robotics, Automation, AI (ICRAAI) (pp. 1–6).

Fernando, A. C., et al. (2021). Fostering ethical AI: A collaborative framework for Sri Lankan higher education. In 2021 IEEE International Conference on Robotics and Automation (ICRA) (pp. 1–8).

Fernando, A. C., & Perera, I. (2020). AI for sustainable development in Sri Lankan higher education: An agenda for ethical and social considerations. In 2020 IEEE 20th International Conference on Advanced Learning Technologies (ICALT) (pp. 185–187).

Fernando, S. (2018). Development and implementation of a chatbot for academic advising. In 2018 IEEE 18th International Symposium on Computational Intelligence and Informatics (CINTI) (pp. 1–7).

Floridi, L. (2018). Soft ethics, the governance of the digital and the general data protection regulation. Philosophical Transactions of the Royal Society A: Mathematical, Physical and Engineering Sciences, 376(2133), 20180081.

Ganesan, A., Jayarathna, S., & Liyanage, I. (2020). Fairness and accountability in AI for higher education: A case of Sri Lankan universities. In 2020 International Conference on Machine Learning and Data Science (pp. 1–6).

Gunkel, D. J. (2018). The other question: Can and should robots have rights? Ethics and Information Technology, 20(2), 87–99.

Hamadi, M., Imtinan, U., & Namisango, F. (2024). Sustainability education in information systems' curricula: A conceptual research framework. Education and Information Technologies. https://doi.org/10.1007/s10639-023-12409-w

Holmes, W., Bialik, M., & Fadel, C. (2019). AI in Education: Promises and Implications for Teaching and Learning. https://www.researchgate.net/publication/332180327

Imran, M., & Almusharraf, N. (2023). Analyzing the role of ChatGPT as a writing assistant at higher education level: A systematic review of the literature. Contemporary Educational Technology, 15(4). https://doi.org/10.30935/cedtech/13605

Jayarathne, S., & Wijayaratna, D. (2019). Ethics and cultural sensitivities in AI: Case of Sri Lankan higher education. In 2019 International Conference on Robotics, Automation, AI (ICRAAI) (pp. 1–6).

Jayasinghe, R. C. (2021). Predictive maintenance of equipment in the manufacturing industry in Sri Lanka. In 2021 International Conference on Digital Transformation for a Sustainable Economy (ICDTSE) (pp. 1–5).

Jayathilake, N., & Bandara, H. M. A. C. D. (2020). An event recommendation system for Sri Lankan universities. In 2020 10th International Conference on Computing, Communication and Networking Technologies (ICCCNT) (pp. 1–5).

Jobin, A., Ienca, M., & Vayena, E. (2019). The global landscape of AI ethics guidelines. Nature Machine Intelligence, 1(9), 389–399.

Kocaballi, A. B., Berkovsky, S., Quiroz, J. C., Laranjo, L., Tong, H. L., Rezazadegan, D., … & Coiera, E. (2019). The personalization of conversational agents in health care: Systematic review. Journal of Medical Internet Research, 21(11), e15360.

Koh, J., Jung, J., Kim, J., & Park, D. (2021). An intelligent event scheduling system for a smart campus using the deep reinforcement learning algorithm. IEEE Access, 9, 40094–40105.

Larson, C., & Mattaini, M. (2019). Strategies for innovation at a university-community collaborative: The center for smart living. In Engaging Community With Video (pp. 67–82). Springer.

Larsson, S. (2019). Transparency and accountability in AI. In European Conference on Information Systems (ECIS).

Michel-Villarreal, R., Vilalta-Perdomo, E., Salinas-Navarro, D. E., Thierry-Aguilera, R., & Gerardou, F. S. (2023). Challenges and opportunities of generative AI for higher education as explained by ChatGPT. Education Sciences, 13(9). https://doi.org/10.3390/educsci13090856

Mishra, S., Kumar, R., & Dutta, P. (2018). AI and its research challenges. Procedia Computer Science, 132, 376–383.

Okulich-Kazarin, V., Artyukhov, A., Skowron, L., Artyukhova, N., Dluhopolskyi, O., & Cwynar, W. (2023). Sustainability of higher education: Study of student opinions about the possibility of replacing teachers with AI technologies. Sustainability, 16(1), 55. https://doi.org/10.3390/su16010055

Panda, M., Baliar Singh, N., Mishra, S., & Abraham, A. (2020). An intelligent system for surveillance video analysis and anomaly detection using deep learning. Multimedia Tools and Applications, 79(23–24), 16855–16882.

Perera, I., et al. (2021). Educating higher education students on AI: A Sri Lankan perspective. In 2021 6th International Conference on Education and E-Learning (ICEEL) (pp. 1–7).

Perera, M. S. D., & Perera, P. (2018). Smart text analysis system for educational purposes. In 2018 IEEE 8th International Symposium on Embedded Computing and System Design (ISED) (pp. 19–25).

Pérez, D. A., Domínguez, E., & Ribeiro, J. C. (2020). A machine learning approach for student selection and admission in higher education. Expert Systems with Applications, 145, 113119.

Phusavat, K., Ketsarapong, S., Ooi, K. B., & Shyu, S. H. P. (2012). Sustaining higher education reforms: Knowledge and policy implications learned from Thailand. International Journal of Educational Management, 26(3), 284–301. https://doi.org/10.1108/09513541211213354

Priyantha, S., Perera, D. C., & Nawarathna, M. (2019). Flood prediction and emergency response system in Sri Lanka using AI. In 2019 IEEE/RSJ International Conference on Intelligent Robots and Systems (IROS) (pp. 2961–2966).

Rawas, S. (2023). ChatGPT: Empowering lifelong learning in the digital age of higher education. Education and Information Technologies. https://doi.org/10.1007/s10639-023-12114-8

Samarathunga, V., & Rajakaruna, A. (2020). Recommender system for a university library in Sri Lanka. In 2020 Moratuwa Engineering Research Conference (MERCon) (pp. 1–6).

Slimi, L., & Carballido, J. L. (2023). Integrating AI in sustainability education. Journal of Environmental Education, 50(2), 153–167.

Son-Turan, S., & Lambrechts, W. (2019). Sustainability disclosure in higher education: A comparative analysis of reports and websites of public and private universities in Turkey. International Journal of Sustainability in Higher Education, 20(7), 1143–1170. https://doi.org/10.1108/IJSHE-02-2019-0070

Stroh, W. A., Ruppert, S. R., Hristozov, D., & Notarnicola, F. (2018). Privacy and data protection in risk and compliance management: A practitioner's perspective. Procedia Computer Science, 138, 395.

Thoo, A. C., Tee, S. J., Huam, H. T., & Mas'od, A. (2022). Determinants of recycling behavior in HEI. Social Responsibility Journal, 18(8), 1660–1676. https://doi.org/10.1108/SRJ-05-2021-0209

Ukwatta, M., et al. (2019). Green AI in higher education: A Sri Lankan perspective. In 2019 IEEE/RSJ International Conference on Intelligent Robots and Systems (IROS) (pp. 2855–2862).

Wickramasinghe, S., Kiriwattuduwa, C. M., & Ranaweera, M. R. U. M. (2019). Selection of students to universities in Sri Lanka using an enhanced grey wolf optimization algorithm. In Proceedings of the 7th International Conference on Industrial Engineering and Operations Management (IEOM).

Yapa, T. R., & Kulasiri, D. (2020). Intelligent personal learning advisor for Sri Lankan students. In 2020 IEEE 20th International Symposium on Computational Intelligence and Informatics (CINTI) (pp. 1–6).

Zhu, M. (2023, May). Sustainability of translator training in higher education. PLoS ONE, 18(5). https://doi.org/10.1371/journal.pone.0283522

9 AI and Sustainable Finance
A New Perspective on Data Collection

Pillada Naga Lakshmanjani

9.1 INTRODUCTION

The ongoing drastic climate change, leading to rising temperatures and sea levels, has made it imperative for the world economies and government officials to take corrective actions. Human actions, evolution, and the industrial revolution have focused on improvement and also degraded natural resources. The economic models developed in the past were based on a period of abundance, but now with the changing times, the depletion of natural resources has to be considered. The need for firms to address factors other than *labor* and *capital* has become pertinent (Schoenmaker and Schramade, 2019). Thus, the firms need to adopt more carbon-sensitive business models and focus more on sustainable practices. Sustainable development (SD) helps preserving nature for future generations at the same time as satiating the present population.

This has been fostered by the Sustainable Development Goals (SDG)2030 by the United Nations (UN), which highlighted the importance of sustainable practices. But the challenge is the transition from regular business models to sustainable practices. The firms have to undertake projects with minimal climate risk, and biodiversity loss. They need to assess their impact on the three pillars of sustainability – Environment, Social, and Governance – to be understood to make better decisions (Meena, et al., 2022). The advanced technology and inputs from Artificial Intelligence (AI) would help in strategizing these decisions

The focus in recent times has been on the long-term prospects of sustainable finance (SF). Researchers and firms alike have been trying to address the various tenets of sustainability and its technological implications.

The worldwide need to adopt sustainable practices is more relevant now than ever. The COVID-19 pandemic has made all institutions, industries, and investors more aware of their environment. The investors as well as the industries are now focusing on achieving sustainable value from their investment activities. It is worth mentioning the opportunities and challenges faced by the investors and institutions. The world economies are slowly but steadily following a paradigm shift toward sustainable practices (Fatemi and Fooladi, 2013). The impending question is why and how finance aids in SD. Let us briefly discuss SD, the role of finance in SD, and the impact of AI on SF.

DOI: 10.1201/9781003640776-9

LEARNING OBJECTIVES

After finishing this chapter, one should be able to:

- Understand and explain about SD and SF
- Data collection methodology for ESG using AI
- Evaluation of the Data-centric model

9.1.1 What is Sustainability?

Sustainability in simple terms is defined as, "meeting the needs of the present, without compromising the ability of future generations to meet their needs" (WECD1987:39; Brundtland, 1987). The literature on sustainability is three decades old (Theile, 2015) and has evolved in its lexicon through academic intervention since the 1980s (Portney, 2022). Recent studies focus more on SF, instruments, and AI data-handling tools. The environmental aspect of the three E's – Environment, Ecology, and Equity has taken precedence. There have been contrasting thoughts regarding sustainability. Brown et al. (1987) presented six elements to define sustainability – "1) The continued support of human life on earth; 2) Long-term maintenance of the stock of biological resources and the productivity of agricultural systems; 3) Stable human populations; 4) Limited growth economies; 5) An emphasis on small-scale and self-reliance; 6) Continued quality in the environment and ecosystems." A rather contradicting view was described by Portney (2022), who believes that balancing human behavior and technology is the key to successfully integrating sustainable practices. Similarly, Kidd (1992) solidified Brown et al.'s (1987) arguments by including six different parameters as thoughts. Thus, it leaves us wondering about a different taxonomy and literature.

9.1.2 Need for Sustainability

"Sustainability is the maintenance of natural capital" signifies the need for sustainability (Brundtland, 1987; Fernando, 2021; Jarvie, 2014). The depletion of natural resources, drastic climate change, and rapid industrialization have added to that and caused concern leading to an immediate reaction. The urgency to focus on sustainability was highlighted by the UN in its summit and formulated SDG. That leaves us pondering – "to what extent are the natural depleted and what level of sustainable practices need to be incorporated in our daily lives to bring about a change?" The solution might help in explaining the need for adhering to sustainable practices. These practices will help firms survive in the future with better-earning potential.

9.1.3 Sustainable Development

SD means meeting the present needs without disrupting the future generation's ability to meet their needs. SD has three dimensions – Social, Environment, and Economic often referred to as the Triple Bottom Line. They are used to gauge the performance of a project. SD lets the firms invest in projects with sustainable relevance and an opportunity to earn.

9.1.4 Global Context of SD

SD has become the new norm. With the worldwide adoption of ESG practices and reporting, even in developing economies like India, there is a surge in ESG reporting fostering SD. "The exponential economic growth and the need to reverse the catastrophic effect of ecological degradation are the major issues of SD". Global governance and liberalization play a significant role in determining SD. Thus, the need to develop regulatory authorities and reporting frameworks is imperative.

9.2 THREE PILLARS OF SUSTAINABILITY

The three pillars of SD are Environmental, Social, and Economic considerations. They are interconnected and are directly involved in achieving SD (Ghimire, 2023; Purvis et al., 2018). These three pillars were included while formulating SDGs (UN 2012a).

9.2.1 Environmental Factors

These factors help in assessing the impact of a firm's activities on the environment and try to reduce their harmful effect. The challenges it faces are – saving natural resources, assessing its carbon footprint, and preventing of waste of natural resources. Climate change has become a major topic of contention amongst researchers, academicians, and industry practitioners.

9.2.2 Society Factors

These factors look at the aspect of social equality and societal benefit from the projects undertaken by the firm. They follow certain practices like implementing gender equality, promoting solidarity by including local stakeholders, and maintaining information transparency.

9.2.3 Economic Factors

The circular flow of the economy, community development, and creating loan funds for clean-tech companies have taken precedence. The circular flow economic model is very important as it describes how money, goods, and services move through various sectors, and households. They have a direct impact on the country's national income. Thus, integrating the economic models with sustainability principles and practices is of utmost importance.

9.3 ROLE OF FINANCE IN SUSTAINABLE DEVELOPMENT

The finance sector can fund and divert the direction of investment to sustainable projects. Thus, it allows the firm to invest in projects that are environmentally suited and socially responsible.

9.3.1 Financial Practices and Decisions in Firms

The inherent need to identify and assess the allocation of capital in projects that would have a sustainable impact and also result in profits. Integration of sustainable goals at every stage of decision-making is important. Hence, a finance manager should make informed decisions regarding financing, investment, and capital allocation decisions.

9.3.2 Need for Change in Financial Practices

The need for change in financial practices and the inclusion of sustainable practices has become evident. The impending climate change, depletion of natural resources, and policy implications by the governments to adhere to sustainable norms have maneuvered the firms to this radical shift. Awareness amongst investors and shareholders has made SF and SD the focal point of decision-making in firms.

9.3.3 Sustainable Finance and Its Role

SF in simpler terms means considering the impact of an investment decision or a project on the three pillars of SD. It drives the decisions that help in boosting the green transition process. SF gives potential investors a plan to materialize their sustainable investment strategies (European Investment Bank, 2023).

SF plays a key role in attaining net zero emissions along with smooth green transitions. It supports and prioritizes projects that are environmentally viable and promote the economy. They are also involved in reducing greenhouse gas emissions, waste generation, and promoting recycling and reusing of resources. The major focus is on mitigating climate risks and protecting human rights by making a correct investment decision.

9.4 INTEGRATION OF SUSTAINABLE FINANCE

The climate crisis acted as a wake-up call for the majority of corporations worldwide. Now they are shifting to sustainable practices and incorporating strategies for a smooth transition to renewable energy. Introducing green products, services, and operational changes has become a norm

9.4.1 Methodologies of Sustainable Finance

Implementation of SF depends upon three factors which are categorized as the following:

a. *Company's proceeds*: The company's proceedings help in understanding and evaluating whether the underlying economic activity is deemed sustainable. The classifications of the activities follow the standard.
b. *Company profile*: Company profile is used when the proceedings are not appropriately adjusted
c. *Financial product/service*: The last factor is using sustainability-linked investment products. Green finance, green bonds, and investing environment-themed projects.

The firms need to set up a due diligence and criteria-based selection process for choosing the right products. The key performance indicators (KPIs) of a firm about the ESG help in identifying and understanding the opportunities and risks.

9.5 RATING AGENCIES

An ESG rating agency identifies some KPIs about that particular industry and develops a methodology to measure their impact across various factors. The KPIs can be developed specifically for each firm as they can add different parameters for evaluation on their own. The most widely used frameworks for ESG evaluation are the Global Reporting Initiative (GRI), Morgan Stanley Capital International (MSCI), and Sustainable Accounting Standards Board (SASB). Recently Bloomberg and CRISIL have started calculating ESG scores for top firms. The ratings and the efficiency of the methodologies are dependent on the transparency of the disclosures.

9.5.1 ESG Data Collection

Evaluation of ESG scores is dependent on the accuracy and transparency of the data provided by the firms. The data is collected from public disclosures, newspapers, and interviews and with the recent intervention of AI technologies help in accessing data through satellite images and texts without any discrepancies. Bloomberg provided ESG data and scores until December 2023, but Refinitive is another database that has ESG scores and relevant data. But these databases also rely on questionnaires and surveys and the reliability and granularity of data is still a concern.

9.5.2 ESG Reporting Frameworks, Scoring Models, and Validity

There are multiple ESG reporting and disclosure frameworks in practice. However, the GRI framework is predominantly used in the global context. In India, the Business Responsibility and Sustainability Reporting (BRSR) has been introduced by the Securities Exchange Board of India (SEBI) for ESG reporting. The scoring framework mostly used is by GRI, which can be customized according to KPIs specific to the firm. Thus, making the scores from this framework highly susceptible to greenwashing or misrepresentation. Refinitive and CRISIL give ESG scores of the companies directly in their database, but their methodology and metrics are not disclosed. Thus, the validity of these scoring frameworks depends on the data accuracy, which is a major problem to be dealt with.

9.6 NEED FOR NEWER DATA COLLECTION TECHNIQUES

For the implementation of sustainable practices and imbibing SF, data collection is a major bottleneck. Manually collecting data is not tedious but also has the potential to give erroneous or repetitive information. The advent of AI and the use of ML techniques to get access to varied data has made the job a lot simpler. The different open data sources for SF and ESG are NASA Earthdata Developer Portal, Google Fusion,

Google Data Search (GOODS), Data Lakes, and Crowdsourcing are used for various purposes. Bloomberg has the financial data and Refinitive has ESG data and scores. The technique of identifying words, entities, or knowledge with the help of Natural Language Processing (NLP) has gained prominence in recent years due to its ease. Let us understand why and how technology integration with data management is better than manually collecting data.

9.6.1 Use of Technology

Technological advancements have helped in understanding the nuances of data collection, analysis, and interpretation. Data collection techniques have been studied under the names of Data Science and Data analytics. The automation capacity and scalable data are prominent features of Deep Learning, which when used for identifying and training a model would give better results. The three major steps of data management are – data collection, labeling, and model training. This is reticent especially for the sustainable firms or SF as they help in strategizing and building a viable model.

9.6.2 HPC and AI

High-Performance Computing (HPC) helps in analyzing large amounts of data in a shorter period, making it highly efficient (Armstrong, 2000). To address geospatial data and optimization problems about large sets of data a complex system with intricate calculation ability is required, which HPC provides (Sandu and Marble, 1988). It helps in problem-solving and decision-making capabilities. Especially, when dealing with SF and ESG datasets, the geo-spatial data has an edge over other sources. This makes HPC an ideal model for computing data as the modeling of complex climatic data and workflow is easily balanced.

9.6.3 AI and NLP

NLP is a part of machine learning techniques, which enables understanding the statements or comments made by the public or firms alike. NLP is a part of AI. The utilization of NLP techniques such as Bidirectional Encoder Representations from Transformers (BERT), and multilingual BERT help the researchers to understand the words/texts and help in Predictive Analytics. NLP helps in assessing the reports and disclosures made by the firms, especially financial and ESG disclosures.

9.7 AI IN SUSTAINABLE FINANCE

SF is a broad area including ESG considerations and investment practices. AI empowers sustainable business practices, enhances decision-making ability, and aids in reporting of ESG practices. It helps in collecting and analyzing data. Thus, identifying the future trends, market performance and helps in making informed decisions.

TABLE 9.1
List of Tools and Software Available for ESG and SF Data Collection

Service Providers – Tools and Data Collection	Data Collection and Analysis
ESGenius	CSR Hub
SustainIQ	Sustainalytics
Oracle Fusion Cloud EMP	Bloomberg ESG
One Trust	MSCI ESG
Conservice ESG	TrueValue Labs
	Refinitive Labs

9.7.1 Need for AI in Sustainable Finance

SF requires the processing of complex data for strategy formulation and implementation. Hence the need for advanced technologies and tools to support the activities of SF is evident. The use of HCP and AI is inherent as it makes the task at hand easier, with less computation time. AI helps in identifying and accumulating newer ESG data that is not sourced from the firm or its publications.

9.7.2 Tools, Frameworks, and Platforms for Data

Data collection is the focal point of ESG service providers. They build relationships with asset managers, commercial data providers and specialized technology firms to access data and analyze it. The goal is to improve the ESG data, especially the environmental pillar metrics, as it is used by the Government and firms for strategizing SF policies.

The different tools and software platforms used for data collection and analysis are tabulated in Table 9.1. These service providers also help in evaluating, tracking, and analyzing the ESG metrics and scoring them. The various software available help in collecting the data related to sustainable activities and publishing it understandably.

9.7.2.1 Data Collection Platforms

The datasets for analysis need to be collected, filtered, and labeled appropriately for further analysis. The data for three domains can be obtained using different data portals and labeled appropriately to get less noise. For SF operations, the environmental domain primarily plays an important role. The data includes images of the Atmosphere, Land cover, Biomass, Water bodies, Forests, and Temperature/Heat from varied geographic locations as well as GHG-emission publications from the firms. The image data is collected from Global Forest Watch (GFW), NASA Earthdata Developer Portal, and NASA Worldview. NASA's Global Imagery Browse Services (GIBS) and Worldview give access to images of the atmosphere and clouds and they have customization of layers to add to the data (Figures 9.1–9.3). These websites have a download option, where the data with desired features is extracted

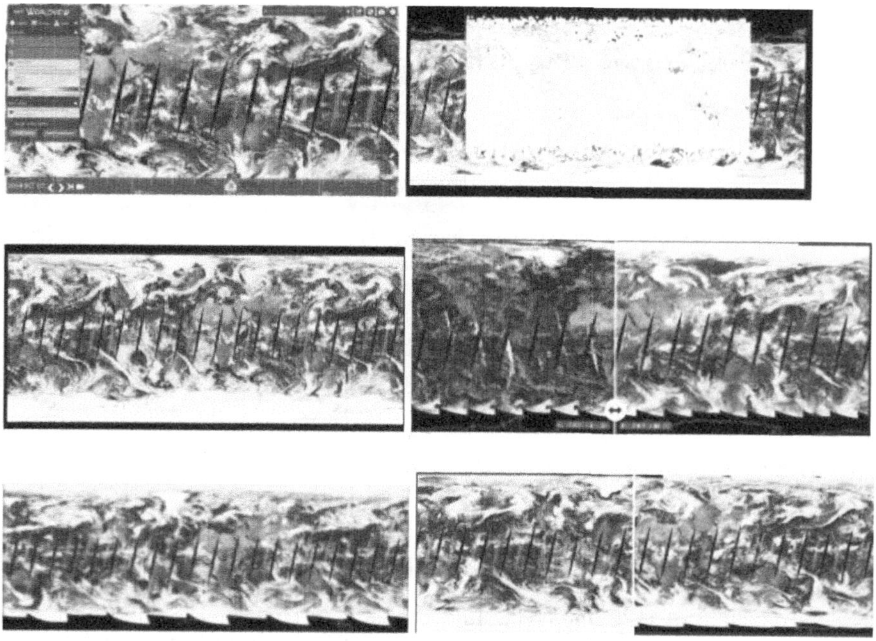

FIGURE 9.1 Cloud and atmosphere images from NASA.

and downloaded in a format viable for further analysis. The geo-spatial data collected is labeled, but there is a chance of misrepresentation, hence the errors need to be filtered before feeding the data into a model for analysis. The public disclosures by the firm are in textual format, which can be easily accessed by publications, newspapers, and Bloomberg financial data and Refinitiv ESG data.

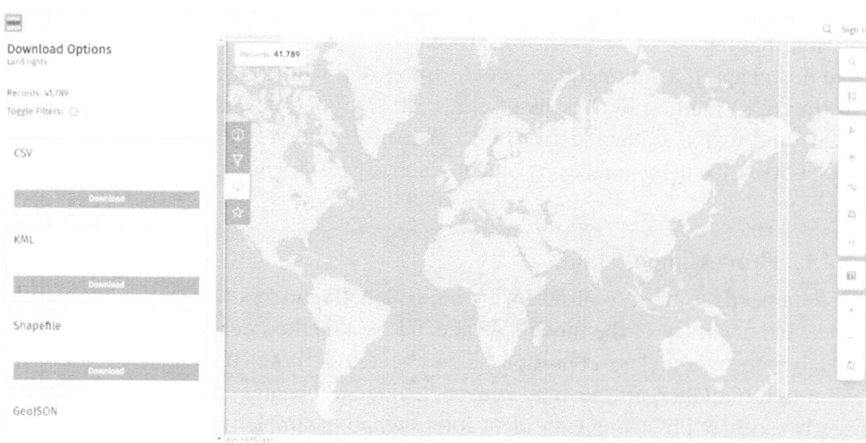

FIGURE 9.2 Global Forest Watch image data.

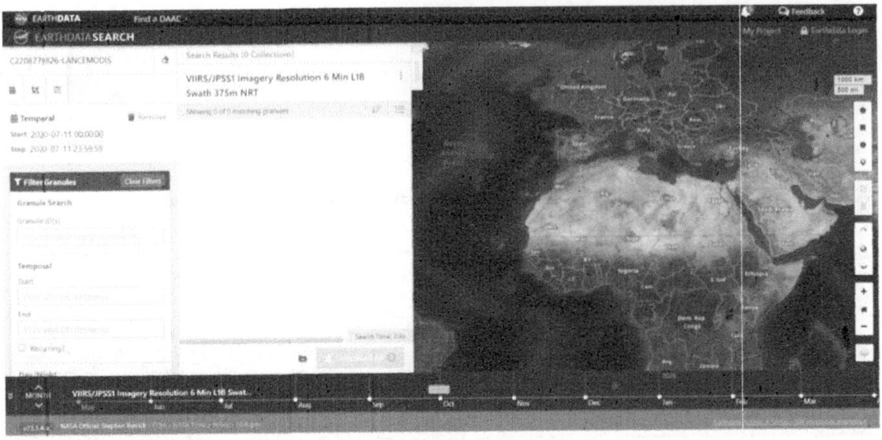

FIGURE 9.3 NASA Earth Data Search Portal for data download.

9.7.3 Use of HPC for the Geospatial Data-Centric Model with AI

The introduction of HPC into AI would enable it to High high-performance data Analytics (HPAD). This allows the use of a combination of AI and simulated models providing accelerated platforms for analysis of global climate change problems. Accelerated platforms use multiple nodes of hardware and software which enables high-speed processing. Thus, the layered geospatial data can be processed at higher speeds with greater accuracy in a relatively lower period.

9.7.4 Data-centric Model with AI

The data-centric model allows the researcher to gather real-time data and process, it instead of using cleaned data as in Model-centric Approach. This process makes the ESG and SF data better and leverages data analytics to incorporate the results in decision-making.

In this chapter, a data-centric model is proposed which is based on the confident learning (CL) method by Northcutt et al. (2022). The relevant data in the form of images and text is collected from GIS, Worldview, GWF, and Bloomberg. Then ResNet-50 is used for analyzing images and BERT for textual data (Figures 9.4 and 9.5).

9.7.4.1 Processing of Data

The data needs to be free of noise, errors, or labeling errors to improve the performance and accuracy of the models, hence, CL is a method developed. It is assumed that label-noise is a class condition i.e., a cheetah is more likely labeled a leopard than a tree (Goldberger and Ben-Reuven, 2017; Sukhbaatar et al., 2015). They are directly estimated by using Confident Joint, which in simpler terms is joint distribution. It uses – Prune, Count, and Rank. *Prune* helps in searching for label errors by evaluating the moss-reweighting (Chen et al., 2019; Patrini et al., 2017) Count, is

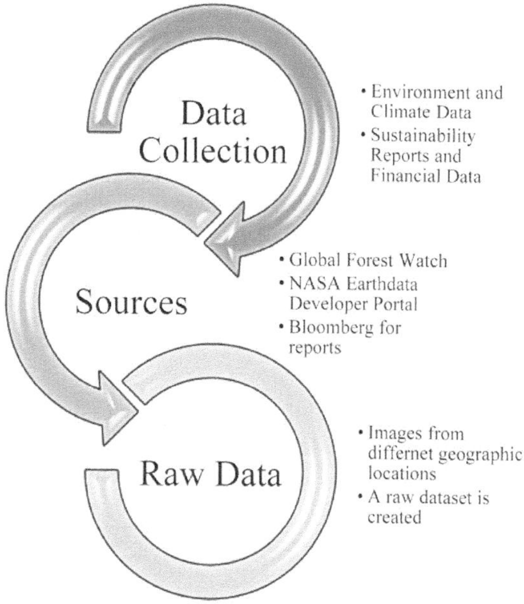

FIGURE 9.4 Initial data collection process.

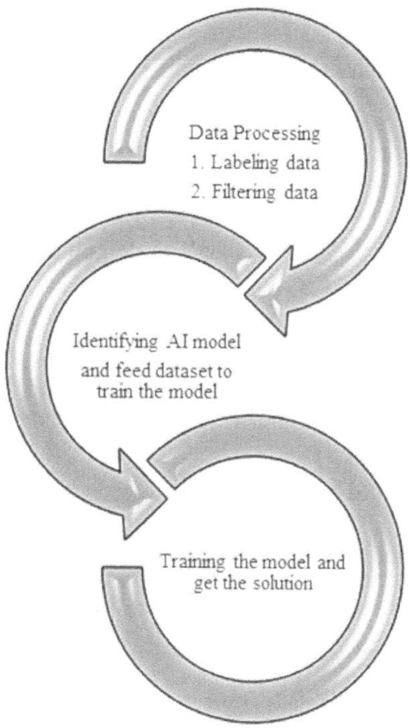

FIGURE 9.5 Data processing.

used to train on clean data and avoid reweighting loss (Natarajan et al., 2017). *Rank* helps in training the model and builds the ideas of curriculum learning (Jiang et al., 2018). The CL approach by Northcutt et al. (2022) is a direct measure of joint distribution between noisy and uncorrupted labels.

Experiment setup: Let us assume there are datasets Y (noisy labels) and Q (true labels) and X is a coupled dataset with cleaned data. It is assumed that there is a possibility of mislabeling and it is reasonable. The class conditional label uncertainty is estimated by joint distribution. The first step is to count the examples that are likely to belong to another class, using the equation

$$C_{y-Q} \epsilon Z_{>0}^{Q*Q}$$

First, the C_{y-y*} errors are estimated then Q_{y-y*} is done to find out the joint distribution of noisy labels, thus producing cleaned data for training. The noisy label is *i* and the true label is *j* and by partitioning *X* into $\hat{X}_{\tilde{y}=i,y^*=\hat{j}}$, where $y^* = j$, the confident joint is determined by per-class threshold t_j

$$C_{\tilde{y},y^*}[i][j] := \left|\hat{X}_{\tilde{y}=i,y^*=j}\right| \quad where$$

$$\hat{X}_{\tilde{y}=i,y^*=j} := \left\{ x \in X_{\tilde{y}=i} : \hat{p}(\tilde{y}=j; x, \theta) \geq t_j,\ j = \underset{l \in [m] \hat{p}(\tilde{y}=l;x,\theta) \geq t_l}{\arg\max}\ \hat{p}(\tilde{y}=l; x, \theta) \right\}$$

$$t_j = \frac{1}{\left|X_{\tilde{y}=j}\right|} \sum_{x \in X_{\tilde{y}=j}} \hat{p}(\tilde{y}=j; x, \theta)$$

The data is ranked and pruned for data cleaning, by employing the following techniques:

a. *Using off-diagonals to count errors*: The diagonals of the $C_{\tilde{y},y^*}$ are counted for labeling errors directly
b. *Use probability ranking*: From the off-diagonals, the probability of error is estimated
c. *Prune by Class C*: Choose the one with the lowest self-confidence
d. *Prune by Noise Rate (NR)*: The noise rate is associated with Q_{y-y*} where the max-margin is estimated
e. *Prune by C+NR*: Combine steps c and d

The missing data is accounted for by reweighting the loss by

$\frac{1}{\hat{p}(\tilde{y}=i|y^*=i)} = \frac{\hat{Q}_{y^*}[i]}{\hat{Q}_{\tilde{y},y^*}[i][i]}$, where $\hat{Q}_{\tilde{y},y^*}[i][i]$ normalizes the data.

9.7.4.2 Working of ResNet-50 Model

ResNet, a Residual network is part of a Convolution Neural Network, which can train up to 150 different layers of data. The data will have different single-label

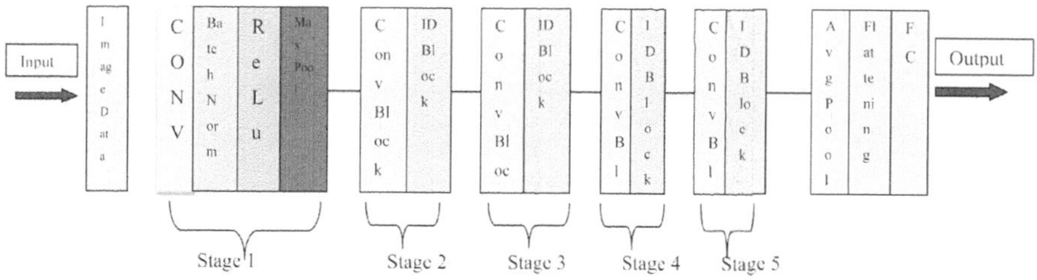

FIGURE 9.6 ResNet-50 model architecture.

networks that predict the atmospheric or ground features. Multi-label data is fed to the ResNet-50 model and scored for the features. The images of the environment are very similar and the chances of the model identifying them as one is very high unless CL is used. Hence, labeling plays a pivotal role in data cleaning. This model helps in evaluating the residual from each layer that is reused and has the potential to categorize images into 1000 object categories. Amongst all the ResNet models (ResNet-18, 35, 50, 152), ResNet-50 is considered superior due to its processing, time generalization ability, and predictability (Lee et al., 2023; Northcutt et al., 2022) (Figure 9.6).

9.7.4.3 Working of ResNet-50 in Data-Centric AI Model

ResNet-50 is a deep network model, which is used for analyzing multi-layer data. In this model, a pooling layer and three dense layers are attached at the end. Importing network structure and downloading pre-trained weights for each network was done with the help of Keras, a Python package. A deep CNN model, with data augmentation layers, was used to develop ResNet. This process includes feeding batches of images and scoring them based on their features. A sigmoid activation function scores each feature between 0 and 1.

This model is developed by Microsoft Research using residual functions to get a stable deep network. It uses a 224×224 image resolution. The Keras callbacks are used to save the model weights during the training to improve the performance and efficiency of the model. Since processing the entire labeled image data at once is difficult, they are loaded in batches. The data is cleaned using CL methodologies discussed previously. Since there is a high probability of acquiring random data, in this model, Stack Overflow was used which allows the processing of labeled dictionary into the generator with a length of 17 binary array values for each geospatial satellite image. Thus, representing its feature labeling. The data was split into training and validation sets to get better efficiency of the k-folds (Gardner and Nichols, 2017).

9.7.4.4 Experiments and Evaluation of the Data-Centric Model

The baseline model and ResNet 50 (CNN model) were used for processing the vanilla data. The model is run on the augmented data and developed as an ensemble model (Figure 9.7).

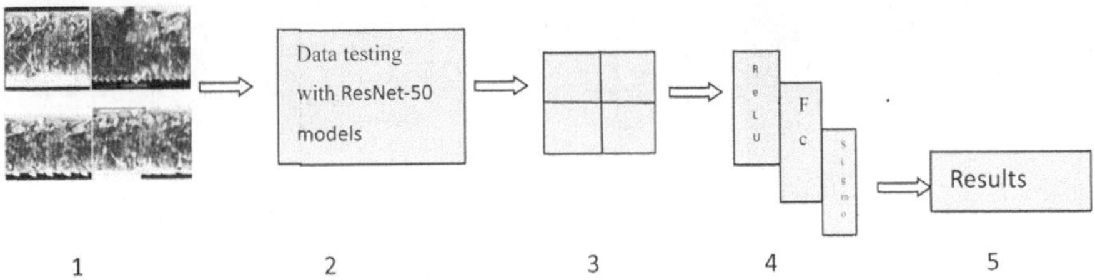

FIGURE 9.7 ResNet 50 working model with geospatial data.

a. *Evaluation*: The evaluation metric chosen for the model is the average F2 score which is defined as

$$F_2 = \left(1+2^2\right) * \left(\left(\text{precision} * \text{recall}\right) / \left(2^2.\text{precision}\right) + \text{recall}\right)$$

$$\text{Precision} = \text{TP}/(\text{TP}+\text{FP}) \text{and} \text{Recall} = \text{TP}/(\text{TP}+\text{FN})$$

It helps in assigning probability false negatives and detecting rare phenomena

b. *Baseline model*: The baseline model has two convolutional layers with ReLu activation with max pooling which is followed by two dense layers. The input feed is raw data, which is not resized. The F2 value is evaluated for the base model (Figure 9.8).
c. *Deep model*: The ResNet 50 model was expected to have a better F2 score than other models, hence it was chosen
d. *Data augmentation and ensembles*: The images were rotated, flipped, and shifted to get augmented data with additional labels. The ResNet-50 model was trained with augmented data and predictions were made using the voting ensemble method.

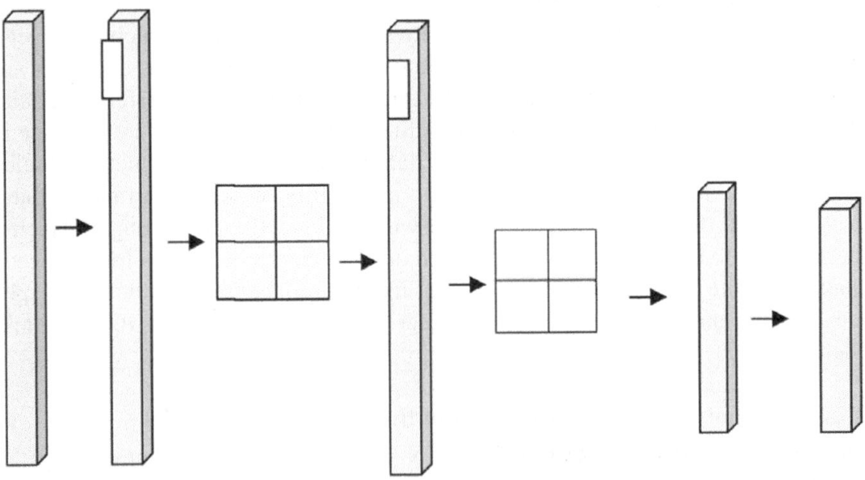

FIGURE 9.8 Baseline model.

e. *Tuning*: The baseline model is trained with an initial setting of 0.5 across classes, and then an exhaustive search is performed to get a uniform threshold for all the classes. The F2 of each class is independent, hence the threshold for all the classes identified is N^n (N is search size, n: classes).

9.7.4.5 Textual Data and Fin-BERT Analysis

There is a lot of textual data available, that can be collected from company disclosures, and newspaper articles. This financial data can be analyzed using the Fin-BERT model which integrates the financial data into layers. Thus, enabling the model to analyze and get relevant interpretations. The textual data collected from Bloomberg, Refinitiv, and public disclosures of the firm are analyzed with the Fin-BERT. They are modeled to understand the firms' sentiment toward SF practices. The codes are available on GitHub and analysis can be done in Google Colab. Mukherjee (2020) has extensively worked on Fin-BERT, trying to formulate a better analytical model for users.

9.8 FUTURE PROSPECTS

Continuous modifications of AL techniques will enhance the data evaluation capabilities. The real question is data collection and handling as these processes require understanding of various technical aspects and require skills that a non-technical person might not possess. Future research should focus on simplifying the process of data collection. Another important aspect is reducing the pricing of the databases, as the majority of small and medium corporations cannot include SF activities and disclosures due to the pricing.

9.9 CONCLUSION

In this chapter, a data-centric AI model was explored, which helps in collecting Geo-satellite data from appropriate sources. These data have several layers and also require appropriate geo-tagging. Despite the data being labeled, there is a high chance of noise in the collected data, as the images are very similar. The databases used for the Geo-satellite data are NASA and Earth and for other public disclosures from the company – Bloomberg and Refinitiv. The analysis is done using ResNet-50 for the imagery data and textual data, and Fin-BERT is used. The labeling errors, if any, are accounted for and cleaned by using pruning and off-diagonal methods. The Res-Net-50 model is used for analyzing geospatial data as it can analyze multiple layered data accurately. Google Colab is used for running the models from both datasets. The results can be used to develop policies or strategize the implementation of SF in firms.

ACKNOWLEDGMENTS

We would like to thank CHRIST (Deemed to be University) and the Bloomberg database for providing timely access to all online library resources for data collection.

BIBLIOGRAPHY

Armstrong, M. P. (2000). Geography and computational science. *Annals of the Association of American Geographers*, *90*(1), 146–156.

Basera, N., (2016). Sustainable development: A paradigm shift with a vision for future. *International Journal of Current Research*, *8*(09), 37772–37777.

Berg, F., Kölbel, J. F., & Rigobon, R. (2020). Aggregate confusion: The divergence of ESG ratings. *Social Science Research Network*. https://doi.org/10.2139/ssrn.3438533

Boloña, C. A. (1973). Donella H. Meadows, Denis L. Meadows, Jorgen Randers y William W. Behrens III, 1972, The Limits to Growth. New York, Potomac Associates Book – Universe Books. *Apuntes: Revista De Ciencias Sociales*, *1*, 106–107. https://doi.org/10.21678/apuntes.1.8

Briere, M., Keip, M., & Berthe, L. T. (2022). *Artificial Intelligence for Sustainable Finance.*

Brown, B. J., Hanson, M. E., Liverman, D. M., & Merideth, R. W. (1987). Global sustainability: Toward definition. *Environmental Management*, *11*(6), 713–719. https://doi.org/10.1007/bf01867238

Brundtland, G. H. (1987). *Report of the world commission on environment and development: Our common future* (p. 41). United Nations. https://sustainabledevelopment.un.org/content/documents/5987our-common-future.pdf

Chen, P., Liao, B. B., Chen, G., & Zhang, S.. (2019). Understanding and utilizing deep neural networks trained with noisy labels. In *International conference on machine learning (ICML).*

Chen, M. K., Von Behren, R., & Mussalli, G. M. (2021). The unreasonable attractiveness of more ESG Data. *The Journal of Portfolio Management*, *48*(1), 147–162. https://doi.org/10.3905/jpm.2021.1.281

Daly, H., & Farley, J. (2011). Ecological economics: principles and applications. Island Press.

European Investment Bank. (2023). *What is sustainable finance?* European Investment Bank. https://www.eib.org/en/stories/what-is-sustainable-finance#:~:text=Sustainable%20finance%20is%20about%20including

Fatemi, A., & Fooladi, I. (2013). Sustainable finance: A new paradigm. *Global Finance Journal*, *24*(2), 101–113. https://doi.org/10.1016/j.gfj.2013.07.006

Fernando, F. (2021). Reconceptualizing natural capital and sustainable use of natural capital through Aldo Leopold's land ethic. *Socio-Ecological Practice Research*, *3*(4), 363–374. https://doi.org/10.1007/s42532-021-00094-3

Gardner, D., & Nichols, D. (2017). *Multi-label Classification of Satellite Images with Deep Learning*. Retrieved September 14, 2023, from http://cs231n.stanford.edu/reports/2017/pdfs/908.pdf

Ghimire, B. (2023). Three pillars of sustainable development: Challenges versus achievements. *Journey for Sustainable Development and Peace Journal*, *1*(02), 132–146. https://doi.org/10.3126/jsdpj.v1i02.58266

Goldberger, J., & Ben-Reuven, E.. (2017). Training deep neural-networks using a noise adaptation layer. In *International conference on learning representations (ICLR).*

Jarvie, M. E. (2014, April 28). *Brundtland report | Sustainable development & global environmental issues*. Encyclopedia Britannica. https://www.britannica.com/topic/Brundtland-Report

Jiang, L., Zhou, Z., Leung, T., Li, L.-J., & Fei-Fei, L. (2018). Mentornet: learning data-driven curriculum for very deep neural networks on corrupted labels. In *International conference on machine learning (ICML).*

Kidd, C. V. (1992). The evolution of sustainability. *Journal of Agricultural and Environmental Ethics*, *5*(1), 1–26. https://doi.org/10.1007/bf01965413

Lee, J., Kim, T.-S., Beak, S., Moon, Y.-J., & Jeong, J. (2023). Real-time pose estimation based on ResNet-50 for rapid safety prevention and accident detection for field workers. *Electronics*, *12*(16), 3513–3513. https://doi.org/10.3390/electronics12163513

Levine, R. L. (2005). Chapter 12: Finance and growth: theory and evidence. In *Handbook of economic growth* (pp. 865–934). Elsevier BV. https://doi.org/10.1016/s1574-0684(05)01012-9

Lipton, Z., Wang, Y.-X., & Smola, A. (2018). Detecting and correcting for label shift with black box predictors. In *International conference on machine learning (ICML).*

Meena, P., Chaturvedi, A., & Gupta, S. (2022). Impact of artificial intelligence on development and growth of entrepreneurship. *Impact of Artificial Intelligence on Organizational Transformation*, 131–146, https://onlinelibrary.wiley.com/doi/abs/10.1002/9781119710301.ch9

Mukherjee, M. (2020, 09 10). ESG-BERT: NLP meets Sustainable Investing. Retrieved from Towards Data Science: https://towardsdatascience.com/nlp-meets-sustainableinvesting-d0542b3c264b

Natarajan, N., Dhillon, I. S., Ravikumar, P., & Tewari, A. (2017). Cost-sensitive learning with noisy labels. *Journal of Machine Learning Research (JMLR), 18*, 155.

Papenbrock, J., Ashley, J., & Schwender, P., (2021). Accelerated Data Science, AI and GeoAI for Sustainable Finance in Central Banking and Supervision.

Patrini, G., Rozza, A., Krishna Menon, A., Nock, R., & Qu, L. (2017). Making deep neural networks robust to label noise: A loss correction approach. In *Conference on Computer Vision and Pattern Recognition (CVPR).*

Portney, K. E. (2022). *Sustainability.* The MIT Press.

Purvis, B., Mao, Y., & Robinson, D. (2018). Three pillars of sustainability: In search of conceptual origins. *Sustainability Science*, *14*(3), 681–695. https://doi.org/10.1007/s11625-018-0627-5

Rogers, D. S., Duraiappah, A. K., Antons, D. C., Munoz, P., Bai, X., Fragkias, M., & Gutscher, H. (2012). A vision for human well-being: Transition to social sustainability. *Current Opinion in Environmental Sustainability*, *4*(1), 61–73. https://doi.org/10.1016/j.cosust.2012.01.013

Sandu, J. S., & Marble, D. F. (1988) An investigation into the utility of the Cray X-MP supercomputer for handling spatial data. In *Proceedings of the Third International Symposium on Spatial Data Handling IGU Sydney, Australia*, pp. 253–266

Schoenmaker, D., & Schramade, W. (2019). *Principles of sustainable finance.* Oxford University Press.

Sukhbaatar, S., Bruna, J., Paluri, M., Bourdev, L., & Fergus, R.. (2015). Training convolutional networks with noisy labels. In *International conference on learning representations (ICLR).*

UN (2012a). *The future we want. Resolution adopted by the general assembly on 27 July 2012 (A/RES/66/288).* United Nations.

United Nations (2015). UN Sustainable Development Goals (UN SDGs) – Transforming our world: the 2030 Agenda for Sustainable Development. A/RES/70/1. New York

Van Rooyen, B., Menon, A., & Williamson, R. C.. (2015). Learning with symmetric label noise: the importance of being unhinged. In *Conference on Neural Information Processing Systems (NeurIPS).*

Wang, S. (2010) A CyberGIS framework for the synthesis of cyberinfrastructure, GIS, and spatial analysis. *Annals of the Association of American Geographers, 100*(3), 535–557.

Wang, S. (2013) CyberGIS: Blueprint for integrated and scalable geospatial software ecosystems. *International Journal of Geographical Information Science*, *27*(11), 2119–2121.

Wang, S. (2019) Cyberinfrastructure. *The geographic information science & technology body of knowledge* (2nd Quarter 2019 Edition), John P. Wilson (Ed.) DOI: 10.22224/gistbok/2019.2.4

10 Artificial Intelligence in Promoting Sustainable Agricultural Practices for Better Economic Growth in India

Asmita Ghosh, Oindrila Acharya, and Surjit Singh

10.1 INTRODUCTION

Sustainable agriculture comprises an integrated and developed system of plant and animal manufacturing techniques with precise applications that, over a long period, will meet the requirements of food and nourishment, improve weather quality, make well-planned and organized use of finite energy resources, and on-farm resources, and centralize relevant natural biological cycles and controls. Additionally, it enhances the way of living for farmers and society at large while maintaining the economic feasibility of farm operations (Velten et al. 2015).

Scale quickly limits sustainability when it is used in agriculture, but resource usage, depletion, and degradation accompany intensification. The environmental issues associated with modern agriculture are numerous and unfortunately difficult to resolve. Agriculture is the backbone of India's economy providing livelihood to more than half of its population (Robertson 2015). The country has always been known for its rich agricultural heritage and diverse crop cultivation practices. The challenges of sustainable agriculture are as follows:

10.1.1 Cultivating an Adequate Amount of Food

While the population is increasing, the amount of productive and fertile land per capita is decreasing. By 2050, the number of basic food resources per person will decrease from 0.21 to 0.15 hectares. In this respect, arable farming is the basis for food requirements and necessities.

10.1.2 Loss of Fertile Soil

Around 97.85 million hectares of cultivation lands are lost per annum for business, commercial, and residential developmental works in India. The remaining portion of land must be put to use more effectively.

DOI: 10.1201/9781003640776-10

10.1.3 Energy

The cultivation of land is becoming increasingly essential in producing renewable energy. Bioenergy can save significant emissions from electricity, heat, and fuel production.

10.1.4 Climate Change

India is the world's fourth worst-affected country in accordance with climatic change. Regions that have lower rainfall, and longer droughts reduce water supply.

In this context, the usage of artificial intelligence (AI) could play an important role. AI is influential enough to change the agricultural sector by providing innovative solutions for precision agriculture (PA), crop monitoring, pest control, weather forecasting, and water management. AI can help increase productivity, reduce costs, and improve resource management, thus improving farmers' livelihoods. This chapter discusses the potential of AI in promoting sustainable agricultural practices for better economic growth in India.

10.2 UNDERSTANDING SUSTAINABLE AGRICULTURE

Sustainable agriculture can be explained as a technique of farming that focuses on long-term productivity while preserving the environment and natural resources. It includes practices such as soil conservation, crop rotation, integrated pest management, and water management. Sustainable agriculture aims to provide a secure and resilient food system that can satisfy current needs without sacrificing the capacity of future generations to satisfy their own wants. Food and other commodities will eventually become less plentiful if we are unable to maintain agricultural production. When profitability declines, extra funds are no longer accessible for maintenance and renovations. Weeds, pests, and chemical residues can contaminate farmland.

10.2.1 Role of Artificial Intelligence in Sustainable Agriculture

AI is defined as the potential of machines to learn from data and perform specific work that usually needs human intelligence. AI links the gap between traditional agricultural practices and sustainable practices which are more efficient and easier to use while decreasing the negative effects. AI is eventually improving the sustainability of agriculture (Kumar et al. 2023).

There is vast scope and opportunity for AI-assisted agricultural practices as their application is restricted and in the beginning stage. A lot has to be explored in terms of the impact verticals of AI in precision farming and agriculture as an entire system. AI can transform the agriculture sector by providing innovative solutions for crop monitoring, pest control, weather forecasting, and water management.

10.2.1.1 Precision Agriculture

PA is the technique that uses data and technology to optimize crop production. PA is a concept-based technique that uses a system approach to restructure the complete system of agriculture toward a low-input, highly potent, sustainable agriculture. PA uses tools like precision irrigation systems, yield mapping and monitoring tools, and information management systems. These tools generate data that is analyzed using advanced analytics engines to provide decisions based on data for low-cost, sustainable agricultural solutions (Zhang et al. 2002).

The Global Positioning System (GPS), also known as a type of navigation system that has high potential and is satellite-based is used to provide precise place and time information in any climatic conditions around the earth's surface. In PA, GPS is an indispensable tool that offers highly accurate location details for mapping and navigation purposes.

A geographical information system (GIS) is a powerful computer software database designed to input, store, retrieve, analyze, and display referenced geographical information in a visually intuitive map-like form. In the context of PA, GIS is utilized to create, store, and analyze spatial data pertaining to farming operations. This invaluable data encompasses field boundaries, topography, soil types, crop types, and a plethora of other critical features (Cropin).

The notion of "precision agriculture" has been developed as a result of the incorporation of AI into farming practices. These types of innovative approaches employ AI to enhance several aspects of farming, boosting productivity, reducing resource waste, and raising crop yields. Since PA is changing the agricultural landscape, the fusion of AI and modern agriculture offers an explanation. Modern farming's success depends on AI technology, including machine learning as well as information analytics. Machine learning algorithms sift through a large number of details collected by sensors, satellites, and drones to look for patterns and relationships. This comprehension based on data enables farmers to take precise actions by equipping them to comprehend the different demands and essentials of their farms.

In the case of PA decision-making and effective agricultural management, timely acquisition of plant status during its development life-cycle is essential. Despite being accurate, traditional manually operated sensing by human sampling in the field is destructive, scattered, laborious, prolonged, and not suitable for contemporary field applications on a larger scale. This is because field spatial heterogeneity necessitates the equipment's users to perform extensive field data collection. Comparing UAV sensing systems to ground-, aircraft-, and satellite-based sensing systems reveals numerous distinct advantages. For instance, while the ground-based manual technique is accurate, it is labor- and time-intensive, expensive, terrain-dependent, and only offers information on specific places. By contrast, UAV sensing may prevent these issues because it offers a larger and greater coverage with less need for human intervention. UAV sensing systems are more adaptable and less dependent on cloud cover than manned aircraft and satellite-based sensing systems. They also have higher cost-effectiveness and accuracy, and flexible multiple-source data acquisition capacity, thanks to a variety of add-on sensing units, and user-defined spectral-spatial-temporal image resolutions (Su 2022).

10.2.1.2 Crop Monitoring

AI can be used to monitor crop health and growth, identify diseases, and predict yields. Image recognition technology can be used to analyze images captured by drones and satellites to identify crop stress and monitor plant growth. Farmers and crop scientists can simply apply the technology of aerial photography. They can comprehend and research the elements affecting crop performance through aerial photography. Small-format drone imagery is an effective tool for identifying patterns of erosion and tracking fleeting changes in vegetation. Identification of diseases of crops and stress is another use for aerial photography (Aber et al. 2019). To recognize agricultural diseases and understand crop changes, infrared aerial photography in black and white or color is utilized. Crop monitoring largely focuses on choosing the best method for spotting any form of illness on crops and ultimately raising their quality. AI suggests a number of methods for an automated evaluation of the condition of the crops. Its development at all phases is crucial for farmers and agricultural management.

Climate-resilient crop monitoring uses cutting-edge technology like remote sensing, the Internet of Things (IoT) (Figure 10.1), and AI to enquire, learn, and address climate-related challenges in agriculture. These tools enable the collection of data on climate trends, quality of soil, and crop health in real-time, supporting farmers in making justifiable decisions and adapting their farming practices in response to changing climatic conditions (TraceX technologies).

AI sensors are currently being used to locate weeds, after which the right pesticides are administered to the region. Instantaneous data monitoring, estimation, and storage are additionally made possible by incorporating IoT sensors and auxiliary

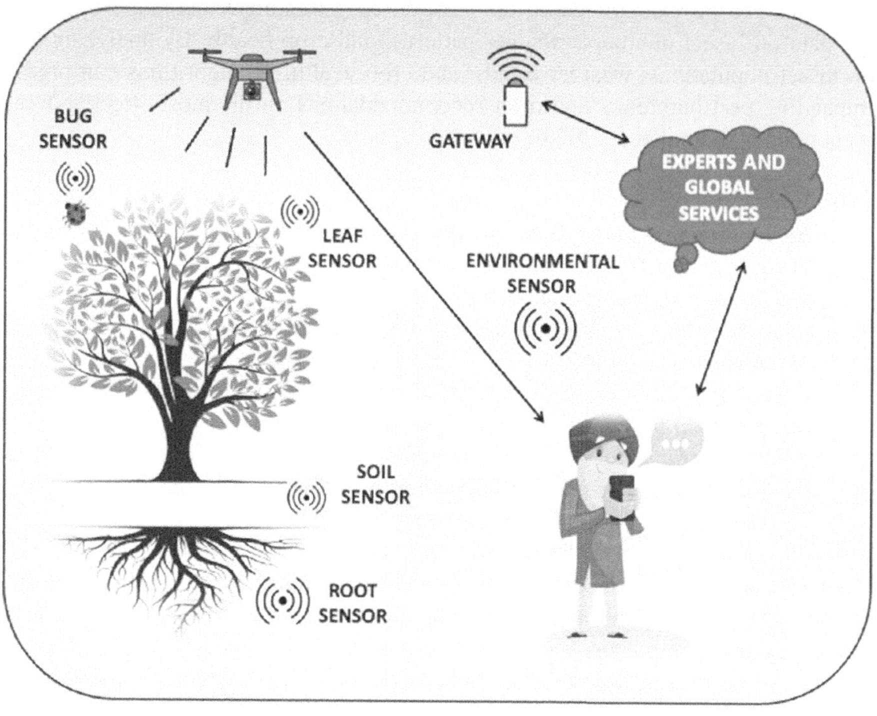

FIGURE 10.1 IoT technology forming networks using different sensors.

machinery such as drones and GISs (Figure 10.1). The aforementioned information can help farmers by illuminating regions that require irrigation, fertilizer, or pesticide application. As a result, they can make well-informed judgments, allocate resources efficiently, and cut back on extravagant expenditures (Balaska et al. 2023).

10.2.1.3 Pest Control

Integrated pest management, also known as integrated pest control is a wide-ranging approach that incorporates both chemical and non-chemical applications for controlling pests. IPM's main goal is to subdue pest populations below the level where they can't cause economic damage.

IPM's goal is to increase the adoption of ecologically friendly farming practices while decreasing the need for chemical pesticides. IPM deployment requires thorough monitoring and decision-making, both of which with the help of AI can be improved. AI can evaluate vast volumes of data and make forecasts based on historical trends to aid farmers in controlling pests more successfully.

Pest monitoring and detection is one of the most significant uses of AI in the control of pests. Both visible surveys and trapping are common, time-consuming methods of detecting pests, yet they only rely on individual perceptions. The incorporation of sensing devices and cameras in AI-based pest monitoring systems allows more accurate and speedy identification of infestations by gathering data on insect populations and behavior. AI also has additional uses, including predicting pest outbreaks and improving pest control. AI algorithms can forecast upcoming pest outbreaks and provide advice on the most efficient treatment methods by examining data on insect numbers, weather patterns, and crop health. By analyzing data on insect populations, weather trends, and crop health, AI algorithms can predict impending pest outbreaks and offer recommendations on the most effective treatment options (Samal et al. 2023).

Advantages

1. *Early detection aids*: Significantly reducing infestation and increasing yield, which improves social and economic health.
2. *Calculating damage*: The farmer can adjust the dosage of pesticides for more nutritious crops and improve human health by measuring the extent of damage caused by pests.
3. *Global applicability*: Because manual labor will be so much less expensive, this will help farmers all across the world.
4. *Increased efficiency:* Gives farmers more time to focus on other vital work that requires greater focus, allowing for innovation.

10.2.1.4 Weather Forecasting

On the basis of several pieces of evidence showing humans are changing the Earth's climate, the effect of climate change is more probable than ever. A shift in each climate system component leads to climate change. The changes in climatic conditions can be caused due to either man-made or natural effects. Climate change will also have an impact on the water cycle. In addition, agriculture will be greatly impacted by climate change. AI algorithms allow for the manipulation of data and the extraction of meaning-filled insights that result in precise conclusions. An inert either inorganic or organic substrate receives nutrient solutions through the use of a revolutionary planting technique called soilless culture. Most likely, the most extensive farming method now in use is to maximize crop yield. AI can analyze the information related to weather and provide accurate forecasts for farmers. This can be helpful for the farmers to make decisions regarding irrigation, pest control, fertilization, etc. Accurate weather forecasting can also help farmers to be prepared to combat critical weather situations like droughts, floods, etc.

Additionally, it is the most intense form of farming practiced when growing greenhouse greens for the market. Hydroponic systems, a subtype of soilless culture, can be run independently thanks to technology. AI's machinery technology is quite useful in this situation. Hydroponic systems, a subtype of soilless culture, can be run independently thanks to the IoT. A subset of AI called machine learning is quite useful in this situation. To predict plant development and water consumption in hydroponic systems, machine learning is employed. Currently, there are a number of techniques for estimating yields that rely on traditional techniques, including statistical frameworks for crop yield assessment and computational models of process-oriented crops.

Water scarcity is a significant challenge in many parts of India. AI can be used to monitor soil moisture levels, predict crop water requirements, and optimize irrigation schedules. This can be helpful for farmers to reduce water wastage and better crop yields.

10.2.1.5 Water Management

The advent of new technologies, devices, and platforms has empowered us to gather and utilize vast volumes of data from various origins, including historical rainfall patterns, aerial imagery, yield records, on-field sensors, and more. Consequently, the synthesized data can undergo processing and integration with forecast data, encompassing factors such as market demand and weather. This integration equips us to make informed decisions characterized by a level of precision and accuracy unparalleled in our access to predictions thus far.

Creating optimal irrigation to schedule and distribute areas that are being overly watered or underwatered is a key question to answer. A routine task, that can be tough to assess and monitor for any farmer or agronomist, is to determine the right amount of water to get the yield and quality in an optimum amount. Depending on the plant type, overwatering also carries huge risks. Therefore, farmers aim to create an optimal irrigation system for their crops to optimize yield and quality while keeping low costs in mind. One of the key metrics is evapotranspiration which creates an irrigation system that is tailored to the needs of a plant. It represents the sum of evaporation from the land surface plus transpiration from plants.

Secondly, discovering irrigation malfunctions or leaks wasting water, especially in areas where it is a scarce resource, is a hugely problematic situation (and expense) for farmers and food growers worldwide. In the past, it might have taken a personal inspection to find a broken piece of equipment or identify a leak. IoT devices in these conditions mean that the software itself can alert when something is wrong or suspicious – and this is only available when devices are interconnected with each other. This way, an irrigation sensor can detect an irregularity and link it to the root issue or variable – especially if it is connected to other data points such as weather or climatic change data so it can rule out other potential causes.

Yield Optimization and Water Footprint Reduction. By optimizing water use and other inputs, AI-driven PA can maximize the crop yields while minimizing environmental impact to a greater extent. This is particularly important as water scarcity and climate change have threatened our global food security. By enabling farmers to produce more with less water, AI has the potential to reduce agriculture's water footprint significantly and provide a better situation to practice cultivation.

10.3 IMPACT OF AI ON AGRICULTURAL PRODUCTIVITY

10.3.1 Increasing Yields

AI is merely the capacity of machines to carry out operations often associated with or performed by human intelligence. Technologies based on AI help to address problems with weeding, irrigation, crop establishment, and crop monitoring, increasing crop productivity and efficiency. The application of AI to guarantee agricultural sustainability has also been spurred by other issues like unpredictable climatic fluctuations, a rapidly expanding population, and food insecurity. In many areas of agriculture, including but not restricted to general agricultural management systems, pest and disease control, soil and irrigated management, weed management, and yield prediction, AI has been employed. In order to monitor soil health, breed seeds, protect crops, feed crops, and harvest crops, AI in agriculture production can be used. Nowadays, farmers deploy robots and drones on their farms for a variety of agricultural tasks (Khan et al. 2022).

In order to lower labor costs and increase agricultural output, farmers must use automation in the management of harvests and produce harvest. Mechanization of crop management and crop harvesting is highly desired by farmers due to its labor- and time-saving benefits. In fields like the use of drones for monitoring crops, the use of robots in agriculture, the use of computational learning and large amounts of data in farming, etc., AI has significantly aided in the mechanization of agriculture. AI has been observed to improve proper crop plant monitoring, consequently promoting crop harvesting, processing, and marketing. This eliminates the need for numerous employees because AI reduces the workload. The majority of produce harvesting, including the harvest of nuts, has been found to be done by robots and AI. Unlike human laborers, robots are programmed so that harvesting is completed more quickly. With the help of sensors to assess their environment, harvesting robots have also been developed as a sort of mechanization to gather produce that is ready to harvest.

10.3.2 Reduced Costs

PA can help farmers reduce costs by optimizing fertilizer water usage. This is useful to reduce waste and increase efficiency. In order to lower labor costs and increase agricultural output, farmers must use automation in the administration of harvests and produce harvests. Mechanization of managing crops and produce harvesting is highly desired by farmers due to its labor- and time-saving benefits. In fields like the application of drones for surveillance of crops, the use of machines in farming, the use of automatic learning and large amounts of data in farming, etc., AI has significantly aided in the mechanization of agriculture. AI has been observed to improve proper crop plant monitoring, consequently promoting crop harvesting, processing, and marketing. The issue of needing several people is resolved since AI reduces the workload. The majority of produce harvesting, including the harvest of nuts, has been found to be done by robots and AI. Unlike human laborers, robots are programmed so that harvesting is completed more quickly. With the help of sensors to assess their environment, harvesting robots have also been developed as a sort of mechanization to gather produce that is ready to harvest (Oluyemi 2022).

10.3.3 Improved Resource Management

We must put in place an irrigation system to ensure that we make adequate use of water resources because over 85% of the freshwater is used for agriculture worldwide. Irrigation is the process of adding water to the soil to keep it moist enough for plant growth. Along with the waste of water resources caused by ineffective irrigation systems, reduced crop yields can also be caused by the leaching of chemicals into the soil. Therefore, it is clear that effective soil and irrigation management is necessary to prevent crop loss and soil degradation. Farmers frequently irrigate crops in agriculture using outdated methods like buckets or watering cans, which should be replaced with more advanced methods utilizing AI. Soil and water management is ensured by applying AI in the machine-based irrigation management system. As a result, a good system for irrigation will increase crop yields and stabilize output, positively promoting crop production, whereas a bad irrigation system will adversely affect crop production. Agricultural monitoring is used in farms to reduce human labor and water use during irrigation. The conventional agricultural irrigation method has been replaced by a machine-driven technology.

AI technology is helpful for weather forecasting and crucial agricultural aspects like groundwater, harvest cycle, and the finding out of plant diseases. Monitoring the health of crops is made feasible by the sensors placed on the soil and plants also multispectral images captured by satellites and drones. Using this data, AI can determine if more complex and complicated unsupervised ML algorithms are. This boosts productivity while reducing crop loss. AI programs may scan data from security cameras or drones for wildlife, birds, and unauthorized individuals that might damage crops.

AI in agriculture uses information and equipment like autonomous tractors, drones, soil detectors, and other technology to help farmers become more productive. Precision farming and statistical analysis are two general uses of AI in the agriculture field. The widespread use of AI in the agriculture sector has changed the whole outcomes of farming techniques mainly agricultural start-ups using AI-enabled approaches to increase the efficiency of agricultural output (Javaid et al. 2023).

10.3.4 Improved Livelihoods

Agriculture is an industry that completely depends upon labor, and as the population is growing and the need for agricultural production is increasing, automation is becoming more important gradually. By the means of technologies and applications, AI is benefitting the farmers. The quality of crops and other supplies is guaranteed through various farming management systems and predictive techniques. Businesses estimate acreage and monitor the condition of crops in real-time using satellite images and weather data. AI is also profitable for businesses to predict prices, estimate production output, and find out pest attacks and diseases. They are eligible to give farmers advice about supply and demands in the market and industry, information about the best crop kinds to plant, the usage of pesticides, and price trends in the industry. Since AI significantly decreases the availability of resources and labor, it indeed will play a powerful role in helping organizations to manage the increasing complexity of the current situation of agriculture. It has become past time for big businesses to make an investment here. AI technology is being used in many sectors to increase production and efficiency. People across many industries are using AI technologies to get beyond traditional barriers. Among the industries that use AI applications are agriculture, finance, transportation, and healthcare.

Since it may give farmers the chance to make better decisions regarding the cultivation of their crops and livestock, using AI is crucial to ensure that agricultural decisions are as efficient and sophisticated as possible. The effective application of AI technology and the dependability of data collection is a clear indication of the progress of the sector of agriculture and the potential for future expansion (Javaid et al. 2023).

10.4 FUTURE PERSPECTIVES

The potential of AI in agriculture is vast, with the continuous advancement of technology and the availability of more data, AI algorithms are becoming increasingly accurate and efficient.

For AI in agriculture to be more widely adopted, challenges with cost, accessibility, data privacy, security, education, and training must be addressed.

The agricultural industry could greatly benefit from AI in the future. AI technology can provide farmers with valuable insights, aid in making better decisions, and optimize resource management. By embracing AI, farmers could potentially increase their productivity, reduce the impact on the environment, and contribute to sustainable food production. However, there are still some challenges that need to be addressed, such as cost, accessibility, data privacy, and education, to ensure that AI adoption is equitable. With continued advancements and collaborative efforts, the integration of AI in agriculture could lead to a future where technology and nature work together to sustainably feed the growing population.

BIBLIOGRAPHY

Aber JS, Marzolff I, Ries JB, Aber SEW. Small Format Aerial Photography and UAS, Imagery: Principles, Techniques and Geoscience Applications. Elsevier, 28 May 2010.

Balaska V, Adamidou Z, Vryzas Z, Gasteratos A. Sustainable Crop, Protection via Robotics and Artificial Intelligence Solutions. *Machines*, 11(8), 774. 2023.

Cropin. 10 Precision Agriculture Tools and Technologies. https://www.cropin.com/precision-agriculture

Javaid M, Haleem A, Khan IH, Suman R. Artificial Intelligence Applications in Agriculture-Understanding the Potential Applications of Artificial Intelligence in Agriculture Sector. *Advanced Agrochem*, 2(2023), 15–30. 2023.

Khan R, Dhingra N, Bhati N. Role of Artificial Intelligence in Agriculture: A Comparative Study. In *Transforming Management with AI, Big-Data, and IoT*, Springer International Publishing, pp. 73–83. 2022.

Kumar AS, Sharma P, Kaur S, Saleh OS, Chennamma HR, Chaturvedi A. AI-Equipped IoT Applications in High-Tech Agriculture Using Machine Learning. In Handbook of Research on AI-Equipped IoT Applications in High-Tech Agriculture (pp. 38–64). IGI Global. 2023.

Oluyemi S. Artificial Intelligence in Produce Harvesting. The Benefits of Artificial Intelligence in Crop Production. Preprint, Simeon Oluyemi, Bournemouth University. 2022.

Robertson GP. *Daedalus* 144(4), 76–89. 2015.

Samal I, Pradhan AK, Bhoi TK. Role of Artificial Intelligence in Integrated Pest Management. *AgroScience Today*, 4(5), 0579–0586. 2023.

Su Y, Liwang M, Chen Z, Du X. Toward Optimal Deployment of UAV Relays in UAV-Assisted Internet of Vehicles. *IEEE Transactions on Vehicular Technology*, 72(10). 2022.

Velten S, Leventon J, Jager N, Newig J. What Is Sustainable Agriculture? A Systematic Review. *Sustainability*, 7(6), 7833–7865. 2015.

Zhang N, Wang M, Wang N. Precision Agriculture—A Worldwide Overview. *Computers and Electronics in Agriculture*, 36(2–3), 113–132. November 2002.

11 The Use of Artificial Intelligence to Enhance Sustainable Development Goals

Public Sector Context

Anna Mempel-Śnieżyk and Petr Hlaváček

11.1 INTRODUCTION

Artificial intelligence (AI) is becoming increasingly vital for the public sector. However, the current state of research is heterogeneous, with thematic and methodological imbalances. Existing studies on AI in the government context primarily focus on changes to existing government structures, governance, and administration (Wirtz et al., 2021). AI is increasingly employed in the public sector to enhance efficiency, transparency, and decision-making (Janssen et al., 2020; Van Noordt & Misuraca, 2020). However, many studies regarding AI tools in the public sector offer limited insight, primarily addressing concerns such as algorithmic bias and privacy issues (Valle-Cruz et al., 2019). Governments use AI to automate routine tasks, potentially improving policy-making processes, public service delivery, and internal administration. AI is used to analyze large amounts of data to identify patterns and trends that can inform policy decisions. Data analysis can help identify areas that need more investment in public infrastructure or help predict the spread of infectious diseases. AI can improve citizen engagement and participation in the decision-making process. AI engagement can support interaction between the government and society by providing information quickly and efficiently. Therefore, implementing AI is seen as an indispensable part of government development in the pursuit of achieving Sustainable Development Goals (SDGs). There is a research gap in the literature on the subject which discusses the mutual relationships between AI and sustainable development. Scholars propose further investigation to understand better the role and impact of various AI technologies and applications within the public sector (van Noordt & Misuraca, 2022).

The proposed study distinguishes itself from previous research for several reasons. It discusses the foundational aspects of AI and readiness in the public sector as a backdrop for sustainable development in European countries. Another unique aspect is the mapping and illustration of differences across countries, providing a foundation for researchers from various scientific areas to delve deeper into investigations and contextualize findings within a specific country.

 DOI: 10.1201/9781003640776-11

The research objective encompasses both conceptual and empirical dimensions. The conceptual aspect pertains to developing a theoretical framework for assessing the readiness of AI by the construction of an Artificial Intelligence Readiness Index (AIR index). The empirical part of the study aims to capture the interrelationships between the level of AIR index deployment and sustainable development outcomes in European countries. In order to identify areas of such relationships, the research component of the study includes several stages of analysis outlined in detail in Section 11.3. An additional value of this study is the mapping and showing of the differences across countries. This will provide a basis for researchers from diverse scientific areas to deepen investigations and contextualize findings within the specificities of a particular country.

11.2 THEORETICAL BACKGROUND

11.2.1 The Link between Digitalization and AI Implementation in the Public Sector

Digital transformation, which is essentially the impact of digital technology on economies and societies, is paving the way for the next stage of development through the use of AI. The ongoing process can be described as a transformation from converting analog information to a digital form. The progression continues with the adoption of cloud computing, Big Data analytics, the Internet of Things (IoT), mobile applications, and the next level of automation. The subsequent stage opens up new possibilities, particularly in terms of boosting productivity and enhancing the well-being of all citizens, all while striving to achieve SDGs.

With technological progress and the evolution of information and communications technology (ICT) and attempts to measure and reflect the state of the economy and society, institutions collecting data propose their indicators, often linked to qualitative research methods such as surveys or mystery shopping. A significant database consists of indicators measuring specific elements of ICT infrastructure, digitized society, or access to infrastructure, as well as those related to e-administration (see Table 11.1). To measure the necessary relationships, we adopted basic measures employed by other institutions and researchers to build indices reflecting the digital economy, society, and government.

11.2.1.1 Unlocking AI in Government: The Digital Infrastructure

Throughout the late 20th century, scholars drew attention to the potential of global information exchange facilitated by advancements in computer communication technologies (Webster, 2006). The relationship between ICT infrastructure and the economy was thoroughly examined by Piore and Sabel (1984), emphasizing the critical connection between technology and market dynamics.

The concept of digitization signifies the progressive augmentation of digital data accessibility Brennen and Kreiss (2016). The concept of digital infrastructure (DI) can be explored from two distinct perspectives: as the technical framework responsible for delivering digital communications to urban centers and regional areas and as a catalyst and facilitator of data-driven services in governments (Barns et al., 2017).

TABLE 11.1
Overview of Indicators for Measuring Digital Development, e-Government and ICT Infrastructure

Index	Description
The E-Participation Index (EPI)	Supplementary index to the United Nations E-Government Survey
Online Service Index (OSI)	Indicator measuring the use of information and communications technology (ICT). OSI values are based on the results of a survey
Telecommunication Infrastructure Index (TII)	Indicator based on data provided by the International Telecommunications Union (ITU)
E-Government Development Index (EGDI)	Based on the TII – data provided by the ITU, on the Human Capital Index (HCI), – data provided by the United Nations Educational, Scientific and Cultural Organization (UNESCO), on the OSI data collected from an independent online assessment, conducted by UNDESA, complemented by a Member State Questionnaire (MSQ)
ICT Development – Index	ICT skills, ICT access, ICT use, ITU World Telecommunication/ICT Indicators database
E-Government Benchmarking	Based on mystery shopping methods concerning user-centricity, transparency, key enablers, cross-border services, European Commission Report
Digital economy and society index	Based on the human capital dimension, connectivity, integration of digital technology, and digital public services dimensions

Source: Own elaboration based on E-Government Benchmark 2022 Synchronising Digital Governments Analyze the Future (2022), United Nations E-Government Survey 2022. The Future of Digital Government (2022), World Telecommunication/ICT Indicators Database online 2022, access online https://www.itu.int/hub/publication/d-ind-wtid-ol-2022/ 12.09.2023, European Commission (2022)

Presently, DI is becoming increasingly crucial for e-government development, especially in the context of delivering and utilizing public-sector services for citizens (Dečman, 2018). This growing significance is reinforced by an OECD report (OECD, 2018), which outlines key strategies for improving digital society (DS). In essence, the OECD's recommendations underscore the multifaceted approach necessary to fully harness the potential of ICT in advancing public services and fostering the development of a DS.

11.2.2 Empowering Citizens in the Age of Technology

The concept of a DS is related to an information society, which has the potential to improve the quality of life and the efficiency of social and economic organization (Bangemann, 1994).

In academic discourse, the term DS is defined as a society characterized by a high level of information in everyday life using common or compatible technology. DS refers to interaction, information sharing, and content dissemination which transcends temporal and spatial constraints. Within this framework, individuals gain access to an extensive array of resources and services that would otherwise remain beyond their reach. Furthermore, they can engage in instantaneous communication, irrespective of geographical boundaries, thus redefining the dynamics of societal interaction. This contemporary understanding of society highlights the transformative potential of technology in fostering connectivity, communication, and accessibility, ultimately reshaping how individuals engage with the world around them. Societies are the users and recipients of public services. Reducing disparities among residents involves creating conditions for access to DI. Simultaneously, there is a need to develop their skills in utilizing this infrastructure, providing residents with the opportunity to avail themselves of increasingly advanced public services and acting against social exclusion.

11.2.3 Building Tomorrow's Government Today: E-Government Context

Most definitions of e-government (understood as digital government (DG) underscore the significance of technology and its potential to transform and enhance public administration processes. According to the definition of OECD, e-government is understood as using ICT, especially the Internet, as a tool to achieve better government (OECD, 2003). Continuing the primary concept of e-administration focuses on granting public institutions access to electronic resources and introducing e-administration as a means to alter the nature of the state and its operations (Dečman, 2018). E-government involves utilizing tools and systems made available through information and communication technology to provide better public services to citizens and businesses. E-government enables all citizens, businesses, and organizations to conduct their activities more easily, rapidly, and cost-effectively, as well as to interact with government authorities. An increasing number of governments are turning to the Internet to deliver public services to their citizens (March, 2010).

This ongoing transformation in public administration manifests as local governments progressively enhance their service delivery mechanisms through the adoption of online platforms, (as discussed by Veeramootoo et al., 2018). Sangki (2018) emphasizes the pressing need for fresh and innovative approaches to government development. His pioneering e-government model is distinctive in its capacity to harmonize both technological and social paradigms and offers a holistic perspective on the evolution of e-government, acknowledging the interplay between technology and society (Sangki, 2018).

11.2.4 AI Solutions in the Public Sector: Paving the Way for a Sustainable Future

The public sector is a relatively new domain for AI solutions and many applications have been implemented as innovative pilot projects, therefore governments and public authorities may not be aware of the full range of possibilities related to the use of AI or the associated challenges (Wirtz et al., 2019). While there are numerous opportunities for applying and implementing AI technology in the public sector to enhance its efficiency, it is essential to acknowledge the associated challenges. These challenges can hinder the successful implementation and use of AI applications in the public sector and are categorized into four groups: AI technology implementation, AI law and regulation, AI ethics, and AI society (Wirtz et al., 2019). In this chapter, we refer to

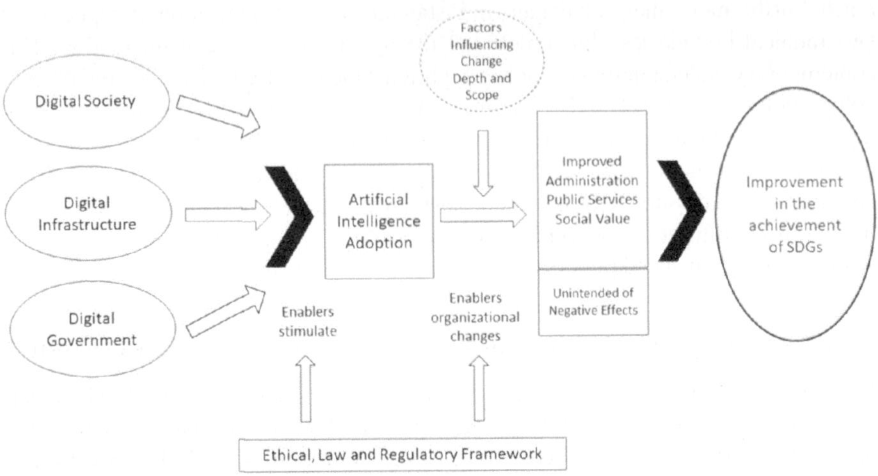

FIGURE 11.1 Conceptual framework for AI impact in the public sector and SDGs. (Own elaboration on the basis of Van Noordt and Misuraca, 2020.)

two of the above-mentioned limitations, specifically addressing the area related to the diversity of countries concerning their readiness to implement AI technology and the recipients of these solutions, measured as DI, DG, and DS (see Figure 11.1).

It is expected that the role of DG will continue to expand and there is a need to monitor the progress of digitalization in government. This monitoring aligns with the EU's recommendation to transition toward a harmonious planet and an evolving digital world. In pursuit of the objectives outlined in the *European Green Deal ESDN Report*, this shift necessitates the adoption of sustainable solutions essential to ensure that every individual, worker, and entrepreneur has an equal opportunity to leverage the benefits of the increasing new solutions. Readiness to implement AI in the economy is a means to improve the growth and well-being of society and the economy (Fetting, 2020).

Governments create policies, regulations, and initiatives that can effectively contribute to achieving sustainable development (SD). They are conscious that ensuring SD is crucial to reducing poverty, ensuring prosperity, creating better educational conditions, and meeting social needs. The indicators used to assess success or failure in achieving SD are not universal and vary depending on the international organizations monitoring SD, such as the OECD, the United Nations, or the EU, as well as in measuring sustainable development at a national or regional level (Megyesiova & Lieskovska, 2018). Considering the study's international focus and the need to include indicators for measuring individual SDGs, we utilize measures developed and monitored by the United Nations (scores are interpreted as a percentage toward optimal SDG performance, the difference between 100 and a country's SDG Index score is the distance, in percentage points, that must be overcome to reach optimum SDG performance).

The researchers believe that the use of AI can help achieve sustainable development (Vinuesa et al., 2020). The increasing economic significance of AI may exacerbate inequality due to the unequal distribution of educational and IT resources worldwide. This stems from the fact that the advantages stemming from the adoption of AI-based technology are likely to primarily benefit individuals who are already well-educated. The issue of digital skills also holds crucial relevance for the application of AI in the public sector. On one hand, the public sector faces the challenge and incentives for implementing AI solutions in public services. On the other hand, there is society, the ultimate recipient of these services, and digital skills, especially in the realm of ICT, emerge as a critical factor for comprehending and efficiently utilizing the available service options.

To validate the adopted research objectives, several stages of analysis were undertaken, namely:

- analyses related to sub-indices of the AIR index, DI, DG, and DS and their relationship with the sustainable development general index score (SDI) in European countries;
- analyses related to sub-indices of the AIR index, DI, DG, and DS and their relationship with particular SDGs in European countries;
- analyses related to the relationship between the AIR index, and SDI in European countries;
- comparison of the above dependencies and cluster analysis of countries.

11.3 METHODS AND MATERIALS

The first part of the study was supported by a traditional literature review to provide detailed information about the components of AI in the public sector to construct an AIR index and its sub-indices namely DI, DG, and DS. The second part referred to the relationship between the AIR index and sustainable development to expand knowledge on the relationship between AI in the public sector and sustainable development (see Figure 11.2). The last part is a comparison of the results between European countries.

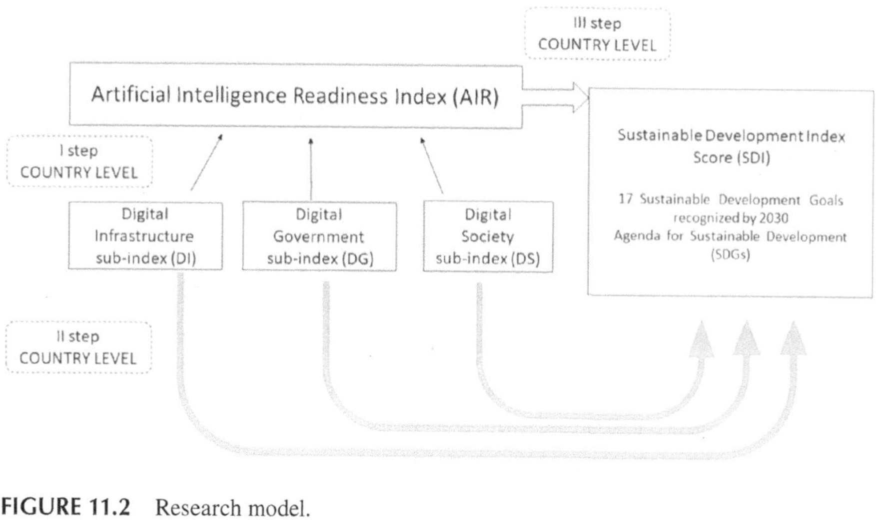

FIGURE 11.2 Research model.

In developing the AIR index and its sub-indices and understanding the components, we studied the basic measures adopted by global statistics such as EUROSTAT, OECD, World Bank, and United Nations reports, the measures in individual databases were consistent. A review of the collected data sets and indicators in the data sources has been conducted, providing the basis for acceptance to follow the proposition of measurement of digitalization within the public sector, digital skills, and infrastructure within the EU. The selection process was meticulously conducted within the framework of our study's objectives and data availability. Our emphasis was placed on choosing data that supported research repeatability and enabled subsequent and comparative analyses by other researchers.

The chosen measures play a key role in assessing technology adoption and penetration, monitoring progress related to internet accessibility and usage, providing a comprehensive framework for evaluating public access to knowledge, information, online services, and referring to the level of digital literacy within a given population. This understanding is of paramount importance for the future adoption of increasingly advanced solutions provided by AI.

The first category of the AIR index, DI, aims to assess the level of technology that forms the foundation for a country's advancement in the direction of AI transformation. This sub-index encompasses aspects related to technological infrastructure, the utilization of AI, the IoT, methods of internet access, security for electronic information exchange, and spending levels on Research and Development (R&D). DI is oriented toward aspects that reflect infrastructure levels and emphasize technology. It reflects the extent to which countries have prepared for the future of the network economy and emerging technology trends. The second sub-index (DG) incorporates a dataset that includes data on accessibility to government services through e-administration channels (citizen and corporate contact with e-government), AI implemented in the public sector (data required from European Commission report), and related to financing R&D. The third category, associated with DS, centers on metrics that mirror the skills within specific societies. This includes how individuals utilize technology, leverage their skills to use AI solutions, and indicators that reflect their choices. Digital skills, encompassing ICT users and ICT specialists, are assessed, reflecting the utilization of DI and DG. (The detailed measures are presented in Tables 11.2–11.4.)

TABLE 11.2
Relationship between Digital Society (DS) Sub-Index Measures – Pearson's Correlation

	(1)	(2)	(3)	(4)	(5)
(1) Individuals used the internet on a mobile device (%)	X				
(2) Employed ICT specialists by educational attainment level (%)	0.10	X			
(3) Employed ICT specialists total (%)	0.69	–0.18	X		
(4) Individuals with basic or above basic overall digital skills (%)	0.79	–0.15	0.63	X	
(5) Individuals who have copied or moved a file or folder (%)	0.54	–0.10	0.40	0.80	X

Note: Significance levels: *** $p < 0.001$, ** $p < 0.01$, * $p < 0.05$.

TABLE 11.3
Relationship between Digital Government (DG) Sub-Index Measures – Pearson's Correlation

	(1)	(2)	(3)	(4)	(5)	(6)	(7)
(1) E-government activities of individuals: submitting completed forms	X						
(2) E-government activities of individuals: obtaining information from public authority's websites	0.88***	X					
(3) E-government activities of individuals: interaction with public authorities	0.94***	0.92***	X				
(4) AI implemented in the public sector (in numbers)	0.45**	0.34	0.36	X			
(5) Share of GBARD in total general government expenditure % of government expenditure	0.51**	0.56**	0.53	0.26	X		
(6) R&D expenditure, by sectors of performance: government sector	–0.06	–0.06	–0.03	0.13	0.40	X	
(7) GERD by sector of performance and fields of R&D: government sectors	–0.06	–0.07	–0.04	0.14	0.40	1	X

Note: Significance levels: *** p < 0.001, ** p < 0.01, * p < 0.05.

The measures were created based on data obtained from a group of 31 European countries. In order to create an AIR index all the detailed measures comprising the AIR index were standardized and then aggregated into a general index composed of sub-indices: DI, DS, and DG. In order to assess whether the constructs (sub-indices DI, DS, DG) constitute a reliable measurement tool, several measures were employed. Cronbach's Alpha values were determined (the value of this measure after the removal of individual items should be relatively high, indicating good internal consistency of the sub-index). Discriminant power was calculated (discriminatory measures should be diverse, signifying that various elements within the sub-index effectively distinguish units from each other). Subsequently, the measures of individual sub-indices were correlated. Cronbach's Alpha values obtained after the removal of specific elements are relatively high, suggesting good internal consistency within the sub-indices. These values typically fall within the range, which is considered an acceptable level. The results were standardized to obtain results on the same scale for all dimensions.

To illustrate the levels of individual sub-indices and the AIR index, maps were prepared using the EUROSTAT tool.

At the next level, Pearson's correlation was used to show the relationship between the AIR index (and sub-indices) and the SD Index Score. An analysis was conducted using Pearson's correlation due to the assumptions of parametric tests (George & Mallery, 2019). The significance level was set at the conventional threshold $\alpha = 0.05$. However, test probability results within the range of $0.05 < p < 0.1$ were interpreted as significant at a statistical trend level.

Due to the fact that analysis was performed on the population of countries and not on a sample, no statistical significance is presented as results are applied to researched countries. The strength of the correlation was indicated by colors – negative relationships

TABLE 11.4
Relationship between Digital Infrastructure (DI) Sub-Index Measures – Pearson's Correlation

	(1)	(2)	(3)	(4)	(5)	(6)	(7)	(8)	(9)	(10)	(11)	(12)	(13)	(14)	(15)	(16)	(17)	(18)
(1) Secure internet servers	X																	
(2) Fixed broadband subscriptions	0.21	X																
(3) Fixed telephone subscriptions	–0.13	0.40	X															
(4) ICT Access and Usage by Businesses	–0.19	0.04	0.24	X														
(5) Enterprises use at least one of the AI technologies	0.48	0.39	0.06	0.56	X													
(6) Internet of Things (enterprise > 10 employees)	–0.26	–0.13	0.12	0.54	0.20	X												
(7) Broadband Internet – more than 100 (Mbps)	0.09	0.27	–0.06	0.02	0.25	–0.05	X											
(8) Cloud computing services by size class of enterprise	0.04	0.31	–0.19	0.56	0.50	0.40	0.17	X										
(9) Big data analysis by size class of enterprise	0.14	0.63	0.18	0.40	0.56	0	0.30	0.61	X									

(10) ICT – Total Enterprise employed ICT/IT specialists	0.22	0.25	0.07	0.37	0.44	0.29	0.12	0.42	0.53	X								
(11) IoT – barriers to use – knowledge	–0.21	–0.12	0.09	–0.29	0	–0.06	0.01	–0.26	–0.17	–0.23	X							
(12) IoT – barriers to use – skills	0.07	0.17	0.25	0.26	0.35	0.18	0.10	0.02	0.12	0.30	0.04	X						
(13) Fibre to the premises (FTTP)	0.29	–0.18	–0.33	–0.33	0.02	–0.32	0.33	–0.18	–0.24	–0.22	0.30	–0.06	X					
(14) Very high-speed digital subscriber line (VDSL)	–0.06	0.21	0.24	0.33	0.03	0.35	–0.05	0.37	0.26	0.33	–0.39	0.12	–0.73	X				
(15) Fifth generation technology (5G)	0.01	0.26	0.20	0.48	0.24	0.22	–0.10	0.28	0.31	0.02	–0.31	–0.09	–0.38	0.39	X			
(16) More than 1 Gbps	0.14	0.34	0.07	0.19	0.38	–0.26	0.50	0.28	0.58	0.23	0.04	0.36	0.30	–0.19	–0.03	X		
(17) Internet coverage	0.34	0.31	–0.03	0.46	0.43	0.20	0.36	0.43	0.48	0.26	–0.28	0.26	0.08	0.23	0.04	0.42	X	
(18) Mobile cellular subscriptions	0.17	–0.10	–0.13	0.40	–0.08	0.08	0.02	0.20	–0.21	0.04	–0.15	–0.11	0.08	0.04	0.13	–0.06	0.04	X

Note: Significance levels: *** $p < 0.001$, ** $p < 0.01$, * $p < 0.05$.

(an increase in one variable corresponded to a decrease in the other variable) were marked with blue colors, and positive relationships (an increase in one variable corresponded to an increase in the other variable) were marked with orange-red colors. Correlations of negligible strength (–0.1 to 0.1) were marked in white. A stronger color signified a stronger correlation.

To compare countries and group them into clusters to better visualize their possible similarity, the cluster analysis method was used and its results were presented in a dendrogram.

11.4 RESULTS

In the first step, the relationships between individual DS indicators for 2021 were examined. As seen in Table 11.2, minimal dependencies were observed for Employed ICT specialists by educational attainment level. The remaining correlations varied from moderately strong to very strong.

Subsequently, a reliability analysis was conducted for the potential overall DS indicator. As expected, indicators employed by ICT specialists by educational attainment level exhibited negligible, negative discriminant power. After removing this dimension, a high level of internal consistency was observed, $\alpha = 0.88$. Therefore, in further analyses, the DS sub-index constructed as the mean of the other four dimensions was used. These observations shed light on the interrelationships between the variables under consideration.

When examining the correlation between the variables individuals (1) and (2), it can be observed that there was no significant interaction between these two variables confirmed. Furthermore, it is assumed that the development of digital services has significantly contributed to the widespread use of the Internet, which is no longer associated with the level of education of ICT professionals. In terms of the calculation of the DS sub-index, the dependence between the level of the national economy and the development of digitalization was confirmed in most countries. The diversity of the DS sub-index across countries is shown in the map in Figure 11.3. The highest values of the DS sub-index were observed in countries such as Finland (1.33), Switzerland, the United Kingdom, and the Netherlands and Sweden (1.05). The lowest indicator values were recorded in Romania (–1.74), Bulgaria (–1.73), and Greece (–1.04).

Particularly significant is the lead of North-Western Europe over Eastern and Southern Europe. This is partly due to the fact that in the post-socialist countries significant investments are still needed in transport and technical infrastructure and the completion of the economic transformation. Then there is a lack of investment in the development of DI and overall digitalization, including public and private services.

In the next step, relationships between individual DG measures for the year 2021–2022 were examined. As evident in Table 11.3, negligible dependencies were observed for dimension (2). The remaining correlations varied from moderately strong to very strong.

Analysis of the DG sub-index looks at the dynamics. The overall high level of internal consistency of the data ($\alpha = 0.79$) suggests that the combination of the seven indicators forms a reliable and consistent model for measuring DG. Table 11.3 shows the range of correlations. Interestingly, the dimension e-government activities of

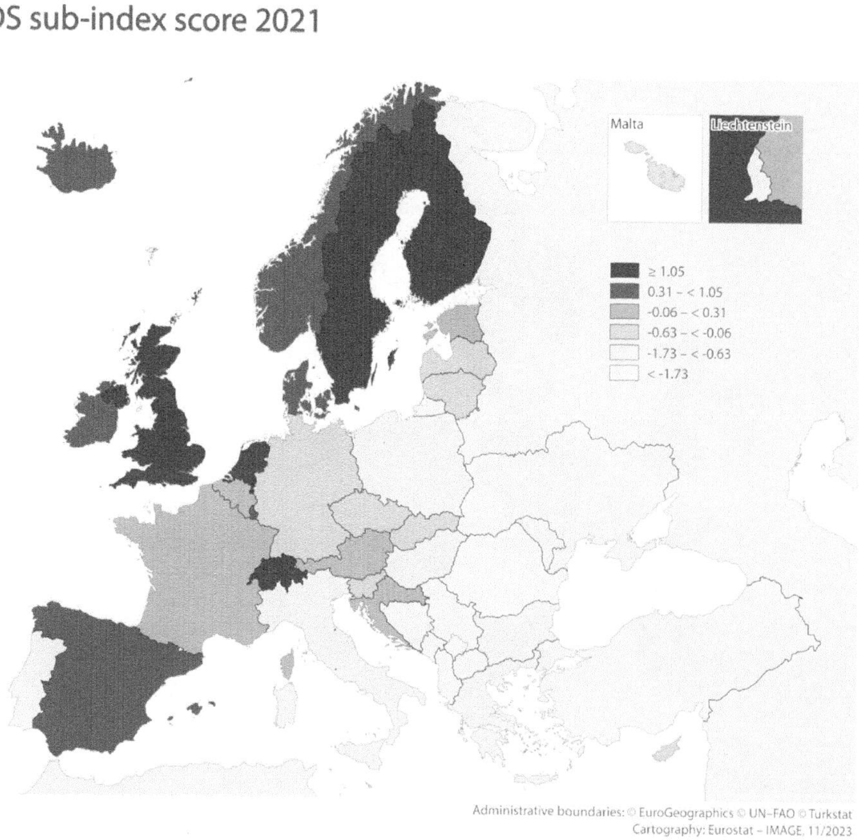

FIGURE 11.3 Digital society (DS) sub-index score for European countries.

individuals: obtaining information from public authority's websites, which relates to e-government activities of individuals in obtaining information from websites, found the most positive correlations. This suggests that states where people interact with the state more using e-government are states with more development of these services, including AI implementation. The characterization of the geographic variation of the DG sub-index is presented in the map in Figure 11.4. The highest values of the indicator were observed in countries such as Switzerland (1.21), Germany (1.08), the Netherlands, Iceland, Denmark, Sweden and France (0.82). The lowest indicator values were recorded in Romania (–1.49), Bulgaria (–1.27), followed by Croatia (–0.73), Slovakia, Cyprus and Italy (–0.5).

In the geographic variation characterization, we can see that countries in the macro regional center of Europe from Scandinavia to France show high DG index scores. This can be attributed to their better DI, which is a consequence of their central geographic location to higher economic development and more effective government policies on digital development. Conversely, the more peripheral regions of Europe show lower DG index scores, with a more pronounced lag in Eastern and Southern Europe, reflecting less government priority on e-government development.

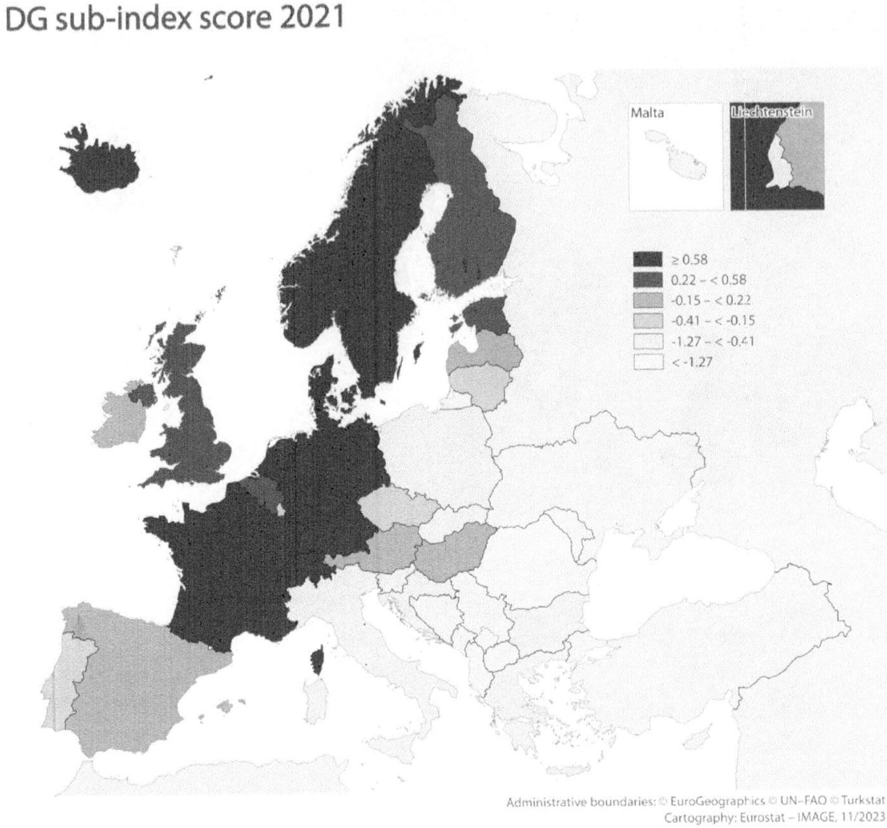

FIGURE 11.4 Digital government (DG) sub-index score for European countries.

The last analysis was conducted for the DI sub-index (see Table 11.4). Due to a lack of data for 2021 concerning the DI indicators, some of the components from 2020 were included in the indicator set. In the 2020–2021 measurement, the scale was constructed from 15 indicators.

A high level of internal consistency was achieved, with $\alpha = 0.79$. Three indicators were excluded due to their negative discriminant power value. Consideration was also given to removing two additional variables – fixed telephone subscriptions and mobile cellular subscriptions; however, in the final model, the discriminant power value of these items exceeded 0.15, and their removal did not significantly increase the level of internal scale consistency.

The analysis of the DI sub-index for the period 2020–2021 included 15 indicators, with the addition of 2020 data in place of some missing 2021 data. The mapping of the DI index for European countries revealed several findings on the state of DI (see Figure 11.5.)

The minimum value of the indicator was −0.97 in Romania, and the maximum was 0.95 in Switzerland, followed by Denmark (0.89), the Netherlands (0.75), and Germany (0.65). First of all, the center of Europe, as the center of the continent,

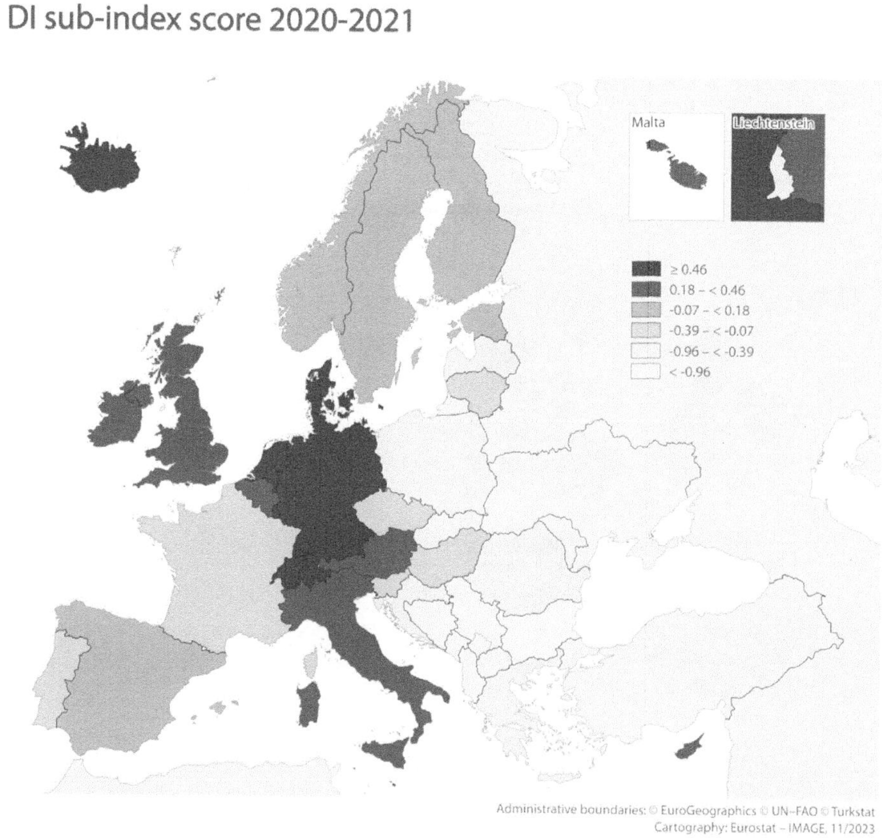

FIGURE 11.5 Digital infrastructure (DI) sub-index score for European countries.

shows a high DI score, which is probably a consequence of its advantageous geographical location which allows better access to digital resources and the associated demand for these resources, determined by a higher population and business concentration. A central location can play a crucial role in the development and availability of DI, especially when stimulated by government policies. It is also interesting to note that Italy has seen a significant improvement in its DI position, indicating the successful implementation of new technologies and policies to support digital development. Conversely, Scandinavia and France have worsened their positions in DI, where in particular the lack of investment in new technologies, outdated infrastructure, or changes in the political and economic environment negatively affect the speed of DI development.

In the next part, the AIR index was constructed as the average of three indicators DG, IS, and DI for the respective years. A high level of internal consistency was observed ($\alpha = 0.87$), and its values are reflected in the map in Figure 11.6.

The minimum value of the indicator was −1.4 in Romania, and the maximum was 1.17 in Switzerland. The next highest AIR index values were in the Netherlands (0.98), Denmark (0.84), and Iceland (0.7). Following closely were Sweden (0.65), United

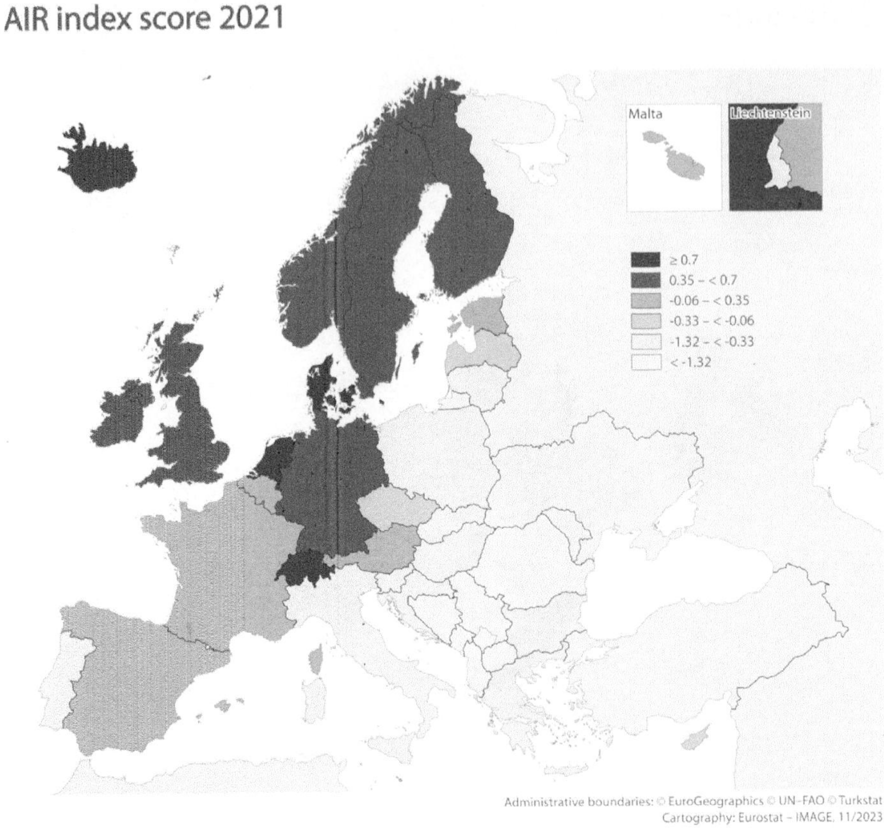

FIGURE 11.6 Artificial Intelligence Readiness index scores for European countries.

Kingdom (0.65), Norway (0.57), Germany (0.46) and Ireland (0.46). The next group was observed countries: France (0.28), Austria (0.2), Spain (0.17), Estonia (0.16), and Belgium (0.16). The following countries can be assigned to the next group: Latvia (–0.33), Slovenia (–0.34), Slovakia (–0.38), Croatia (–0.4), Italy (–0.41), Portugal (–0.41), Lithuania (–045), Greece (–0.61), and Poland (–0.66). The lowest indicators were observed in Bulgaria (–1.32) and the previously mentioned Romania.

From the map, a clear division in the north-western and east-central parts of Europe emerges. The highest indicators were recorded by Northern Europe, as well as Switzerland and Germany. This reflects the values which these countries have achieved in sub-indices.

Additionally, to group countries a classification of countries based on three indicators was performed using hierarchical clustering; the average linkage method with a squared Euclidean distance. The results are presented in the form of dendrograms (Figure 11.7).

The dendrogram shows differences between groups of states in the development of digitalization: differences are manifested between northern and western states on one hand and southern and eastern EU states on the other hand.

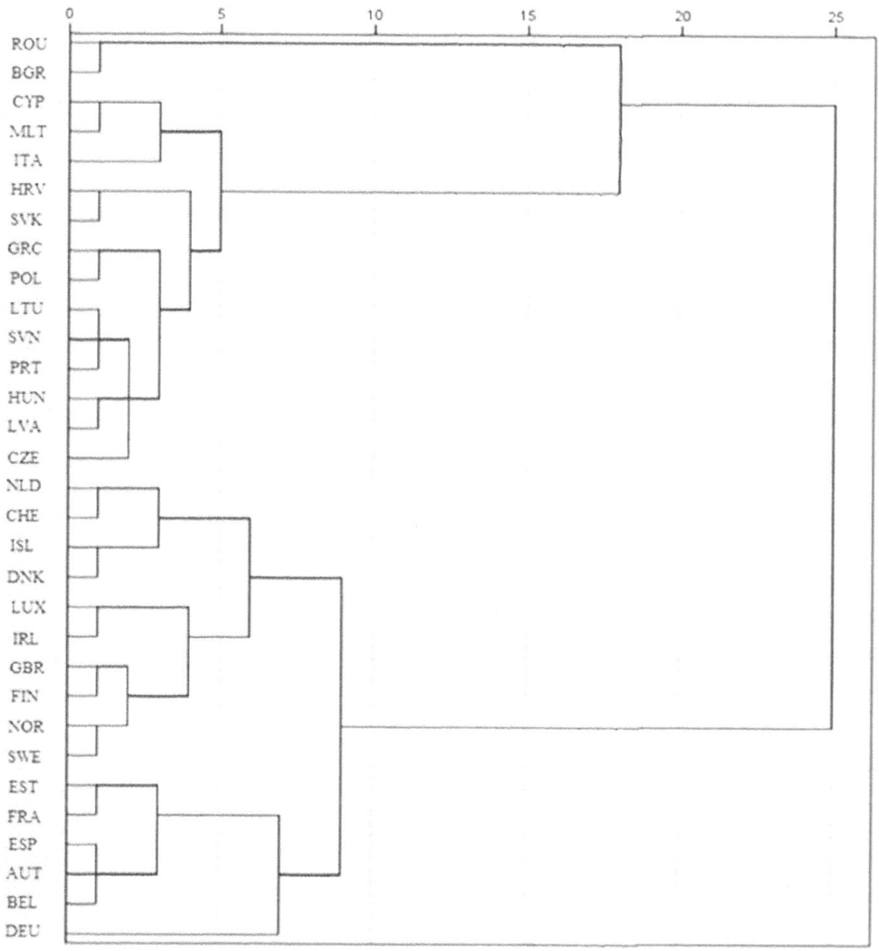

FIGURE 11.7 Combined rescaled distance clusters.

North-western Europe demonstrates a significant advancement in DI. This region, known for its robust economies, showcases a sophisticated level of AI integration, extensive deployment of IoT systems, and strong investment in R&D. These characteristics indicate a strategic alignment with the future of emerging technological trends. Conversely, the Southern and Eastern European countries exhibit a developmental lag in this area. Their technological infrastructure is less advanced, characterized by lower levels of AI and IoT integration and reduced R&D investment, reflecting a slower pace in embracing technological advancements.

When it comes to DG, North-western European countries likely lead in integrating digital processes into government services. This is evidenced by their extensive e-administration services, which facilitate efficient and effective digital interactions between government entities and citizens. This high degree of digitalization in public administration points to a sophisticated incorporation of digital technologies in governmental operations. In contrast, Southern and Eastern European countries may have less developed DG services, potentially due to infrastructural and policy limitations, impacting the accessibility and efficiency of DG services.

The disparity is also evident in DS. The population in North-western European countries is expected to display a higher proficiency in digital skills, covering both general ICT usage and specialized areas. This suggests a well-integrated digital education framework and widespread access to digital technologies. On the other hand, the Southern and Eastern European regions might display a relative deficiency in these competencies. This gap could be attributed to various factors, including differences in educational standards, limited access to advanced technology, and economic constraints that impede the widespread dissemination of digital technologies.

11.4.1 Artificial Intelligence Readiness Index vs. Sustainable Development

To examine the relationships between the AIR index with the SDG Index Score and other individual goals, a series of Pearson correlation analyses were conducted. As seen in Table 11.5, all relationships examined were statistically significant.

TABLE 11.5
Relationship within the AIR Index (and Sub-Indices) between SDG Index Score and SDGs – Pearson's Correlation

	DG	DS	DI	AIR Index
SDG Index Score	0.53**	0.6***	0.25	0.53**
No Poverty	0.14	0.07	0.04	0.11
No Hunger	−0.22	−0.11	−0.17	−0.19
Good Health and Well-Being	0.79***	0.73***	0.83***	0.86***
Quality Education	0.58***	0.64***	0.6***	0.67***
Gender Equality	0.75***	0.79***	0.58***	0.79***
Clean Water and Sanitation	0.35^	0.38*	0.04	0.31^
Affordable and Clean Energy	0.35^	0.45*	0.12	0.36*
Decent Work and Economic Growth	0.28	0.24	0.17	0.26
Industry, Innovation, and Infrastructure	0.72***	0.83***	0.74***	0.84***
Reduced Inequalities	0.42*	0.38*	0.33^	0.42*
Sustainable Cities and Communities	0.73***	0.68***	0.61***	0.75***
Responsible Consumption and Production	−0.6***	−0.54**	−0.68***	−0.66***
Climate Action	−0.61***	−0.56**	−0.57***	−0.64***
Life Below Water	0.07	−0.06	−0.31	−0.07
Life on Land	−0.33^	−0.36*	−0.44*	−0.4*
Peace, Justice, and Strong Institutions	0.66***	0.68***	0.59***	0.72***
Partnerships for the Goals	0.34^	0.47**	0.3	0.41*
Life on Land	−0.33	−0.36	−0.44	−0.40
Peace, Justice, and Strong Institutions	0.66	0.68	0.59	0.72
Partnerships for the Goals	0.34	0.47	0.30	0.41

Note: Significance levels: *** $p < 0.001$, ** $p < 0.01$, * $p < 0.05$.

In the overall context, the AIR index positively correlates with the SD index score at a level of 0.53. The correlations between sub-indices were positive (if DG, DS, and DI increase the level of the SDG index score also increased). Different results were obtained when analyzing the DG, IS, and DI indicators in relation to specific SDGs.

The strongest positive relationships existed between AIR and Good Health and Well-Being (0.86), Industry, Innovation and Infrastructure (0.84), Gender Equality (0.79), Sustainable Cities and Communities (0.75), and Peace, Justice, and Strong Institutions (0.72). A slightly weaker but still positive relationship was noted in connection with certain SDGs. The strongest negative correlation was observed for Responsible Consumption and Production, followed by Climate Action such as Quality Education.

In the case of the goal of Good Health and Well-Being, all three DS, DI, and GD exhibit a strong positive correlation. DG shows a correlation of 0.79, indicating that the development of digital public administration can contribute to improving the health and well-being of society. DS also demonstrates a strong positive correlation with this goal (0.73), suggesting that the advancement of the information society can contribute to better health and well-being. DI shows the strongest positive correlation with this goal (0.83), implying that investments in DI yield benefits in the realm of health and well-being. Similarly, regarding the goal: Industry, Innovation, and Infrastructure, DS displays the highest correlation with this goal (0.83), emphasizing the role of the DS in the development of industry, innovation, and infrastructure. DI also has a strong positive correlation with the goal (0.74), implying that the development of DI is associated with progress in industry, innovation, and infrastructure. DG also exhibits a favorable correlation with this goal (0.72), signifying that the development of digital public administration supports development in these areas. It is also worth mentioning the positive significant correlations between the goal of Sustainable Cities and Communities and indicators (DG 0.66, DI 0.59, DS 0.68). This highlights a strong relationship between these digitalization factors and the pursuit of sustainable urban development.

DI demonstrates a strong negative correlation with the goal of Responsible Consumption and Production (–0.68), suggesting that the development of DI may not necessarily support sustainable consumption and production patterns. Both DG and DS also display negative correlations with the goal (–0.60 and –0.54), indicating that the development of digital public administration and the information society may conflict with objectives related to responsible consumption and production. DI and DS show negative correlations with Life Below Water (DI: –0.31, IS: –0.06), implying that the development of DI and the information society may negatively affect aquatic life. DG displays a slight positive correlation (0.07) with this goal. DI, DG, and DS exhibit negative correlations with Life on Land and also exhibit negative correlations with Climate Action. This implies that focusing on sustainable consumption and climate mitigation may not necessarily be accompanied by high levels of digital governance.

11.5 DISCUSSION

The researchers demonstrated that the application of sustainability theory in current public sector research is lacking and the utilization of the concept is mostly arbitrary and superficial. The majority of public sector – in particular e-government – papers concentrate solely on one aspect of sustainability, whereas papers that encompass and incorporate other dimensions are scarce (Larsson & Grönlund, 2014). Jankowski discusses the state of research between SDGs and digitalization of government, society, and infrastructure and confirms that this connection is missing. He offers trials to check connections between the digitalization of government and SDGs. In the results, he confirms the connections of the SDGs with digital technology and points out that some of them directly relate to digital technology and 15 require digital technology as a tool to support other technological developments (Janowski, 2016).

It is worth mentioning that government initiatives in the field of digitization can contribute to the efficiency and transparency of public administration, while at the same time supporting innovation and economic growth. Digitization, as part of innovation strategies (Rodriguez-Pose, 2013), can be key to identifying and utilizing the specific research and innovation potentials of a state or region. In this context, it is crucial that governments recognize the importance of investing in DI and education, which are key factors in achieving sustainable development and increasing competitiveness. The asymmetry between states in the development of digitization is also influenced by the quality of public management and its services. According to Charron (2016), states with higher government efficiency, stronger rule of law, and lower corruption develop better, thereby growing more compared to other states with worse governance characteristics (Charron, 2016), which is also confirmed by Iammarino et al. (2019). In new areas of the economy in particular, thanks to the specific needs of new industries (Isaksen & Trippl, 2016), the difference between states can deepen as new growth industries also require higher digital competencies of residents and companies and an innovative digitized environment. Development processes can then proceed more selectively, which can further strengthen asymmetric differentiation between states and regions (Grillitsch et al., 2018) according to the level of digitalization in the private and public sectors, which can also lead to the growth of differentiations in innovation and economic performance.

The strategies concerning new technologies in the public sector encompass several essential components, including raising awareness of the pivotal role of ICT and the Internet in societal development. This involves educating the public and decision-makers about the profound and far-reaching impacts of digital technologies. Additionally, to promote DS, there is a need for systematic and focused support for the development of DI, services, and capabilities that benefit all of society. This is closely linked to ensuring high-speed access to the open Internet for all members of society. Such measures are crucial for bridging the digital divide and ensuring equitable access to digital resources and opportunities (OECD, 2018). Implementing new technologies, systems, and applications confers a spectrum of direct benefits. These advantages concern both local government authorities and extend to residents and entrepreneurs. It has been substantiated that embracing innovative solutions equates to cost reduction and promotes more effective financial management within the public sector. Conversely, for end-users of public services, such as residents and entrepreneurs, these benefits manifest as cost savings and heightened convenience. This alignment with the principles of sustainable development underscores the importance of these advancements, fostering a more sustainable and efficient public service framework. Additionally, e-government development strengthens the bond between government institutions and their citizens. Furthermore, e-government has the potential to yield specific policy outcomes by enabling stakeholders to share information, exchange ideas, and contribute to shaping policy decisions (Putra et al., 2018). This aligns with the findings of Welch, Hinnant, and Moon, indicating high levels of public satisfaction with e-government implementation. With the myriad of benefits that internet-based communication with public authorities affords, a continued upward trajectory in its adoption is anticipated in the near future (Welch et al., 2005).

Research conducted by the European Union underscores that progress in e-government has a direct and positive influence on the attainment of the SDGs. This progress contributes significantly to the achievement of various SDGs and their associated targets. The researchers studying the overview of the influence of AI in general on 17 SDGs and (169 targets) suggest that AI may act as an enabler on 134 targets (79%) across all SDGs, generally through technological improvement, but 59 targets (35%, also across all SDGs) may experience negative impacts from the development of AI (Vinuesa et al., 2020). This is in accordance with our research which indicates that there is a correlation between the digital progress readiness of countries to adopt AI solutions (AIR index) and sustainable development.

11.6 CONCLUSIONS

The findings of this study contribute to the current discourse on the ongoing phases of the digitalization process and utilization of AI in the public sector. The chapter extends the existing body of work on AI in the public sector by developing the AIR index. The research suggests that geographical, economic, and political factors can significantly influence digital progress and infrastructure in various regions, which is crucial for the formulation of effective digital development policies and strategies for AI implementation. The mapping and grouping of countries revealed a distinctive division between Northern and Western Europe and Southern and Central Europe. Furthermore, the study indicates that a country's readiness for AI can influence sustainable development. Through an examination of the AIR index and its sub-indices, the study confirmed a positive relationship between the level of DI, society and DG, and SDGs.

However, limitations may arise from the scope and availability of indicators across countries. Correlation does not imply causation, and the study does not establish a causal link; therefore, further research is required. Additionally, the study focuses on European countries, and generalizing the findings to other regions or global contexts may pose challenges.

Our study opens up several avenues for further research. While certain aspects of AI implementation in shaping the world's future may be challenging to measure directly, we believe that following trends and utilizing appropriate indicators can assist in developing targeted actions. These actions can steer the process in the right direction and maximize benefits, not only for younger generations but also for the economy and society as a whole.

BIBLIOGRAPHY

Bangemann, M. (1994). *Recommendations to the European Council Europe and the Global Information Society.*

Barns, S., Cosgrave, E., Acuto, M., & Mcneill, D. (2017). Digital infrastructures and urban governance. *Urban Policy and Research, 35*(1), 20–31. https://doi.org/10.1080/08111146.2016.1235032

Brennen, J. S., & Kreiss, D. (2016). *Digitalization. The international encyclopedia of communication theory and philosophy.* Wiley-Blackwell.

Charron, N. (2016). Diverging cohesion? Globalisation, state capacity and regional inequalities within and across European countries. *European Urban and Regional Studies, 23*(3), 355–373. https://doi.org/10.1177/0969776413512844

Dečman, M. (2018). The analysis of e-government services adoption and use in Slovenian information society between 2014 and 2017. *Central European Public Administration Review, 16*(2), 193–215. https://doi.org/10.17573/cepar.2018.2.10

European Commission, Directorate-General for Communications Networks, Content and Technology. (2022). eGovernment Benchmark 2022: Synchronising Digital Governments – Insight Report. Publications Office of the European Union. https://data.europa.eu/doi/10.2759/488218

eGovernment Benchmark 2022 Synchronising Digital Governments Analyze the Future. (2022).

European Commission. (2022). *Digital economy and society index – DESI.* European Comission, 0–3. https://digital-strategy.ec.europa.eu/en/library/digital-economy-and-society-index-desi-2022

Fetting, C. (2020). *The European Green Deal. ESDN Report*, December, 2(9), 53.

George, D., & Mallery, P. (2019). *IBM SPSS statistics 26 step by step: A simple guide and reference.* Routledge. https://doi.org/10.4324/9780429056765

Grillitsch, M., Asheim, B., & Trippl, M. (2018). Unrelated knowledge combinations: The unexplored potential for regional industrial path development. *Cambridge Journal of Regions, Economy and Society, 11*(2), 257–274. https://doi.org/10.1093/cjres/rsy012

Iammarino, S., Rodriguez-Pose, A., & Storper, M. (2019). Regional inequality in Europe: Evidence, theory and policy implications. *Journal of Economic Geography, 19*(2), 273–298. https://doi.org/10.1093/jeg/lby021

Isaksen, A., & Trippl, M. (2016). *Innovation drivers and regional innovation strategy* (D. Parrilli, R. Fitjar, & A. Rodriguez-Pose (Eds.); pp. 66–84). Routledge.

Janowski, T. (2016). Implementing sustainable development goals with digital government – Aspiration-capacity gap. *Government Information Quarterly, 33*(4), 603–613. https://doi.org/10.1016/j.giq.2016.12.001

Janssen, M., Brous, P., Estevez, E., Barbosa, L. S., & Janowski, T. (2020). Data governance: Organizing data for trustworthy artificial intelligence. *Government Information Quarterly, 37*(3), 101493. https://doi.org/10.1016/j.giq.2020.101493

Larsson, H., & Grönlund, Å. (2014). Future-oriented eGovernance: The sustainability concept in eGov research, and ways forward. *Government Information Quarterly, 31*(1), 137–149. https://doi.org/10.1016/j.giq.2013.07.004

March, P. W. (2010). Six sigma DMAIC quick reference. *Government Information Quarterly, 18*(2), 1–6. https://doi.org/10.1016/S0740-624X(01)00066-1

Megyesiova, S., & Lieskovska, V. (2018). Analysis of the sustainable development indicators in the OECD countries. *Sustainability (Switzerland), 10*(12). https://doi.org/10.3390/su10124554

OECD. (2003). *The E-Government Imperative,* OECD e-Government Studies, OECD Publishing, Paris, https://doi.org/10.1787/9789264101197-en.

OECD. (2018). *Bridging the Digital Gender Divide*: Include, upskill, innovate. OECD Publishing. https://eulacfoundation.org/system/files/digital_library/2023-07/bridging-the-digital-gender-divide.pdf

Piore, M. J., & Sabel, C. F. (1984). *The second industrial divide* (2nd ed.). Basic Books.

Putra, D. A. D., Jasmi, K. A., Basiron, B., Huda, M., Maseleno, A., Shankar, K., & Aminudin, N. (2018). Tactical steps for e-government development. *International Journal of Pure and Applied Mathematics*, *119*(15), 2251–2258.

Rodriguez-Pose, A. (2013). Do institutions matter for regional development? *Regional Studies*, *47*, 1034–1047.

Sangki, J. (2018). Vision of future e-government via new e-government maturity model: Based on Korea's e-government practices. *Telecommunications Policy*, *42*(10), 860–871. https://doi.org/10.1016/j.telpol.2017.12.002

United Nations E-Government Survey 2022. The Future of Digital Government. (2022). https://publicadministration.un.org/egovkb/en-us/

Valle-Cruz, D., Sandoval-Almazan, R., Ruvalcaba-Gomez, E. A., & Ignacio Criado, J. (2019). A review of artificial intelligence in government and its potential from a public policy perspective. In *ACM International Conference Proceeding Series*, 91–99. https://doi.org/10.1145/3325112.3325242

van Noordt, C., & Misuraca, G. (2022). Artificial intelligence for the public sector: Results of landscaping the use of AI in government across the European Union. *Government Information Quarterly*, *39*(6). https://doi.org/10.1016/j.giq.2022.101714

Van Noordt, C., & Misuraca, G. (2020). Evaluating the impact of artificial intelligence technologies in public services: Towards an assessment framework. In *ACM International Conference Proceeding Series, September*, 8–16. https://doi.org/10.1145/3428502.3428504

Veeramootoo, N., Nunkoo, R., & Dwivedi, Y. K. (2018). What determines success of an e-government service? Validation of an integrative model of e-filing continuance usage. *Government Information Quarterly*, *35*(2), 161–174. https://doi.org/10.1016/j.giq.2018.03.004

Vinuesa, R., Azizpour, H., Leite, I., Balaam, M., Dignum, V., Domisch, S., Felländer, A., Langhans, S. D., Tegmark, M., & Fuso Nerini, F. (2020). The role of artificial intelligence in achieving the Sustainable Development Goals. *Nature Communications*, *11*(1), 1–10. https://doi.org/10.1038/s41467-019-14108-y

Webster, F. (2006). The information society revisited. In *Handbook of new media: Social shaping and social consequences of ICTs* (pp. 443–457). https://doi.org/10.4135/9781446211304.n22

Welch, E. W., Hinnant, C. C., & Moon, M. J. (2005). Linking citizen satisfaction with e-government and trust in government. *Journal of Public Administration Research and Theory*, *15*(3), 371–391. https://doi.org/10.1093/jopart/mui021

Wirtz, B. W., Weyerer, J. C., & Geyer, C.. (2019). Artificial intelligence and the public sector—Applications and challenges. *International Journal of Public Administration*, *42*(7), 596–615. https://doi.org/10.1080/01900692.2018.1498103

Wirtz, B. W., Langer, P. F., & Fenner, C. (2021). Artificial intelligence in the public sector – A research agenda. *International Journal of Public Administration*, *44*(510), 1–26.

12 Artificial Intelligence, Energy, and Environment

Necmi Altin and Süleyman Emre Eyimaya

12.1 INTRODUCTION

Artificial intelligence (AI) is the ability of machines to perceive, synthesize, and infer information, as opposed to the natural intelligence exhibited by humans and non-human animals [Hasan & Hasan, 2023]. Speech recognition, computer vision, inter-language translation, and other mappings of inputs are a few examples of tasks where this is done. AI has become an important tool for solving complex problems in many fields. AI applications affect all areas of life, from health to social areas. In addition, with the increase in digitalization, the application areas of AI are constantly expanding. One of the critical areas that AI can contribute to is energy and the environment. By using AI in energy systems, it is possible to increase energy efficiency and cost and optimize renewable energy sources. While doing this, it is also possible to contribute to the green environment by reducing carbon emissions [Ahmad et al., 2021].

AI applications applied to an energy system have a very important effect on the performance of the energy system. Various AI applications have been developed to make the energy system more stable, reliable, and effective. AI technologies have been used in various research studies and industrial applications in the energy area, such as production and consumption predictions for different energy resources, control of ground source heat pumps, optimal determination and distribution of the generation units and their power, and energy management in smart buildings [Zhang et al., 2014].

In addition, AI applications are applied in different fields, such as modeling and optimization of multiple energy systems, energy monitoring in smart buildings, data-based energy modeling for buildings, short-term forecasting of wind and solar photovoltaic (PV) system potential, detection of damage in PV modules, and determination of biodiesel and engine characteristics. Different AI methods have been applied to solve different problems in energy applications such as [Tahmasebi & Hezarkhani, 2012, Senthilselvi et al., 2021; Hamdia et al., 2021]:

- Fuzzy Logic
- Genetic Algorithms
- Artificial Neural Networks
- Neural Fuzzy Logic Inference System
- Machine Learning

In order to use these methods, data is needed in the system. The data must be sufficient in number, be representative of the subject to be studied, and have sufficient variables. For instance, when working on renewable energy applications such as

 DOI: 10.1201/9781003640776-12

wind and solar energy, latitude, longitude, and other climate data must be collected to provide sufficient data. Therefore, there is a need to clearly define the parameters affecting the problem. To achieve healthy results in AI applications, it is important to define the variables, understand the physical basis of the problem, and determine all parameters that affect the problem.

Improving energy efficiency and optimizing energy consumption are also important areas that AI can be used in many ways. For instance, energy management systems supported with AI can monitor and manage energy usage and can identify potential energy saving opportunities. AI algorithms can also optimize the operation of various systems (or subsystems), such as heating, ventilation, and air conditioning (HVAC) systems; software configurations; electronic circuit designs; illumination; buildings; and computer systems, thereby reducing energy consumption [Siegmund et al., 2022]. AI can also be used in microgrids, which are small-scale power grids that can operate independently or collaboratively with other small power grids. Microgrids have their local generation and storage units. These systems are gaining popularity, particularly in remote and off-grid locations. With AI, the management of the energy production and distribution in a microgrid can become more efficient, stable, and flexible [Talaat et al., 2023].

Several studies have highlighted the potential of AI technologies in the energy industry [Wang et al., 2020; Dudnik et al., 2021; Cheng & Yu, 2019]. In the energy industry, studies are carried out to improve energy efficiency and power quality by using AI technologies [Chen et al., 2021; Ahmad et al., 2022]. A study has pointed out that AI can improve the accuracy of the measurement of power quality, an important aspect of the energy generation process. Accurate power quality analysis can lead to more reliable, efficient, and safe operation of power plants [Ibrahim & Morcos, 2002].

Renewable energy resources such as solar and wind energy conversion systems can also benefit from AI applications. For example, AI can be used to predict the possible generatable power of solar PV modules or wind turbines based on weather conditions, and thus, energy generation, use of storage units, and load planning can be optimized accordingly [Sabzehgar et al., 2020]. AI can also be used in the smart grid network to manage the distribution of electricity from renewable resources more effectively. Planning the renewable generation and storage units and determining the size and location of these units to achieve better utilization and decrease the cost is another area where AI can be used. Another aspect where AI can make a significant impact is the design and construction of buildings. AI algorithms can predict the potential energy use and consumption of a building before it's constructed [Baduge et al., 2022]. The design of the building can then be adjusted to optimize energy efficiency. Monitoring the energy use of buildings and providing feedback to occupants to encourage more energy-efficient behavior patterns is one other possible application for the AI.

The integration of AI in the energy industry is still in its early stages. However, there is significant potential for future developments. One area that AI could play a crucial role in is energy storage [He et al., 2022]. Energy storage is crucial in ensuring the stability and reliability of the power grid. AI can optimize energy storage systems by predicting energy demand and adjusting energy supply accordingly. One of the growing areas that can be potential application areas for AI is electric vehicles.

The adoption of electric vehicles is expected to grow significantly in the coming years. AI can be used to optimize the charging process of electric vehicles, thereby reducing the energy consumption of charging stations and their negative effects on the power system.

There has been a rise in interest in figuring out how AI may affect climate action as AI is used more widely in society. Researchers are developing a comprehensive and practical understanding of the various ways AI can impact climate change mitigation and adaptation strategies, both positively and negatively. Thus, AI can be clearly and consistently considered in long-term climate and energy projections, enabling the design of appropriate policies [Kaack et al., 2022]. Estimating macro-scale effects, identifying underlying dynamics and trends, and prioritizing actions to align AI with climate strategies can all be difficult. A methodical framework for classifying the various effects of AI on global greenhouse gas (GHG) emissions, including compute-related impacts, the immediate effects of AI applications, and the system-level changes AI causes, is given in Figure 12.1.

This chapter, entitled "Artificial Intelligence, Energy and Environment", will explain in detail the applications of AI in energy and its impact on the environment. First, the concept of AI will be explained, and some well-known AI technologies will be introduced. Then, AI applications in energy applications will be examined, advantages and disadvantages and application areas will be explained. The environmental impact of AI applications in the energy industry will also be explained in detail. While

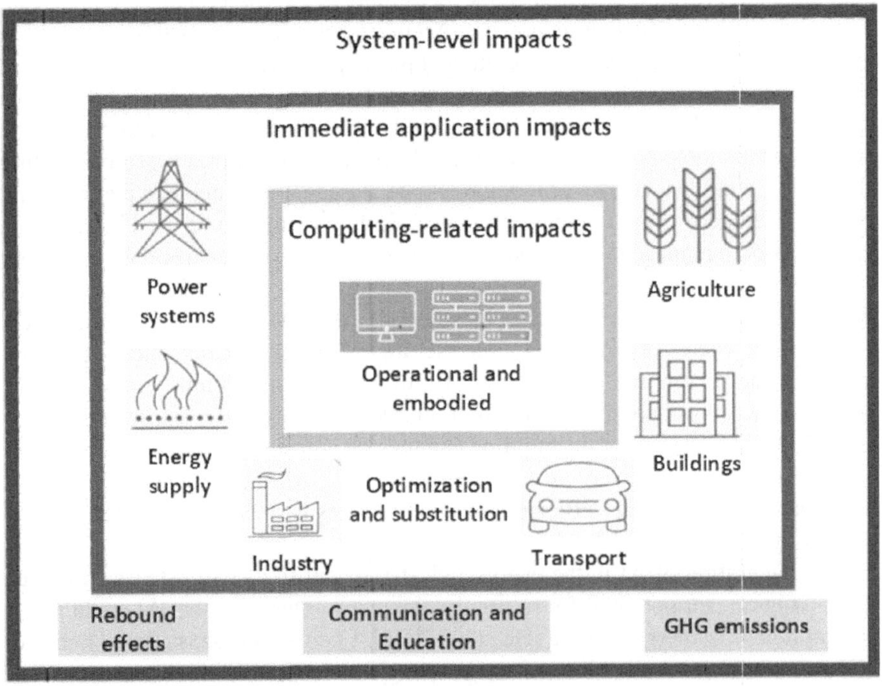

FIGURE 12.1 Framework for assessing impacts of AI on the greenhouse gas emission.

examining the latest trends, prospects and potential problems in this technology will be discussed. Finally, this section will be completed with the conclusion section.

12.2 ARTIFICIAL INTELLIGENCE (AI)

AI is the type of intelligence displayed by machines, as opposed to the natural intelligence displayed by animals and humans. AI has become a technology that closely affects industries, institutions, societies, and the future of people in all parts of life. AI is the driving force in the development of technologies, such as Big Data, robotics, autonomous systems, sensor technologies and the Internet of Things. AI will continue to be one of the most important tools that offer technological innovation in the foreseeable future.

A correct understanding of the concepts of intelligence and AI is very important to interpret the future impact of this technology more accurately. The term AI has undergone some changes since its beginning. The first ideas put forward to create intelligent machines or intelligent computer programs date back to the 1950s. Especially until the 1980s, the focus was on the computer's ability to think. Later, with the introduction of expert systems, the era of creating computers that behave like humans began. The development of some systems, software, and robots that imitate the characteristics of human intelligence and achieve human-level intelligence has begun to be presented as AI. Especially recently, it has also presented itself as a technology that develops autonomous systems that can make decisions on their own and operate without any human intervention.

AI has many application areas, as seen in Figure 12.2. With the improvements of AI technologies and computer systems, AI applications have successfully fulfilled

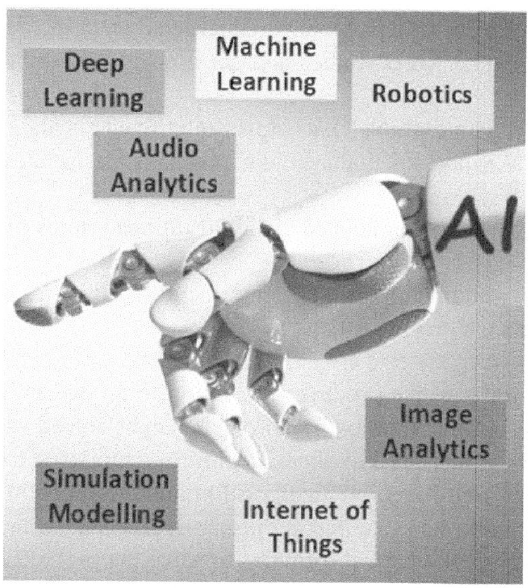

FIGURE 12.2 Applications of AI.

many challenging tasks. The current state of AI applications can be summarized as follows:

- It can produce solutions to complex problems that computers cannot solve with known methods.
- It can beat humans in chess.
- It can control a spacecraft.
- It can talk to humans and other machines with speech recognition systems.
- Robots can make comments, solve problems, establish relationships, make decisions, read text, make sense of it, perceive events, and prioritize them.

These achievements have led researchers to focus on new tasks as given below:

- Automatic language translation can be carried out on websites.
- AI can serve as a member of boards of directors.
- Virtual organs can be produced.
- It forms the basis for the creation of driverless (autonomous) vehicles.
- It can detect unusual situations (traffic accidents, wanted persons, etc.) with face/image/shape recognition systems.

The developments and progress achieved on these applications prove that successful results can be achieved in the following subjects soon:

- Ability to talk to each other (information protocols)
- Ability to aim at the same goal (purpose/sensor modeling)
- Socializing, helping each other and supporting each other (emotional intelligence)
- Ability to teach events to each other (intelligent teaching systems)
- Ability to conduct R&D studies and act innovatively (modeling scientific discoveries)
- Ability to perform multiple tasks alone (intelligent agents)
- Ability to take part in management positions in businesses (intelligent factors)
- Ability to create personalized education/training systems (intelligent teaching systems)
- Ability to communicate with the interlocutor in his/her native language (natural language processing)

Just as human intelligence produces a solution to an event, AI applications are trying to produce a similar solution. If a problem can be solved with any mathematical formula, that is, if there is a mathematical formula to solve the problem, a computer program is written based on an algorithm and the problem is solved, but this is not an AI application. AI is a computer program that is more unstructured, that is, it does not have any mathematical formulas to solve the problem. It can solve problems how people solve using their own intuition, knowledge, and experience. Many problems around us are already non-structural problems. For instance, there is no

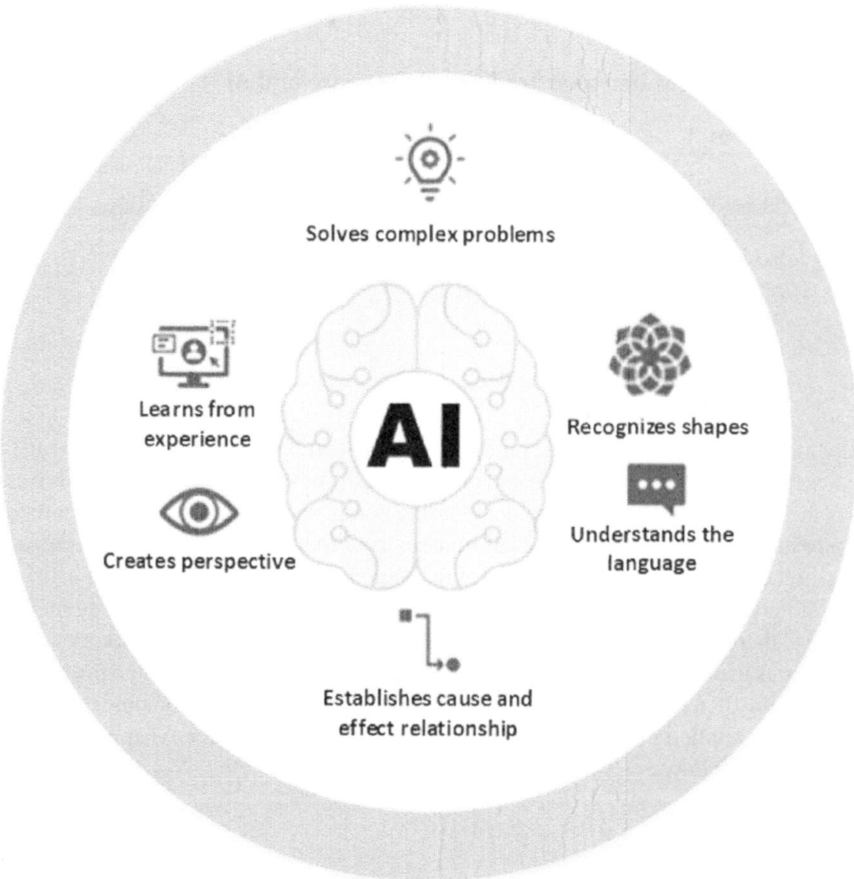

FIGURE 12.3 Decision-making ability of the artificial intelligence system.

formula that can be followed step by step in a recruitment process and yield the best employee results. A similar situation applies to many events. With AI, decisions are made as in Figure 12.3, using intuitive information and depending on the information in hand, without following any formula or step-by-step method as in traditional computer programs.

Table 12.1 presents the differences between the traditional program and AI comparatively. In traditional programs, there is mostly data and algorithms, and the data is displayed numerically. In AI, work is based on information rather than data. Although AI and machine learning work by collecting and relying on data, they are actually trying to access the information hidden behind the data. AI evaluates that information and makes some decisions.

In the field of AI, we encounter concepts, such as machine learning, deep learning, and statistical learning, which are related to each other, as shown in Figure 12.4. Machine learning is a branch of AI and deals with algorithms and statistical models that enable computer systems to learn. It enables a specific task to be performed

TABLE 12.1
Differences between Traditional Software and AI

Features	Traditional Software	AI
Source	Data	Information
Processing method	Algorithmic	Heuristic
Source structure	Numerical	Symbolic
Incomplete information processing ability	No	Yes
Ability to process ambiguous information	No	Yes
Program error	No	Yes
Behaving adaptively	No/Static	Yes/Dynamic

autonomously and without direct instructions. Statistical learning is a branch of statistics that emphasizes modeling and prediction. In summary, statistical learning can provide tools for modeling and understanding complex data sets. In general, statistics is a branch of mathematics that is ultimately used to collect, organize, analyze, and interpret data. Deep learning is a set of machine learning methods that use artificial neural networks. Artificial neural networks are considered a deep learning method because there are many layers between the input and output of these networks. Deep learning is used especially in speech recognition, translation, and image processing.

Defining different concepts in the field of AI is important to understand the framework of the applied methods. In this context, the definitions of the AI approaches are explained as follows:

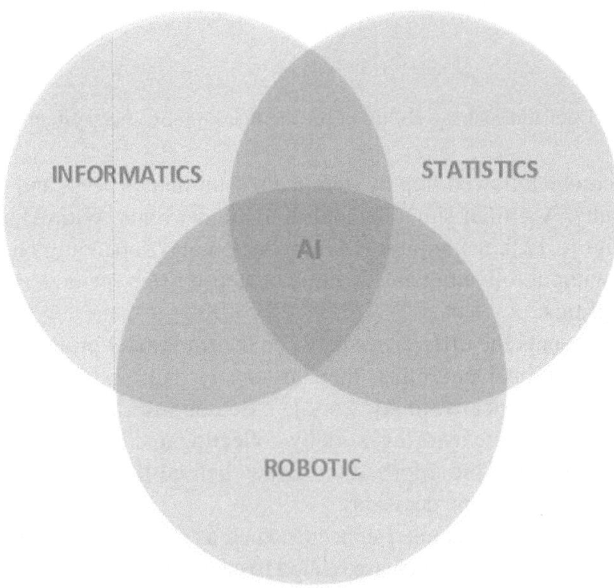

FIGURE 12.4 Topics related to AI.

Fuzzy Logic: It is a computational method that is based on human thought and operates by transforming this thought into mathematical functions. It provides the structure that we use in our daily lives and interprets our behavior. The basis of fuzzy logic is a fuzzy set. In the classical set approach, elements either belong to that set (meaning "1") or do not (meaning "0"). However, in the fuzzy logic approach, the belonging of the elements to that cluster (or membership values in fuzzy sets) varies between 0 and 1. Here, 0 is wrong and 1 is absolutely right. For instance, any temperature degree may be either hot or not hot compared to the classical set. According to the fuzzy set, this temperature has a certain degree of membership in the set it belongs to. As an example, the temperature value of 5°C may belong to the very low cluster with a membership degree of 0.5 and to the low cluster with a membership degree of 0.667. While modeling, sets and rules are defined by associating all inputs with outputs. In a way, it can be thought of as the way the mathematical cause-effect function works. Specific to the problem, input information is expressed using linguistic variables, such as very low, low, medium, high, and very high. Then, the input information is converted into fuzzy logic information with membership functions. The membership functions are represented in geometric shapes, such as triangles and trapezoids. The rule base consists of "IF-THEN" rules created to map the input-output relationship according to the expert knowledge. The inference engine generates the fuzzy output variable by using the fuzzy input information and the rule base.

The most common application area of fuzzy sets and fuzzy logic theory is control systems. Fuzzy logic control does not need the mathematical model of the plant and enables designers to design a control system by using expert knowledge. With this feature, it is widely used in the control of systems whose mathematical models are difficult to obtain.

Genetic Algorithm: It works by imitating the natural life process and is frequently used in optimization problems. The first point in imitating nature is that it is a repetitive process. Each iteration represents one generation for the genetic algorithm. The genetic algorithm searches by creating new generations until the termination condition is met. In each generation, genetic algorithm operators are applied again, and thus a new generation is created. Another point in imitating nature is expressed as the principle of "survival of those who adapt to the environment". The conditions that are meant by environment are determined by the objective function within the genetic algorithm, that is, the environment to which individuals must adapt is the objective function itself. Each individual forming the community has the opportunity to take part in the next generations and create new individuals to the extent that he/she can adapt to the environment, that is, the objective function. In fact, this is the way to transfer the knowledge to the next step (generation), and thus the best solution or results are obtained after some generations.

Artificial Neural Networks: Artificial neural networks are computer programs designed to automatically emulate certain cognitive functions of the human brain, such as the ability to generate and discover new information on their own. The mathematical modeling of the learning process using the human brain as an example led to the development of artificial neural networks. It mimics the design of biological neural networks in the brain as well as their capacity for learning, recollection, and generalization. Artificial neural networks use examples to carry out the learning process. Rules are established, and information about input and output is provided during learning. It is widely used in many fields, especially since its solutions provide successful results in nonlinear problems. It is used in credit scoring and algorithmic trading in the field of computational finance. Image processing, face recognition, gesture recognition, and object recognition studies are another important application area for artificial neural networks. It is also widely used in the fields of biology, health, energy, automotive, and aviation.

It consists of artificial nerve cells called neurons that are simple processing elements and connected to each other as in the human nervous system. Neurons are grouped as layers. An artificial neural network has at least two layers called input layer and output layer. The number of neurons in the input layer is equal to the number of inputs. Similarly, the number of neurons in the output layer is equal to the number of outputs. However, with these two layers, the learning, prediction and classification ability of the network is limited. Therefore, hidden layers are added between these two layers. The number of hidden layers and the number of neurons in each hidden layer are determined according to the problem. Many artificial neural network architectures and learning algorithms have been developed and applied to various applications.

Machine Learning: It is the process of machines that can perform logical operations, accepting the data obtained through observation and measurement methods as experience and producing meaningful relationships from these experiences through mathematical algorithms. Data sets correspond to past experiences, and thanks to learning algorithms, a model suitable for the problem to be solved is created from the relationships between the data and results.

The study of AI aims to develop a computer system that can simulate human intelligence. Algorithms used by the AI system take into account human intelligence. It includes deep learning neural networks and reinforcement learning algorithms for machine learning. A computer system can use historical data to predict the future or make specific decisions without being explicitly programmed thanks to machine learning. A machine learning model can produce accurate results or make predictions based on this data because machine learning makes extensive use of structured and semi-structured data. Machine learning algorithms are characterized as algorithms that allow computers to perform cognitive operations without being explicitly programmed. Algorithms that fall into this definition have historically replaced the hard-coded AI algorithms that emerged before. The feature that distinguishes machine learning from hard-coded symbolic AI algorithms is that the algorithm learns entirely from data.

12.3 AI IN ENERGY

The use of conventional fossil-based energy resources has contributed to a significant problem that the world is currently facing: global warming and climate change [Eyimaya et al., 2021; Tarigan, 2018; Thakur et al., 2017; Khan & Halder, 2016]. There is currently a trend to rely on renewable energy sources rather than conventional fossil-based resources as a result of the ongoing depletion of traditional energy resources and widespread concern over environmental pollution [Rehmani et al., 2018].

Due to the need to address climate change issues and ensure the effective use of current energy resources, strategies for the energy transition and sustainable development have become more prevalent in recent years. Modern infrastructures and technologies, as well as the active management and control of various energy resources, would become essential in this regard.

Attempts are being made to combine renewable resources into isolated microgrids to power remote areas far from the main power grid or to integrate them into the grid to increase efficiency, reliability, and stability. The integration of renewable energy resources has increased significantly in terms of strategic importance in solving energy problems. Integration of renewable resources faces numerous problems and challenges that need to be solved to reduce energy losses due to the diversity of renewable energy resources and the various factors that renewable energy resources depend on for energy generation [Polleux et al., 2022; Choudhury, 2022]. In addition, the irregular energy generation characteristics of renewable energy resources have caused some problems [Altin & Eyimaya, 2018]. The energy storage units have been installed to the energy systems to overcome the problems related to the irregular characteristics of renewable resources and improve the system efficiency, reliability, and power quality.

In energy systems that include renewable energy and distributed resources, problems related to the co-operation of these resources are being studied [Altin et al., 2023]. Active operation and control of energy systems with different types of demands and energy resources are very important in terms of cost-benefit efficiency. In order to pave the way for the active use of energy systems, advanced technologies such as AI have become a necessity, as well as efficient infrastructure. Technologies that communicate with the energy resources of the energy system are known as energy management systems.

Numerous distributed energy resources are combined in energy systems. These resources include synchronous generators, solar PV modules, energy storage devices, and wind turbines. While the energy system is benefiting from these different resources, they also come with a number of drawbacks, such as the need for complex energy management and control and the volatility, uncertainty, and unreliability of renewable energy resources. Energy management systems are intelligent automatic systems that contribute to reducing energy system costs as well as reducing/replacing energy consumption, for example, at critical moments. Even though the use of energy management systems may take other goals like lowering CO_2 emissions or self-sufficiency, they primarily use optimization techniques. Energy management systems can also control the grid connection of the system. It can enable grid-connected mode, where a bidirectional energy exchange can be obtained with the power grid, or stand-alone mode (also called islanded mode), where the system operates on its own. This capability has made microgrids an appealing option for enhancing energy efficiency, resilience, and sustainability. It also coincides with the growth of renewable energy resources and distributed power generation [Aberilla et al., 2020]. AI technologies are a promising solution for realizing and improving energy management in energy systems [Albarakati et al., 2021]. AI is one of the main components that make renewable energy resources a key component of efficient energy systems. The integration of distributed resources and AI in energy systems is shown in Figure 12.5.

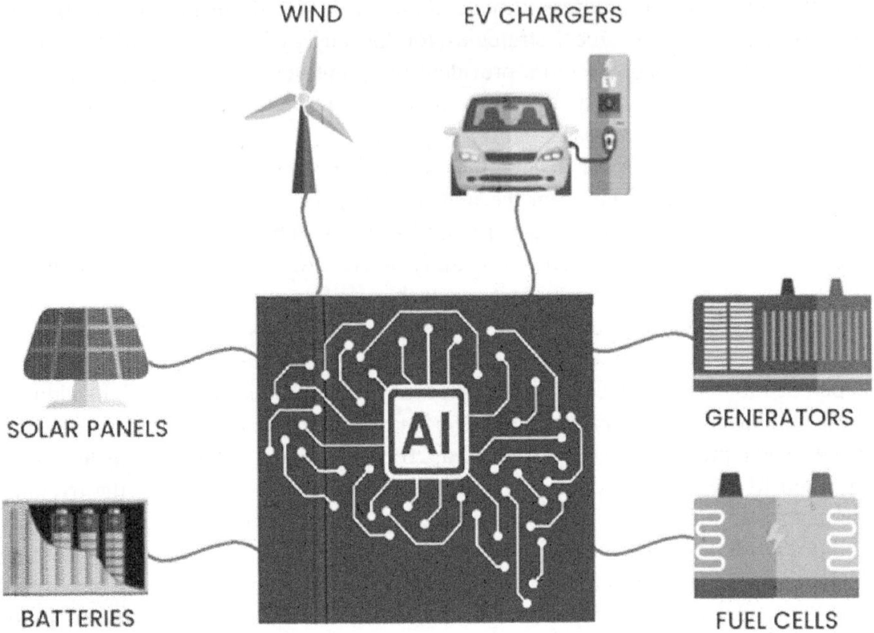

FIGURE 12.5 AI and distributed energy resources.

The use of various AI-based algorithms in energy systems for a variety of tasks, including energy management, load forecasting, renewable energy forecasting, fault detection and classification, and cyber-attack detection, has been discussed in the literature [Esmalifalak et al., 2014]. In the literature, it has been discussed how many AI-based algorithms can be used in microgrids. These studies mainly concentrated on significant contemporary issues like managing supply and demand in the energy sector, estimating the load and power produced by renewable energy sources, cyber security, fault detection, and fault classification [Alimi et al., 2020]. Additionally, uses of AI techniques in power systems have been investigated within the scope of demand-side management of energy [Antonopoulos et al., 2020]. Natural factors like wind speed and solar irradiation make it difficult for renewable energy sources used in power systems to maintain a balance between constantly changing production power and demand power that is constantly changing over time. However, using AI in power systems is not a viable option for achieving this balance. Energy management, load factor, demand response, and fault detection are just a few of the parameters that have been reviewed for smart grids or power systems [Zhang et al., 2018].

AI is also used to strengthen the methods used in energy systems. For instance, the limitations of centralized control method are eliminated by using artificial neural networks in an energy system with various renewable resources [Albarakati et al., 2021]. As more applications are developed and more research is done in this field, AI technologies in microgrids are promising. One of the major trends is the fusion of blockchain and AI technologies, which enables the safe and open transfer of data and energy between microgrids and the main grid. Peer-to-peer energy trading and the ability for microgrid owners to profit from their excess energy are two additional benefits of this strategy. Another trend is the use of explainable AI, which can make AI-based systems easier to understand, more transparent, and more trustworthy. Additionally, AI technologies are used in the microgrid for energy management, control, optimization, and monitoring [Singh & Lather, 2022].

12.3.1 AI in Renewable Energy and Energy Systems

Many renewable energy resources are used together in an energy system. In order to use renewable energy resources efficiently, all components of these resources must be controlled effectively. AI technologies are widely used to control these systems. In the microgrid system, which includes many renewable energy resources, a system that controls the efficient operation of these resources is designed [Altın & Eyimaya, 2023]. Energy systems that include renewable energy resources use machine learning, deep learning, and other AI algorithms to analyze large volumes of data generated by sensors and other devices [Mohammadi et al., 2022]. They can also be used for prediction, optimization, control, and monitoring in systems containing renewable energies.

- *Predictive Analytics*: Predictive analytics is a subset of data analytics that analyzes historical data and forecasts future trends, patterns, and events using machine learning and other AI techniques. Based on weather forecasts, geographic location, seasonality, and other factors, predictive analytics can be used in energy systems to forecast the output of renewable energy resources like solar and wind power. The operation of the system can then be optimized, and the need for backup generators and other non-renewable resources can be reduced [Elmouatamid, 2020]. In addition, production and consumption power predictions are made in energy systems, ensuring efficient operation of the system. For instance, energy consumption in agriculture is predicted by using AI and mathematical models in Bolandnazar et al. (2020).
- *Optimization*: Optimization is the process of finding the best solution to a problem for certain constraints and goals. Optimization in energy systems can be used to minimize installation cost and energy costs, to improve the power quality, to reduce carbon emissions, and to increase the efficiency, the reliability and durability of renewable energy resources. In addition, optimization algorithms can also be used to balance energy supply and demand in real time, which is critical to system operation [Abdolrasol et al., 2021].
- *Control*: Control refers to the ability to manage and regulate the behavior of renewable energy resources and other system components in energy systems. AI-based control systems can predict the energy demand and generation capacity of systems and adjust the power output of renewable energy resources accordingly. These systems can also detect and respond to emergencies, such as power outages, equipment failures, and natural disasters.

Detection of critical and non-critical loads in systems and how the system will operate in emergency situations can be controlled by AI. In addition, the relationship and control of energy storage systems with renewable energy sources in the system have also been discussed.

- *Monitoring*: Monitoring is the process of keeping an eye on and evaluating the effectiveness and condition of renewable energy resources and the various parts of the energy system. AI-based monitoring systems can spot anomalies like system failures, cyberattacks, and device malfunctions and initiate the proper actions, like shutdowns, preventive maintenance, and backup systems [Mallesham et al., 2012].

Optimization algorithms are commonly used to solve the problems related to the energy management because energy management is designed to minimize or maximize an objective depending on the objectives of the parties involved in the energy system and the asset management strategy. According to the kind of problem, a variety of optimization techniques have been introduced. Convex and non-convex optimization techniques can be broadly categorized into two groups. The type of optimization technique can be properly chosen based on the characteristics of the problem. Convex problems predominate in energy management, or problems are defined in such a way that convex methods can be applied to solve them. This is because convex problems provide better convergence performance compared to non-convex problems.

Due to the nature of renewable energy resources, there may also be a lot of uncertainty in energy system operation. For example, intermittent renewable components such as wind turbines and solar PV units and their unpredictable demand can create these uncertainties. However, these uncertainties can be eliminated through some well-known mathematical and statistical techniques when defining optimization problems for energy management. Three different types of optimization methods—deterministic, stochastic, and robust—have been proposed to analyze the effect of uncertainty in data. Robust and stochastic optimization solutions are thought to be the most effective techniques in energy management problems, which are illustrated in detail in the following subsections, even though the deterministic approach to defining an optimization problem may be useful for comparing the results of the problem with other approaches.

Every potential input led to a single output in deterministic problems. Variations in wind speed or solar irradiation over time, for example, could have a significant impact on the output power of wind turbines or PV systems. Therefore, the amount of energy produced by these renewable resources would vary for different values of wind speed and solar irradiation. The power generation function of these renewable energy sources, however, could be described as deterministic, which means that the output power of wind and PV units is taken into account as certain values for any wind speed and solar irradiation. Additionally, this approach might be helpful if the goal is to understand the major system operating principles under a specific circumstance.

The issue of managing energy could be presented by a statistical objective function in stochastic optimization. By keeping this in mind, it is possible to model the problem's uncertain parameters as the well-known probability distribution functions, such as the output power of renewable energy resources. Because renewable resources like solar irradiation and wind energy differ in their nature, these distribution functions may be different. They might also differ because of the uncertainties resulting from consumers' stochastic behavior, including characteristics of load profiles, drivers' actions, and charging habits. However, since their sources are largely predictable, all these uncertainties can be regarded as the most common distribution functions.

In order to serve as an alternative for modeling problems with uncertain parameters, the robust optimization method has been introduced and used in numerous studies as one of the most effective approaches to energy management. When there is a limited amount of data and a number of uncertainties, robust optimization is used to solve energy management problems. Unlike stochastic optimization, which considers multiple scenarios, this optimization method only takes into account one scenario, so no probability distribution function is required. When it comes to uncertain situations during the optimization process, this scenario is thought to be the worst case. The worst-case scenario in energy management issues is the one that is thought to result in the most serious consequences when it actually occurs. In other words, it is assumed that the uncertain parameters are in their worst state when using this method. This could help in developing a realistic paradigm for the actual situation, and if possible, it could enhance the optimization's performance in comparison to stochastic techniques.

12.4 THE IMPACT OF AI APPLICATIONS IN ENERGY ON THE ENVIRONMENT

The effects of energy on the environment have been the subject of research for years in literature. Efforts are being made to design systems that do not neglect protecting the environment while using energy efficiently. AI applications have also been studied for this subject for years. However, with the increasing use of AI, the growth of data centers and the complexity of algorithms also increase energy consumption. Therefore, AI systems have an energy cost. Research on AI applications also brings up various research issues in terms of energy. AI's provision of efficiency in energy production, energy saving, and control of consumed energy have become the main research topics.

When the policy documents published in recent years are examined, a green agenda (Green Agreement) published by the European Union in December 2019 stands out [A European Green Deal, European Commission, 2019]. There are many achievements under various subheadings in the green agenda, which essentially aims at a prosperous and healthy world and providing better conditions for future generations:

- Clean air, clean water, healthy soil, and biodiversity;
- Renovated and energy-efficient buildings;
- Healthy and accessible food opportunities;
- Greater use of public transport;

- Cleaner energy and the use of cutting-edge innovative clean technologies;
- The use of longer-lasting products that can be repaired, recycled, and reused; and
- Expansion of a globally competitive and resilient industry.

The eight topics identified to achieve these outcomes are as follows: climate, energy, agriculture, industry, environment and oceans, transport, finance and regional development, and research and innovation. When we look at the determined actions, almost all of them are directly or indirectly related to energy. In parallel with the green agenda published by the European Union, the UK published its innovation strategy document in July 2021 [UK Innovation Strategy, 2021]. Following this, a new strategy document called "Innovate UK" was published in the UK in August 2021 regarding the industrialization of AI applications [Ipsos MORI, 2021]. Finally, in September 2021, a new expanded AI strategy was published in the UK [National AI Strategy, 2023]. In this expanded document, a lot of emphasis is placed on energy and there are important topics on energy. Energy has been put forward as one of the priority areas in AI, and they have tried to determine some application areas related to it. The prominent issues regarding energy in the AI strategy document can be summarized as follows:

- Developing innovative technologies such as AI for energy;
- Rapidly increasing the efficiency of energy systems and reducing emissions related to climate change with advances in AI;
- Possible AI applications related to energy and climate change;
- Machine vision for monitoring the environment;
- Forecasting electricity production and demand and using machine learning to control its distribution around the grid;
- Data analysis to identify inefficiencies in carbon-intensive industries;
- AI applications to analyze complex systems such as climate models.

The report also shares the results of research conducted by Microsoft and PwC. Accordingly, it is stated that a 4% contribution to the green economy can be made by using AI in carbon emission and energy saving studies. If this application is expanded further, it is estimated that it could contribute around 4.5% to the world's gross national product. According to the report in this strategy document, energy expenditures can be reduced by up to 25% by optimizing electricity and therefore energy systems with AI. In October 2021, in parallel with the green agendas in the USA and Europe, the "net zero strategy" was published in the UK. The concept of "Green Industrial Revolution" was used here for the first time in the world. The concept of the Green Industrial Revolution was essentially put forward as an alternative to the fourth industrial revolution (Industry 4.0) and digital transformation. The Green Industrial Revolution includes suggestions for reducing carbon emissions by using AI in many different fields, especially energy. With this strategy document, 2030 and 2050 targets are defined. Digitalization and smart applications are no longer a priority, and instead, the goal of becoming greener and directing the economy in this way comes to the fore.

There is a mixed effect in the relationship between AI and climate change. AI can both help and harm the environment. While companies use AI to increase factory efficiency and reduce energy costs, training AI algorithms requires a lot of energy. The energy consumption of AI has reached levels that may cause environmental problems. Data centers and large AI models consume large amounts of energy and have harmful effects on the environment. From this perspective, questions arise about whether AI reduces the carbon footprint and whether AI helps or harms the environment. Companies can use AI to help the environment, including preventing forest fires and reducing factory waste, but the operation of the AI algorithm causes a carbon footprint.

Weather and climate forecasting is very important in energy production. Weather and climate change forecasting uses scientific methods to predict the future state of the atmosphere. While weather forecasting covers short-term (a few hours or days) changes, climate forecasting, on the other hand, also covers long-term (months, years, or decades) changes. Weather and climate change forecasting plays an important role in many areas such as natural disasters that affect people's lives, agriculture, energy, transportation, and health. There are many studies on AI technologies used in weather and climate change forecasting. Weather forecasting is done using mathematical models based on the physical laws of the atmosphere. Supercomputers are required to solve these models. However, weather forecasts may not be completely accurate due to the limitations of the models and the lack of data. Therefore, it is possible to use AI technologies in weather forecasting. Similarly, climate change prediction is made using mathematical models that take into account the effects of human activities on the atmosphere, such as greenhouse gas emissions. It also requires supercomputers to solve these models. However, due to the uncertainties of the models and the inadequacy of the data, climate change predictions may not be completely accurate. Therefore, it is possible to benefit from AI technologies in climate change prediction.

Energy efficiency is the use of energy resources in a way that provides the highest benefit with the least loss and waste. Energy efficiency is an important issue both economically and environmentally. AI is used in different areas to reduce energy consumption and save energy. AI saves energy by analyzing energy consumption patterns and optimizes the distribution of energy resources. Smart buildings equipped with AI increase energy efficiency by automatically adjusting systems such as heating, cooling, and lighting. AI can also save energy by controlling energy-consuming devices. For example, a system developed with AI reduces the electricity bill by intelligently managing the operating hours and power levels of electrical devices at home. In addition, AI can save energy by optimizing energy-consuming vehicles. For example, a system developed with AI increases fuel efficiency by analyzing the speed, route, and fuel consumption of vehicles.

In addition, AI is used in different fields to increase energy generation and reduce energy loss. AI is improving the production and storage of renewable energy sources. For example, wind turbines developed with AI produce maximum energy by predicting wind speed and direction. In addition, smart grids supported by AI prevent energy loss by balancing electricity demand and supply. AI also increases nuclear energy efficiency. A system developed with AI produces the most efficient configuration by optimizing the operating parameters of the nuclear reactor. AI can also increase the efficiency of fossil fuels. For example, a system developed with AI optimizes production by monitoring the condition of oil wells.

AI is used in different fields to reduce waste production and develop waste prevention strategies. AI saves materials and energy by optimizing production processes. Yarn production, fabric production and coloring are carried out with AI-based methods in the textile industry. Thus, fabric waste is reduced by improving the processing processes of the textile industry and optimizing textile production [Sikka et al., 2024]. AI can prevent waste by analyzing consumption habits. By using an AI-based system, food production and distribution processes can be managed efficiently, and operational competence can also be improved. AI can improve the quality of restaurants, cafes, online delivery food chains, hotels, and food outlets by increasing production using different adaptation algorithms for sales forecasting. AI can significantly improve packaging, extend shelf life, provide menu combinations using AI algorithms, and ensure food safety by creating a more transparent supply chain management system. In addition, waste is separated at the source with AI, and smart garbage bins can recognize waste with image recognition technology and can be recycled or separated organically [Kumar et al., 2021].

12.5 CONCLUSION

In this chapter, the applications of AI in the field of energy and its impact on the environment are explained in detail. First, the concept of AI was discussed, and some well-known AI technologies were introduced. Then, AI applications in energy applications were examined; their advantages, disadvantages, and application areas were explained. The environmental impact of AI applications in energy was also discussed in detail. While the latest trends were examined, prospects and possible problems with this technology were also discussed. The transformative potential of AI in the energy sector will continue to increase day by day. New applications and new beneficiary areas will arise with the increasing adaptation of AI technologies in energy applications. Additionally, AI will continue its critical role in solving environmental challenges.

BIBLIOGRAPHY

A European Green Deal, European Commission. (2023, September 25). Accessed https://commission.europa.eu/strategy-and-policy/priorities-2019-2024/european-green-deal_en

Abdolrasol, M. G., Mohamed, R., Hannan, M. A., Al-Shetwi, A. Q., Mansor, M., & Blaabjerg, F. (2021). Artificial neural network based particle swarm optimization for microgrid optimal energy scheduling. *IEEE Transactions on Power Electronics*, *36*(11), 12151–12157.

Aberilla, J. M., Gallego-Schmid, A., Stamford, L., & Azapagic, A. (2020). Design and environmental sustainability assessment of small-scale off-grid energy systems for remote rural communities. *Applied Energy*, *258*, 114004.

Ahmad, T., Zhang, D., Huang, C., Zhang, H., Dai, N., Song, Y., & Chen, H. (2021). Artificial intelligence in sustainable energy industry: Status Quo, challenges and opportunities. *Journal of Cleaner Production*, *289*, 125834.

Ahmad, T., Zhu, H., Zhang, D., Tariq, R., Bassam, A., Ullah, F., …, & Alshamrani, S. S. (2022). Energetics systems and artificial intelligence: Applications of industry 4.0. *Energy Reports*, *8*, 334–361.

Albarakati, A. J., Boujoudar, Y., Azeroual, M., Jabeur, R., Aljarbouh, A., El Moussaoui, H., …, & Ouaaline, N. (2021). Real-time energy management for DC microgrids using artificial intelligence. *Energies*, *14*(17), 5307.

Alimi, O. A., Ouahada, K., & Abu-Mahfouz, A. M. (2020). A review of machine learning approaches to power system security and stability. *IEEE Access*, *8*, 113512–113531.

Altin, N., & Eyimaya, S. E. (2018). A combined energy management algorithm for wind turbine/battery hybrid system. *Journal of Electronic Materials*, *47*, 4430–4436.

Altin, N., & Eyimaya, S. E. (2023, June). *Artificial intelligence applications for energy management in microgrid.* 11th International Conference on Smart Grid, Paris, 1–6.

Altin, N., Eyimaya, S. E., & Nasiri, A. (2023). Multi-agent-based controller for microgrids: An overview and case study. *Energies*, *16*(5), 2445.

Antonopoulos, I., Robu, V., Couraud, B., Kirli, D., Norbu, S., Kiprakis, A., …, & Wattam, S. (2020). Artificial intelligence and machine learning approaches to energy demand-side response: A systematic review. *Renewable and Sustainable Energy Reviews*, *130*, 109899.

Baduge, S. K., Thilakarathna, S., Perera, J. S., Arashpour, M., Sharafi, P., Teodosio, B., …, & Mendis, P. (2022). Artificial intelligence and smart vision for building and construction 4.0: Machine and deep learning methods and applications. *Automation in Construction*, *141*, 104440.

Bolandnazar, E., Rohani, A., & Taki, M. (2020). Energy consumption forecasting in agriculture by artificial intelligence and mathematical models. *Energy Sources, Part A: Recovery, Utilization, and Environmental Effects*, *42*(13), 1618–1632.

Chen, C., Hu, Y., Karuppiah, M., & Kumar, P. M. (2021). Artificial intelligence on economic evaluation of energy efficiency and renewable energy technologies. *Sustainable Energy Technologies and Assessments*, *47*, 101358.

Cheng, L., & Yu, T. (2019). A new generation of AI: A review and perspective on machine learning technologies applied to smart energy and electric power systems. *International Journal of Energy Research*, *43*(6), 1928–1973.

Choudhury, S. (2022). Review of energy storage system technologies integration to microgrid: Types, control strategies, issues, and future prospects. *Journal of Energy Storage*, *48*, 103966.

Dudnik, O., Vasiljeva, M., Kuznetsov, N., Podzorova, M., Nikolaeva, I., Vatutina, L., …, & Ivleva, M. (2021). Trends, impacts, and prospects for implementing artificial intelligence technologies in the energy industry: The implication of open innovation. *Journal of Open Innovation: Technology, Market, and Complexity*, *7*(2), 155.

Elmouatamid, A. (2020). MAPCAST: An adaptive control approach using predictive analytics for energy balance in micro-grid systems. *International Journal of Renewable Energy Research*, *10*(2), 945–954.

Esmalifalak, M., Liu, L., Nguyen, N., Zheng, R., & Han, Z. (2014). Detecting stealthy false data injection using machine learning in smart grid. *IEEE Systems Journal*, *11*(3), 1644–1652.

Eyimaya, S. E., Altin, N., & Bal, G. (2021, July). *Design of an energy management system with power fluctuation mitigation capability for PV/wind hybrid renewable energy sources.* 13th International Conference on Electronics, Computers and Artificial Intelligence, Pitesti, 1–6.

Hamdia, K. M., Zhuang, X., & Rabczuk, T. (2021). An efficient optimization approach for designing machine learning models based on genetic algorithm. *Neural Computing and Applications*, *33*, 1923–1933.

Hasan, M., & Hasan, F. (2023). Relationship between artificial intelligence and human intelligence. *International Journal of Research and Analytical Reviews*, *10*(3), 993–996.

He, Z., Guo, W., & Zhang, P. (2022). Performance prediction, optimal design and operational control of thermal energy storage using artificial intelligence methods. *Renewable and Sustainable Energy Reviews, 156*, 111977.

Ibrahim, W. A., & Morcos, M. M. (2002). Artificial intelligence and advanced mathematical tools for power quality applications: A survey. *IEEE Transactions on Power Delivery, 17*(2), 668–673.

Ipsos MORI, 2021. Impact review of Innovate UK's AI-related activity (2023, September 25). Accessed https://www.ukri.org/wp-content/uploads/2021/08/UKRI-190821-ImpactReviewAIPortfolio-InterimReport.pdf

Kaack, L. H., Donti, P. L., Strubell, E., Kamiya, G., Creutzig, F., & Rolnick, D. (2022). Aligning artificial intelligence with climate change mitigation. *Nature Climate Change, 12*(6), 518–527.

Khan, I., & Halder, P. K. (2016). Electrical energy conservation through human behavior change: Perspective in Bangladesh. *International Journal of Renewable Energy Research, 6*(1), 43–52.

Kumar, I., Rawat, J., Mohd, N., & Husain, S. (2021). Opportunities of artificial intelligence and machine learning in the food industry. *Journal of Food Quality, 2021*, 1–10.

Mallesham, G., Mishra, S., & Jha, A. N. (2012, July). *Automatic generation control of microgrid using artificial intelligence techniques*. IEEE Power and Energy Society General Meeting, California, 1–8.

Mohammadi, E., Alizadeh, M., Asgarimoghaddam, M., Wang, X., & Simões, M. G. (2022). A review on application of artificial intelligence techniques in microgrids. *IEEE Journal of Emerging and Selected Topics in Industrial Electronics, 3*(4), 878–890.

National AI Strategy. (2023, September 25). Accessed https://www.gov.uk/government/publications/national-ai-strategy

Polleux, L., Guerassimoff, G., Marmorat, J. P., Sandoval-Moreno, J., & Schuhler, T. (2022). An overview of the challenges of solar power integration in isolated industrial microgrids with reliability constraints. *Renewable and Sustainable Energy Reviews, 155*, 111955.

Rehmani, M. H., Reisslein, M., Rachedi, A., Erol-Kantarci, M., & Radenkovic, M. (2018). Integrating renewable energy resources into the smart grid: Recent developments in information and communication technologies. *IEEE Transactions on Industrial Informatics, 14*(7), 2814–2825.

Sabzehgar, R., Amirhosseini, D. Z., & Rasouli, M. (2020). Solar power forecast for a residential smart microgrid based on numerical weather predictions using artificial intelligence methods. *Journal of Building Engineering, 32*, 101629.

Senthilselvi, A., Duela, J. S., Prabavathi, R., & Sara, D. (2021). Performance evaluation of adaptive neuro fuzzy system (ANFIS) over fuzzy inference system (FIS) with optimization algorithm in de-noising of images from salt and pepper noise. *Journal of Ambient Intelligence and Humanized Computing*, 1–6. https://link.springer.com/article/10.1007/s12652-021-03024-z#citeas

Siegmund, N., Dorn, J., Weber, M., Kaltenecker, C., & Apel, S. (2022). Green configuration: Can artificial intelligence help reduce energy consumption of configurable software systems?. *Computer, 55*(3), 74–81.

Sikka, M. P., Sarkar, A., & Garg, S. (2024). Artificial intelligence (AI) in textile industry operational modernization. *Research Journal of Textile and Apparel, 28*(1), 67–83.

Singh, P., & Lather, J. S. (2022). Artificial neural network-based dynamic power management of a DC microgrid: A hardware-in-loop real-time verification. *International Journal of Ambient Energy, 43*(1), 1730–1738.

Tahmasebi, P., & Hezarkhani, A. (2012). A hybrid neural networks-fuzzy logic-genetic algorithm for grade estimation. *Computers & Geosciences, 42*, 18–27.

Talaat, M., Elkholy, M. H., Alblawi, A., & Said, T. (2023). Artificial intelligence applications for microgrids integration and management of hybrid renewable energy sources. *Artificial Intelligence Review, 56*, 1–55.

Tarigan, E. (2018). Simulation and feasibility studies of rooftop PV system for university campus buildings in Surabaya, Indonesia. *International Journal of Renewable Energy Research*, *8*(2), 895–908.

Thakur, A., Kumar, L., Romana, H. K., & Malik, R. K. (2017). Energy consumption attributes in residential buildings-a case study of replacing conventional electrical appliances with energy efficient appliances. *International Journal of Renewable Energy Research (IJRER)*, *7*(4), 1950–1955.

UK Innovation Strategy. 2021. (2023, September 25). Accessed https://www.gov.uk/government/publications/uk-innovation-strategy-leading-the-future-by-creating-it

Wang, B., Yang, Z., Xuan, J., & Jiao, K. (2020). Crises and opportunities in terms of energy and AI technologies during the COVID-19 pandemic. *Energy and AI*, *1*, 100013.

Zhang, Y., Balochian, S., Agarwal, P., Bhatnagar, V., & Housheya, O. J. (2014). Artificial intelligence and its applications. *Mathematical Problems in Engineering*, 840491, 1–10.

Zhang, D., Han, X., & Deng, C. (2018). Review on the research and practice of deep learning and reinforcement learning in smart grids. *CSEE Journal of Power and Energy Systems*, *4*(3), 362–370.

13 Revamping Agricultural Entrepreneurship through Artificial Intelligence

A Sustainability Perspective

Pushpam Singh, Madhuri Yadav, and Sukanta Kumar Baral

13.1 INTRODUCTION

The agriculture sector being, the source of rural development, provides a strong basis for addressing agricultural entrepreneurship. For generations, it has served as a backbone of the global economy, ensuring worldwide sustainability (Arafat et al., 2020). The World Bank data shows that the agriculture sector contributes around 4% of global gross domestic product (GDP). Specifically in underdeveloped and highly impoverished areas, entrepreneurial agriculture possesses the potential to create value-added benefits through employment creation. Although early research on entrepreneurship in the 19th century focused mostly on the agricultural sector, the empirical research in this area has been ignored for a long time and instead concentrated on areas like manufacturing, high technology, and service. In general, agriculture was considered a low-tech sector with little dynamics (Dias et al., 2019). The deterioration of employment rates in many developing nations has drawn more attention to an expansion of agricultural entrepreneurship as it has a favourable long-term impact on employment (Saghaian et al., 2022). It is estimated that there will be 8.6 billion people in the globe by 2030, according to the United Nations Department of Economic and Social Affairs, and if this increasing population is not effectively managed, the economy will suffer severely. To sustain the population, the agricultural sector needs to be structured effectively for which innovative technology would serve best to rejuvenate agricultural entrepreneurship. Modern digital technologies are rapidly evolving into every facet of our lives and are an inevitable core of enterprise. Artificial intelligence (AI) has revolutionized the practical implications of current entrepreneurial studies and aided strategic advancements (Li et al., 2022). As there are an increasing number of obstacles to the agriculture sector for its resources, the policies and actions should prioritize meeting the needs to ensure economic, social, and environmental sustainability. A digital revolution is an approach that drives the transformation

 DOI: 10.1201/9781003640776-13

of agricultural activities by influencing factors (Hrustek, 2020). In agriculture, the most significant benefit of contemporary technology is the eradication of information discrepancies by giving stakeholders the ability to retrieve information, which subsequently enhances accountability and fosters the effective exchange of information among stakeholders in the value chain at cheaper expenses (Kumar et al., 2023). Employing digital solutions to decrease manual and paper processing or data entry errors will lower operational and transaction expenses. Increased market accessibility through direct connections between farmers and customers through AI will reduce the need for middlemen, improve the price of farmers' produce, and provide savings to consumers. Increasing access to credit for farmers who previously lacked it by assessing their creditworthiness using alternative data can be rectified through AI (Goh, 2022). By integrating digital technology, the agricultural sector is set to undergo the fourth revolution, or "Agriculture 4.0", which will make it increasingly effective and environmentally friendly. Various technological breakthroughs have been devised in the field of agriculture to enhance sustainability and optimize agricultural practices to achieve higher productivity (Javaid et al., 2022). The fourth revolution in agriculture will build a value network that incorporates the enterprise, its customers, and other participants through the use of technological advancements in agricultural operations and alterations in the way individuals work (Sott et al., 2020). The implementation of digital systems such as the Internet of Things (IoT) and AI can enhance the agricultural sector by providing more precision and understanding of the obtained data and executing agricultural practices accurately by reducing manual work (Subeesh & Mehta, 2021). The agriculture sector still has a lot of potential to explore how AI applications can influence agricultural processes, practices, and the industry as a whole. AI holds the capacity to execute internal operations of agriculture, such as crop harvesting, quality upgradation, production volume increment, cost saving, and data compilation from smart sensors (Alreshidi, 2019). The targets set by the UN for sustainable development pertain to the notion of accurate, enhanced, and smart agriculture for better infrastructure, ethical resource utilization, and environmental conservation. Thus, entrepreneurial agriculture and sustainability are gradually picking up pace in people's eyes and are being given more importance in their research and execution (Sargani et al., 2020).

Agricultural entrepreneurship has previously been researched under different contexts by numerous authors, addressing its economic impact, agriculture training initiatives, policy framework, and unemployment mitigation. However, the studies examining AI practices in agricultural enterprises and their calls for action to revamp agricultural entrepreneurship for sustainable viability are lacking in the existing literature. This systematic review intends to provide a thorough examination of currently published articles on AI approaches used in agricultural processes. It strives to outline a research plan and provide a framework of reference for related subsequent research. This study reviews the present scenario of agricultural entrepreneurship as well as the extent to which AI has been adopted in current entrepreneurial activities. It also examines the advances associated with AI that could help revive this sector and promote a sustainable economy. The design of the research objectives has been driven by the necessity for a thorough comprehension of AI applications in the field of agricultural entrepreneurship. The additional contents of this study have been organized into sections. After a brief introduction, the research objectives of this study are presented in Section 13.2. The methodology of the research is discussed in Section 13.3, results and discussion are discussed in Section 13.4, and the conclusion is delivered in Section 13.5.

13.2 OBJECTIVES OF THE STUDY

- To scrutinize the current state of research about AI in the context of agricultural entrepreneurship;
- To determine the roles of AI in enhancing agricultural entrepreneurship.

13.3 RESEARCH METHODOLOGY

This study employs a thorough review of the related scholarly publications through a systematic process. Specifically, the PRISMA or Preferred Reporting Items for Systematic Reviews and Meta-Analyses is a standard for systematically reporting results of such studies assisted in answering the research objectives. This method contains an in-depth reviewing process which is applied to conduct a comprehensive literature search for this study. The PRISMA statement was designed to assist researchers in summarizing the findings from systematic reviews and meta-analyses. It features a four-stage process flowchart and a checklist with 27 items (Moher et al., 2010). The four stages are identification, screening, eligibility, and inclusion. The Scopus bibliographic repository, which includes a large number of reputable publications, is used in this study to highlight the present state of research on the subject throughout the globe. The search keywords are agricultural entrepreneurship, AI, agriculture startups, and agriculture enterprise. This methodology is dependent upon the use of certain inclusion and exclusion conditions that are stated in Table 13.1.

A total of 124 papers were obtained throughout the identification process. Out of those, three were spotted to be duplicate papers that were removed as per the

TABLE 13.1
Search Parameters

Inclusion Criteria	
Database type	Scopus
Search base	"Title, abstract, and keywords"
Search keywords	"Artificial Intelligence AND Agricultural Entrepreneurship OR Agriculture Startups OR Agriculture enterprise"
Document types	Book chapter, article, conference paper, and review
Publication years	2018–2023
Exclusion Criteria	
Paper in other languages apart from English	
Paper duplication	

Source: Authors' work.

exclusion criteria. As the identified papers at the first stage were not in huge numbers, it was decided to count all documents for further evaluation, excluding duplicate papers. The second process involved paper screening, where 121 documents were checked based on abstracts. The abstracts having languages other than English were excluded as per the exclusion criteria. Also, the abstracts that do not relate to the objectives were excluded for further review. The number of papers excluded after screening was 70. The third process is an eligibility check, where full-fledged papers are taken into consideration. Out of 51 papers, 21 papers were excluded due to the non-availability of full papers, and some papers do not have specific data for attaining the expectancy of research. Finally, 30 papers were considered suitable for review study in the inclusion stage.

This study also employed Word Cloud analysis by taking 30 selected papers to exhibit the words with the highest frequency. The Word Cloud has become a popular and striking means of text visualization. They are used in various research areas as a way to summarize texts by removing all words except those that appear most frequently (Heimerl et al., 2014). The Word Cloud method has been executed through an open-source software called Voyant Tools, which is primarily designed for interpreting textual materials and data visualization. The Voyant Tools proves to be particularly effective when working with extensive textual information collections (Schumann, 2022). This software uses the Cirrus tool to generate word frequency diagrams from a corpus. The collocated graph has been visually shown with the help of the Links view, which exhibits keywords that appear together as a network graph. The Terms view displayed the frequency of each word within an entire corpus in the form of a table.

13.4 RESULTS AND DISCUSSION

13.4.1 Results

Figure 13.1 shows the inclusion of 30 datasets based on quality content for the research review. As shown in Figure 13.2, the four document types, namely review, article, book chapter, and conference paper, opted for paper selection.

It depicts that the reviews and articles have contributed equally to the datasets, with nine (30%) each. The conference papers provided ten (33.33%) datasets, and lastly, the book chapter has the least number of datasets, which is two (6.66%). The number of records in the conference paper reflects the relevance of entrepreneurial agriculture and technology in a way that is taken as a discussion and important theme for academic research. The number of articles published in high-impact journals shows the quality of content and acceptance of AI in agricultural entrepreneurship for future studies.

The amount of research done was high in the year 2022, with 11 documents, as shown in Figure 13.3, which signifies that interest in exploring the role of AI in entrepreneurial agriculture has grown and evolved in recent times. The papers selected for review were retrieved from 2018 to 2023. The lowest number of papers was in 2018, which was only one. The Industrial Revolution had a significant influence on agricultural practices, leading to a spike in academic research in this field, which subsequently contributed to a rise in the number of articles indexed in Scopus.

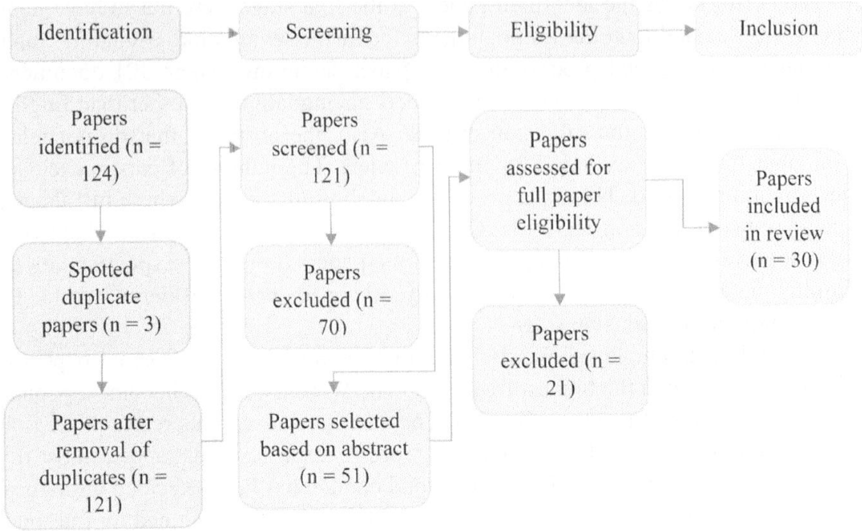

FIGURE 13.1 Selection process flowchart through the PRISMA method. (Authors' work.)

Figure 13.4 shows that the European countries have the highest number of publications, with Russia being the most prominent among them. Since Russia is a major exporter of food production, they are consequently carrying out research studies to devise crop production methods that are efficient and cost-effective. Research on technological innovations in agriculture is also on the rise in Asia, with five academic publications from India signifying the country's dominance in this sector (Table 13.2).

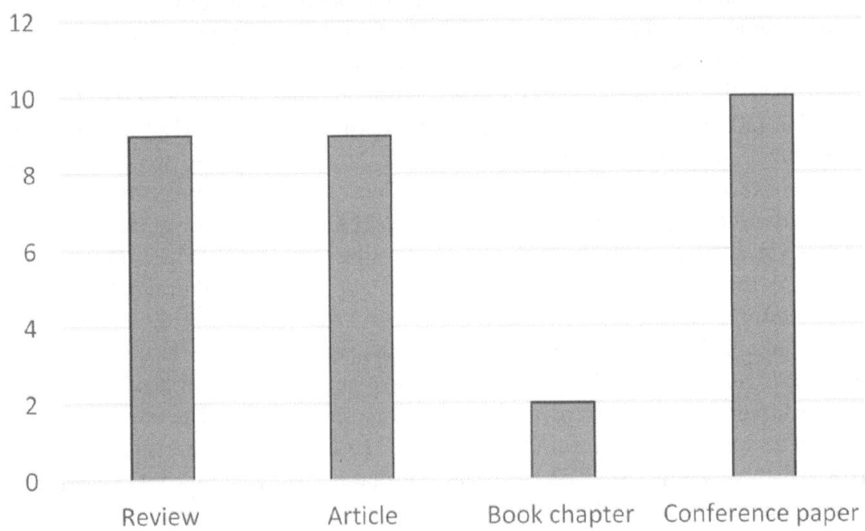

FIGURE 13.2 Types of documents selected. (Authors' compilation.)

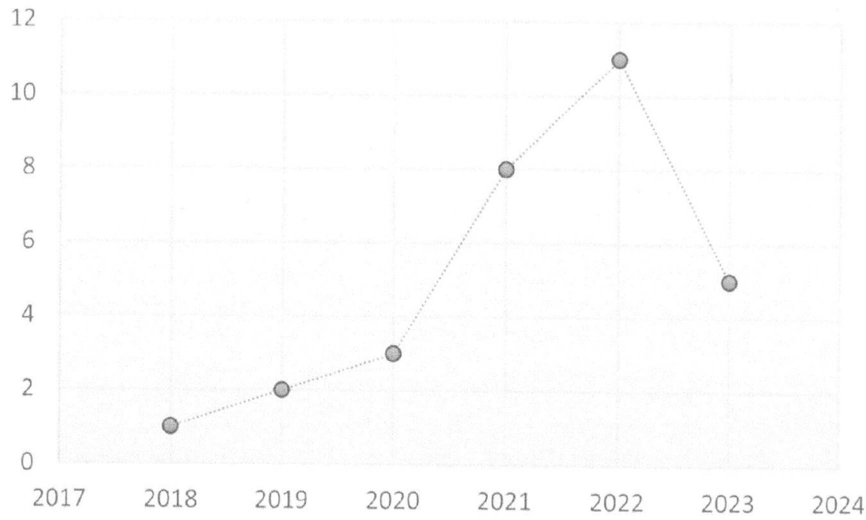

FIGURE 13.3 Number of publications per year. (Authors' compilation.)

This analysis characterizes crucial words as those that initially occurred inside a 45-word context. The chosen 30 papers were uploaded to the Voyant Tools software to recognize frequently appearing terms. Figure 13.5 demonstrates that the Cirrus view expresses significant terms such as agriculture, data, technologies, development, smart, IoT, management, systems, digital, monitoring, and many more. The word context in the Cirrus view was restricted to 45 words with a reason to include the most crucial frequent terms. The analysis of the Word Cloud serves as a useful

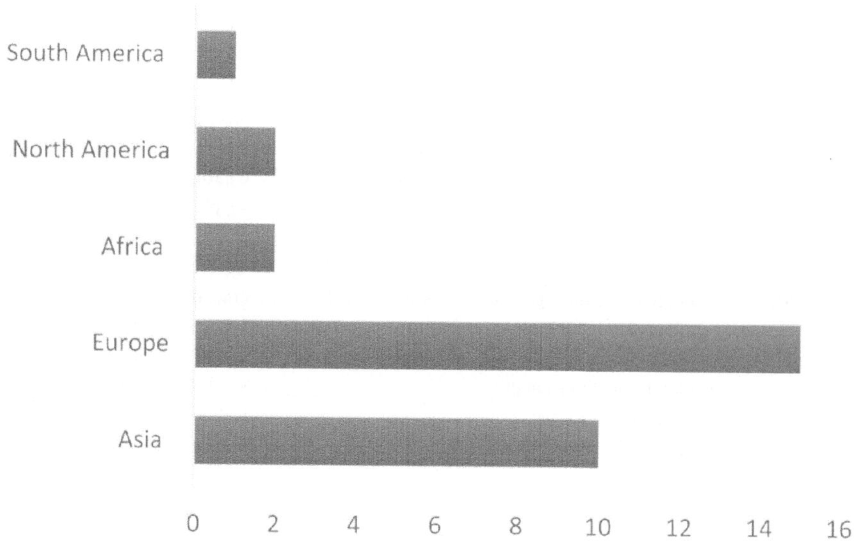

FIGURE 13.4 Country-wise number of publications. (Authors' compilation.)

TABLE 13.2
An Overview of Selected Documents

References	Research Objectives	Agri-Tech Trends	Findings
Mochalova et al. (2022)	• Comparing the regional growth rates of different agriculture segments before and after the widespread adoption of digital devices.	Detection of vehicles used in agriculture via satellite connection.	Evaluated the key factors impacting agricultural production and developed a digital agriculture project that necessitates infrastructural, financial, and authoritative assistance.
Akinfiev and Tsvirkun (2021)	• Boosting long-term viability and decreasing risks for agricultural SMEs using the proposed financial decision support system.	The TEO-INVEST Agro software facilitates financial decisions in agribusiness.	Several agricultural firms employ this technique to decrease financial risks and promote the steady growth of SMEs.
Lezoche et al. (2020)	• Reviewing the ways of enhancing the efficacy of the supply chain process for farmers through new technologies.	Agriculture robots, IoT, Blockchain, Big Data, and Knowledge Model Approaches for sustainable agri-food systems.	Although new technologies have significant beneficial effects, they also present new challenges, and their precision is still in its nascent stages.
Cavazza et al. (2023)	• Present a future research agenda by mapping the current status of artificial intelligence (AI) implications in agriculture, including its benefits, drawbacks, and potential to inspire innovative business ideas.	Machine learning, cloud computing, drones, geographical indication systems, and decision support systems.	The literature and practical implementation are still ongoing with the testing of further solutions and applications.
Monteiro and Barata (2021)	• Discern research clusters pertaining to intelligent agri-food; • Learning how AI contributes to the global agri-food supply chain.	Deep Neural Network, unmanned aerial vehicles, convolutional neural network, Support Vector Machine.	The influence of AI on food production is growing, and there is a need to expand its contributions across the whole supply chain.
Remondino and Zanin (2022)	• Examining the ways to improve the management of supply chains and resources for digitization; • Identifying the strategic implications for the agri-food sector.	UAV drones, vision picking, Virtual Reality, Augmented Reality.	Logistics management is crucial in the agri-food business due to its perishable nature and long-distance services for which digital technology comes to play a role, especially in nations with inefficient infrastructure.

(Continued)

TABLE 13.2 *(Continued)*
An Overview of Selected Documents

References	Research Objectives	Agri-Tech Trends	Findings
Subeesh and Mehta (2021)	• Reviewing the most promising IoT and AI tools in the agriculture field.	Support Vector Machines, KNN model, naive Bayes for crop monitoring.	IoT and AI play a crucial role in agricultural automation, optimizing pre- and post-harvest procedures and simplifying farmers' lives.
Voronin et al. (2022)	• Reviewing modern technologies used in farms for production optimization.	Geographic Information Systems such as Panorama AGRO, Geo-Agro, and GeoPlan for information sensing; Afimilk system for cows' movement.	Various technological advancements have been made in the agriculture field, but attention should be given to rural regions with an immense shortage of skilled farmers.
Kolmykova et al. (2021)	• Reviewing sustainable digital innovations in the agriculture sector.	Cloud data storage.	The use of cloud technology has both pros (optimized operations) and cons (high implementation cost).
Lu (2021)	• Reviewing the growth pattern and potential of online enterprises run by farmers in the digital age; • Examine the challenges of farmers in digital entrepreneurship.	Rural e-commerce for farmer entrepreneurs.	The study suggested various strategic ways to enact the new e-commerce model for rural farmers.
Kumbhar et al. (2022)	• Review the recent relevant studies that use geospatial data to enhance agricultural activities.	Spatial Data Mining and soil map model.	Results for agricultural production forecasting using the ANN model are more accurate than decision trees and conventional vegetation indicators.
Sultanov and Ishankhodjayev (2022)	• Evaluate how well current infrastructure in agriculture enterprises are performing and developing smart information devices.	IISDS model for modernizing agriculture enterprises.	The DRS analysis revealed a generalization and advancement of conventional data models in the entity-relationship model since it is the only model with 4-level portrayals of entities and relationships.
Bouguettaya et al. (2023)	• Examine new developments in UAV-based agricultural disease detection and management using computer vision approaches.	RGB, spectral, and thermal infrared cameras are used for crop disease identification.	It analysed the prominent deep learning-based machine vision classifications for crop disease detection that are assisting researchers and farmers in picking the best models and tools for their study contexts.

(Continued)

TABLE 13.2 *(Continued)*
An Overview of Selected Documents

References	Research Objectives	Agri-Tech Trends	Findings
Kumari et al. (2021)	• Discusses the aspects and constraints of digitalization in agriculture.	Telematics, NDVI, Variable Rate Applications, and autonomous tractors.	Precision farming technologies are briefly discussed, along with their advantages and challenges. Creating affordable internet solutions can enable farmers to experience the effect of digitalization on their crops.
Stehel et al. (2019)	• Assessing the current performance of agricultural enterprises using AI.	Using Kohonen networks to evaluate and forecast the growth of agricultural firms.	The analysis of agriculture enterprises exhibits favourable attributes that include ideal asset levels, finance structures, and acceptable economic outcomes.
Lassoued et al. (2023)	• Providing insights into the marketing of innovative agricultural tools.	Dot SeedMaster technology.	Agtech enterprises' innovation depends on aspects such as economic benefit, organizational strategic aim, market size, and competitiveness in the target market. Most of these variables are external to the system and cannot be influenced by government action.
Raut et al. (2022)	• Performing comprehensive study review of AI applications in drying methods and food quality enhancements.	KGS09 model for data-driven soft sensors.	The study found little application of AI and related approaches in the convective drying process.
Kaldarova et al. (2023)	• Detecting weeds by applying AI and machine algorithms.	Mask R-CNN AI software for weed scanning.	The software achieved high-quality weed identification results, which detects weeds in 0.2 seconds, eradicating human error with 0.98 learning accuracy and 1.43% data loss.
Rowan et al. (2022)	• Explaining the transition towards adopting smart technology through paludiculture-based sustainable innovation.	Agri-photonics technology for measuring crop health.	Wet peatland innovation is developing to provide green jobs and balance economic, social, and ecological sustainability.

(Continued)

TABLE 13.2 *(Continued)*
An Overview of Selected Documents

References	Research Objectives	Agri-Tech Trends	Findings
Shivaprakash et al. (2022)	• Provide a worldwide account of the state of AI study and application to the fields of forestry and conservation of biodiversity.	Outland Analytics and Terramonitor for monitoring deforestation.	Technological advancements are mostly used in rich nations and a few developing countries that manage forests for economic interests.
Skobelev et al. (2019)	• Developing a conceptual framework for smart farming.	Virtual "round table" model for assisting farmers with decision-making.	With the use of smart planning services, farmers may divide up scarce resources throughout their fields and create strategies for seasonal crop rotation.
Kour and Arora (2020)	• Reviewing current technologies in the agriculture sector.	Robotic harvesting, IoT for irrigation.	Existing research indicates that 90% of data is self-acquired using wireless sensors. The data included soil, pH, humidity, light, water, and photos.
Beloev et al. (2021)	• Designing a robot prototype for small-scale agriculture.	Raspberry Pi model for agricultural robot.	The study proposed a small-scale agriculture robot prototype for precision farming. Despite early examination, it outperformed expectations and accomplished core operations.
Inshakova et al. (2022)	• Stating the potentiality of automation in agricultural activities.	A "Skif" cargo-type drone is a "flying tractor" used in agriculture.	The Federal Law needs to be amended to give incentives and advantages for digital technology developers and users to optimize food supply chains and deliver accurate consumer information.
Gupta et al. (2020)	• Examine the challenges of maintaining privacy and data integrity for precision agriculture.	SCADAfarm enables remote monitoring of water and energy use, irrigator locations, soil moisture, and weather data; Software Defined Network in smart farming.	There are insufficient cyber insurance plans in the food supply chain. Cyber insurance firms struggle to forecast and measure security risks in these networks.
Pivoto et al. (2018)	• Specifying smart farming and its prospects in Brazil.	"Telemetry" for agricultural monitoring.	Brazil adopts smart farming technology but does not significantly contribute to its development, putting potential advantages at risk.

(Continued)

TABLE 13.2 *(Continued)*
An Overview of Selected Documents

References	Research Objectives	Agri-Tech Trends	Findings
Alfred et al. (2021)	• Reviewing the trends of Big Data, ML, and IoT in rice production.	Optimized Fuzzy Inference System for detecting paddy rice disease; AdaBoost algorithm for categorizing the samples of paddy rice.	The use of ML algorithms can detect rice blasts early and support the use of biocidal chemicals or microbes that destroy fungal parasites or their mites.
Tombe and Smuts (2023)	• Analysing potential advantages and obstacles of Society 5.0 in the agriculture supply chain.	Data automation in agriculture.	Limited infrastructure, skills, and expertise hinder the adoption of digitization in the agricultural value chain, particularly in developing nations.
Vorozhtsov et al. (2022)	• To ascertain the adoption of compact tractors in agricultural farms.	Robotic tractors.	As agricultural robots become more prevalent, mini-tractors should be developed to keep up with the trend of robotizing operations.
Siregar et al. (2022)	• Reviewing the vertical farming and its technological trends.	RNG k-epsilon model for the vegetable plant; digital twins.	Currently, most use cases are at the prototype stage. This is because indoor farming, particularly soilless agriculture, requires sophisticated design and management with varying dimensions and conditions.

Source: Authors' compilation.

tool for figuring out the arrangement of specific words and their associated conceptual relevance among the selected papers for this review study. This analysis characterizes crucial words as those that initially occurred inside a 45-word context. The chosen 30 papers were uploaded to the Voyant Tools software to recognize frequently appearing terms.

Figure 13.5 demonstrates that the Cirrus view expresses significant terms such as agriculture, data, technologies, development, smart, IoT, management, systems, digital, monitoring, and many more. The word context in the Cirrus view was restricted to 45 words with a reason to include the most crucial frequent terms. The analysis of the Word Cloud serves as a useful tool for figuring out the arrangement of specific words and their associated conceptual relevance among the selected papers for this review study.

The Collocates diagram displayed in the Links view, as shown in Figure 13.6, functions as a connectivity graph that highlights the keywords that have close associations with one another in a network. The Collocates diagram conveys that blue terms are associated with orange terms.

FIGURE 13.5 Word Cloud analysis. (Authors' compilation using the Voyant Tools.)

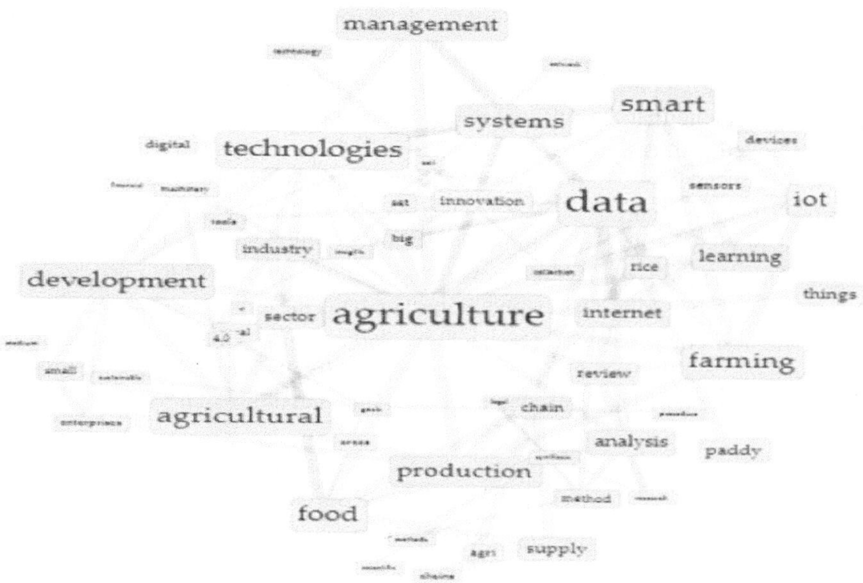

FIGURE 13.6 The Collocates graph depicts a close association of terms. (Authors' compilation using the Voyant Tools.)

	Term	Count	Trend
1	Agriculture	2582	
2	Data	2550	
3	Smart	1600	
4	Technologies	1447	
5	Agricultural	1430	
6	Development	1316	
7	Food	1262	
8	Farming	1257	
9	IoT	1205	
10	Systems	1138	

FIGURE 13.7 Terms having the highest frequency. (Authors' compilation using the Voyant Tools.)

Figure 13.6 shows the link of each term with many different collocates such as the term agriculture is linked to development, technologies, AI, management, IoT, sensors, data, production, smart devices, farming, and many more. Likewise, the term technology is linked to data, digital, development, agriculture, systems, management, and many other collocates. As per the diagram, terms such as agriculture, technologies, development, smart, and data are widely associated with different collocates, conveying that the selected research papers revolve around all these terms and are linked with each other.

The Terms view is a frequency table of all terms used across the whole corpus. Figure 13.7 shows a corpus view of the terms used to describe AI in the agricultural sector. It provides a precise compilation of frequently occurring terms with their count. Here, the highest count of terms is "agriculture" with 2582 that is used in the selected research papers. The second highest count is the term "data" with 2550. The top 10 highest count terms are agriculture, data, smart technologies, agricultural development, food, farming, IoT, and systems. The trend of term depicts the number of times a particular term is used in a selected individual research paper.

13.4.2 Discussion

With the help of technology and AI, agriculture has the optimum potential to increase agricultural accuracy and, hence, fulfil the growing food demand of the future. Major shifts in the scale and structure of smart farming will be brought about by the combination of these Big Data technologies and the forecasting capacity of predictive machine learning software. IoT applications include weather and soil analysis, agricultural yield and disease prediction, irrigation system management, and remote control of cars and robots (Alfred et al., 2021). Society 5.0 is an idea that emphasizes the need to combine technology and society to foster long-term agricultural sustainability and resilience. The knowledge exchange on agricultural practices and supply chain management are instances of how digital technology may aid in the development of agriculture that is both productive and environmentally friendly. Further, digital technology may advance social justice by allowing previously unprivileged farmers to get remote access to market data and operational support. The lack of technical capabilities among farmers and the technological gap are two impediments to using innovations in sustainable agriculture (Tombe & Smuts, 2023). The growing rivalry in both international and local markets necessitates cost reduction in product manufacturing which may be attainable by making economically feasible AI robotic systems (Vorozhtsov et al., 2022).

13.5 CONCLUSION

This study delivers valuable input to the existing research studies on agricultural entrepreneurship, particularly in the context of supporting the implementation of Agriculture 4.0. There are ample technologies in agriculture that have been discussed in the past studies. While doing a systematic review, 30 documents were retrieved from the Scopus database which implies that the study of AI in relation to agricultural entrepreneurship is proliferating as most of the studies were conducted during recent years. The first objective was to find out the current state of research, which was analysed using the PRISMA approach, and the Word Cloud tools were applied to determine the frequency of terms used in the selected 30 research papers using the Voyant Tools. The second objective was to determine the implications of AI in enhancing agricultural entrepreneurship. The inclusion of AI systems in agriculture is still at its nascent stage. Poor farmers and small-scale entrepreneurs have insufficient access to efficient digital tools, thereby depending on conventional agricultural practices. The availability of AI devices at cheaper prices would serve their need, and adequate training for its usage is necessary. Undoubtedly, there are many AI innovations made in agricultural practices, but AI's approach to rural areas is low. It is crucial to train the farmers and entrepreneurs regarding such smart devices. The study opted for the Scopus database to retrieve papers, which resulted in obtaining limited results. Adding more search databases would have provided more results.

BIBLIOGRAPHY

Akinfiev, V., & Tsvirkun, A. (2021). Decision support systems for stable development of agricultural SMEs. *IFAC-PapersOnLine*, *54*(13), 289–292. https://doi.org/10.1016/j.ifacol.2021.10.461

Alfred, R., Obit, J. H., Chin, C. P. Y., Haviluddin, H., & Lim, Y. (2021). Towards paddy rice smart farming: A review on Big Data, machine learning, and rice production tasks. *IEEE Access*, *9*, 50358–50380. https://doi.org/10.1109/ACCESS.2021.3069449

Alreshidi, E. (2019). Smart sustainable agriculture (SSA) solution underpinned by Internet of Things (IoT) and artificial intelligence (AI). *International Journal of Advanced Computer Science and Applications*, *10*(5), 93–102. https://doi.org/10.14569/IJACSA.2019.0100513

Arafat, M. Y., Saleem, I., Dwivedi, A. K., & Khan, A. (2020). Determinants of agricultural entrepreneurship: A GEM data based study. *International Entrepreneurship and Management Journal*, *16*, 345–370. https://doi.org/10.1007/s11365-018-0536-1

Beloev, I., Kinaneva, D., Georgiev, G., Hristov, G., & Zahariev, P. (2021). Artificial intelligence-driven autonomous robot for precision agriculture. *Acta Technologica Agriculturae*, *24*(1), 48–54. https://doi.org/10.2478/ata-2021-0008

Bouguettaya, A., Zarzour, H., Kechida, A., & Taberkit, A. M. (2023). A survey on deep learning-based identification of plant and crop diseases from UAV-based aerial images. *Cluster Computing*, *26*, 1297–1317. https://doi.org/10.1007/s10586-022-03627-x

Cavazza, A., Dal Mas, F., Paoloni, P., & Manzo, M. (2023). Artificial intelligence and new business models in agriculture: A structured literature review and future research agenda. *British Food Journal*, *125*(13), 436–461. https://doi.org/10.1108/BFJ-02-2023-0132

Dias, C. S., Rodrigues, R. G., & Ferreira, J. J. (2019). Agricultural entrepreneurship: Going back to the basics. *Journal of Rural Studies*, *70*, 125–138. https://doi.org/10.1016/j.jrurstud.2019.06.001

Goh, L. (2022). How AgriTech is transforming traditional agriculture in emerging markets. In H. Kharas, J. W. McArthur & I. Ohno (Eds.), *Breakthrough: The promise of frontier technologies for sustainable development* (pp. 125–147). Brookings Institution Press.

Gupta, M., Abdelsalam, M., Khorsandroo, S., & Mittal, S. (2020). Security and privacy in smart farming: Challenges and opportunities. *IEEE Access*, *8*, 34564–34584. https://doi.org/10.1109/ACCESS.2020.2975142

Heimerl, F., Lohmann, S., Lange, S., & Ertl, T. (2014). Word Cloud Explorer: Text Analytics Based on Word Clouds. *47th Hawaii International Conference on System Sciences* (pp. 1833–1842). IEEE. https://doi.org/10.1109/HICSS.2014.231

Hrustek, L. (2020). Sustainability driven by agriculture through digital transformation. *Sustainability*, *12*(20), 1–17. https://doi.org/10.3390/su12208596

Inshakova, A. O., Ryzhenkov, A. Y., Pon'ka, V. F., & Davudov, D. A. (2022). Current issues of agriculture digitalization in the Russian federation. In A. O. Inshakova & E. I. Inshakova (Eds.), *New technology for inclusive and sustainable growth* (pp. 125–135). Springer. https://doi.org/10.1007/978-981-16-9808-8_14

Javaid, M., Haleem, A., Singh, R. P., & Suman, R. (2022). Enhancing smart farming through the applications of Agriculture 4.0 technologies. *International Journal of Intelligent Networks*, *3*, 150–164. https://doi.org/10.1016/j.ijin.2022.09.004

Kaldarova, M., Akanova, A., Nazyrova, A., Mukanova, A., & Tynykulova, A. (2023). Identification of weeds in fields based on computer vision technology. *Eastern-European Journal of Enterprise Technologies*, *4*(2), 44–52. https://doi.org/10.15587/1729-4061.2023.284600

Kolmykova, T. S., Obukhova, A. S., Klykova, S. V., Mashegov, P. N., Zaitsev, A. G., & Popova, O. V. (2021). Features and benefits of digital technologies in agricultural enterprises. *E3S Web of Conferences*, *247*, 1–4. https://doi.org/10.1051/e3sconf/202124701018

Kour, V. P., & Arora, S. (2020). Recent developments of the Internet of Things in agriculture: A survey. *IEEE Access*, *8*, 129924–129957. https://doi.org/10.1109/ACCESS.2020.3009298

Kumar, A. S., Sharma, P., Kaur, S., Saleh, O. S., Chennamma, H. R., & Chaturvedi, A. (2023). AI-equipped IoT applications in high-tech agriculture using machine learning. In *Handbook of research on AI-equipped IoT applications in high-tech agriculture* (pp. 38–64). IGI Global.

Kumari, S., Parasher, Y., Mehra, S., & Singh, P. (2021). Digitization in agriculture: insight into the networked world. In P. Tomar & G. Kaur (Eds.), *Artificial intelligence and IoT-based technologies for sustainable farming and smart agriculture* (pp. 1–24). IGI Global. https://doi.org/10.4018/978-1-7998-1722-2.ch001

Kumbhar, V., Maru, A., & Kumari, S. (2022). spatial data mining-a tool for spatial decision support system in agriculture management. *Journal of Engineering Science & Technology Review*, *15*(1), 128–133. http://dx.doi.org/10.25103/jestr.151.16

Lassoued, R., Phillips, P. W., & Smyth, S. J. (2023). Exploratory analysis on drivers and barriers to Canadian prairie agricultural technology innovation and adoption. *Smart Agricultural Technology*, *5*, 1–10. https://doi.org/10.1016/j.atech.2023.100257

Lezoche, M., Hernandez, J. E., Díaz, M. D. M. E. A., Panetto, H., & Kacprzyk, J. (2020). Agri-Food 4.0: A survey of the supply chains and technologies for the future agriculture. *Computers in Industry*, *117*, 1–35. https://doi.org/10.1016/j.compind.2020.103187

Li, X., Long, Y., Fan, M., & Chen, Y. (2022). Drilling down artificial intelligence in entrepreneurial management: A bibliometric perspective. *Systems Research and Behavioral Science*, *39*(3), 379–396. https://doi.org/10.1002/sres.2855

Lu, Y. (2021). Analysis of the impact of the internet on Farmers' intelligent selection under the era of Big Data and cloud computing. *Journal of Physics: Conference Series*, *1982*(1), 1–7. https://doi.org/10.1088/1742-6596/1982/1/012211

Mochalova, Y. V., Ermakova, A. N., Levushkina, S. V., Vavakina, O. B., Savvateev, E. V., Aimen, A. T., Atashev, D., & Kabanov, O. V. (2022). Application of digital technologies to increase the economic efficiency of agribusiness in Russia. *Procedia Environmental Science, Engineering and Management*, *9*(2), 601–606.

Moher, D., Liberati, A., Tetzlaff, J., & Altman, D. G., & Prisma Group. (2010). Preferred reporting items for systematic reviews and meta-analyses: The PRISMA statement. *International Journal of Surgery*, *8*(5), 336–341. https://doi.org/10.1016/j.ijsu.2010.02.007

Monteiro, J., & Barata, J. (2021). Artificial intelligence in extended Agri-food supply chain: A short review based on bibliometric analysis. *Procedia Computer Science*, *192*, 3020–3029. https://doi.org/10.1016/j.procs.2021.09.074

Pivoto, D., Waquil, P. D., Talamini, E., Finocchio, C., Dalla Corte, P. S., & de Vargas Mores, V. F. G. (2018). Scientific development of smart farming technologies and their application in Brazil. *Information Processing in Agriculture*, *5*(1), 21–32. https://doi.org/10.1016/j.inpa.2017.12.002

Raut, S., von Gersdorff, G., Schemminger, J., Adolphs, J., & Sturm, B. (2022). Improving Food Processing Through Integration of Artificial Intelligence in the Drying Process: A Perspective. In *42nd GIL-Jahrestagung, Künstliche Intelligenz in der Agrar- und Ernährungswirtschaft*, 231–236. Gesellschaft Fur Informatik.

Remondino, M., & Zanin, A. (2022). Logistics and agri-food: Digitization to increase competitive advantage and sustainability. Literature review and the case of Italy. *Sustainability*, *14*(2), 1–21. https://doi.org/10.3390/su14020787

Rowan, N. J., Murray, N., Qiao, Y., O'Neill, E., Clifford, E., Barceló, D., & Power, D. M. (2022). Digital transformation of peatland eco-innovations ('Paludiculture'): Enabling a paradigm shift towards the real-time sustainable production of 'Green-Friendly' products and services. *Science of the Total Environment*, *838*, 1–20. https://doi.org/10.1016/j.scitotenv.2022.156328

Saghaian, S., Mohammadi, H., & Mohammadi, M. (2022). Factors affecting success of entrepreneurship in agribusinesses: Evidence from the City of Mashhad, Iran. *Sustainability*, *14*(13), 1–12. https://doi.org/10.3390/su14137700

Sargani, G. R., Zhou, D., Raza, M. H., & Wei, Y. (2020). Sustainable entrepreneurship in the agriculture sector: The nexus of the triple Bottom line measurement approach. *Sustainability*, *12*(8), 1–24. https://doi.org/10.3390/su12083275

Schumann, F. R. (2022). Using Voyant Tools for data mining social media comments about a destination: A Guam study. *Journal of Hospitality & Tourism*, *20*(2), 106–118.

Shivaprakash, K. N., Swami, N., Mysorekar, S., Arora, R., Gangadharan, A., Vohra, K., Jadeyegowda, M., & Kiesecker, J. M. (2022). Potential for artificial intelligence (AI) and machine learning (ML) applications in biodiversity conservation, managing forests, and related services in India. *Sustainability*, *14*(12), 1–20. https://doi.org/10.3390/su14127154

Siregar, R. R. A., Seminar, K. B., Wahjuni, S., & Santosa, E. (2022). Vertical farming perspectives in support of precision agriculture using artificial intelligence: A review. *Computers*, *11*(9), 1–19. https://doi.org/10.3390/computers11090135

Skobelev, P., Larukchin, V., Mayorov, I., Simonova, E., & Yalovenko, O. (2019). smart farming–Open multi-agent platform and eco-system of smart services for precision farming. In Y. Demazeau, E. Matson, J. M. Corchado & F. D. L. Prieta (Eds.), *Advances in practical applications of survivable agents and multi-agent systems* (pp. 212–224). Springer. https://doi.org/10.1007/978-3-030-24209-1_18

Sott, M. K., Furstenau, L. B., Kipper, L. M., Giraldo, F. D., Lopez-Robles, J. R., Cobo, M. J., Zahid, A., Abbasi, Q. H., & Imran, M. A. (2020). Precision techniques and Agriculture 4.0 technologies to promote sustainability in the coffee sector: State of the art, challenges and future trends. *IEEE Access*, *8*, 149854–149867. https://doi.org/10.1109/ACCESS.2020.3016325

Stehel, V., Horák, J., & Vochozka, M. (2019). Prediction of institutional sector development and analysis of enterprises active in agriculture. *Economics and Management*, *22*(4), 103–118. http://hdl.handle.net/11025/36040

Subeesh, A., & Mehta, C. R. (2021). Automation and digitization of agriculture using artificial intelligence and Internet of Things. *Artificial Intelligence in Agriculture*, *5*, 278–291. https://doi.org/10.1016/j.aiia.2021.11.004

Sultanov, M., & Ishankhodjayev, G. (2022). Development of Intelligent Information Decision Support Systems. *Proceedings of the 6th International Conference on Future Networks & Distributed Systems*, 1–7. https://doi.org/10.1145/3584202.3584203

Tombe, R., & Smuts, H. (2023). Society 5.0-inspired digitalization framework for resilient and sustainable agriculture. *Proceedings of Society 5.0 Conference*, *93*, 216–227. https://doi.org/10.29007/xc5q

Voronin, B. A., Kukhar, V. S., Chupina, I. P., Voronina, Y. V., & Simachkova, N. N. (2022). Artificial intelligence in agriculture as a basis for increasing the competitiveness of Russian enterprises. *BIO Web of Conferences*, *51*, 1–8. https://doi.org/10.1051/bioconf/20225105003

Vorozhtsov, O. V., Plaksin, I. E., & Trifanov, A. V. (2022). The use of small-sized tractors in agriculture. *IOP Conference Series: Earth and Environmental Science*, *979*(1), 1–9. https://doi.org/10.1088/1755-1315/979/1/012034

14 AI and Sustainability
Its Recent Trends and Future Prospects

Gaganpreet Kaur, Swati Malik, Kiran Deep Singh, Sunil Khullar, Senthil Kumar A. V., and Jatin Arora

14.1 INTRODUCTION

The relationship between artificial intelligence (AI) and sustainability is growing as more organisations, institutions, and people realise that AI has the potential to alleviate many of the world's environmental problems (Vinuesa et al., 2020; Entezari et al., 2023). With an increase in businesses focusing on supply chain, sustainability, agriculture-tech, and climate, sustainability and achieving the United Nations Sustainable Development Goals (SDGs) will be a major trend in 2023. According to research published in Nature, it was suggested, that AI is used to achieve 79% of the SDGs (Chen et al., 2023). This technology has the potential to be a key tool for promoting a circular economy and building smart cities with minimal resource consumption (Tyagi et al., 2023). Following are some recent advancements and forecasts in AI and sustainability:

- *Energy Efficiency*: By anticipating demand and controlling energy consumption in real time, AI can optimise energy use (Nti et al., 2022). As a result, there may be considerable cost savings and a decrease in greenhouse gas emissions.
- *Climate Simulation*: AI can enhance climate modelling by making more precise forecasts of weather patterns and how they will affect ecosystems. This can lessen the consequences of climate change and lower the probability of natural disasters while also assisting communities and policymakers in better preparing for extreme weather events. To better understand climate patterns and forecast weather, this entails using machine learning algorithms to analyse huge datasets, such as satellite imagery and weather sensor data (Nishant et al., 2020; Kar et al., 2022).
- *Precision Agriculture*: By giving real-time information on the weather, soil moisture, and plant health, AI can assist farmers in boosting agricultural yields and decreasing waste. This may result in more environmentally friendly agricultural methods, thereby promoting long-term food security (Rosário & Dias, 2022).
- *Smart Cities*: By maximising energy use, cutting waste, and enhancing transportation infrastructure, AI can assist cities in becoming more

DOI: 10.1201/9781003640776-14

sustainable (Dhamija and Bag, 2020). As a result, metropolitan areas could become healthier and cleaner, and citizens' quality of life could improve.

- AI can support a cyclical economy by making it possible to track and manage materials effectively throughout their life cycles (Hsu et al., 2022). This could contribute to a more sustainable and robust economy by reducing waste and improving resource efficiency.
- By forecasting energy supply and demand and improving energy storage (Sharma et al., 2020), AI is also used to optimise renewable energy sources, such as wind and solar.
- Resource management is a crucial area where AI is used for sustainability. By spotting waste-reduction opportunities and increasing the effectiveness of processes like manufacturing and agriculture (Lee, 2021), AI can help maximise resource consumption. This may result in considerable decreases in greenhouse gas emissions as well as other negative effects on the environment (Feroz et al., 2021).
- The use of AI to enable more resilient and sustainable cities is also gaining popularity. This includes utilising AI to enhance urban planning and design, decrease traffic congestion and emissions, and increase traffic flow (Mehmood et al., 2019; Moodaley & Telukdarie, 2023; Talari et al., 2024). In order to better endure extreme weather conditions and other disturbances, AI can also be utilised to increase the resilience of vital infrastructure, such as power grids and transportation systems.

Utilising AI for sustainability could increase our ability to deal with the urgent social and environmental problems our world is currently facing.

It is essential to ensure that new technologies are created and applied in a responsible and equitable manner (Kaur & Kaur, 2022) with a focus on maximising the results and reducing potential risks and unanticipated repercussions.

14.2 PRELIMINARIES

This section provides an overview of the three categories – sustainability, AI, sustainable development, and finally the role of AI in sustainability that make up the framework for research.

14.2.1 Sustainability

Sustainability is the ability to improve or maintain current social, economic, and environmental conditions over time without endangering the needs of coming generations (Leal Filho et al., 2023). It is a philosophy that underlines the necessity to balance economic development and progress with the preservation of ecosystems and natural resources (Ainapure et al., 2022) as well as the welfare of society as a whole.

14.2.2 Machine Intelligence

The invention of computer systems and programmes that can do tasks that usually require intelligence from people, such as speech recognition, natural language processing, visual perception, and decision-making, is referred to as AI (Andeobu et al., 2022; Liao et al., 2022).

AI is a system of systems that can learn from their experiences and improve their abilities with the use of machine learning (Kaur & Kaur, 2022; Kaur et al., 2023), neural networks, deep learning (Kaur et al., 2023), and various other techniques (Yigitcanlar et al., 2021). AI is also used in a wider range of businesses, which include transportation, natural language processing, picture and video identification, and healthcare (Di Vaio et al., 2020). As AI is advancing these days, it is expected to have a large impact on society, potentially changing a number of industries and creating new opportunities for innovation and development.

14.2.3 Sustainable Development Goals

SDGs stand for Sustainable Development Goals. The UN established these 17 goals, as a part of the 2030 Agenda for Sustainable Development in 2015. The SDGs are an appeal to all countries, organisations, and individuals to work in accordance with a sustainable future for all people and address issues including poverty, inequality, climate change, and environmental degradation (Sakshi et al., 2020; Kumar et al., 2021; Mhlanga, 2021). The SDGs can be divided into three categories: environment, economics, and society (Vinuesa et al., 2020; Entezari et al., 2023). The classification of the SDGs into the three categories of economy, society, and environment is shown in Figure 14.1 and Table 14.1.

14.3 AI: PLAYING MAJOR ROLE IN DIFFERENT DISCIPLINES

AI has gained amazing success in recent years in a variety of fields, including recommendation systems, natural language processing, computer vision, intelligent sensing, and condition monitoring systems. It plays a significant role in enhancing productivity and efficiency (Chen et al., 2023). From Figure 14.2, it is clear that AI is becoming more prevalent across a variety of application fields, which include telecommunications (Schoormann et al., 2021), environmental science, material science, and others, in addition to its traditional home in computer science.

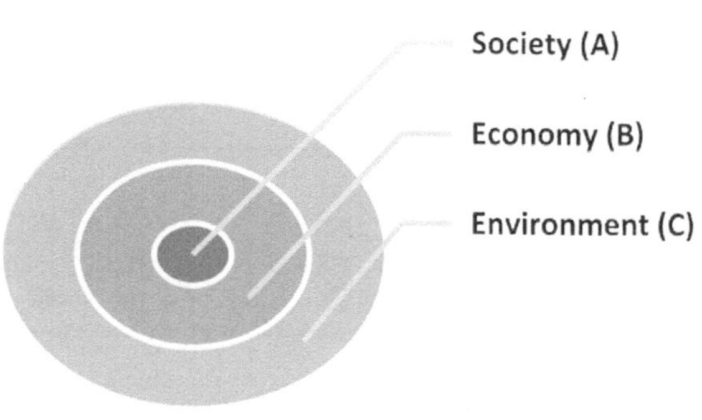

FIGURE 14.1 Various SDG's categorisation.

TABLE 14.1
Division of 17 Available SDGs into Three Categories

Society (A)	Economy (B)	Environment (C)
Zero Poverty (1)	*Economic Growth and Decent Work (8)*	*Climate Change (13)*
No Hungry (2)	*Infrastructure, Business, and Innovation (9)*	*Life Above Water (14)*
A good quality of life (3)	*Decreased Inequality (10)*	*Life Below Water (15)*
Quality Education (4)	*Consumption and production with responsibility (12)*	
Equal Opportunity (5)	*Collaborations for the Goals (17)*	
Sanitation and clean water (6)		
Low-cost, clean energy (7)		
Healthy Communities and Cities (11)		
Justice, peace, and powerful institutions (16)		

14.3.1 Interlinkage of Various SDGs

There is an interlinkage between all SDGs. The interconnection of the 17 global goals is their defining feature. It is found that a reduction in hygienic practices and an uptick in health problems are likely to follow an increase in poverty (Owe & Baum, 2021). Additionally, it is seen that poverty makes it harder for people to attend school and makes it easier for violence to happen.

So, it can be rightly said that the components of sustainability are interdependent and need one another to function, just like our body system. The state of the

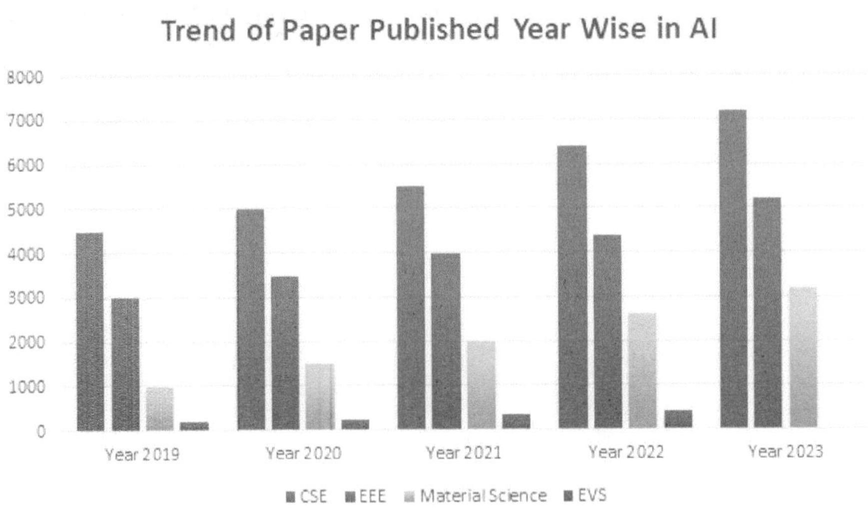

FIGURE 14.2 Increasing trend of AI research papers [3].

economy affects society, which in turn affects how we treat the environment. The objectives were always intended to demonstrate that society, which is heavily dependent on the environment, cannot grow without having an impact on the economy.

14.4 TECHNOLOGY'S NECESSITY FOR SDGs

Information and Communication Technology (ICT) infrastructure is seen as a crucial means of implementation that supports the achievement of all goals. Economic growth, social inclusion, and environmental preservation are the three pillars of sustainable development. ICT is a key enabler for each of them. The 17 SDGs can be accomplished but only with faster, broader, and more equal development.

14.4.1 Use of Artificial Intelligence Revolution for Sustainable Development Goals (SDGs)

Applications of AI are playing a major role in reengineering a quality environment. According to various published reports, AI could be used to construct a successful society. The use of AI has gradually permeated both urban and rural environments. AI is also addressing environmental changes (Louman et al., 2019), food and water security, and ecological-economic urban communities, promoting human prosperity by reducing human error in many manual tasks, and hence promoting energy use efficiency (Khagram et al., 2003).

The era of digital technology today propels amazing breakthroughs at a spectacular rate. Humans will be able to use massive amounts of data to harness AI innovation and achieve ground-breaking improvements in sectors like healthcare, agriculture, education, and transportation (Nti et al., 2022).

There are three ways that AI, when developed ethically and used responsibly, can assist in achieving the SDGs:

14.4.1.1 AI Working as an Accelerator

With a variety of disciplines, and skill sets, we can accomplish some challenging objectives. We needed to support three different groups: (1) those who were integrating AI technologies; (2) those who were adopting AI technologies in various processes; and (3) partnerships to deliver AI technologies and AI-driven results.

14.4.1.2 Augmenting Intelligence with AI

The realisation came when we were interested in learning more about the profound impact that widespread adoption of AI will have on the advancement of research (Entezari et al., 2023). Use of vast data sets to learn from them and then finally enhance a product. Instead of trying to replace the researcher's intelligence, this is meant to enhance it.

14.4.1.3 AI as a Solver

With real-time problem-solving abilities, you may leave the support to a computer that can think independently but for your benefit, leaving you to focus just on your goals. Many bright minds are working in AI to improve our quality of life. It would be much simpler to concentrate on the more significant aspects of life if you had someone to take care of your daily requirements (Vinuesa et al., 2020). The integration of AI into our daily lives has been explored for many years, and Mantra AI has made significant investments in it.

14.5 FACTORS AFFECTING ARTIFICIAL INTELLIGENCE AND SUSTAINABLE DEVELOPMENT GOALS

AI has a positive and negative impact on society when using the SDGs. According to the three pillars of sustainable development: society, economy, and environment, the SDGs are categorised into three groups, as discussed in Table 14.1. The SDGs and 169 targets, that are set in the 2030 Sustainable Development Agenda (Vinuesa et al., 2020), if worked upon, may be affected by AI in all facets of sustainable development. It has been found that AI may affect the capacity to achieve all SDGs. The AI is affecting the three SDGs as follows:

14.5.1 AI as Positive Enabler

An analysis of the pertinent data reveals that AI may operate as a facilitator on 134 targets across all SDGs, typically through a technological advancement that may allow it to get beyond some current constraints (Barnett & Dovers, 2001). The percentage in the figures corresponds to the impact of AI on SDGs across society, the economy, and the environment as a whole. In Figures 14.1–14.3, it is shown that the SDGs: Zero Poverty (1), Quality Education (4), Sanitation and clean water (6), Low-cost, clean energy (7), and Healthy Communities and Cities (11) have a positive impact on society to the fullest with the help of AI. From Figure 14.4, it is found that the SDGs Infrastructure, Business, and Innovation (9) are positively affecting the economy using AI. It is evident from Figure 14.5 that SDG 15 (Life Below Water) is positively affecting the environment using AI,

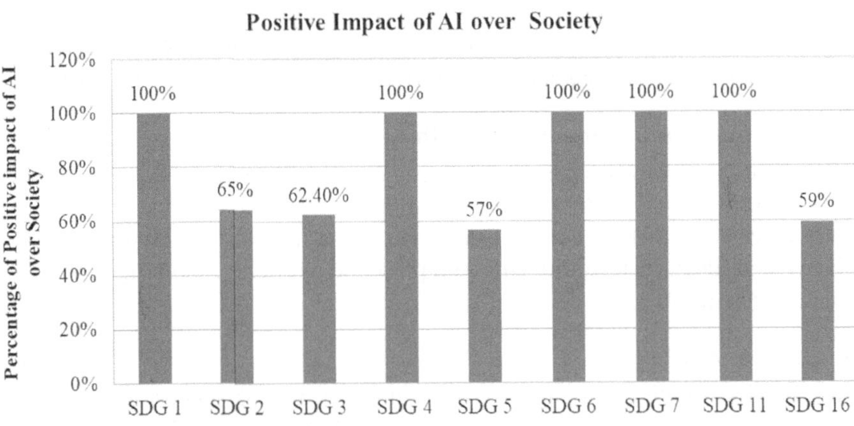

FIGURE 14.3 Percentage of the positive impact of AI on society using SDGs.

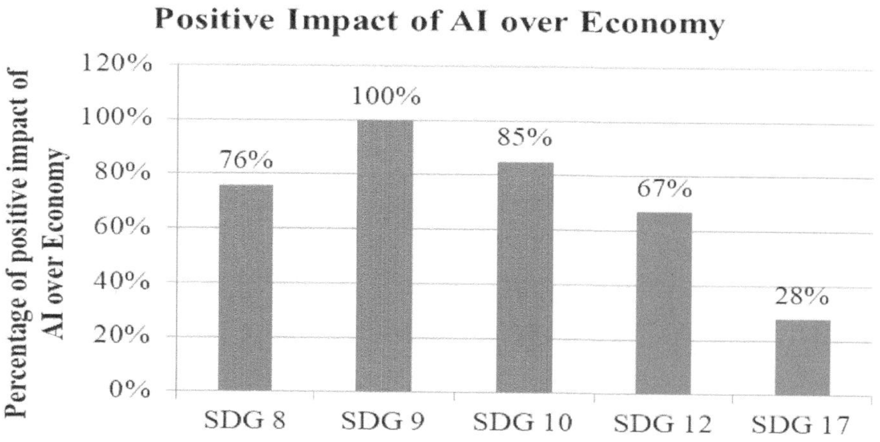

FIGURE 14.4 Percentage of positive impact of AI on the economy using SDGs.

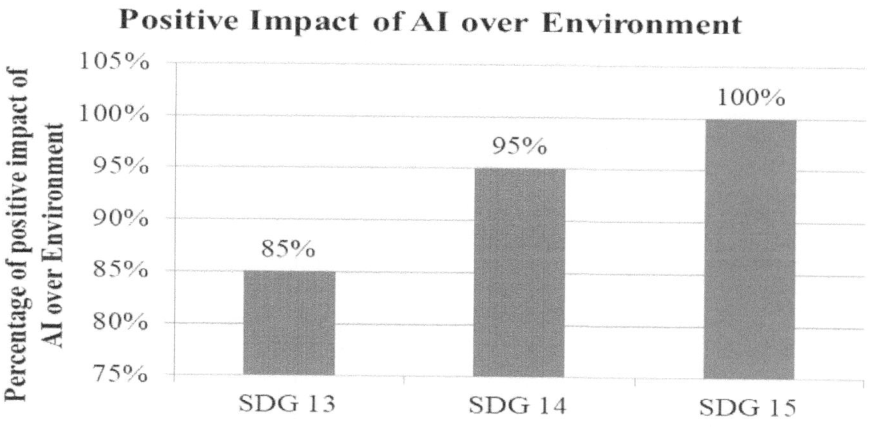

FIGURE 14.5 Percentage of positive impact of AI on the environment using SDG.

while SDGs (Climate Change) and 14 (Life Above Water) are partially affecting the environment.

14.5.2 AI as a Negative Enabler

The development of AI could have a detrimental effect on various targets. In Figure 14.6, it is shown that SDGs are having a negative impact on society with the use of AI. From Figure 14.6, it is found that the SDGs: Zero Poverty (1), Quality Education (4), Sanitation and clean water (6) are having a negative impact on society. Further from Figure 14.7, the SDGs Decreased Inequality (10) and Infrastructure, Business, and Innovation (9) are negatively affecting the environment using AI, while SDG Life Below Water (15) is affecting the environment which is evident from Figure 14.8.

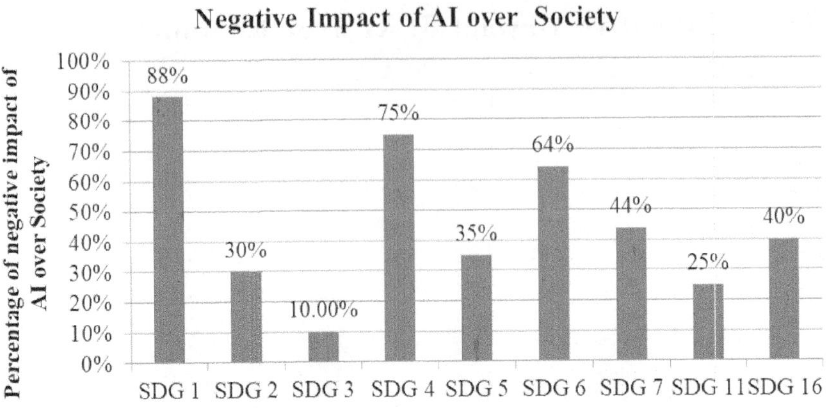

FIGURE 14.6 Percentage of the negative impact of AI on society using SDGs.

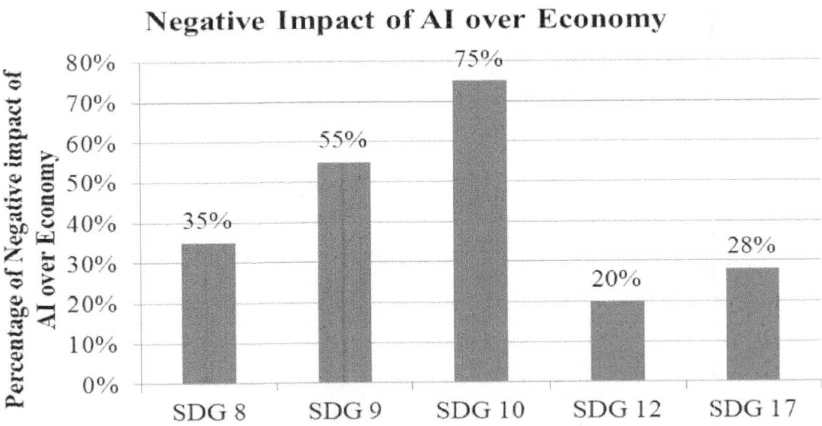

FIGURE 14.7 Percentage of negative impact of AI on the economy using SDGs.

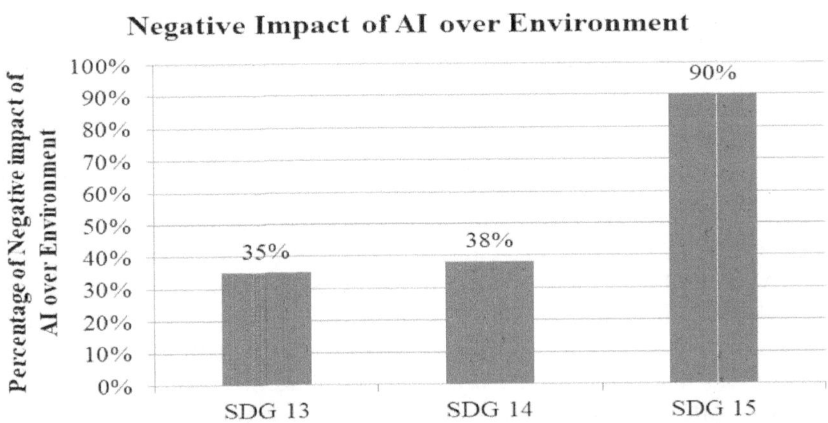

FIGURE 14.8 Percentage of negative impact of AI on the environment using SDGs.

14.6 FRAMEWORK TO INTEGRATE AI AND SUSTAINABILITY

The integration of AI with sustainability can be accomplished using a variety of models and frameworks. The Triple Bottom Line (TBL), which evaluates sustainability based on three pillars, economic, social, and environmental, is a widely used concept (Yigitcanlar & Cugurullo, 2020). The following model can be taken into account while using the TBL framework for AI:

14.6.1 Financial Stability

- *AI for Efficiency*: Create AI systems that optimise energy use, supply chain management, and resource allocation in various industries to cut costs and improve economic sustainability.
- Using AI in green finance make use of AI algorithms to assist financial institutions with impact evaluation, risk assessment, and sustainable investment decisions.

14.6.2 Social Responsibility

- Use AI in healthcare systems to expand access to care, personalise treatment programmes, and improve diagnostics in order to improve social well-being.
- Apply AI technologies to educational systems to improve individualised instruction, flexible tutoring, and universal access to education.

14.6.3 Artificial Intelligence for Environmental Monitoring

- Utilise AI-powered systems to monitor and analyse environmental data, including air quality, water availability, and weather patterns (Nti et al., 2022), to aid in conservation and sustainable decision-making.
- Use AI algorithms to optimise the production of renewable energy (Chen et al., 2023), increase grid efficiency (Mehmood et al., 2019), and facilitate a better integration of renewable sources into the energy system.

14.6.4 Responsible and Ethical AI

- *Governance of AI*: To assure justice, accountability, transparency, and privacy in AI systems, establish ethical norms, rules, and frameworks for AI development and implementation.
- *Bias Reduction*: Create methods to spot and correct biases in AI systems to avoid discriminatory outcomes and guarantee fair treatment for all populations (Khagram et al., 2003; Yu et al., 2021).

These are just a few examples of how AI can be used to advance environmental initiatives. The setting, objectives, and resources at hand will determine the precise model and strategy. The possible social, economic, and environmental effects of AI applications must be carefully considered, and they must be in line with the Sustainable Development Goals.

14.7 MODEL FOR SUSTAINABLE SYSTEMS

The basic model for defining an algorithm for sustainable systems is as follows:

- *Define the Sustainability Goals*: Make it crystal clear what the system's sustainability goals are (Vinuesa et al., 2020). These can involve lessening trash production, increasing renewable energy sources, or advancing social fairness.
- *Data Gathering and Preparation*: Assemble pertinent information about the system's social, economic, and environmental aspects. To make sure the data is high-quality and suitable for AI analysis, clean and pre-process it.
- *Engineering and Feature Choice*: Find the essential elements or parameters that have the most bearing on the sustainability objectives. Make use of feature engineering and selection to produce relevant input variables for the AI model.
- *Choose AI Algorithms*: Decide which AI algorithms are best suited to solve the current sustainability problem (Chen et al., 2023). Depending on the nature of the issue, this can involve regression models, classification models, clustering techniques, or deep learning structures.
- *Model Education*: Utilise the prepared dataset to train the chosen AI model. To improve the performance of the model, alter its hyperparameters, such as the learning rate or network design.
- *A Model's Performance Evaluation*: Using appropriate evaluation measures, rate the effectiveness of the AI model that has been trained. This guarantees that the patterns and relationships between the variables are properly captured by the model.
- *Utilise the Trained AI Model:* To offer decision support for sustainability-related tasks.
- *Decision Support and Optimisation*: This may entail streamlining decision-making procedures, pinpointing problem areas, or optimising resource allocation.
- *Monitoring and Feedback*: Constantly keep an eye on the system's performance and solicit input on how AI-driven judgments turned out. This aids in model improvement and necessary strategy modification.
- *Constant Development and Adaptation*: By utilising AI insights and feedback, you can promote a culture of continuous improvement. To maintain sustained sustainability, modify the system and its tactics in accordance with changing conditions and needs.

14.8 AI ALGORITHMS FOR SUSTAINABILITY IN DIFFERENT DOMAINS

By streamlining procedures, cutting waste, and assisting with informed decision-making, AI algorithms can significantly contribute to the advancement of sustainability (Chen et al., 2023). Here are some ways AI algorithms support sustainability in different domains:

14.8.1 Energy Optimisation

AI algorithms are capable of analysing the patterns of energy use in a variety of systems, including buildings, factories, and transportation networks (Mehmood et al., 2019; Mustapha et al., 2021; Entezari et al., 2023). AI can assist in reducing energy waste and lowering carbon emissions by finding inefficiencies and offering changes.

14.8.2 Management of the Smart Grid

AI algorithms can be used to better control the grid and distribute electricity, balancing the supply and demand for it. With the use of these algorithms, a more efficient and sustainable energy infrastructure can be created by integrating renewable energy sources, predicting trends in energy usage (Yigitcanlar et al., 2021) and reducing power outages.

14.8.3 Waste Management

AI algorithms are capable of analysing vast volumes of data to spot trends and improve waste management procedures. AI can assist in reducing landfill trash and promoting recycling and composting by forecasting waste creation rates, streamlining collection routes, and detecting recycling opportunities.

14.8.4 Environmental Analysis

AI algorithms may interpret data from a variety of sources, including satellites, sensors, and drones, to monitor and assess the state of the environment (Yigitcanlar et al., 2021). This can aid in the prompt detection and response to problems including deforestation, air and water pollution, and the effects of climate change.

14.8.5 Agriculture That is Sustainable

By examining information on crop health, weather patterns, and soil conditions, AI systems can support precision agriculture techniques (Kaur et al., 2023), AI has the potential to save water, use fewer chemicals, and increase crop yields by supplying insights regarding the best times to plant, the need for irrigation, and pest management.

14.8.6 Sustainable Transportation

AI algorithms that analyse traffic patterns, recommend effective routes, and enable ridesharing can optimise transportation networks (Nti et al., 2022), Congestion, fuel use, and greenhouse gas emissions can all be decreased as a result.

14.8.7 Supply Chain Optimisation

By examining data on inventory levels, demand projections, and logistics of transportation, AI algorithms can improve supply chain operations. AI can reduce resource consumption and the carbon footprint by enhancing efficiency and cutting waste in the supply chain.

The use of AI algorithms should be accompanied by ethical considerations and close supervision to ensure that they are consistent with sustainability goals and do not unintentionally damage people or reinforce biases, despite the fact that they have great potential to be sustainable.

14.9 CHALLENGES AND RISK IN IMPLEMENTATION OF AI IN SUSTAINABILITY

While AI applications in sustainability show enormous potential, there are a number of difficulties and dangers that must be taken into account when putting them into practice. To guarantee that AI is used responsibly and effectively for sustainable development, it is crucial to solve these concerns. The following are some significant dangers and concerns connected to AI in sustainability:

- Data bias and quality

For training and decision-making, AI systems significantly rely on vast datasets. Inaccurate or unjust results may result if the data utilised to train these algorithms is inadequate, biased, or of poor quality. For instance, skewed statistics can promote current resource use habits or prolong social and environmental injustices.

- Ethics

AI raises a number of ethical challenges, including privacy, security, and transparency (Khagram et al., 2003). Only with the proper authorisation and security precautions in place should personal information be gathered and utilised. Transparent decision-making processes and accountability measures should be used to ensure that AI systems are fair, and intelligible, and do not violate ethical standards.

- Impact on society and job displacement

As automation replaces some tasks, the widespread use of AI in many industries may result in employment displacement. While AI may open up new job prospects, programmes for retraining and upgrading skills are necessary to ensure a fair transition for people. Furthermore, to minimise any potential negative effects on vulnerable people, the socioeconomic ramifications of AI deployment should be carefully studied.

- Energy use and carbon emissions

The creation and use of AI technology requires a substantial amount of computational power (Entezari et al., 2023), which could result in higher energy use and carbon emissions. As AI systems proliferate, efforts should be taken to reduce the environmental impact of AI by creating energy-efficient algorithms, improving infrastructure, and investigating renewable energy sources.

- Absence of regulatory frameworks

The creation of thorough regulatory frameworks has lagged behind the quick development of AI. Without the right rules and laws, there is a danger that AI may be used without sufficient control, which could result in abuse or unforeseen effects. Establishing reliable governance procedures that guarantee responsible AI deployment and guard against hazards is essential.

- Accessibility and equity

Especially in developing countries or marginalised areas, the affordability and accessibility of AI technologies may present difficulties. To stop the escalation of already existing disparities, it is crucial to guarantee equitable access to AI resources, expertise, and benefits. The digital divide needs to be closed, and diversity in AI deployment should be promoted.

A multidisciplinary strategy encompassing stakeholders from academics, industry, civil society, and policymakers is necessary to address these issues and hazards. To create rules, regulations, and standards that support moral, inclusive, and sustainable AI practices, cooperation is required. We can utilise AI's potential for sustainability while reducing its risks by proactively addressing these issues.

14.10 CONCLUSION

The chapter "AI and Sustainability: Its Recent Trends and Future Prospects" emphasises how AI and sustainability are evolving together as well as how AI has the capacity to solve pressing societal and environmental problems. The chapter looks at the most recent innovations for AI applications that promote sustainability across diverse industries. How AI is being utilised to improve resource consumption and boost energy efficiency is the chapter's first subject. Machine learning algorithms can evaluate large datasets to uncover patterns that can be utilised to maximise the use of energy in buildings, transportation networks, and industrial operations. This reduces costs while also reducing carbon emissions and ecological footprints. It also looks at how AI can improve environmental monitoring and conservation initiatives. AI-powered systems can examine satellite pictures, sensor data, and other data to track wildlife populations, monitor deforestation, and pinpoint places vulnerable to natural disasters. AI supports proactive decision-making for environmental protection and conservation by offering real-time information and early warnings. AI algorithms can evaluate crop data, weather patterns, and soil conditions to improve farming methods, use less water and pesticides, and produce more crops. The chapter also looks at a framework to integrate AI and sustainability. Despite the prospective uses of AI in sustainability, the chapter emphasises the difficulties involved in putting it into practice. It is important to carefully analyse ethical issues like employment displacement, algorithmic bias, and privacy. The chapter focuses on the potential for AI and sustainability in the future. Unlocking the full potential of AI in tackling global sustainability concerns requires ongoing study, development, and collaboration between academia, industry, and policymakers. We can work towards a more sustainable and resilient future for the environment and society at large by using AI technology responsibly and ethically.

BIBLIOGRAPHY

Ainapure, B., Khamparia, S., Varshney, A., & Baheti, N. (2022). IoT enabled smart water ATM with digital payment. In Proceedings of 3rd International Conference on Intelligent Engineering and Management, ICIEM 2022 (pp. 189–194), doi: 10.1109/ICIEM54221.2022.9853074.

Andeobu, L., Wibowo, S., & Grandhi, S. (2022). Artificial intelligence applications for sustainable solid waste management practices in Australia: A systematic review. *Science of the Total Environment, 834*, 155389.

Barnett, J., & Dovers, S. (2001). Environmental security, sustainability and policy. *Pacifica Review: Peace, Security & Global Change, 13*(2), 157–169.

Chen, Z., Wu, M., Chan, A., Li, X., & Ong, Y. S. (2023). Survey on AI sustainability: Emerging trends on learning algorithms and research challenges. *IEEE Computational Intelligence Magazine, 18*(2), 60–77.

Dhamija, P., & Bag, S. (2020). Role of artificial intelligence in operations environment: A review and bibliometric analysis. *The TQM Journal, 32*(4), 869–896.

Di Vaio, A., Boccia, F., Landriani, L., & Palladino, R. (2020). Artificial intelligence in the agri-food system: Rethinking sustainable business models in the COVID-19 scenario. *Sustainability, 12*(12), 4851.

Entezari, A., Aslani, A., Zahedi, R., & Noorollahi, Y. (2023). Artificial intelligence and machine learning in energy systems: A bibliographic perspective. *Energy Strategy Reviews, 45*, 101017.

Feroz, A. K., Zo, H., & Chiravuri, A. (2021). Digital transformation and environmental sustainability: A review and research agenda. *Sustainability, 13*(3), 1530.

Hsu, L. P., Huang, Y. K., & Chang, Y. C. (2022). The implementation of artificial intelligence in dentistry could enhance environmental sustainability. *Journal of Dental Sciences, 17*(2), 1081.

Kar, A. K., Choudhary, S. K., & Singh, V. K. (2022). How can artificial intelligence impact sustainability: A systematic literature review. *Journal of Cleaner Production, 376*, 134120.

Kaur, B., & Kaur, G. (2022). Heart disease prediction using modified machine learning algorithm. In International Conference on Innovative Computing and Communications: Proceedings of ICICC 2022, Volume 1 (pp. 189–201). Singapore: Springer Nature Singapore.

Kaur, G., Adhikari, N., Krishnapriya, S., Wawale, S. G., Malik, R. Q., Zamani, A. S., & Osei-Owusu, J. (2023). Recent advancements in deep learning frameworks for precision fish farming opportunities, challenges, and applications. *Journal of Food Quality, 2023.*

Khagram, S., Clark, W., & Raad, D. F. (2003). From the environment and human security to sustainable security and development. *Journal of Human Development, 4*(2), 289–313.

Kumar, A., Sharma, S., Goyal, N., Singh, A., Cheng, X., & Singh, P. (2021). Secure and energy-efficient smart building architecture with emerging technology IoT. *Computer Communications, 176*, 207–217.

Leal Filho, W., Yang, P., Eustachio, J. H. P. P., Azul, A. M., Gellers, J. C., Gielczyk, A., …, & Kozlova, V. (2023). Deploying digitalisation and artificial intelligence in sustainable development research. *Environment, Development and Sustainability, 25*(6), 4957–4988.

Lee, K. (2021). A systematic review on social sustainability of artificial intelligence in product design. *Sustainability, 13*(5), 2668.

Liao, M., Lan, K., & Yao, Y. (2022). Sustainability implications of artificial intelligence in the chemical industry: A conceptual framework. *Journal of Industrial Ecology, 26*(1), 164–182.

Louman, B., Keenan, R. J., Kleinschmit, D., Atmadja, S., Sitoe, A. A., Nhantumbo, I., …, & Morales, J. P. (2019). SDG 13: Climate action—impacts on forests and people. In Sustainable development goals: Their impacts on forests and people (pp. 419–444). Cambridge University Press.

Mehmood, M. U., Chun, D., Han, H., Jeon, G., & Chen, K. (2019). A review of the applications of artificial intelligence and big data to buildings for energy-efficiency and a comfortable indoor living environment. *Energy and Buildings, 202*, 109383.

Mhlanga, D. (2021). Artificial intelligence in the industry 4.0, and its impact on poverty, innovation, infrastructure development, and the sustainable development goals: Lessons from emerging economies? *Sustainability, 13*(11), 5788.

Moodaley, W., & Telukdarie, A. (2023). Greenwashing, sustainability reporting, and artificial intelligence: A systematic literature review. *Sustainability, 15*(2), 1481.

Mustapha, U. F., Alhassan, A. W., Jiang, D. N., & Li, G. L. (2021). Sustainable aquaculture development: A review on the roles of cloud computing, Internet of Things and artificial intelligence (CIA). *Reviews in Aquaculture, 13*(4), 2076–2091.

Nishant, R., Kennedy, M., & Corbett, J. (2020). Artificial intelligence for sustainability: Challenges, opportunities, and a research agenda. *International Journal of Information Management, 53*, 102104.

Nti, E. K., Cobbina, S. J., Attafuah, E. E., Opoku, E., & Gyan, M. A. (2022). Environmental sustainability technologies in biodiversity, energy, transportation and water management using artificial intelligence: A systematic review. *Sustainable Futures, 4*, 100068.

Owe, A., & Baum, S. D. (2021, December). The ethics of sustainability for artificial intelligence. In Proceedings of the 1st International Conference on AI for People: Towards Sustainable AI (CAIP 2021b) (pp. 1–17).

Rosário, A. T., & Dias, J. C. (2022). Sustainability and the digital transition: A literature review. *Sustainability, 14*(7), 4072.

Sakshi, Shashi, Cerchione, R., & Bansal, H. (2020). Measuring the impact of sustainability policy and practices in tourism and hospitality industry. *Business Strategy and the Environment, 29*(3), 1109–1126.

Schoormann, T., Strobel, G., Möller, F., & Petrik, D. (2021). Achieving sustainability with artificial intelligence-a survey of information systems research. In Proceedings of the 42nd International Conference on Information Systems (ICIS 2021).

Sharma, G. D., Yadav, A., & Chopra, R. (2020). Artificial intelligence and effective governance: A review, critique and research agenda. *Sustainable Futures, 2*, 100004.

Talari, P., Bharathiraja, N., Kaur, G., Alshahrani, H., Al Reshan, M. S., Sulaiman, A., & Shaikh, A. (2024). Hybrid feature selection and classification technique for early prediction and severity of diabetes type 2. *PLoS One, 19*(1), e0292100.

Tyagi, R., Bagchi, S., Kaur, G., Sharma, N., Khan, M. N. A., & Prabha, C. (2023, April). Cyber security architecture for safe data storage and retrieval for Smart City pplications. In 2023 International Conference on Computational Intelligence and Sustainable Engineering Solutions (CISES) (pp. 580–585). IEEE.

Vinuesa, R., Azizpour, H., Leite, I., Balaam, M., Dignum, V., Domisch, S., & Fuso Nerini, F. (2020). The role of artificial intelligence in achieving the sustainable development goals. *Nature Communications, 11*(1), 1–10.

Yigitcanlar, T., & Cugurullo, F. (2020). The sustainability of artificial intelligence: An urbanistic viewpoint from the lens of smart and sustainable cities. *Sustainability*, *12*(20), 8548.

Yigitcanlar, T., Mehmood, R., & Corchado, J. M. (2021). Green artificial intelligence: Towards an efficient, sustainable and equitable technology for smart cities and futures. *Sustainability*, *13*(16), 8952.

Yu, K. H., Zhang, Y., Li, D., Montenegro-Marin, C. E., & Kumar, P. M. (2021). Environmental planning based on reduce, reuse, recycle and recover using artificial intelligence. *Environmental Impact Assessment Review*, *86*, 106492.

15 Implementation of Sustainable Goals Using Artificial Intelligence

Recent Trends and Future Prospects

Madhavi Shamkuwar, Vidya Kadam, Deepanshu Sharma, and Jayesh Katkar

15.1 INTRODUCTION

The new Goals are distinctive in that they urge action from all nations—rich and poor alike—to advance development while preserving the environment. They understand that confronting climate change and environmental protection must coexist with initiatives that promote economic growth and fulfil a variety of social needs, such as those related to education, health, social protection, and job opportunities.

Governments are expected to assume ownership and create national frameworks for achieving the 17 Goals even though the SDGs are not legally obligatory. Countries are primarily responsible for monitoring and evaluating the progress made in implementing the Goals, which calls for the timely, accurate, and high-quality gathering of data. The technologies are changing how the SDGs can be implemented by all the stakeholders—the government, politicians, people in the public, and decision-makers—in a beneficial way. The technologies are the block chain, artificial intelligence (AI), green computing, cloud computing, Internet of Things, etc. The rise of AI and its gradually increasing impact on several industries need an evaluation of its influence on the attainment of Sustainable Development Goals (SDGs). It is imperative for today's businesses to adapt the changing nature of digitalization for sustainability. AI has risen to the top of the global debate in recent years. Due to their potential to materially enhance the future, sustainable development and AI have recently received a lot of attention. The 17 UN SDGs and 169 targets are part of the UN's 2030 Vision for Sustainable Development, which 193 Member States endorsed in an effort to 'Leave nobody Behind.' Everyone must participate in development of all aspects. This is mainly relevant for those who are most marginalized and at risk. This all-encompassing plan acknowledges that it is no longer adequate to only focus on economic growth but also on creating safer, more prosperous communities.

AI can help to achieve 17 SDGs. The achievement of the SDGs internationally relied heavily on India. The world and environment will be significantly affected by

DOI: 10.1201/9781003640776-15

the sustainable development of one-sixth of humanity. It will be with fewer obstacles, more optimism, and greater certainty of success. Leveraging the power of AI has enormous promise to promote positive transformation and expedite the transition to a sustainable future. A tremendous potential to address complex challenges like climate change, resource scarcity, urbanization, and food security exists at the junction of AI and sustainable development. AI systems are able to evaluate enormous volumes of data, identify patterns, and make defensible conclusions. As a result, they provide creative solutions and optimize resource usage in previously unthinkable ways. The new Goals are distinctive in that they urge action from all nations—rich and poor alike—to advance development while preserving the environment. They understand that confronting climate change and environmental protection must coexist with initiatives that promote economic growth and fulfil a variety of social needs, such as those related to education, health, social protection, and job opportunities.

Governments are expected to assume ownership and create national frameworks for achieving the 17 goals even though the SDGs are not legally obligatory. Countries are primarily responsible for monitoring and evaluating the progress made in implementing the Goals, which calls for the timely, accurate, and high-quality gathering of data. Based on national-level analysis, regional follow-up and review will help with follow-up. The purpose of sustainable development has become a global priority, from nations to organizations to balance the economic growth, environmental protection, and social equity. In this situation, to accelerate the achievement of the United Nations SDGs the integration of AI technologies embraces immense potential. In a various types of industries, from energy mitigation and climate change to agriculture and healthcare sectors. This chapter discovers recent trends and future prospects in the implementation of sustainable goals using AI, highlighting key applications, challenges, and opportunities.

The sustainable development has become a top concern on a global scale as nations and institutions see the need to establish a balance between economic growth, social justice, and environmental protection. The achievement of the SDGs of the United Nations has the potential to be significantly sped up by the use of AI technologies. In this chapter, the use of AI to achieve sustainable goals is reviewed, with a focus on key applications, challenges, and opportunities.

The chapter examines the role of AI in achieving SDG, positive effects, and opportunities that might result from the fusion of AI with sustainable development. It also shows revolutionary effects of AI on accomplishing sustainable development objectives and outlining likely upcoming difficulties and possibilities.

15.1.1 Role of AI in Achieving Sustainable Development Goals

Artificial intelligence-driven (AI-Driven) digital technologies (DT) are inherently intertwined with the ability to engage, comprehend, and interact with individuals, enterprises, economies, and the broader spectrum of human existence(Zhang et al, 2021). The concept of AI can be grasped as a holistic fusion and amalgamation of various applications with other 'Digital Technologies,' aiming to develop machines endowed with the capacity to emulate human thinking processes (Bozkurt et al, 2021 & Di Vaio et al., 2020). The economic and societal ramifications of AI-Driven

DTs are steadily growing, and more recently, they have taken on a significant role within the context of the SDGs outlined in Agenda 2030 (Jurgilevich et al, 2016). Implementing these technologies are becoming a pivotal decision for both developed and developing nations. We are currently teetering on the edge of a fourth industrial revolution that promises to reshape how we connect, work, and live in profound ways. The opportunities and advantages presented by AI are immense, often surpassing our wildest imaginations (Lei & Wang, 2020). As we step into the era of sustainable development, marked by the guidance of the 17 SDGs shaping nations worldwide, there is a significant anticipation that AI and DT like digital twins, block chain, virtual and augmented reality, and big data, among others, hold tremendous potential to elevate economic, environmental, and societal aspects in the global pursuit of SDG objectives.

To maximize the impact of AI on SDGs, certain priorities and key elements have been identified in Pereira and Santos (2013), including: empowering AI-driven DT with ubiquitous and dependable data accessibility; strengthening the dialogue between science, industry, and government for the transfer of technology and knowledge; tailoring and coordinating action plans to fit the unique circumstances of each country and context; and develop alternative standards to facilitate the evaluation of SDG progress.

Currently, the global discourse revolves around the feasibility of pursuing and attaining this objective. Additionally, AI is geared towards addressing historical challenges associated with handling vast amounts of data, which have traditionally been regarded as unwieldy and difficult to manage (Wu & Hu, 2018) In the present day, AI-based systems have emerged that can efficiently handle large datasets while ensuring a certain degree of security, thanks to innovative data storage solutions like HDFS, no SQL, and decentralized block chain data storage (Djenouri et al, 2021).

Numerous studies have also highlighted the benefits of employing AI-Driven DT in economic and environmental assessments. These technologies, particularly in industry segments as indicated in references (Meet, 2020), facilitate cleaner production processes, resulting in increased productivity, less toxic and more biodegradable products, and improved efficiency in the utilization of raw materials, water, and energy. The ultimate objective is to reduce or eliminate waste generation through non-generation, reduction, or recycling. Given the widespread impact of climate change on many nations, environmental sustainability is gaining paramount importance in global business operations. Sustainability, a universally recognized concept, encompasses three key dimensions: environmental, economic, and social (Dwivedi et al, 2022). In today's fiercely competitive market, thriving economies and environmental degradation are incompatible, and achieving environmental sustainability is associated with inherent risks that can affect business operations and prospects.

The commitment of the UK Government to implement the International Norm for Event Sustainability Management Systems (Nishant et al., 2020) underscores the leadership and ambition of countries in the realm of sustainable event management. However, environmental sustainability is a multifaceted challenge fraught with trade-offs, often oversimplified by self-serving solutions. Trade can exert both positive and negative influences on the environment, with economic growth often resulting in increased pollution and natural resource depletion. Here, AI plays a pivotal role in addressing these environmental sustainability challenges, with far-reaching implications for various sectors (Nandi & Sarkar, 2019).

The Governmental Agri-Food Transformation Fund aims to encourage the global adoption of precision farming practices (Silver & Le, 2017). Additionally, timely initiatives for workforce up skilling, delivered through technical and vocational education and training (TVET) and micro-credentials across sectors and industries, are essential. AI can contribute significantly to personalized learning for quality education (Luengo-Oroz et al, 2012). In the pursuit of efficient food production, AI can play a crucial role in reducing waste through optimized supply chains (WHO, 2021). Automated food delivery systems that predict daily orders based on consumer big data contribute to ingredient logistics and minimize food waste, promoting a more sustainable food system. Implementing circular economy principles within the food system is of paramount importance (Chen & Liu, 2014) with transformative potential, particularly for large fast-food chains worldwide, to optimize resource utilization.

Another transformative shift involves transitioning from animal-based to plant-based proteins, which holds the promise of significantly reducing greenhouse gas emissions (Rolnick et al., 2019).

1. *Eradicating Poverty and Hunger*: AI can contribute to destroy poverty by enhancing education, healthcare, and financial services. By using data analysis, AI systems can able to identify patterns of poverty and food paucity, allowing targeted interventions and resource optimization for efficient allocation.
2. *Ensuring Health and Well-Being*: AI has made transformations in healthcare by developing diagnostics, treatment plans, and disease control. By using machine learning (ML) algorithms, AI is analysing medical data, and predicted diseases. This proactive strategy transforms the effective healthcare management and high-quality services access.
3. *Promoting Quality Education*: AI provides adaptive learning experiences, which make education more accessible and individualized. Virtual classrooms and educational chat bots can assist learners in acquiring knowledge skills and bridging gaps in education quality.
4. *Fostering Sustainable Cities and Communities*: AI-driven technologies can optimize urban planning, energy consumption, and transportation systems, leading to smarter cities with reduced environmental impact. Intelligent systems can manage traffic flow, optimize energy usage, and enhance waste management, promoting sustainable and resilient communities.
5. *Combating Climate Change*: AI plays a vital role in analysing vast amounts of environmental data and generating insights for climate modelling, prediction, and mitigation strategies. ML algorithms can optimize renewable energy systems, enable smart grids, and facilitate efficient resource management, contributing to climate change adaptation and mitigation.
6. *Ensuring Responsible Consumption and Production*: AI-powered supply chain management systems can enhance transparency, traceability, and sustainability in production and distribution processes. By monitoring and

optimizing resource usage, reducing waste, and identifying sustainable alternatives, AI helps achieve responsible consumption and production patterns. Revolutionary Effects and Future Possibilities:

To gain multiple dimensions on the above said topic, the book chapter is organized into multiple topics and subtopics.

15.1.1.1 Journey of Global Goals

It comprises about the Journey of the Global goals, its historical significance and the evolution. The history, present and future of Global goals, will be described in the section.

The Global goals, commonly referred to as the SDGs, are an international call to action to eradicate poverty, safeguard the environment, and provide prosperity for everyone. In September 2015, the UN formally endorsed them, building on the achievements and knowledge gained from the Millennium Development Goals (MDGs). The SDGs have subsequently spread throughout the world, serving as a model for governments, corporations, and civil society organizations, heralding a fundamental shift towards a more sustainable and just future.

The 17 SDGs include a wide range of goals, each of which focusses on a different facet of sustainable development. These objectives are linked together in recognition of the complex relationships that exist between social inclusion, economic progress, and environmental conservation. The path to accomplishing these objectives is characterized by advancement, difficulties, and a common commitment to leave no one behind (United Nations (UN), 2015).

Goal 1: No Poverty—By 2030, SDG 1 aspires to end poverty in all of its manifestations. Due to targeted policies, investments, and economic development across many areas, substantial progress has been made in decreasing extreme poverty globally since the adoption of the SDGs (United Nations (UN), G1, 2015a).

Goal 2: Zero Hunger SDG 2 is focussed on attaining food security, putting an end to hunger, and advancing sustainable agriculture. Improvements to agricultural practices and food delivery networks are assisting in reducing hunger in many countries despite issues like climate change and food insecurity (United Nations (UN), G2, 2015b).

Goal 3: Good Health and Well-Being—SDG 3 aims to guarantee healthy lifestyles and advance wellbeing for everyone. With the COVID-19 pandemic showing the need for affordable healthcare and robust public health systems, this objective has taken on new relevance (United Nations (UN), G3, 2015c).

Goal 4: Quality Education—SDG 4 aims to offer all people access to inclusive, high-quality education. Although there has been progress in increasing educational access, there are still issues with guaranteeing educational fairness, particularly in marginalized areas (United Nations (UN), G4, 2015d).

Goal 5: Gender Equality—SDG 5 advocates for women's empowerment and gender equality. Despite more awareness and support for gender equality, violence and discrimination against women remain plague many areas (United Nations (UN), G5, 2015e).

Goal 6: Clean Water and Sanitation SDG 6 aims to provide everyone with access to clean water and sanitation. Although access to sanitary facilities and clean water has increased, inequities still exist, especially in rural regions (United Nations (UN), G6, 2015f).

Goal 7: Affordable and Clean Energy Affordable and clean energy sources are a requirement of SDG 7. Energy efficiency initiatives and the switch to renewable sources of energy are progressing, but the world's energy system is still complicated (United Nations (UN), G7, 2015g).

Goal 8: Decent Work and Economic Growth SDG 8 aims to advance steady, inclusive, and environmentally friendly economic growth. Unemployment, unregulated labour markets, and income inequality remain problems (United Nations (UN), G8, 2015h).

Goal 9: Industry, Innovation, and Infrastructure SDG 9 aspires to advance inclusive and sustainable industrialization, boost innovation, and create resilient infrastructure. Economic growth is primarily fuelled by infrastructure and innovation investments (United Nations (UN), G9, 2015i).

Goal 10: Reduced Inequality SDG 10 is concerned with eliminating inequality both within and between nations. Even if improvements have been achieved, economic, service, and opportunity, inequities still exist and call for focussed interventions (United Nations (UN), G10, 2015j).

Goal 11: Sustainable Cities and Communities Goal 11 seeks to create inclusive, secure, resilient, and sustainable cities and human settlements. It talks on things like housing, transportation, and environmental deterioration in cities (United Nations (UN), G11, 2015k).

Goal 12: Responsible Consumption and Production Goal 12 promotes sustainable consumption and production patterns. It calls for reducing waste generation, promoting resource efficiency, and ensuring sustainable management of natural resources (United Nations (UN), G12, 2015l).

Goal 13: Climate Action Goal 13 emphasizes taking urgent action to combat climate change and its impacts. It calls for strengthening resilience to climate-related hazards and integrating climate measures into national policies (United Nations (UN), G13, 2015m).

Goal 14: Life Below Water Goal 14 focusses on conserving and sustainably using oceans, seas, and marine resources. It talks about things like protecting marine habitats, overfishing, and marine pollution (United Nations (UN), G14, 2015n).

Goal 15: Life on Land The protection, restoration, and promotion of biodiversity, forests, and sustainable use of terrestrial ecosystems are the objectives of Goal 15. It addresses problems including habitat loss, land degradation, and deforestation (United Nations (UN), G15, 2015o).

Goal 16: Peace, Justice, and Strong Institutions Goal 16 is concerned with fostering inclusive and peaceful communities, ensuring that everyone has access to justice, and creating efficient, transparent, and responsible institutions. It talks about things like access to justice, corruption, and violence (United Nations (UN), G16, 2015p).

Goal 17: Partnerships for the Goals Goal 17 emphasize the importance of global partnerships to achieve the other SDGs. It calls for enhanced international cooperation, technology transfer, and support for developing countries (United Nations (UN), G17, 2015q).

The SDGs' path is characterized by a shared resolve to address some of the most critical issues facing the globe. Beyond governments, corporations, civil society groups, and people are also bound by this promise. The 2030 Agenda acknowledges that in order to achieve these objectives, multi-stakeholder collaboration, innovation, and global cooperation are necessary. The SDGs are a massive worldwide initiative to build a more just and sustainable society. Although there will be progress and obstacles along the way to accomplishing these goals, the trip is worthwhile. It is vital to keep in mind that, as we move closer to 2030, the SDGs will only be successful if individuals, communities, and countries work together. We can ensure that future generations have a brighter future by adopting the spirit of these objectives.

15.2 THE UMBRELLA OF AI

The creation of computers and systems that are capable of carrying out activities that traditionally require human intellect is the focus of the large discipline of computer science known as AI. The goal of AI, an interdisciplinary field of computer science, is to create devices, programmes, and algorithms that resemble human cognitive processes in order to address challenging information processing issues that are intractable with current techniques (Doherty & Esmaeili, 2020). Computer systems are mostly used in AI to mimic human thought processes. This field has a broad research focus and has been used in a variety of contexts. AI covers the wide view of various domain, though it specifically relies on computer science, but now it applicable to many more such as linguistics, philosophy, and mathematics (Zhao & Feng, 2018). The MYCIN programme, a demonstration of a deductive AI system, aids medical professionals in the diagnosis of infections. Therefore, by rewriting some portions of the programme and using it on a new database, the fundamental reasoning capabilities of MYCIN might be extended to various topics (Bernhard, 1980).

The term 'artificial intelligence' (AI) refers to a broad variety of innovations, methods, and disciplines that are all intended to simulate or duplicate certain facets of human intellect and cognitive abilities. These disciplines and technologies frequently fall under the purview of AI. The AI has significantly curtailed the human efforts. The contribution of AI is in the monitoring and diagnostic function's enhanced automation, particularly in the duty of complicated and time-consuming data correlation and interpretation moving from a human operator to a computer (Melamed, 1991).

AI is significantly booming in almost all the sectors and which is now considered as ubiquitous. AI can be integrated with almost all the domains among which unification of AI and optimization is very prevalent and majorly supports in decision making. The complete amalgamation of both gives the framework for unified programming (Lee, 1996). In the military, the advancement of AI has progressively reached the preliminary application stage, but there are still at least there are some conundrums which prevents to use the AI capabilities to the fullest. Though AI provides a great support in military applications such as strategic planning, cyber security, and autonomous weapon system (Zhang et al, 2020).

The following are some of the important disciplines and technologies that are frequently linked to AI:

ML: ML is a subset of AI that focusses on the development of algorithms and models that enable computers to learn from and make predictions or decisions based on data. Supervised learning, unsupervised learning, and reinforcement learning are some common ML approaches.

Deep Learning: Deep learning is a specialized branch of ML that uses artificial neural networks, particularly deep neural networks (DNNs) with multiple layers (deep architectures), to solve complex problems, such as image and speech recognition. For many contemporary applications of AI, DNNs represent the cutting edge. You have undoubtedly experienced the effects of one of them. Personal digital assistants like Siri, Cortana, Alexa, and Google Assistant, as well as automated album creation in Google Photos; all tag contacts in Facebook automatically (Garg & Agarwal, 2019).

Natural Language Processing (NLP): NLP is the field of AI dedicated to the interaction between computers and human language. It includes tasks like language translation, sentiment analysis, and chatbots.

Computer Vision: Computer vision involves teaching machines to interpret and understand visual information from the world, including image and video analysis, object detection, and image classification.

Robotics: Robotics is the integration of AI with physical machines, enabling robots to perceive their environment, make decisions, and take actions. This includes both industrial and service robots. A novel idea called AI Brick, which enables the construction of specialized tools with AI at their core, was put out in the context of cloud robotics (Sabol & Sincak, 2018).

Expert Systems: Expert systems use knowledge-based techniques to solve problems in specific domains. They encode human expertise and logic to make decisions or provide recommendations. Numerous engineering applications, notably in industrial and civil engineering, have called for the use of expert systems. They have been used most successfully in circumstances with straightforward guidelines (Sadiku, 1989).

AI in Healthcare: AI in health sector is persistently burgeoning and highly encouraging. AI technologies are being used to assist with medical diagnoses, drug discovery, and personalized treatment plans. The most important conclusions from the use of AI in health preservation are that they are attempting to address one of the major issues in health—a lack of information. They change the consumer's data collection and focus/activity around the way in which their conduct influences the emerging determinants of health, while also replacing the consumer's 'trial and error' activity in discovery (Godber, 2018).

AI used as a trusted adviser in the medical industry would enhance human potential and lead to exponential advancements. The implementation of AI in areas such as robotic surgery, nursing assistants, predictive diagnosis, image analysis, and administrative workflow produces excellent outcomes despite clinical judgements that place it at a lower level, revolutionizing healthcare in the process (Titu & Stanciu, 1998).

Autonomous Vehicles: AI plays a crucial role in the development of self-driving cars, enabling them to perceive their surroundings and make driving decisions.

Recommender Systems: Recommender systems use AI algorithms to provide personalized recommendations in various domains, such as e-commerce and content streaming services.

AI Ethics and Governance: As AI technologies advance, there is a growing focus on ethical considerations, transparency, and responsible AI development and deployment.

AI in Education: With the advent of AI, education system is blessed with all the major breakthroughs which AI brought. It has the ability to induce the intelligence teaching system, examination system, and personalized learning.

AI gives instructors a platform for self-expression and professional growth, inspiring them to continually enhance their teaching materials, preventing the waste of human resources, and more effectively encouraging the creation of teaching resources (Lei & Wang, 2020).

These are just a few examples of the technologies and areas that fall under the AI umbrella. AI has applications in nearly every industry, and its impact on society continues to grow as research and development in the field advance. Somehow, these domains assist in leveraging the sustainable development. AI imparts a major impact on the sustainability and persistently enhancing its capabilities.

15.2.1 Implementation of AI in SDG

This section will be related to the effective usage of AI in meeting the sustainable goals.

15.2.1.1 An Overview to Sustainable Development

Sustainable development is a concept and approach that seeks to balance the economic, social, and environmental dimensions of human development to meet the needs of the present without compromising the ability of future generations to meet their own needs. This concept is substantially ensures the harmony between the resources and enable us to use the same wisely. Decision-making places a strong emphasis on sustainable development, and system performance is optimized to save fundamental resources. Through user interfaces, humans may monitor the autonomous functioning and, if necessary, make changes or physically operate the devices (Riekki & Mämmelä, 2021).

The three pillars viz. social equality, environmental sustainability, and economic success can lead to sustainable development. All economic and social sectors, as well as the government and other social organizations, must contribute in order to accomplish it (Nam, 2016).

Sustainable development has a core control over the resources and its utilization. However, the degree of living quality is indirectly influenced by product quality, which defines one of the elements of sustainable development. Product quality is enhanced by maintaining production's rhythm and continuity (Voitko et al, 2020).

It is a holistic and long-term perspective on development that aims to create a harmonious and equitable society while also preserving the planet's natural resources and ecosystems. There are three sub-parts which incorporates the economic, ecological, and social sustainable development and they all are dependent and mutually conditioned on each other (Heng, 2011).

15.2.1.2 Technological Innovation Ameliorates Sustainable Development

The technology has ground breaking victories which successfully bolster the concept of sustainable development. Science and technology has phenomenal ways to exploit the different mechanisms to maintain the effective sustainable development.

Majorly AI comes under as an influential contrivance and with dominant capabilities to leverage sustainability. Biotechnology, membrane separation technology, high gradient magnetic separation technology, remote sensing technology, nuclear technology, activated carbon technology, and other advancements in science and technology have all had a significant impact on environmental management and offer great potential (Ashtaiwi, 2020).

15.2.1.3 Leveraging Sustainable Development Using Artificial Intelligence

AI is one of the most remarkable finding which has a capability to stimulate the human-like intelligence and enhances the ease of every domain. The potentiality of AI is considerably conquering the commercial markets and it advances every processes and also addresses the umpteen loopholes in the existing systems.

The goal of AI research is to develop robots with human-like cognition and reasoning patterns. The majority of AI is made up of ML. The goal of ML is to create prediction models by teaching computers to recognize and extrapolate patterns in datasets (Gandhi et al, 2020). AI can reduce waste and resource consumption by optimizing resource allocation and supply chain management. This contributes to sustainability and is applicable to sectors like manufacturing and logistics. This way it ensures the optimality of resources and maintains a track of resources.

AI is the partner that sustainable development requires to more efficiently plan, build, and execute the future of our planet and its sustainability. Among many other things, technology like AI will help us construct more effectively, use resources responsibly, and decrease and manage the trash we make. It also focusses on the algorithm for adjusting traffic signals based on the volume of vehicles in order to lessen congestion, give passengers speedier transit, and cut down on pollution (State gov., 2023). AI has the potential to enhance healthcare outcomes and access, supporting sustainable development. Telemedicine, health monitoring systems, and diagnostic tools powered by AI can reach disadvantaged groups and ease the strain on the healthcare system.

In one of the ministerial side event organized in New York, where different parts of the world made commitments on harnessing the AI to accelerate the sustainable development. Japan provided an example of how to achieve synergies between several sustainable development objectives by utilizing AI to optimize supply and demand balance stability in the domestic renewable energy sector (Active, 2023).

Traffic management is an obvious example of how AI contributes to sustainability. Urban mobility with AI enables the prediction of traffic congestion and the recommendation of other routes. This technique forecasts vehicle demand by zone and time for shared mobility. This implies that businesses may plan how many automobiles are available to residents based on those individuals' requirements. This method minimizes the environmental effect of transportation while simultaneously facilitating it.

AI has substantially strengthening the sustainable development by meeting the abilities for all defined SDGs in sustainability. We have defined 17 global goals which are standardized and formulated by members of United Nations. SDG has the potential to address the global criticalities and establish a future that is more ethical and sustainable for both people and the environment. All 17 global goals have their motive and they all somehow interconnected to each other.

A research that appeared in Nature suggests that AI might assist in achieving 79% of the SDGs as per the study published in Nature (Fernández-Aller et al, 2021). AI immensely supports all the domains such as healthcare, smart city, city pollution, and many more. It has a considerable prestige which can aid in almost all the sectors. By assisting in the population's access to services for food, health, water, and energy, AI may serve as an enabler for all the aims. It may also promote low-carbon systems, such as promoting the development of circular economies and resource-efficient smart cities.

There has been a huge considerably on achieving SDGs and sustainable development in Europe. A normative framework at the European level will probably be necessary to achieve the goal of an inclusive, sustainable, and human-centred AI in Europe. There has been going a huge hits and trials with AI to escalate the concept of sustainable development. To encourage SDG-driven AI and public-private partnership in the sharing of technology and data, financial and regulatory incentives are needed (Vinuesa et al, 2020).

We can also make use of data mining and ML which supports the potential of AI. The improvement of data mining and ML methods for event prediction is the focus of in-depth research and applications of AI technology to the SDGs. Applications like anticipating severe weather or recidivist criminal behaviour fall under this category (Mehmood & Mahadeo, 2020).

There has been a water-related disasters or a lingering situation of bad water quality which affects the sustainability to a larger extent. AI has a potential to forecast the water-related disasters, assessing the water quality, etc. Water management systems with AI-IoT capabilities enable facility managers to track water demand and usage and evaluate water system efficiency in real-time (Gambín et al, 2021). Also, there water quality hugely affects the marine life at coastal areas for which costal water management is a necessity. Numerous studies on issues related to coastal sustainability have revealed ways that Earth Observation (EO) data and technologies can assist coastal management initiatives, particularly in relation to environmental monitoring, such as the detection of harmful algal blooms (HABs), disaster response aided by early warning systems, flood monitoring, maritime safety, and security issues like the detection of vessels and oil spills, and sea-state forecasting (Fisher, 2011).

15.2.2 Key Principles and Elements of Sustainable Development Include

15.2.2.1 Environmental Sustainability

This aspect emphasizes the importance of protecting and conserving natural resources and ecosystems, reducing pollution and waste, and mitigating the negative impacts of human activities on the environment. There are intelligent controls for usage phases as well as planning and scheduling issues for manufacturing, such cutting supply chains to lessen their impact on the environment. Another emerging trend is AI for sustainable design, such as cradle-to-cradle design, that gamuts the holistic view of sustainability and aims to reduce waste using low-energy reclamation procedures (Vladimirovich & Valeryevna, 2020).

15.2.2.2 Economic Sustainability

Sustainable development seeks to promote economic growth and prosperity, but in a way that is inclusive, equitable, and does not deplete resources or harm the environment. It often involves sustainable business practices and responsible resource management. The system of management choices and actions that underpins possessory risk management methods and provides competitive advantage through strategic application is the foundation of a company's economic sustainability (Cunha et al, 2021).

15.2.2.3 Social Sustainability

This dimension focusses on improving the well-being and quality of life for all members of society. It involves addressing social inequalities, promoting social cohesion, and ensuring access to basic services such as education, healthcare, and clean water. There is a dire need to set up initiatives for social innovation and there might exist some which can guides and empowers the citizens, moreover induces the potential to serve their needs wisely (Yufang, 2010).

Regarding awareness, we can also include some social responsibility into business culture so that everyone has a strong feeling of social duty through employee education and training, so that we may successfully safeguard the company's sustainable development (Tamburri, 2020).

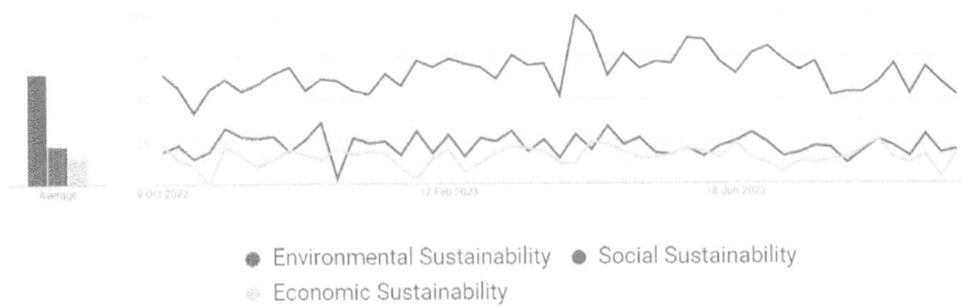

15.2.3 Other Principles of Sustainable Development

15.2.3.1 Inter-Generational Equity

Sustainable development recognizes the rights and needs of future generations and aims to ensure that the choices made today do not compromise their ability to meet their own needs and enjoy a high quality of life. It also enhances the standard of living by catering all the needs and simultaneously preserve for the future generation.

15.2.3.2 Stakeholder Engagement

It is important to involve all relevant stakeholders, including governments, businesses, civil society organizations, and local communities, in decision-making processes related to development to ensure that diverse perspectives and interests are considered. Stakeholder engagement become the substantial factor when it comes to software evolution and anything pertaining to that and the capacity to change a software system in response to stakeholders' shifting needs. Software sustainability ensures the harmonious relation between the consumption of resources and meeting the software requirements needs (Theodorou et al, 2019).

The United Nations' 2030 Agenda for Sustainable Development, which has 17 SDGs that address a variety of social, economic, and environmental challenges, is frequently linked to sustainable development. These objectives offer a worldwide framework for tackling the most serious issues facing the planet and building a more sustainable and just future. There has been a framework called Sustainable Game (SG) which helps in tracking the percentage of time of an individual's consumption, collection of items, food collecting, etc. and also suggests where and how much should one put their money which is quite intricate for a present system (Hui et al, 2011).

Sustainable growth is constrained by non-renewable energy resources, and the development of energy-saving technologies makes it difficult to address the issues of scarcity. Many nations observe both an increase in resource depletion and an increase in efficiency. It indicates that ongoing increase of the energy supply is necessary for sustainable growth, particularly in industrializing nations, and that this may be accomplished primarily through energy diversification rather than oil extraction (Miller et al, 2020). Energy diversification is one of the key factor for sustainable economic growth as it directly influences it in many ways.

A multidisciplinary and integrated strategy that takes into consideration the intricate relationships between economic, social, and environmental aspects is necessary in practice to achieve sustainable development. To reconcile immediate demands with long-term objectives and make sure that development gains are dispersed equally throughout society, it also entails making thoughtful decisions and trade-offs.

An interdisciplinary research programme on the application of AI methods to assist SDI (Sustainable Development Index) measurements, employing both ML approaches to model SDI measurements and explainable AI approaches to deliver the results in a human-friendly manner (IEEEXplore).

All sectors will benefit from using AI and sustainable development to create a better planet that meets present demands without endangering future generations as a result of climate change or other significant issues. However, its also imperative to consider the ethical and social ramifications such as data privacy and unauthorized access etc. when we implement sustainability with AI. In conclusion, AI proved to be a successful contrivance to augments the sustainable development.

15.3 RESEARCH TRENDS

'Research trends' is an upward wave in the predominant and emerging areas in the academic-research domain. Researchers often track these inclinations to stay abreast with the latest developments, discover new research prospects, and contribute to the body of knowledge in their respective domains. Research gives the breakthroughs of various emerging technologies, industry opinions, social issues and is further magnified by the lens of research trends. Research trends is analysed with multiple parameters each highlighting the one or few aspects of the study. Understanding research trends is crucial for staying informed about the current state of knowledge and for making informed decisions about where to direct research efforts and investments. The book chapter highlights the change in research trends over a specific period of time. The time period considered for the research is 2000–2023 the over the IEEE xplore search. IEEE xplore (ieeexplore.ieee.org) is the digital research database which consists of various research domains in the field of information technology, computer, electrical engineering, and electronic engineering. For the study, an advanced search is being conducted for the year 2000–2022 with the search keywords as 'artificial intelligence' and 'sustainable goals' specified in the abstract of the research article. Abstract is being considered over other parameters such as title of paper, title of publication, metadata, and keywords. The reason behind is the gist of the paper is given in the abstract, this helps to provide the research direction. This section will cover the bibliometric analysis a quantitative method used to learn several facets of scientific literature, scholarly communication, and thereby increase in the productivity of research. It is basically a structured and systematic analysis of research publication to mine meaningful research patterns, track trends; gauge research impact, research decision-making, perform research gap analysis and relationships among academic and scientific literature characteristics.

Bibliometric analysis is a quantitative research method used to evaluate and analyse scholarly publications, typically in the form of academic papers, articles, books, and conference proceedings. It involves the use of bibliometric indicators and statistical techniques to gain insights into the patterns, trends, and impact of research output in a particular field or by a specific author, institution, or country.

As shared already the research trend is analysed using multiple parameters, one parameter is the article citation count. It refers to the number of time the article is being cited by other research articles such as research papers, white papers, books, and other scholarly works. A research articles impact is measured and relevance by the Citation counts. Figure 15.1 provides the citation count over the year 2000–2023. As shown there is a significant upward citation trend till year 2019 and after that the citation count is lowered down.

When a research article is being framed it uses multiple other research articles as a reference in their scholarly work. In other words, the count of research papers considered to support current research paper to support their study, research, arguments, discussions, claims, identify influential works and conclusions is termed a reference

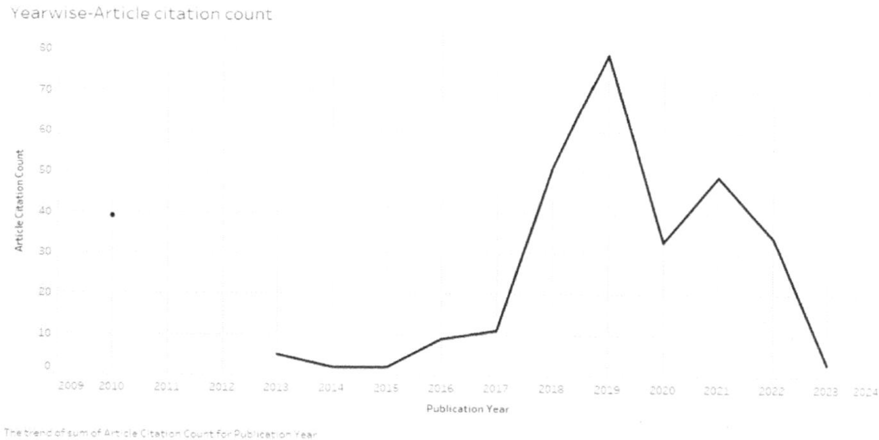

FIGURE 15.1 Yearwise article citation count.

count. Furthermore, ithelps for scholarly engagement, source verification and provide academic integrity. From Figure 15.2, it is a evident that around 20 papers have approx. 50 reference count. This histogram suggests that the ideal reference count is 50 to lay a significant impact for the current study.

In the field of AI and sustainable goals, most of the conferences are organized in countries such as India, China, Malaysia, USA, UK, and Bangladesh (Figure 15.3). India has the maximum number of conferences, it holds 35% of the organized conferences among the top five countries.

Furthermore, research trends are analysed on the basis of top ten publications topics. For the study, the topics are sustainable development, renewable energy, learning AI, energy conservation, optimization, power grids, Internet of Things, decision making, distributed systems and educational development (Figure 15.4). The above topics are given in the descending order of association among AI and sustainable goals.

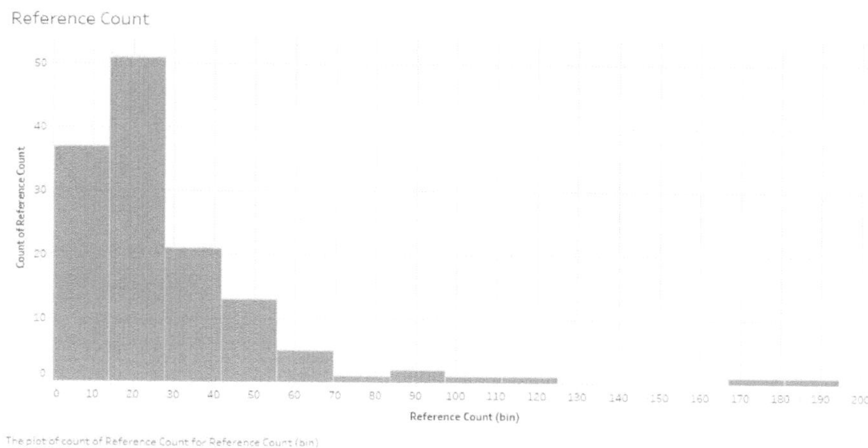

FIGURE 15.2 Yearwise article reference count.

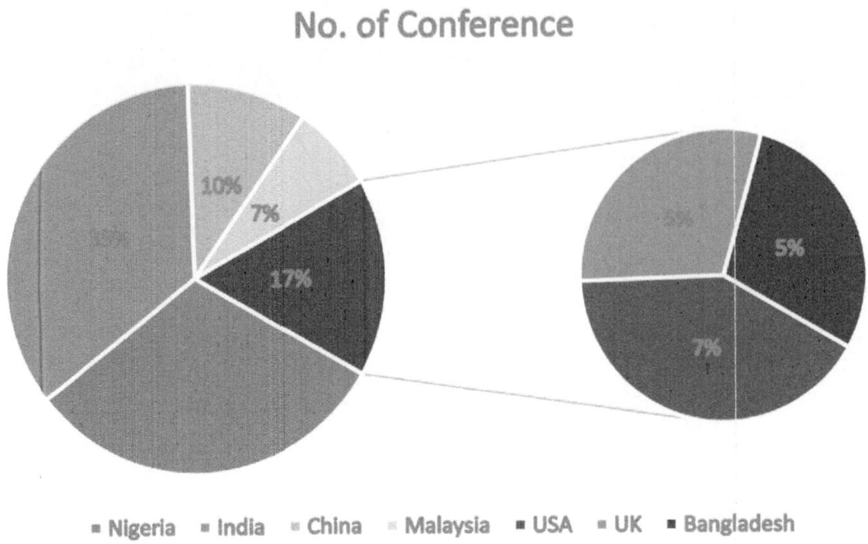

FIGURE 15.3 Conferences location from 2010 to 2023 from IEEE Xplore database.

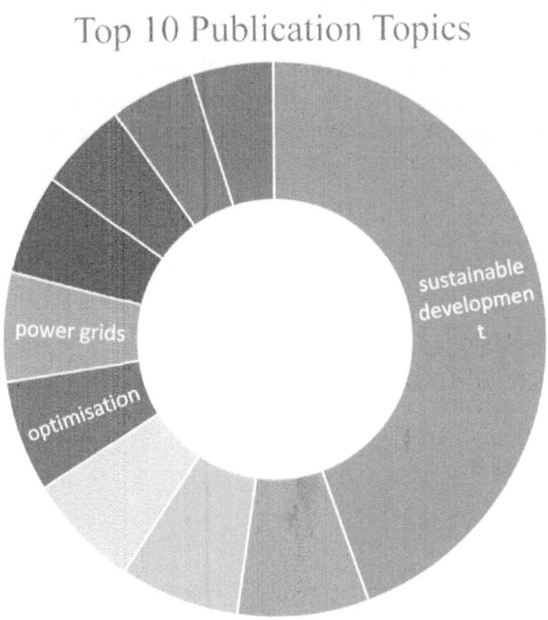

FIGURE 15.4 Top 10 publication topics, 2010–2023 from IEEE Xplore database.

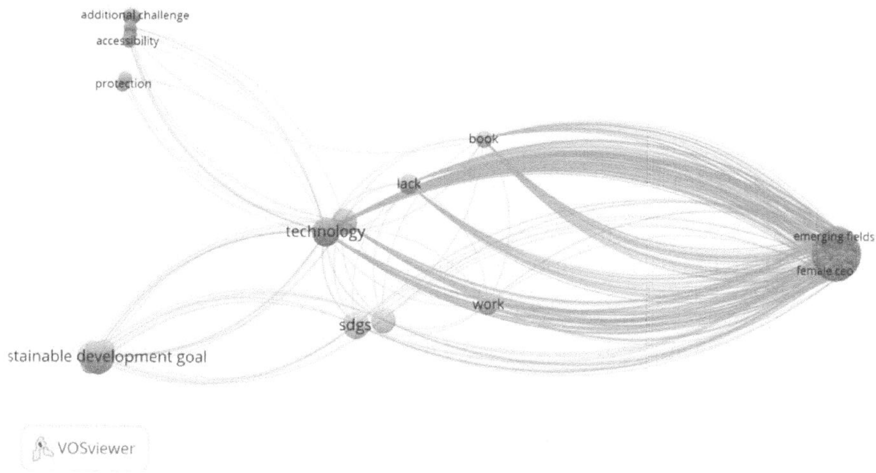

FIGURE 15.5 Bibliometric analysis using VOSviewer 2010–2023 from IEEE Xplore database.

VOSviewer is a popular and user-friendly software tool used for performing bibliometric analysis and visualization of scientific literature. VOSviewer is a valuable tool for researchers, institutions, and policymakers who want to gain insights into scientific literature, collaboration patterns, and emerging research trends (vosviewer.com). When the csv file was uploaded on VOSviewer, it generate following visualization, as given in Figure 15.5.

As given in Figure 15.5, clusters of various colours are being formed 'red' being most significant one. It is found out that the red clusters consists of various terms which are considered to be more relevant; the terms are: decision impact, disaster monitoring, associated vulnerability, broader usage, critical infrastructure. cybersecurity, mobile communication, qualified competency, rural network, and universal accessibility.

15.4 CONCLUSION

This section will be help the note the future roadmap for implementing AI in sustainable goals. The implementation of SDGs using AI is a promising and rapidly evolving field that holds great potential for addressing some of the world's most pressing challenges. Recent trends and future prospects in this area indicate a positive trajectory towards achieving sustainability targets. In conclusion, the integration of AI into the pursuit of SDGs presents a multifaceted opportunity to address complex global challenges. While there have been notable achievements, ongoing collaboration, ethical considerations, and addressing challenges are crucial to unlock AI's full potential in promoting sustainable development and leaving no one behind. The future prospects are bright, but continued dedication and responsible AI deployment will be key to realizing these prospects. Despite these challenges, the potential benefits of AI for sustainability are great. By addressing the challenges and working together, we can harness the power of AI to create a more sustainable future. The future prospects for AI in sustainability are bright. As AI technology continues to develop, it is likely to play an even greater role in addressing the world's most pressing challenges. AI has the potential to revolutionize the way we achieve SDGs.

BIBLIOGRAPHY

https://ieeexplore.ieee.org/Xplore/home.jsp19, 285.

https://www.vosviewer.com

Ashtaiwi, A. (2020). Artificial Intelligence Is Transforming the World Development Indicators. In 2020 IEEE/ITU International Conference on Artificial Intelligence for Good (AI4G) (pp. 122–128). Geneva, Switzerland. https://doi.org/10.1109/AI4G50087.2020.9311079

Bernhard, R. (1980). An electronic advisor/companion: Computers able to function as personal consultants require breakthroughs in the field of artificial intelligence. IEEE Spectrum, 17(9), 39–44. https://doi.org/10.1109/MSPEC.1980.6368385

Bozkurt, A., Karadeniz, A., Baneres, D., Guerrero-Roldán, A. E., & Rodríguez, M. E. (2021). Artificial intelligence and reflections from educational landscape: A review of AI studies in half a century. Sustainability (Switzerland), 13, 1–16. https://doi.org/10.1007/s43621-021-00064-5

Chen, M., Mao, S., & Liu, Y. (2014). Big Data: A survey. Mobile Networks and Applications, 19(2), 171–209.

Cunha, J., Ferreira, C., Araújo, M., Nunes, M. L., & Ferreira, P. (2021). Understanding the Linkage between Social Innovation and Sustainable Development Goals: Some Insights of Field Research. In 2021 IEEE International Conference on Industrial Engineering and Engineering Management (IEEM) (pp. 1142–1146). Singapore, Singapore. https://doi.org/10.1109/IEEM50564.2021.9672961

Di Vaio, A., Boccia, F., Landriani, L., & Palladino, R. (2020). Artificial intelligence in the agri-food system: Rethinking sustainable business models in the COVID-19 scenario. Sustainability (Switzerland), 12, 4851.

Djenouri, Y., Srivastava, G., Belhadi, A., & Lin, J. C. (2021). Intelligent blockchain management for distributed knowledge graphs in IoT 5G environments. Transactions on Emerging Telecommunications Technologies. https://doi.org/10.1002/ett.4332

Doherty, M., & Esmaeili, B. (2020). Application of Artificial Intelligence in Electrical Safety. In 2020 IEEE IAS Electrical Safety Workshop (ESW) (pp. 1–6). Reno, NV, USA. https://doi.org/10.1109/ESW42757.2020.9188324

Dwivedi, Y. K., et al. (2022). Climate change and COP26: Are digital technologies and information management part of the problem or the solution? An editorial reflection and call to action. International Journal of Information Management, 63, 102456.

Fisher, D. H. (2011). Computing and AI for a sustainable future. IEEE Intelligent Systems, 26(6), 14–18. https://doi.org/10.1109/MIS.2011.98

Gambín, Á. F., Angelats, E., González, J. S., Miozzo, M., & Dini, P. (2021). Sustainable marine ecosystems: Deep learning for water quality assessment and forecasting. IEEE Access, 9, 121344–121365. https://ieeexplore.ieee.org/document/9525388

Godber, E. (2018). Uses of Artificial Intelligence in Health. In 2018 International Conference on Artificial Intelligence Applications and Innovations (IC-AIAI) (pp. 31–36). Nicosia, Cyprus. https://doi.org/10.1109/IC-AIAI.2018.8674444

Hui, Z., Danxiang, A., & Chengke, Z. (2011). Energy Diversification and Sustainable Economy Growth. In 2011 International Conference on E-Business and E-Government (ICEE) (pp. 1–4). Shanghai, China. https://doi.org/10.1109/ICEBEG.2011.5882134

Jurgilevich, A., et al. (2016). Transition towards circular economy in the food system. Sustainability (Switzerland), 8, 1–14.

Lee, J. K. (1996). Unification of Artificial Intelligence with Optimization for Decision Support: UNIK Approach. In 1996 IEEE International Conference on Systems, Man and Cybernetics. Information Intelligence and Systems (pp. 2546–2551, vol. 4). Beijing, China. https://doi.org/10.1109/ICSMC.1996.561330

Lei, Z., & Wang, L. (2020). Construction of organisational system of enterprise knowledge management networking module based on artificial intelligence. Knowledge Management Research & Practice, 1–13. https://doi.org/10.1080/14778238.2020.1831892

Luengo-Oroz, M. A., Arranz, A., Frean, J., & Crowcroft, J. (2012). Crowdsourcing malaria parasite quantification: An online game for analyzing images of infected thick blood smears. Journal of Medical Internet Research, 14(6), e167.

Meet GIUSEPPE, our AI chef. (2020). Retrieved from https://notco.com/us/giuseppe

Mehmood, H., Liao, D., & Mahadeo, K. (2020). A Review of Artificial Intelligence Applications to Achieve Water-Related Sustainable Development Goals. In 2020 IEEE/ITU International Conference on Artificial Intelligence for Good (AI4G) (pp. 135–141). Geneva, Switzerland. https://doi.org/10.1109/AI4G50087.2020.9311018

Melamed, A. (1991). Distributed systems management on Wall Street-AI technology needs. In Proceedings First International Conference on Artificial Intelligence Applications on Wall Street (pp. 206–212). New York, NY, USA. https://doi.org/10.1109/AIAWS.1991.236600

Nam, V. T. (2016). Environmental Pollution – The Barrier to Sustainable Development on Breeding Industrial Chicken in Southeast Provinces of Vietnam. In 2016 3rd International Conference on Green Technology and Sustainable Development (GTSD) (pp. 63–68). Kaohsiung, Taiwan. https://doi.org/10.1109/GTSD.2016.25

Nandi, S., & Sarkar, S. (2019). IoT-based precision agriculture: A review of recent advances and future directions. Precision Agriculture, 20(5), 693–710.

Nishant, R., Kennedy, M., & Corbett, J. (2020). Artificial intelligence for sustainability: Challenges, opportunities, and a research agenda. International Journal of Information Management, 53, 102104.

Pereira, T., & Santos, H. (2013). The matrix of quality dimensions of knowledge management: Knowledge management assessment models review. Knowledge Management: An International Journal, 12(1), 33–41. https://doi.org/10.18848/2327-7998/cgp/v12i01/50839

Riekki, J., & Mämmelä, A. (2021). Research and education towards smart and sustainable world. IEEE Access, 9, 53156–53177. https://doi.org/10.1109/ACCESS.2021.3069902

Rolnick, D., Veit, A., Belongie, S., Shavit, N., & Durand, T. (2019). Tackling Climate Change with Machine Learning. arXiv preprint arXiv:1906.05433.

Sabol, P., & Sincak, P. (2018). AI Bricks: A Microservices-Based Software for a Usage in the Cloud Robotics. In 2018 World Symposium on Digital Intelligence for Systems and Machines (DISA) (pp. 207–212). Košice, Slovakia. https://doi.org/10.1109/DISA.2018.8490532

Sadiku, M. N. O. (1989). Artificial intelligence. IEEE Potentials, 8(2), 35–39. https://doi.org/10.1109/45.31596

Silver, D., & Le, H. (2017). Mastering chess and shogi by self-play with a general reinforcement learning algorithm. Nature, 551(7676), 354–359.

State gov. (2023). https://www.state.gov/artificial-intelligence-for-accelerating-progress-on-the-sustainabledevelopment-goals-addressing-societys-greatest-challenges

Tamburri, D. A. (2020). Sustainable MLOps: Trends and Challenges. In 2020 22nd International Symposium on Symbolic and Numeric Algorithms for Scientific Computing (SYNASC) (pp. 17–23). Timisoara, Romania. https://doi.org/10.1109/SYNASC51798.2020.00015

Theodorou, A., Bandt-Law, B., & Bryson, J. J. (2019). The Sustainability Game: AI Technology as an Intervention for Public Understanding of Cooperative Investment. In 2019 IEEE Conference on Games (CoG) (pp. 1–4). London, UK. https://doi.org/10.1109/CIG.2019.8848058

United Nations (UN). (2015a). Goal 1: No Poverty. Retrieved from https://sdgs.un.org/publications/transforming-our-world-2030-agenda-sustainable-development

United Nations (UN). (2015b). Goal 2: Zero Hunger. Retrieved from https://sdgs.un.org/goals/goal2

United Nations (UN). (2015c). Goal 3: Good Health and Well-Being. Retrieved from https://sdgs.un.org/goals/goal3

United Nations (UN). (2015d). Goal 4: Quality Education. Retrieved from https://sdgs.un.org/goals/goal4

United Nations (UN). (2015e). Goal 5: Gender Equality. Retrieved from https://sdgs.un.org/goals/goal5

United Nations (UN). (2015f). Goal 6: Clean Water and Sanitation. Retrieved from https://sdgs.un.org/goals/goal6

United Nations (UN). (2015g). Goal 7: Affordable and Clean Energy. Retrieved from https://sdgs.un.org/goals/goal7

United Nations (UN). (2015h). Goal 8: Decent Work and Economic Growth. Retrieved from https://sdgs.un.org/goals/goal8

United Nations (UN). (2015i). Goal 9: Industry, Innovation, and Infrastructure. Retrieved from https://sdgs.un.org/goals/goal9

United Nations (UN). (2015j). Goal 10: Reduced Inequality. Retrieved from https://sdgs.un.org/goals/goal10

United Nations (UN). (2015k). Goal 11: Sustainable Cities and Communities. Retrieved from https://sdgs.un.org/goals/goal11

United Nations (UN). (2015l). Goal 12: Responsible Consumption and Production. Retrieved from https://sdgs.un.org/goals/goal12

United Nations (UN). (2015m). Goal 13: Climate Action. Retrieved from https://sdgs.un.org/goals/goal13

United Nations (UN). (2015n). Goal 14: Life Below Water. Retrieved from https://sdgs.un.org/goals/goal14

United Nations (UN). (2015o). Goal 15: Life on Land. Retrieved from https://sdgs.un.org/goals/goal15

United Nations (UN). (2015p). Goal 16: Peace, Justice, and Strong Institutions. Retrieved from https://sdgs.un.org/goals/goal16

United Nations (UN). (2015q). Goal 17: Partnerships for the Goals. Retrieved from https://sdgs.un.org/goals/goal17

Vinuesa, R., Azizpour, H., Leite, I., et al. (2020). The role of artificial intelligence in achieving the Sustainable Development Goals. Nature Communications, 11, 233. https://doi.org/10.1038/s41467-019-14108-y

Vladimirovich, K. M., & Valeryevna, K. E. (2020). Developing Possessory Risk Management Systems as the Basis for Economic Sustainability of Russian Companies in the Context of Pandemic. In 2020 Fourth World Conference on Smart Trends in Systems, Security and Sustainability (WorldS4) (pp. 203–207). London, UK. https://doi.org/10.1109/WorldS450073.2020.9210261

Voitko, S., Gaidutskiy, I., & Skorobogatova, N. (2020). Industry 4.0 and Next Normality in Ensuring Sustainable Development. In 2020 III International Conference on High Technology for Sustainable Development (HiTech) (pp. 1–2). Sofia, Bulgaria. https://doi.org/10.1109/HiTech51434.2020.9363981

WHO (World Health Organization). (2021). The State of Food Security and Nutrition in the World 2021: Transforming Food Systems for Food Security, Improved Nutrition, and Affordable Healthy Diets for All.

Wu, I.-L., & Hu, Y.-P. (2018). Open innovation-based knowledge management implementation: A mediating role of knowledge management design. Journal of Knowledge Management, 22(8), 1736–1756. https://doi.org/10.1108/JKM-06-2016-0238

Yufang, W. (2010). Study on Social Responsibilities of State-Owned Forestry Enterprises during the Sustainable Development. In International Conference on Information Management, Innovation Management and Industrial Engineering (pp. 138–141). Kunming, China. https://doi.org/10.1109/ICIII.2010.39

Zhang, P., et al. (2021). Nanotechnology and artificial intelligence to enable sustainable and precision agriculture. Nature Plants, 7, 864–876.

Zhang, Y., Dai, Z., Zhang, L., Wang, Z., Chen, L., & Zhou, Y. (2020). Application of Artificial Intelligence in Military: From Projects View. In 2020 6th International Conference on Big Data and Information Analytics (BigDIA) (pp. 113–116). Shenzhen, China. https://doi.org/10.1109/BigDIA51454.2020.00026

Zhao, H., Li, G., & Feng, W. (2018). Research on Application of Artificial Intelligence in Medical Education. In 2018 International Conference on Engineering Simulation and Intelligent Control (ESAIC) (pp. 340–342). Hunan, China. https://doi.org/10.1109/ESAIC.2018.00085

16 Artificial Intelligence and Sustainable Agriculture

Prabhakara S. and Shruthi S. P.

16.1 INTRODUCTION

The challenges of feeding an increasing world population, the impacts of climate change on agriculture, and the growing concern over how to fulfil the rising food demand while simultaneously assuring food and nutritional security will lead to sustainable agriculture as a solution. Artificial intelligence (AI) is needed for sustainable development to plan, develop, and implement the future of our planet and its sustainability more effectively. Know-how like AI will, among many other things, help human beings to develop more efficiently, use resources sensibly, and lessen and manage the trash we produce. Using AI with sustainable development makes a better world that satisfies current needs without risking future generations because of climate change or other important concerns to all sectors including agriculture. This chapter tries to discuss AI in achieving sustainable agriculture.

16.2 DEFINITION OF SUSTAINABLE AGRICULTURE AND ITS MEANING

Adopting business models that address the UN 2030 Agenda on the Sustainable Development Goals (SDGs) may be made possible by the adoption of innovative technologies. Economic, environmental, and social factors are its three main components, and they are all linked (Elkington, 2013). "Agricultural practises that ensure fulfilment of present and future food and nutritional requirements of the society, while maximising the net advantage towards the ecosystem, society, and earth," is how Tilman et al. (2002) defined sustainable agriculture. Among the several elements of sustainable agriculture are SDGs relating to agriculture, like "No Hunger." Goal number two is to "eliminate hunger, achieve food security, improve nutrition, and support sustainable agriculture." AI can contribute by smart agriculture, combining historical knowledge of crop rotation, natural fertilisation, and plant symbiosis with various optimisation approaches, forecasting, wise water usage, and optimal collection and distribution.

16.3 CONCEPT OF ARTIFICIAL INTELLIGENCE (AI) AND ITS TYPES

"Machines will be capable of doing any work a man can do," stated in 1965 by Herbert Simon, a Nobel laureate in economics. His visionary viewpoint has come true in the present day through remarkable achievements on account of AI

DOI: 10.1201/9781003640776-16

applications (Taneja et al., 2023). AI refers to the ability of machines or computer programmes to undertake tasks that typically require human intelligence, such as learning, problem-solving, reasoning, and decision-making (Taneja et al., 2023). The phrase "Artificial Intelligence" was first coined by John McCarthy in 1959. It involves the improvement of computational models and algorithms that facilitate machines to process and analyse large amounts of data, identify patterns and relationships, and make predictions or decisions based on that analysis (Taneja et al., 2023). Natural language processing (NLP), machine learning (ML), computer vision, robotics, deep learning, and cognitive computing are a few of the subfields of AI. AI is being used a lot these days in a variety of sectors, such as finance, healthcare, retail, transportation, manufacturing, and agriculture (Palomares et al., 2021; Taneja et al., 2023).

The different types of AI as mentioned by Yadav et al. (2023) include (1) ANI (artificial narrow intelligence), which is all over the place, like Google Maps, and it is great for discovering efficient routes to places when driving, or it can be compared to a chess programme. It is also characterised as "weak AI," because it only applies AI to select activities. Alexa, Siri, Sofia, and self-driving cars are just a few examples. (2) AGI (artificial general intelligence): imagine a computer that is as intelligent as a person in every aspect. So, anything we can do with our brain, including learning, is possible. (3) ASI (artificial super intelligence): AI is becoming more powerful every day, with applications leading to machines and systems leading to more advanced AI.

16.4 STATUS/ROLE OF AI APPLICATIONS IN AGRICULTURE

The FAO reports that more people are experiencing hunger and malnutrition than ever before (Kakaei et al., 2022). The AI has important applications in agriculture in many areas including crop selection and yield improvement, pest detection and weed management, precision agriculture (PA) and smart farming, and post-harvest activities. However, the agriculture sector can address numerous issues that affect production and enhance the quality and quantity of raw materials accessible to the food business by implementing AI and ML in the management of crops and using high-tech automated systems (Taneja et al., 2023). To enhance agricultural practices like irrigation, fertilisation, and pest management, AI can be applied in PA to assess data from satellites, drones, and sensors. This could lead to reduced expenses, increased yields, and less of an impact on the environment (Ben Ayed & Hanana, 2021; Zhang et al., 2021). Using precision agricultural techniques such as site-specific application, farmers can spray herbicides only where necessary, minimising the amount of chemicals used and lowering the risk of contamination (Kumar et al., 2023). The development of AI-based technologies that use ML algorithms and computer vision techniques to detect and classify different types of weeds in crop fields has the potential to increase agricultural productivity and sustainability, in addition to decreasing the need for herbicides and increasing crop yields (Liakos et al., 2018).

Robotic weed control systems often use ML and computer vision algorithms to identify and locate weeds in agricultural fields before using robotic arms or other mechanical equipment to remove or kill the weeds. These technologies can work in a range of agricultural settings, such as greenhouses, where traditional weed control methods like pesticides would not be appropriate or efficient (Wu et al., 2020; Allmendinger et al., 2022). Cultivars with finger weeders or elastic tines can be used to control weeds both within and between rows (Wu et al., 2020). A part of precision farming is precision weed management, which is predicated on the application of information technology for site-specific weed control analysis. (Christensen et al., 2009).

To find and identify weed species in agriculture fields, it can be highly helpful to use artificial neural networks (ANN) and multispectral/hyperspectral imaging technology. The weed *Silybum marianum* was discovered using counter propagation ANN (CP-ANN) and multispectral images obtained by unmanned aircraft system (UAS) (Pantazi et al., 2017). Multispectral imaging entails taking pictures of crop fields at various light wavelengths, whereas CP-ANN is a kind of artificial neural network that can be utilised for pattern identification applications. These technologies worked together to enable pinpointing the presence of the weed with extreme precision. Crop and weed species recognition was developed using hyperspectral imaging and ML approaches (Pantazi et al., 2016). By photographing agricultural fields using a variety of light wavelengths, a process known as hyperspectral photography, it is possible to learn more about the spectral characteristics of various plant species. ML algorithms were applied to analyse these photos and categorise various plant species, including both crops and weeds. Additionally, a support vector machine (SVM)-based approach for the classification of different weed species in grassland cropping systems was developed using images captured by unmanned aerial vehicles (UAVs) (Binch & Fox, 2017).

AI for weed management reduces the need for unwanted plants in shorter amounts of time and reduces the usage of fertilisers and herbicides, which degrade the soil and pollute it (Sachithra & Subhashini, 2021). AI can be used in soil management to create soil maps that assist illustrating the relationships between soil and landscape features as well as the different soil layers and soil content beneath (Zha, 2020). AI is also used in accurate data analysis and prediction, storage and farm management, and precise application of inputs (Elijah et al., 2018). AI weed identification systems have been tried in labs for weed management to determine the precise amount of spray to use and to accurately spray on the target location, which also lowers expenses and the danger of injuring crops (Partel et al., 2019; Zha, 2020).

PA is a management concept that can maximise agricultural output while minimising environmental stress, such as temperature and humidity changes, for a specific site. It can recognise variability within the soil environment. Several technologies have been created to utilise in PA to increase crop output and decrease resource waste. Drones, computers, data analytics, robots, and other technologies are among them (Misra et al., 2020). In precision farming, irrigation management is essential and considering the benefits to people linked, AI-driven agriculture concentrates on methods to optimise land (Nguyen et al., 2019; Oliveira et al., 2021) soil (Nguyen et al., 2019; Paliwal et al., 2019), and water/irrigation (Kakani et al., 2020; Jung et al., 2021). One of the most popular methods for precision farming is smart farming. Precision farming entails the distribution of a specific quantity of inputs, such as soil, water, and fertiliser, at a precise time and location, such as weed control (Snyder, 2017). The industrial technology company Trimble Agriculture (Westminster, CO, USA) has developed a system called Weed Seeker spot spray, which is a novel approach to effective and targeted weed management. By using sensors to detect the presence of weeds and a spray nozzle to apply a precise amount of chemicals, the system can help reduce the use of herbicides and lessen the environmental impact of weed management (Wu et al., 2020; Allmendinger et al., 2022). With modest adjustments, this device can even be put on conventional spraying equipment. It works best in places where weeds grow intermittently.

Smart farming may be made possible by the internet of things (IoT), a modern technology that allows devices to connect remotely. The IoT has begun to have an impact on a wide range of enterprises, including those in the health, trade, communications, energy, and agriculture sectors to increase efficiency and performance across all sectors (Dhanaraju et al., 2022). A novel method that uses cutting-edge technologies to improve the quality and output of agricultural products, "smart farming," has emerged because of the use of modernised technologies in agriculture. AI advocates the replacement of traditional agricultural practices and methodology with smart farming, a sustainable way that helps to prevent resource waste (such as fertilisers and pesticides) and achieve sustainable development (Rejeb et al., 2022). Smart farming enables farmers to make better decisions about their crops and to optimise their production processes by giving them detailed information on specific crops, such as soil nutritional deficiencies, moisture levels, and hyperspectral data to prevent damage (Chukkapalli et al., 2020).

Climate-based irrigation is another component of smart farming. The Specialty Crop Research Initiative-Managing Irrigation and Nutrients with Distributed Sensing (SCRI-MINDS) project was developed to boost plant production efficiency while limiting the overuse of nutrients and irrigation water (Dhanaraju et al., 2022). Microsoft (Redmond, Washington, USA) has also created an AI-based sowing tool that offers suggestions for the best time to sow seeds and how to prepare the soil for agriculture, among other things. To anticipate crop yields at every step of farming, a mobile phone software model employs remote sensing data from geo-stationary satellite photos. The moisture adequacy index was created to identify the ideal sowing window. Historical sowing area, productivity, yield, and meteorological data are among the input data. Participating farmers receive seeding advice from the app regarding the best time to sow. The farmers do not need to put any sensors in their fields or invest in any capital equipment – all they need is a feature phone that can receive text messages (Meshram et al., 2021).

For improved global food security, less resources (such as water, fertiliser, and pesticides) may be used in agriculture, losses may be avoided, and food products' shelf life may be prolonged (Misra et al., 2020). For the protection of natural resources and sustainable agriculture, many more computer-aided technologies, such as low-altitude spectrum imaging for detecting pest infestation, nutrient, or moisture insufficiency, are being adopted. Smart farming uses low-altitude airborne hyperspectral photography and deployed sensors to monitor farm conditions (Akhtman et al., 2017). To pick fruits and vegetables without damaging the plants, robotic technology (robot arm) has been found to be a successful tool (Hespeler et al., 2021).

Several technologies use computer vision systems for the inspection of grains in the agricultural sector, including examination of milled rice grains using SVM; computerised wheat quality assessment system; and development of a method using hyperspectral imaging system for the detection of *Fusarium*-infected wheat grains (Zareiforoush et al., 2015; Singh & Chaudhury, 2016). Computer vision technologies are increasingly being used for grain inspection. These systems examine grain images and look for defects or impurities like cracked kernels, foreign objects, or fungal infestations using cutting-edge imaging techniques and ML algorithms (Mir et al., 2023 as cited in Taneja et al., 2023). Computer vision systems can assist in the precise and automated monitoring of various plant phenological stages, including seedling emergence, leaf unfolding, flowering, and fruit ripening. Additionally, they can aid in the early detection of illness and plant stress, enabling prompt treatments and averting crop losses, a computer vision system that uses disease-specific image processing algorithms to identify the presence and severity of leaf spot diseases in rice plants (Peruzzi et al., 2017).

For the classification and identification of grains and other agricultural products, ML approaches such as ANN, dense scale-invariant feature transform (DSIFT) algorithm, and SVMs have been successfully used in the agriculture industry (Taneja et al., 2023). According to their visual properties, such as shape, size, and colour, ANNs are used to categorise various wheat species (Sabanci et al., 2016). The DSIFT algorithm is a computer vision technology that can recognise characteristics of wheat grains, such as their size, shape, and texture, and use these to categorise the grains into several groups (Patrício & Rieder, 2018). Another ML method is SVM, which is used to classify wheat grains, identify fungal species in rice, analyse milled rice grains, and identify germinated wheat grains.

For the identification and classification of crop diseases, backpropagation neural networks (BPNN) have been employed in conjunction with other technologies like wavelets and fuzzy inference systems (Bellocchio et al., 2012). Real-time phenotyping and ML techniques were used to examine the dangers of chlorosis brought on by an iron deficiency in soyabean plants (Naik et al., 2017). Early detection and monitoring of iron deficiency stress in soyabean plants using this technology can enhance iron fertilisation and boost crop yields (Guo et al., 2015; Lu et al., 2015; Lu et al., 2016; Sadeghi-Tehran et al., 2017).

AI-based systems for product sorting can assist in locating flaws, pollutants, and irregularities in the items, facilitating wise decision-making, and raising the overall standard of the products. With the aid of datasets, deep learning – a branch of ML and a branch of AI – helps classify the apples using pattern recognition and judgement. In the fruit and food industries, thermal imaging, a non-contact, developing technique, is becoming more and more used for assessing fruit quality. It provides a non-destructive alternative to extraction, which can permanently harm the thing being examined. By monitoring the difference in temperature between undamaged and damaged tissues, infrared thermal imaging can identify damage or flaws in fresh fruits and vegetables (Gowen et al., 2010). To predict the shelf life of goods, ANNs and other AI and ML approaches have been frequently used. Based on respiration rate and levels of ripeness under various supply chain scenarios, AI models for predicting the shelf-life of mangoes stored under diverse settings were built.

16.5 OPPORTUNITIES AND CHALLENGES OF IMPLEMENTING AI-BASED APPROACHES IN AGRICULTURE

There are opportunities to use AI-based solutions in agriculture, including cutting-edge concepts based on autonomous and intelligent robots for plant and soil sample retrieval, effective livestock management, and precision farming (Linaza et al., 2021), among others. By lowering the usage of fertiliser and pesticides, increasing the precision of pest and disease detection, and enabling the automated grading of crops, AI applications have the potential to improve farming practices and increase their sustainability. Additionally, the management of farm operations, planting, and harvesting are all aided by combining data on soil qualities, weather, and other meteorological aspects and interpreting them through ML software (Cook & O'Neill, 2020). Farmers in many countries, including India, rely on the monsoon for their crop production. Rain-fed agriculture mostly relies on forecasts from several departments regarding the weather. The AI will be beneficial for predicting the weather as well as other aspects of agriculture, such as the quality of the land, the availability of groundwater, the cycle of the crops, and pest attacks. Most of the farmers' worries will be alleviated by an accurate projection or prediction made with the aid of AI. AI-driven sensors are incredibly helpful for capturing crucial information about agriculture. The information will help increase output. These sensors have a lot of potential in agriculture (Talaviya et al., 2020). ML and big data have been linked into sensors that focus on agricultural output, yield forecasting, disease detection, and features that are available to provide improved information for decision-making and movement (Kler et al., 2022).

High-tech greenhouses are equipped with different standard sensors for monitoring light, temperature, humidity, and CO_2 and for actively controlling different actuators (e.g., lighting, screening, heating, ventilation, cooling, CO_2 dosing, fogging, dehumidification, irrigation, and fertiliser dosing) to control all growth factors important for crop production at every moment. Dynamic climate models have been developed (Vanthoor et al., 2011) which act as digital twins of real greenhouses. Since experienced and well-trained crop managers are scarce, crop simulation models can play a role in decision-making. Farming operations will be improved by the deployment of AI-based expert systems, providing support for decision-making and paving the way for data-driven agriculture, if massive field data become accessible. Crop health management involves detection and actuation. Lately, technologies such as the use of Big Data, Cloud Computing, Remote Sensing, Agri-robotics, and the IoT sensors, combined with the use of AI, are increasingly used in every aspect of the agri-food supply chain (AFSC).

Crop planning at micro and macro levels can be improved through AI-enabled models that link weather forecasts, dynamic soil data, warehousing and logistics infrastructure, and market conditions. Smart farming solutions, including IoT-enabled irrigation and dynamic soil health mapping at the farm level, while leveraging AI in remote sensing and automatic weather station data are possible. Crop health can be managed more effectively through AI-powered pest control, agriculture input advisory platforms, and drone-enabled farm mapping and agriculture input applications. IoT can be used to enhance warehousing and logistics, and AI, spectroscopy, and blockchain to enhance quality and traceability, and market linkage platforms. AI has the potentiality to used in Intelligent Crop Planning, smart farming, farm gate-to-fork (including agriculture (i.e., land cultivation and crop production), production processes, packaging, warehousing systems, distribution, transportation, and marketing (Santoso et al., 2021) and data-driven agriculture). Emerging technologies, such as AI, IoT, blockchain, and drones – further enabled by unlocking key datasets – offer an unprecedented and unparalleled opportunity to boost the efficiency and effectiveness of agriculture production systems.

Challenges of AI in field crop production include infrastructure resources required, system-wide challenges, system dynamics and continuous improvement, concept drift, model generalisations or overfitting, convincing reliability, training the farming population, mechanisation as a service, and crop protection (EU, 2023). The current challenge is to give meaningful interpretation to sensor data and to transform that into decision support systems (DSS) or even autonomous control for growers. Given the complexity of greenhouse production, the use of different technological tools in an integrated approach is the key to optimum crop management to reach optimum yield, while minimising the use of resources, including the reduction of energy and water use and pest and pathogen management. Current challenges lie in the high dimensionality of greenhouse growing systems due to the various designs and various crops. Associated costs of the development of high-fidelity digital twins are high and a selection of minimum assets covering the market demands is required. A balance between highly detailed information and more general twins can lower development costs. The successful deployment of AI throughout agricultural equipment, with the purpose of making it "intelligent" and efficient to execute automated functions, may be threatened and hindered by the many challenges, which can limit or even ruin their practical implementation and acceptance. These challenges include the higher cost inherent in advanced technology, the monetary cost of purchasing, and the time cost of learning, which may be compensated by equipment sharing in farmer associations or cooperatives, but there are still many professionals who are not willing to share their equipment (EU, 2023).

Systematic data collection is one of the main challenges to the implementation of AI in agriculture (Linaza et al., 2021). Before large-scale agricultural AI implementation can be successful, the farm's data infrastructure will need to become more robust and IT-equipped. Other difficulties could include a future in which mechanisation is distributed unevenly, inconsistencies between control experiments and real-world applications, and security and privacy issues (Linaza et al., 2021). While AI is ideally suited for PA, it may be used more quickly for the creation of new seeds, fertilisers, or crop protection products. The issue is not with AI deployment and development; it is with the lack of compatibility between the two environments when it comes to validation and testing. ML and AI are still a long way from being able to forecast crucial agricultural outcomes solely based on machines' cognitive capacities. The issue with AI's success is not that it does not function; it is that the industry has not spent enough time recognising that agriculture operates in a highly volatile environment (Yadav et al., 2023).

Plant variety, underlying genetics, and environmental elements (light, temperature, irrigation) all affect the plants' shape and morphology. Digital plant phenotyping is the term used to describe the use of computers to measure plant traits using digital sensors. Plant physiological processes are crucial for crop monitoring after plant morphology. The operational efficiency of greenhouse horticulture is notable for being quite high and requiring strong administrative abilities. To assist yield predictions, scalable and general ML analytics are now applied in addition to expert-based methods. The identification of plant infections and pests will be crucial in the future. Nothing can be done to help a plant unless the cause is identified.

The ML, a subfield of AI, is the idea that machines can learn from data, recognise models on their own, and make judgements with little assistance from humans (Klumpp, 2017; Di Vaio et al., 2020). For example, in the field of agriculture, agronomists can identify the nature of a plant's problem by using smartphone apps that have been "enhanced" by AI (Boshkoska et al., 2019). Robots (both physical and software) are sophisticated devices that can resolve challenging issues. For instance, robotic agriculture expedites the most monotonous chores, such as picking weeds and picking fruit or packaging. The use of self-driving tractors and drones has made precision agricultural techniques possible (Xu et al., 2019). Agri-food production systems, or all the operational procedures, are being transformed by PA in several ways. Robots can determine the precise state of the soil and crops, or they may connect to satellites to determine how much water is required, efficiently. Using data on soil, temperature, humidity, agricultural equipment, animals, fertilisers, soil, and sown crops, farmers are also able to use less water, chemicals, and other resources (Di Vaio et al., 2020).

16.6 AI IN ACHIEVING SUSTAINABLE AGRICULTURE

AI, one of the core fields of technology, is changing the agriculture sector by reducing input and resource usage (Ruiz-Real et al., 2020). By utilising AI technologies, the agri/food sector has the prospective to experience early sustainability and revolution in a variety of ways. For farmers, food producers, and distributors, it can support improved decision-making, higher efficiency, waste reduction, and increased sustainability and food security (Taneja et al., 2023).

As agriculture is said to be the common thread that bonds the 17 SDGs together, from eradicating hunger and poverty to maintaining natural resources and combating climate change, it is a crucial element in the Agenda for Sustainable Development 2030 to achieve the SDGs. Despite increasing production, agriculture nevertheless encounters new problems that endanger human civilisation globally. Due to increasing population and climate change complexities, the sector has been forced to switch from industrial methods to data-driven management and automation to increase food production while using fewer crucial inputs. AI is increasingly being used in the agri/food sector to boost output, effectiveness, and sustainability. It has the potential to change several areas, including crop monitoring, PA, predictive analytics, supply chain optimisation, processing of food, control of food quality, individualised nutrition, and food safety in agriculture (Taneja et al., 2023). The platforms working in this area include Gobasco which provides yield prediction and procurement optimisation and Jivabhumi which connects farmers directly with consumers as well as institutional buyers (Manaware, 2020). AI for PA, which concentrates on soil and weed control, has the potential to be very important (Linaza et al., 2021).

AI has the potential to increase the efficiency and sustainability of agriculture to a great extent. AI algorithms can assist farmers in making informed decisions regarding crop productivity, water use, and pest management by gathering and analysing data from multiple sources. AI can reduce the use of pesticides and other toxic chemicals, boost crop yields, and reduce water waste (Talaviya et al., 2020; Anil Chougule & Mashalkar, 2022; Arnault & Patissier, 2022). Reduced crop quality and crop loss can result from improper irrigation and soil management. Examples of such systems include those that estimate soil moisture content, assess the design and operation of microirrigation systems, and suggest crops based on maps of the suitability of the area. It has been discovered that these AI-based solutions are efficient at enhancing irrigation and soil management procedures. The agricultural sector has the potential to significantly enhance food production sustainability and the environment. AI has been used to forecast crop diseases and control measures. Additionally, hybrid systems that combine AI and image processing have been developed. For instance, the web-based expert system "Dr. Wheat" (in Pakistan) employs AI to identify problems affecting wheat (Arnault & Patissier, 2022).

The different facets of farming, including an unskilled and skilled workforce, image sensing for mapping of yield, prediction of yield, improving output, and decision-support for farmers and producers, could be transformed using AI in sustainable agriculture (Talaviya et al., 2020). To make more sustainable agriculture, AI is frequently used in monitoring climate, automatically controlling greenhouses, monitoring crop quality, management of livestock, predictive analysis, and integrated farm management systems (Alreshidi, 2019). Chatbots to assist with knowledge of cultivation practices, digital applications of plant health diagnosis, tools of remote sensing, and solutions for irrigation management are among the AI products that are in high demand from consumers with a background in sustainable agriculture (Partel et al., 2019).

To achieve sustainable agriculture utilising AI approaches, Klyushin and Tymoshenko (2021) suggested a methodology for drip irrigation system optimisation. Using AI and nanotechnology to discover sustainable solutions in agriculture, Zhang et al. (2021) placed emphasis on informatics and material science. Aggarwal and Singh (2021) argued that technology can help with PA and examined the effects of the IoT and AI in agriculture to determine the need for fertilisers, humidity, and other factors. By using a design science methodology, Spanaki et al. (2020) explored the problems with food security and suggested an AI technology as a way out. Using a technological acceptance model, Mohr and Kühl (2021) looked at the challenges to AI adoption in agriculture. However, Mahto et al. (2021) compared the performance of the ARIMA (auto-regressive (AR) integrated (I) moving average (MA)) model (a forecasting model) for sustainable agriculture with that of their approach and employed ANN to estimate prices of agricultural commodities (Mahto et al., 2021; Bhagat et al., 2022).

ML is described as computational methods that use historical data and prior experiences to change, enhance, repair, and accurately forecast performance in future in the 2018 book "Foundations of Machine Learning" (Mohri et al., 2018). The most recent applications of ML in sustainable agriculture include improving supply chains (Sharma et al., 2020), field monitoring (Li et al., 2021), soil temperature prediction (Zeynoddin et al., 2020; Bhagat et al., 2022), and sustainable soil management (Motia & Reddy, 2021). Some of the ML know-hows that can be used to promote sustainable production include polynomial prediction algorithms, K-nearest neighbours' neural networks, and decision trees (Balducci et al., 2018). ML technologies are becoming more and more popular for big projects involving assessments of land/soil suitability assessments because of costly and time-consuming traditional methods of assessing soil suitability for sustainable agriculture, especially in far-off areas where data about the properties of the soil is unavailable (Taghizadeh et al., 2020).

The AI and deep neural network method of ML was a popular choice across all categories of agricultural processes, particularly in the categories of soil management, water management, and livestock management, according to Liakos et al. (2018). Ju et al. (2019) compared four different ML techniques for estimating maize and soybean yields and found that the convolutional neural network, or CNN, was the most accurate method.

In agriculture, robotics is mostly used to speed up boring and repetitive processes including, sowing, spraying, weed control, mowing, harvesting/picking, and lastly product sorting and packaging. Fresh produce supply chains have found use for the automation that robotics, cloud computing, blockchain, and big data enable. To replace the need for dangerous and excessive chemical spraying on crops and soil, field robots are utilised in PA to perform functions of targeted weed control (Wu et al., 2020). The "Agriculture 5.0," refers to the employment of robotics and AI in data-driven farming and has gained popularity (Saiz-Rubio & Rovira-Más, 2020).

The Smart Machine for Agricultural Solutions High-tech (SMASH) project at its design stages of an AgroBot with four modules working together to control weeds and safeguard crops were reported by Sarri et al. (2020). Robotic solutions are well-liked not just by researchers but also by businesspeople who want to invest in and use these eco-friendly technologies (Cavallone et al., 2020; Bhagat et al., 2022). Due to its extensive utility, safe human-robot interactions in agricultural contexts are becoming a growing area of academic interest. Benos et al. (2023) raised concerns about human safety on account of automation and programmed robots and advised them to take measures to make robots more sensitive to sensing human presence and ensure risk-free work environment for labourers. The article by Linaza et al. (2021) outlined recent robotics research initiatives in the European Union and emphasised using robots not only to make precise work but also to address workforce constraints brought on by an increase in the average age of farmers. The use of robotics in agriculture can assist resolve serious food scarcity challenges and contribute to the achievement of UN SDGs without decreasing non-renewable resources (Oláh et al., 2020; Mondejar et al., 2021). However, to commercialise robotic technologies, various hurdles including increased speed and precision must be surmounted. The lower body of research in this area and the slow and small-scale development to implementation process can be attributed to the lack of financing for research when compared to investments in manufacturing and military equipment (Shamshiri et al., 2018; Sokil et al., 2018; Gyenge et al., 2021).

The See & Spray technique is one of the successful case studies for the use of AI in sustainable farming. It has created the first tools in the world that enable farmers to enhance each plant in their field using robotics and ML. With the help of the Blue River Technology system, farmers may spray herbicide only on weeds and hence use less than a tenth of the herbicide typically used for traditional weed control methods. Another successful case is The Application of Sowing. Microsoft and ICRISAT are utilising AI in agriculture to improve crop production. It confirmed a new sowing application for Farmers paired with a Personalised Village Advisory Dashboard for the Indian state of Andhra Pradesh. It yielded the 30% better average yield per hectare. The sowing app was developed to help farmers produce their best crops by suggesting the best time to sow based on the weather, soil, and other variables. The pilot study was conducted in June 2016 in Kurnool's Devanakonda Mandal, and the groundnut crop was the only crop to which the guidance was applicable (Hasan et al., 2023).

The other AI techniques that can be used to ensure sustainability in food production include predictive analytics, DSS, genome tracking, ANN, fuzzy logic, neuro-fuzzy logic, Bayesian networks, and remote sensing. Advanced biosensing know-hows in sustainable farming may make it easier to identify plant infections and illnesses early, even in asymptomatic plants, which will reduce crop and productivity losses (Ali et al., 2021). UAVs (drones) and advanced ML provide continuous weed management by reducing the spread of pesticides in the environment and facilitating decision-making (Esposito et al., 2021). Rasmussen et al. (2018) also investigated the impact of using UAVs that receive data from satellite imagery to perform weed mapping of a specific variety of weed and the findings indicated that it produces images with higher resolution and enables the detection of a specific variety of weed in crops.

With genetic history data for creating precise forecasts, research in AI and genomics can improve the detection of defects and gains in productivity per unit of time. On the other hand, technologies like fuzzy logic and ANN can be trained to create sustainable agriculture forecasting models. Other uses of AI in agriculture include AI-based data fusion for monitoring of crops, agricultural digital twins for geospatial monitoring, robotics for precision viticulture, olive tree prediction using phenotypic data, simultaneous localisation and mapping (SLAM), use of advanced imaging techniques and ML algorithms to identify defects or impurities and analyse images of grain, computer vision, and ML methods are frequently used by robotic weed control systems to recognise and identify weeds, IoT and big data in smart farming, irrigation, and nutrients management with distributed sensing (SCRI-MINDS), AI in the processing of food, AI in food quality and food safety, management of food quality in fresh fruits and vegetables, food waste management, and AI in the personalised nutrition management.

16.7 CONCLUSION

The applications of AI in agriculture include (1) IoT, (2) site-specific/precision farming, (3) Use of Drone Technology, (4) AI for the Production of Image-Based Insight, (5) Optimal Mix for Agronomic Products Using AI, (6) Application of AI to Remote

Sensing, (7) The Automatic Irrigation System with AI, (8) Potato Sorting System using AI for Quality Grading, (9) AI in Driverless Tractors, Self-Driving Cars, and Autonomous Navigation 100 ML in Expert Systems, (10) The use of AI in DSS, (11) Computer vision technology that incorporates AI, (12) Gas Fermentation System with AI, (13) Use of AI in Predictive Agriculture Analytics, (14) Supply Chain Efficiency with AI (Yadav et al., 2023).

AI has the potential to transform agriculture by enhancing productivity, fostering sustainability, and improving efficiency. However, there are certain issues with the use of AI in agriculture in the future. For instance, there are possibilities that AI would eliminate jobs in rural areas and worsen inequality. The high cost of developing AI systems is an important barrier. For small and medium-sized firms, investing significantly in software and hardware infrastructure, and training is highly expensive. Concerns exist regarding the precision and dependability of AI systems as well, mostly when it comes to making decisions on agricultural use.

A few examples of how AI and ML are applied in agriculture to increase efficiency, productivity, and sustainability include smart, robotic farming. With a variety of possible applications in agriculture more specifically cultivation, control of insects and pests, processing of food, control of quality, packaging, extending shelf-life, and supply chain management, ML and AI technologies are likely to define the future of agriculture. While AI has enormous potential to revolutionise agriculture and make it more effective, innovative, and sustainable, it also raises significant social, legal, and ethical implications that must be considered carefully and need to be resolved. To secure long-term benefits from AI, it is crucial to make sure they are created and used in a sustainable and ethical manner.

The improvement and application of AI technology, the laws and rules that are applicable in their usage, and how society adjusts to the changes that AI brings are just a few of the variables that will affect how long AI will be around. A wide range of environmental, societal, and economic considerations all have a role in AI sustainability. The future and sustainability of AI need consider several important factors. To develop and implement AI systems in a responsible and sustainable manner, there is a need to close the gap in skills and ensure the availability of a sufficient pool of experts. This necessitates spending on educational and training initiatives that can give people the abilities and information needed to work around AI. Although there are still many issues including issues with data privacy, high costs, moral dilemmas, and the requirements for specialised training to be resolved, the future of AI in agriculture is bright. In the years to come, one can anticipate tremendous advancements in food production and distribution as more and more farmers employ AI-powered devices.

BIBLIOGRAPHY

Aggarwal, N. & Singh, D. (2021). Technology assisted farming: Implications of IoT and AI. IOP Conference Series: Materials Science and Engineering, 1022(1), 012080. https://doi.org/10.1088/1757-899X/1022/1/012080

Akhtman, Y., Golubeva, E., Tutubalina, O. & Zimin, M. (2017). Application of hyperspectural images and ground data for precision farming. Geography, Environment, Sustainability, 10(4), 117–128. https://doi.org/10.24057/2071-9388-2017-10-4-117-128

Ali, Q., Ahmar, S., Sohail, M.A., Kamran, M., Ali, M., Saleem, M.H., Rizwan, M., Ahmed, A.M., Mora-Poblete, F., do Amaral Júnior, A.T., Mubeen, M. & Ali, S. (2021). Research advances and applications of biosensing technology for the diagnosis of pathogens in sustainable agriculture. Environmental Science and Pollution Research, 28, 9002–9019. https://doi.org/10.1007/s11356-021-12419-6

Allmendinger, A., Spaeth, M., Saile, M., Peteinatos, G.G. & Gerhards, R. (2022). Precision chemical weed management strategies: A review and a design of a new CNN-based modular spot sprayer. Agronomy, 12, 1620. https://doi.org/10.3390/agronomy12071620

Alreshidi, E. (2019). Smart sustainable agriculture (SSA) solution underpinned by Internet of things (IoT) and artificial intelligence (AI). International Journal of Advanced Computer Science and Applications, 10(5), 93–102.

Anil Chougule, M. & Mashalkar, A.S. (2022). Chapter 10. A comprehensive review of agriculture irrigation using artificial intelligence for crop production. In: Computational Intelligence in Manufacturing (pp. 187–200). Elsevier. https://doi.org/10.1016/B978-0-323-91854-1.00002-9

Arnault, P. & Patissier, C. (2022). Towards Sustainable Artificial Intelligence: An Overview of Environmental Protection Uses and Issues. In 12th International Multidisciplinary Conference on Economics, Business, Technology and Social Sciences (pp. 1–8), Dec 2022, Tbilisi, Georgia. https://doi.org/10.48550/arXiv.2212.11738

Balducci, F., Impedovo, D. & Pirlo, G. (2018). Machine learning applications on agricultural datasets for smart farm enhancement. Machines, 6(38), 1–22. http://dx.doi.org/10.3390/machines6030038

Bellocchio, F., Ferrari, S., Piuri, V. & Borghese, N.V. (2012). Hierarchical approach for multiscale support vector regression. IEEE Transactions on Neural Networks and Learning Systems, 23(9), 1448–1460.

Ben Ayed, R. & Hanana, M. (2021). Artificial intelligence to improve the food and agriculture sector. Hindawi Journal of Food Quality, 2021, 1–7, Article ID 5584754. https://doi.org/10.1155/2021/5584754

Benos, L., Moysiadis, V., Kateris, D., Tagarakis, A.C., Busato, P., Pearson, S. & Bochtis, D. (2023). Human-robot interaction in agriculture: A systematic review. Sensors, 23, 6776. https://doi.org/10.3390/s23156776

Bhagat, P.R., Naz, F. & Magda, R. (2022). Artificial intelligence solutions enabling sustainable agriculture: A bibliometric analysis. PLoS ONE, 17(6), e0268989. https://doi.org/10.1371/journal.pone.0268989

Binch, A. & Fox, C.W. (2017). Controlled comparison of machine vision algorithms for Rumex and Urtica detection in grassland. Computers and Electronics in Agriculture, 140, 123–138. http://dx.doi.org/10.1016/j.compag.2017.05.018

Boshkoska, B.M., Liu, S., Zhao, G., Fernandez, A., Gamboa, S., Del Pino, M., Zarate, P., Hernandez, J. & Chen, H. (2019). A decision support system for evaluation of the knowledge sharing crossing boundaries in agri-food value chains. Computers in Industry, 110, 64–80. https://doi.org/10.1016/j.compind.2019.04.012

Cavallone, P., Botta, A., Carbonari, L., Viscont, C. & Quaglia, G. (2020). The Agri.q mobile robot: Preliminary experimental tests. In Advances in Italian mechanism science. In Proceedings of the 3rd International Conference of IFToMM, Naples, Italy, Niola V., Gasparetto A. Eds., 524–532. https://doi.org/10.1007/978-3-030-55807-9_59

Christensen, S., Sogaard, H.T., Kudsk, P., Nørremark, M., Lund, I., Nadimi, E.S. & Jørgensen, R. (2009). Site-specific weed control technologies. European Weed Research Society Weed Research, 49, 233–241. https://doi.org/10.1111/j.1365-3180.2009.00696.x

Chukkapalli, S.S.L., Mittal, S., Gupta, M., Abdelsalam, M., Joshi, A., Sandhu, R. & Joshi, K. (2020). Ontologies and artificial intelligence systems for the cooperative smart farming ecosystem, IEEE Access, 8, 164045–164064. https://doi.org/10.1109/ACCESS.2020.3022763

Cook, P. & O'Neill, F. (2020). Artificial Intelligence in Agribusiness is Growing in Emerging Markets, IFC, a member of the World Bank Group, https://documents1.worldbank.org/curated/en/198451596436781534/pdf/Artificial-Intelligence-in-Agribusiness-is-Growing-in-Emerging-Markets.pdf

Dhanaraju, M., Chenniappan, P., Ramalingam, K., Pazhanivelan, S. & Kaliaperumal, R. (2022). Smart farming: Internet of Things (IoT)-based sustainable agriculture. Agriculture, 12, 1745. https://doi.org/10.3390/agriculture12101745

Di Vaio, A., Boccia, F., Landriani, L. & Palladino, R. (2020). Sustainability, 12, 4851. https://doi.org/10.3390/su12124851

Elijah, O., Abd Rahman, T., Orikumhi, I., Leow, C.Y. & Hindia, M. (2018). An overview of Internet of things (IoT) and data analytics in agriculture: Benefits and challenges. IEEE Internet of Things Journal, 5(5), 3758–3773. https://doi.org/10.1109/JIOT.2018.2844296

Elkington, J. (2013). Enter the triple bottom line. In: The Triple Bottom Line (pp. 23–38, Vol. 7). Routledge: London. https://johnelkington.com/archive/TBL-elkington-chapter.pdf

Esposito, M., Crimaldi, M., Cirillo, V., Sarghini, F. & Maggio, A. (2021). Drone and sensor technology for sustainable weed management: A review. Chemical and Biological Technologies in Agriculture, 8(18). https://doi.org/10.1186/s40538-021-00217-8

EU (2023) Artificial intelligence in the agri-food sector: Applications, risks, and impacts. https://www.europarl.europa.eu/RegData/etudes/STUD/2023/734711/EPRS_STU(2023)734711_EN.pdf

Gowen, A.A., Tiwari, B.K., Cullen, P.J., Mcdonnell, K. & O'Donnell, C. (2010). Applications of thermal imaging in food quality and safety assessment. Trends in Food Science & Technology, 21, 190–200. https://doi.org/10.1016/j.tifs.2009.12.002

Guo, W., Fukatsu, T. & Ninomiya, S. (2015). Automated characterization of flowering dynamics in rice using field-acquired time-series RGB images. Plant Methods, 11(1), 7. https://doi.org/10.1186/s13007-015-0047-9

Gyenge, B., Mátě, Z., Vida, I., Bilan, Y. & Vasa, L. (2021). A new strategic marketing management model for the specificities of e-commerce in the supply chain. Journal of Theoretical and Applied Electronic Commerce Research, 16, 1136–1149. https://doi.org/10.3390/jtaer16040064

Hasan, M., Shamael, M., Akter, A., Hossain, M.S. & Islam, S. (2023). An Artificial Intelligence-Based Framework to Achieve the Sustainable Development Goals in the Context of Bangladesh. https://doi.org/10.48550/arXiv.2304.11703

Hespeler, S.C., Nemati, H. & Dehghan-Niri, E. (2021). Non-destructive thermal imaging for object detection via advanced deep learning for robotic inspection and harvesting of chili peppers. Artificial Intelligence in Agriculture, 5, 102–117. https://doi.org/10.1016/j.aiia.2021.05.003

Ju, S., Lim, H. & Heo, J. (2019). Machine Learning Approaches for Crop Yield Prediction with Modis and Weather Data. In 40th Asian Conference on Remote Sensing: Progress of Remote Sensing Technology for Smart Future, ACRS (pp. 1–4), Daejeon: Asian Association on Remote Sensing.

Jung, J., Maeda, M., Chang, A., Bhandari, M., Ashapure, A. & Bowles, J.L. (2021). The potential of remote sensing and artificial intelligence as tools to improve the resilience of agriculture production systems. Current Opinion in Biotechnology, 70, 15–22.

Kakaei, H., Nourmoradi, H., Bakhtiyari, S., Jalilian, M. & Mirzaei, A. (2022). Effect of COVID-19 on food security, hunger, and food crisis. In: COVID-19 and the Sustainable Development Goals (pp. 3–29). https://doi.org/10.1016/B978-0-323-91307-2.00005-5

Kakani, V., Nguyen, V.H., Kumar, B.P., Kim, H. & Pasupuleti, V.R. (2020). A critical review on computer vision and artificial intelligence in food industry. 2, 1–12. https://doi.org/10.1016/j.jafr.2020.100033

Kler, R., Elkady, G., Rane, K., Singh, A., Hossain, M.S., Malhotra, D., Ray, S. & Bhatia, K. (2022). Machine learning and artificial intelligence in the food industry: A sustainable approach. Journal of Food Quality, 2022. https://doi.org/10.1155/2022/8521236

Klumpp, M. (2017). Automation and artificial intelligence in business logistics systems: Human reactions and collaboration requirements. International Journal of Logistics Research and Applications. https://doi.org/10.1080/13675567.2017.1384451

Klyushin, D. & Tymoshenko, A. (2021). Optimization of drip irrigation systems using artificial intelligence methods for sustainable agriculture and environment. In: A.E. Hassanien, R. Bhatnagar & A. Darwish (Eds.), Artificial Intelligence in Sustainability Agricultures, Artificial Intelligence for Sustainable Development: Theory, Practice and Future Applications, Studies in Computational Intelligence (pp. 3–18, Vol. 912). Springer Nature: Switzerland. https://doi.org/10.1007/978-3-030-51920-9_1

Kumar, A.S., Sharma, P., Kaur, S., Saleh, O.S., Chennamma, H.R. & Chaturvedi, A. (2023). AI-equipped IoT applications in high-tech agriculture using machine learning. In: Handbook of Research on AI-Equipped IoT Applications in High-Tech Agriculture (pp. 38–64). IGI Global: Hershey, PA.

Li, K.-Y., Burnside, N.G., de Lima, R.S., Peciña, M.V., Sepp, K., Cabral Pinheiro, V.H., de Lima, B., Yang, R.C.A., Vain, M.-D. & Sepp, A. (2021). An automated machine learning framework in unmanned aircraft systems: New insights into agricultural management practices recognition approaches. Remote Sensing, 13, 3190. https://doi.org/10.3390/rs13163190

Liakos, K., Busato, P., Moshou, D., Pearson, S. & Bochtis, D. (2018). Machine learning in agriculture: A review. Sensors, 18(8), 2674. https://doi.org/10.3390/s18082674

Linaza, M.T., Posada, J., Bund, J., Eisert, P., Quartulli, M., Döllner, J., Pagani, A., Olaizola, I. G., Barriguinha, A., Moysiadis, T., et al. (2021). Data-driven artificial intelligence applications for sustainable precision agriculture. Agronomy, 11, 1227. https://doi.org/10.3390/agronomy11061227

Lu, H., Cao, Z., Xiao, Y., Fang, Z., Zhu, Y. & Xian, K. (2015). Fine-grained maize tassel trait characterization with multi-view representations. Computers and Electronics in Agriculture, 118, 143–158. http://dx.doi.org/10.1016/j.compag.2015.08.027

Lu, H., Cao, Z., Xiao, Y., Li, Y. & Zhu, Y. (2016). Region-based colour modelling for joint crop and maize tassel segmentation. Biosystems Engineering, 147, 139–150. https://doi.org/10.1016/j.biosystemseng.2016.04.007

Mahto, A.K., Alam, M.A., Biswas, R., Ahmed, J. & Alam, A.I. (2021). Short-term forecasting of agriculture commodities in context of Indian market for sustainable agriculture by using the artificial neural network. Journal of Food Quality, 2021, 9939906, Article ID. https://doi.org/10.1155/2021/9939906

Manaware, D. (2020). Artificial intelligence: A new way to improve Indian agriculture. International Journal of Current Microbiology and Applied Sciences, 9(3), 1095–1102. https://doi.org/10.20546/ijcmas.2020.903.128

Meshram, V., Patil, K., Meshrama, V., Hanchate, D. & Ramkteke, S.D. (2021). Machine learning in agriculture domain: A state-of-art survey. Artificial Intelligence in the Life Sciences, 1, 100010. https://doi.org/10.1016/j.ailsci.2021.100010

Misra, N.N., Dixit, Y., Al-Mallahi, A., Bhullar, M.S., Upadhyay, R. & Martynenko, A. (2020). IoT, big data and artificial intelligence in agriculture and food industry. IEEE Internet of Things Journal, 1–19. https://doi.org/10.1109/JIOT.2020.2998584

Mohr, S. & Kühl, R. (2021). Acceptance of artificial intelligence in German agriculture: An application of the technology acceptance model and the theory of planned behavior. Precision Agriculture, 22, 1816–1844. https://doi.org/10.1007/s11119-021-09814-x

Mohri, M., Rostamizadeh, A. & Talwalkar, A. (2018). Foundations of Machine Learning (2nd ed.). The MIT Press: Cambridge, MA; London.

Mondejar, M.E., Avtar, R., Diaz, H.L.B., Dubey, R.K., Esteban, J., Gómez-Morales, A., Hallam, B., Mbungu, N.T., Okolo, C.C., Prasad, K.A., She, Q. & Garcia-Segura, S. (2021). Digitalization to achieve sustainable development goals: Steps towards a Smart Green Planet. Science of the Total Environment, 794, 148539. https://doi.org/10.1016/j.scitotenv.2021.148539

Motia, S. & Reddy, S. (2021). Exploration of machine learning methods for prediction and assessment of soil properties for agricultural soil management: A quantitative evaluation. Journal of Physics: Conference Series, 1950, 012037. https://doi.org/10.1088/1742-6596/1950/1/012037

Naik, H.S., Zhang, J., Lofquist, A., Assefa, T., Sarkar, S., Ackerman, D., Singh, A., Singh, A.K. & Ganapathysubramanian, B. (2017). A real-time phenotyping framework using machine learning for plant stress severity rating in soybean. Plant Methods, 13(23), 1–12. https://doi.org/10.1186/s13007-017-0173-7

Nguyen, T.H., Nong, D. & Paustiana, K. (2019). Surrogate-based multi-objective optimization of management options for agricultural landscapes using artificial neural networks. Ecological Modelling, 400, 1–13. https://doi.org/10.1016/j.ecolmodel.2019.02.018

Oláh, J., Aburumman, N., Popp, J., Khan, M.A., Haddad, H. & Kitukutha, N. (2020). Impact of Industry 4.0 on environmental sustainability. Sustainability, 12, 4674. https://doi.org/10.3390/su12114674

Oliveira, L.F., Moreira, A.P. & Silva, M.F. (2021). Advances in agriculture robotics: A state-of-the-art review and challenges ahead. Robotics, 10, 52. https://doi.org/10.3390/robotics10020052

Paliwal, N., Vanjani, P., Liu, J.-W., Saini, S. & Sharma, A. (2019). Image processing-based intelligent robotic system for assistance of agricultural crops. International Journal of Social and Humanistic Computing, 3(2), 190–204.

Palomares, I., Martínez-Cámara, E., Montes, R. et al. (2021). A panoramic view and swot analysis of artificial intelligence for achieving the sustainable development goals by 2030: Progress and prospects. Applied Intelligence, 51, 6497–6527. https://doi.org/10.1007/s10489-021-02264-y

Pantazi, X.E., Moshou, D. & Bravo, C. (2016). Active learning system for weed species recognition based on hyperspectral sensing. Biosystems Engineering. https://doi.org/10.1016/j.biosystemseng.2016.01.014

Pantazi, X.E., Tamouridou, A.A., Alexandridis, T.K., Lagopodi, A.L., Kashefi, J. & Moshou, D. (2017). Evaluation of hierarchical self-organising maps for weed mapping using UAS multispectral imagery. Computers and Electronics in Agriculture, 139, 224–230. http://dx.doi.org/10.1016/j.compag.2017.05.026

Partel, V., Kakarla, S., Charan & Ampatzidis, Y. (2019). Development and evaluation of a low-cost and smart technology for precision weed management utilizing artificial intelligence. Computers and Electronics in Agriculture, 157, 339–350. https://doi.org/10.1016/j.compag.2018.12.048

Patrício, D.I. & Rieder, R. (2018). Computer vision and artificial intelligence in precision agriculture for grain crops: A systematic review. Computers and Electronics in Agriculture, 153, 69–81. https://doi.org/10.1016/j.compag.2018.08.001

Peruzzi, A., Martelloni, L., Frasconi, C., Fontanelli, M., Pirchio, M. & Raffaelli, M. (2017). Machines for non-chemical intra-row weed control in narrow and wide-row crops: A review. Journal of Agricultural Engineering, XLVIII(583), 57–70. https://doi.org/10.4081/jae.2017.583

Rasmussen, J., Nielsen, J., Streibig, J.C., Jensen, J.E., Pedersen, K.S. & Olsen, S.I. (2018). Pre-harvest weed mapping of *Cirsium arvense* in wheat and barley with of-the-shelf UAVs. Precision Agriculture. https://doi.org/10.1007/s11119-018-09625-7

Rejeb, A., Rejeb, K., Zailani, S., Keogh, J.G. & Appolloni, A. (2022). Examining the interplay between artificial intelligence and the agri-food industry. Artificial Intelligence in Agriculture, 6, 111–128. https://doi.org/10.1016/j.aiia.2022.08.002

Ruiz-Real, J.L., Uribe-Toril, J., Torres Arriaza, J. & de Pablo Valenciano, A. (2020). A look at the past, present and future research trends of artificial intelligence in agriculture. Agronomy, 10, 1839. https://doi.org/10.3390/agronomy10111839

Sabanci, K., Kayabasi, A. & Toktas, A. (2016). Computer vision-based method for classification of the wheat grains using artificial neural network. https://doi.org/10.1002/jsfa.8080

Sachithra, V. & Subhashini, L.D.C.S. (2021). How artificial intelligence uses to achieve the agriculture sustainability: Systematic review. Artificial Intelligence in Agriculture, 8, 46–59. https://doi.org/10.1016/j.aiia.2023.04.002

Sadeghi-Tehran, P., Sabermanesh, K., Virlet, N. & Hawkesford, M.J. (2017). Automated method to determine two critical growth stages of wheat: Heading and flowering. Frontiers in Plant Science, 8(252). https://doi.org/10.3389/fpls.2017.00252

Saiz-Rubio, V. & Rovira-Más, F. (2020). From smart farming towards Agriculture 5.0: A review on crop data management. Agronomy, 10(207), 1–21. https://doi.org/10.3390/agronomy10020207

Santoso, I., Purnomo, M., Sulianto, A.A. & Choirun, A. (2021). Machine learning application for sustainable agri-food supply chain performance: A review. International Conference on Green Agro-Industry, and Bioeconomy, IOP Conference Series: Earth and Environmental Science, 924, 012059. https://doi.org/10.1088/1755-1315/924/1/012059

Sarri, D., Lombardo, S., Lisci, R., De Pascale, V. & Vieri, M. (2020). AgroBot Smash a robotic platform for the sustainable precision agriculture. In A. Coppola, G. Di Renzo, G. Altieri & P. D'Antonio (Eds.), Innovative Biosystems Engineering for Sustainable Agriculture, Forestry and Food Production. MID-TERM AIIA 2019. Lecture Notes in Civil Engineering (Vol. 67). Springer: Cham. https://doi.org/10.1007/978-3-030-39299-4_85

Shamshiri, R.R., Weltzien, C., Hameed, I.A., Yule, I.J., Grift, T.E., Balasundram, S.K., Pitonakova, L., Ahmad, D. & Chowdhary, G. (2018). Research and development in agricultural robotics: A perspective of digital farming. International Journal of Agricultural and Biological Engineering, 11(4), 1–14. https://doi.org/10.25165/j.ijabe.20181104.4278

Sharma, R., Kamble, S.S., Gunasekaran, A., Kumar, V. & Kumar, A. (2020). A systematic literature review on machine learning applications for sustainable agriculture supply chain performance. Computers & Operations Research, 119, 104926. https://doi.org/10.1016/j.cor.2020.104926

Singh, K. & Chaudhury, S. (2016). Efficient technique for rice grain classification using back-propagation neural network and wavelet decomposition. IET Computer Vision, 1–8. https://doi.org/10.1049/iet-cvi.2015.0486

Snyder, C.S. (2017). Enhanced nitrogen fertiliser technologies support the '4R' concept to optimise crop production and minimise environmental losses. Soil Research, 55, 463–472. http://dx.doi.org/10.1071/SR16335

Sokil, O., Zhuk, V. & Vasa, L. (2018). Integral assessment of the sustainable development of agriculture in Ukraine. Economics and Management of National Economy, Economic Annals-XXI, 170(3–4), 15–21.

Spanaki, K., Karafili, E., Sivarajah, Despoudi, S. & Irani, Z. (2020). Artificial intelligence and food security: Swarm intelligence of AgriTech drones for smart AgriFood operations. Production Planning and Control, 33. https://doi.org/10.1080/09537287.2021.1882688

Taghizadeh, M.R., Nabiollahi, K., Rasoli, L., Kerry, R. & Scholten, T. (2020). Land suitability assessment and agricultural production sustainability using machine learning models. Agronomy, 10(573), 1–20. https://doi.org/10.3390/agronomy10040573

Talaviya, T., Shah, D., Patel, N., Yagnik, H. & Shah, M. (2020). Implementation of artificial intelligence in agriculture for optimisation of irrigation and application of pesticides and herbicides. Artificial Intelligence in Agriculture, 4, 58–73.

Taneja, A., Nair, G., Joshi, M., Sharma, S., Sharma, S., Jambrak, A.R., Roselló-Soto, E., Barba, F.J., Castagnini, J.M., Leksawasdi, N., et al. (2023). Artificial intelligence: Implications for the agri-food sector. Agronomy, 13, 1397. https://doi.org/10.3390/agronomy13051397

Tilman, D., Cassman, K.G., Matson, P.A., Naylor, R. & Polasky, S. (2002). Agricultural sustainability, and intensive production practices. Nature, 418(6898), 671–677. https://doi.org/10.1038/nature01014. PMID: 12167873.

Vanthoor, B.H.E., de Visser, P.H.B., Stanghellini, C. & van Henten, E.J. (2011). A methodology for model-based greenhouse design: Part 2, description, and validation of a tomato yield model. Biosystems Engineering, 110(4), 378–395. https://doi.org/10.1016/j.biosystemseng.2011.08.005

Wu, X., Aravecchia, S., Lottes, P., Stachniss, C. & Pradalier, C. (2020). Robotic weed control using automated weed and crop classification. Journal of Field Robotics, 1–19. https://doi.org/10.1002/rob.21938

Xu, B., Agbele, T. & Jiang, R. (2019). Biometric blockchain: A better solution for the security and trust of food logistics. IOP Conference Series: Materials Science and Engineering, 646, 12009. https://doi.org/10.1088/1757-899X/646/1/012009

Yadav, V., Kumar, A. & Yadav, P. (2023). Artificial intelligence and its applications in agriculture. Agriallis, 5(3), 11–23.

Zareiforoush, H., Minaei, S., Alizadeh, M.R. & Banakar, A. (2015). A hybrid intelligent approach based on computer vision and fuzzy logic for quality measurement of milled rice. Measurement, 66, 26–34. http://dx.doi.org/10.1016/j.measurement.2015.01.022

Zeynoddin, M., Ebtehaj, I. & Bonakdari, H. (2020). Development of a linear based stochastic model for daily soil temperature prediction: One step forward to sustainable agriculture. Computers and Electronics in Agriculture, 176, 105636. https://doi.org/10.1016/j.compag.2020.105636

Zha, J. (2020). Artificial intelligence in agriculture. Journal of Physics: Conference Series, 1693, 012058.

Zhang, P., Guo, Z., Ullah, S., Melagraki, G., Afantitis, A. & Lynch, I. (2021). Nanotechnology and artificial intelligence to enable sustainable and precision agriculture. Nature Plants, 7(7), 864–876. https://doi.org/10.1038/s41477-021-00946-6

Index

Note: Locators in *italics* represent figures and **bold** indicate tables in the text.

B

C

F

G

J

K

L

R

S